MW01251318

Learn Advanced Internet Relay Chat

Kathryn Toyer

Wordware Publishing, Inc.

Library of Congress Cataloging-in-Publication Data

Toyer, Kathryn.
Learn advanced Internet relay chat / by Kathryn Toyer.
p. cm.
Includes index.
ISBN 1-55622-604-7 (pbk)
1. Internet Relay Chat. I. Title.
TK5105.886.T688 1997 97-41787
005.7'1376--dc21 CIP

Copyright © 1998, Wordware Publishing, Inc.

All Rights Reserved

2320 Los Rios Boulevard
Plano, Texas 75074

No part of this book may be reproduced in any form or by any means without permission in writing from Wordware Publishing, Inc.

Printed in the United States of America

ISBN 1-55622-604-7
10 9 8 7 6 5 4 3 2 1
9711

Product names mentioned are used for identification purposes only and may be trademarks of their respective companies.

All inquiries for volume purchases of this book should be addressed to Wordware Publishing, Inc., at the above address. Telephone inquiries may be made by calling:

(972) 423-0090

Acknowledgement

I'd like to thank Kirk Weatherman for his assistance in writing about the Pirch PIL scripts, mIRC scripts, and the section on creating bots. His assistance was invaluable and helped to make this book whole. Thank you, Kirk, for answering my endless questions and for all your help.

— Katy

Contents

Introduction . . . 1
Software . . . 3
Nets . . . 8

Chapter 1 Aliases . . . 14
What are Aliases? . . . 14
mIRC. . . . 15
Pirch . . . 17
How to Create Aliases . . . 17
mIRC. . . . 18
Pirch . . . 21
Exercises . . . 25

Chapter 2 Popups . . . 27
What are Popups in mIRC and Pirch? . . . 27
How to Create Popups in mIRC and Pirch . . . 27
mIRC. . . . 28
Pirch . . . 33
Exercises . . . 37

Chapter 3 Remotes and Events . . . 38
What are Remotes and Events? . . . 38
How to Create Events, Commands, etc. in mIRC . . . 39
Users . . . 39
Variables . . . 42
Commands . . . 43
Events . . . 47
Raw . . . 55
How to Create Events and Controls in Pirch . . . 56
Exercises . . . 64

Chapter 4 Operator's Status . . . 65
What is Operator's Status? . . . 65
Responsibilities of Operator's Status . . . 66
What Channel Operators Do . . . 67
Exercises . . . 72

Chapter 5 Advanced Commands . . . 74
What Commands Are . . . 74
Client Commands . . . 75
mIRC . . . 75
Pirch . . . 79
Foiling Stalkers and Hackers . . . 83
IRC Commands . . . 88
Exercises . . . 89

Chapter 6 Splits and Lags . . . 90
What is Lag? . . . 90
What are Splits? . . . 91
How to Alleviate Lag . . . 94
What to Do About Splits . . . 94

Chapter 7 DCC and Sound . . . 96
What is DCC? . . . 96
Sounds . . . 102
Exercises . . . 102

Chapter 8 Advanced Pirch . . . 103
Autoexec Commands . . . 104
Colors . . . 105
File Servers . . . 107
Video . . . 109
Text to Speech . . . 110
Miscellaneous . . . 110
Exercises . . . 112

Chapter 9 Advanced mIRC . . . 113
Colors . . . 114
Address Book . . . 116
File Servers . . . 117
Text to Speech . . . 121
On Connect Perform . . . 123
Exercises . . . 124

Chapter 10 VIRC . . . 125
What is VIRC? . . . 125
How to use VIRC . . . 126
Exercises . . . 134

Chapter 11 Multiple Channels and Nets . . . 135
How to Manage Multiple Channels in mIRC . . . 136
How to Manage Multiple Channels in Pirch . . . 137

How to Manage Multiple Nets in mIRC . . . 138
How to Manage Multiple Nets in Pirch . . . 139
Exercises . . . 140

Chapter 12 **Web Chat and Other Chat Programs** . . . 141
Web Chat Programs . . . 141
3-D Chat Programs . . . 146
The Palace . . . 147
Microsoft V-Chat . . . 151
Active Worlds Chat . . . 152
OnLive Traveler . . . 156
Other Chat Programs . . . 159
LOL Chat . . . 160
Comic Chat . . . 163
Internet TeleCafé . . . 166
OrbitIRC Chat . . . 171

Chapter 13 **Scripts** . . . 174
What are Scripts? . . . 174
How to Create Scripts in mIRC . . . 175
How to Create Scripts in Pirch—PIL . . . 184
Example 1: A simple PIL . . . 186
Example 2: Using variables within the Command() function . . . 187
Example 3: If Statement . . . 188
Example 4: Play a Wave Script . . . 189
Exercises . . . 196

Chapter 14 **Bots** . . . 197
What are Bots? . . . 197
Channel Bots . . . 198
Personal Bots . . . 199
War and Protection Bots . . . 200
How to Use Bots . . . 200
Channel Bots . . . 201
Tips on Using Bots . . . 206
Personal, War, and Protection Bots . . . 207
How to Create Bots . . . 208
How to Create a Bot in mIRC . . . 209
Automatic Bot Functions . . . 211
How to Create a Bot in Pirch . . . 215
Running Your Bot . . . 219

Chapter 15 **CUSeeMe** . . . 220
What is CUSeeMee? . . . 220
How to Use CUSeeMe . . . 222

Chapter 16 PowWow 227
What is PowWow? 227
How to Use PowWow. 229

Chapter 17 Voice Chat 236
What is Voice Chat? 237
Voice Chat Programs and How to Use Them. 238
Gather Talk 238
InterPhone 240
Televox 241
Internet Phone. 243
Iris Phone 246
VDO Phone. 247
HoneyComb 248

Chapter 18 Internet Teleconferencing 251
What is Internet Teleconferencing?. 251
Tools for Internet Teleconferencing and How to Use Them 253
NetMeeting. 254

Chapter 19 Putting It All Together 260
Putting It All Together in mIRC 260
Aliases 261
Popups 262
Remotes and Events 262
Putting It All Together in Pirch 263
Aliases 263
Popups 264
Events and Controls 264

Index 267

Introduction

IRC can be just simple text-based chat or it can be much more. What used to involve typing Unix commands to perform even the simplest tasks has evolved into sophisticated clients that afford you easy point-and-click interfaces. When IRC began it was limited to text chat in black and white only. Today, IRC lets you add colors to your text and ASCII art, listen to sounds or the voices of your friends online, and even get a live video feed of those friends as they're chatting with you.

If you have been chatting for several months or even as long as a year, you have tried your hand at creating some aliases, remotes, and events. But now you thirst for more—for more of a challenge. This book is designed for you.

In this introductory chapter you learn about the software that is available to you and the software we detail in this book—Pirch and mIRC. Then you learn about the various nets and some of the servers that go with them.

Chapter 1 teaches you how to set up some of the more complicated aliases. These include many of the colorized activities you see displayed on channels. By the time you finish this chapter and the exercises you will be an expert in aliases.

Chapter 2 teaches you about popups and how you can create sophisticated popups to amaze and astound your IRC friends. By the time you are finished with this chapter and the exercises you will be the envy of all your friends and be in demand for your unique and eye-catching popups.

In Chapter 3, you learn about remotes and events. This chapter teaches you how to set up the more complicated remotes and events to handle some IRC functions for you. The exercises help you put what you learn in this chapter to use in creating your own remotes, events, and commands.

Chapter 4 explains operator status. In this chapter you learn about the various things you can do as an operator and the responsibilities and your obligations as an operator on a channel with an assigned channel bot. The exercises for this chapter teach you how to manage your channel bot and keep peace and tranquillity reigning throughout your IRC kingdom.

Chapter 5 teaches you about advanced commands. In this chapter you learn about all the different commands you can use—client-specific commands and IRC commands. You also learn about hackers, harassers, and stalkers and ways to combat them.

In Chapter 6 you learn about splits and lags. This chapter teaches you measures you can take to alleviate or get around this often frustrating aspect of life on IRC.

Chapter 7 covers DCC and sounds. In this chapter you learn how to set up events to automate many of the activities you normally perform in these two functions of IRC. The exercises are designed to help you learn and become an expert in these activities.

In Chapter 8, you learn the advanced activities you can partake in using Pirch. We teach you how to set up autoexec commands, use colors, set up your file server, and send and receive live videos, and give you exercises to help you in the learning process.

Chapter 9 covers mIRC in detail. You learn advanced remotes, events, colors, and how to set up your file server. The exercises help you take what you learn and apply it to actual IRC activities.

In Chapter 10 you learn about one more popular IRC client—VIRC. This chapter teaches you how to use this client and some activities you can perform with it.

Chapter 11 details how to manage multiple channels and nets in these two IRC clients—Pirch and mIRC. This chapter also teaches you how to manage multiple nets on each of these clients. The exercises help you become proficient in these activities.

In Chapter 12 you learn about some of the other chat programs including some of the web chat programs. This chapter teaches you how to use some of these programs and explores what each has to offer.

Chapter 13 teaches you about scripts. You learn what scripts are, and how to create and use them in Pirch and mIRC. The exercises help you take what you learn and apply it to your IRC clients to enhance many of your events and remotes.

In Chapter 14 you learn about bots. We teach you how to use them, where to get some bots you can use, and how to create your own bots. You also learn about channel bots and how you can get and manage one of your own. The exercises are designed to assist you in mastering bots.

Chapter 15 covers CUSeeMe, a program that lets you hold chat and live video sessions with other users. This chapter explains what CUSeeMe is and how to use it.

In Chapter 16 you learn about PowWow, another enhancement program for IRC. This client lets you conference with several people at a time while also exploring sites on the web.

Chapter 17 teaches you how to use Internet phones with IRC. This chapter covers some of the products and programs available and how to use them to talk live to friends and family around the world.

Chapter 18 shows you how to use IRC for teleconferencing. It covers the software you need and how to use that software and the channels and nets to set up and conduct teleconferencing on the Internet.

In Chapter 19 we put it all together. This chapter takes everything you learned in previous chapters and puts it into easy steps to guide you through learning to use some of the more advanced features and activities of IRC.

Before we get into the fundamentals of IRC activities, let's learn about some of the software and the nets that are available to you.

Software

In early 1995, Khaled Mardam-Bey of London designed an IRC program called mIRC. If you have been using IRC for a while, you are familiar with this client. You may even use it. If not, I'm sure you have heard its name bandied about. If you don't have a copy of it, we have included a copy on the CD-ROM at the back of this book. You can also download it or any of the other software covered in this section at: http://www.tucows.com.

Mardam-Bey added some very nice enhancements to mIRC. He added a feature that lets you send and receive sound files as either waves with the extension of .wav, or midis with the extension of .mid. He also added something called a URL catcher. This enhancement saves web site addresses into a separate window. It also opens your browser and lets you view the web page by activating your web browser from IRC. This feature saves you the trouble of writing down these web site addresses every time someone gives them out on IRC. You also no longer have to type them in yourself after you take the time to open up your web browser. Mardam-Bey added several more features like colorized text, scripting commands, and drag and drop for sending files. The current version and the one discussed in this book is mIRC 5.11 See Figure I-a for an example of a login window for mIRC.

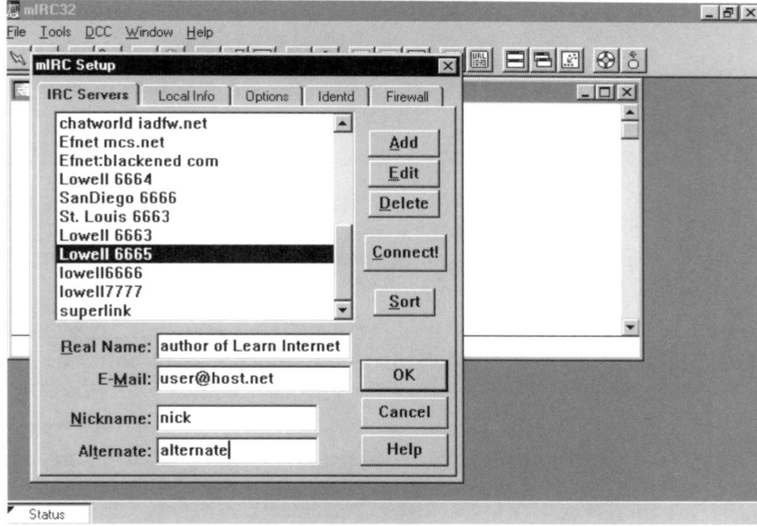

Figure I-a. mIRC login window

In November of 1995 Northwest Computer Services created another new software program for IRC called Pirch. This program is similar to mIRC in many ways but has some added features and enhancements. It has the same sound exchange functions and a URL catcher. In addition to these, it has added features. One of these lets you connect to more than one server at a time, allowing you to be on more than one net at the same time. This is all accomplished within the same application window. mIRC only lets you do this if you open the program twice and then you have more than one mIRC applications window for each server rather than one application window with a separate window within it for each server that you have with Pirch. Pirch also has a live video viewer and sender to let you see a video feed of other users and send one of yourself. See Figure I-b for an example of a login window for Pirch. A copy of Pirch is on the CD-ROM included with this book.

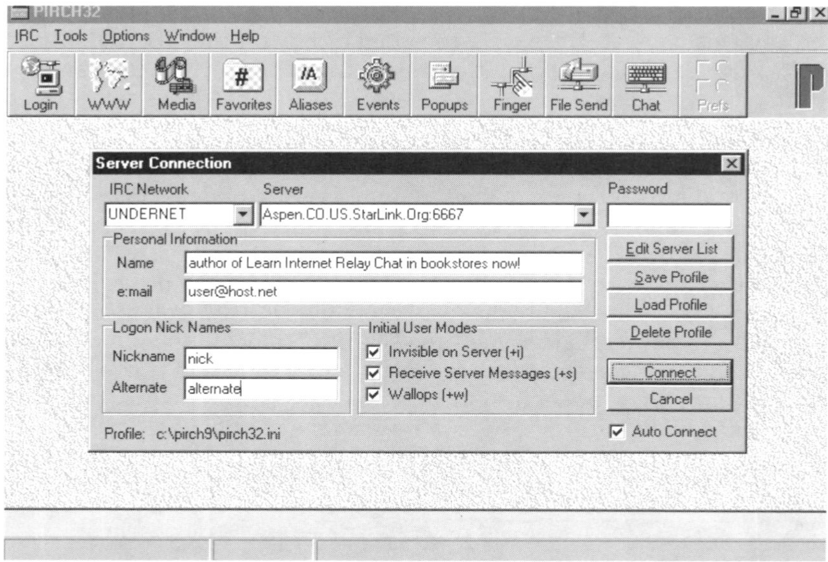

Figure I-b. Pirch login window

Both of these IRC clients are excellent. They provide you with excellent features to make your time on IRC easier and more pleasant. They come in both 16-bit and 32-bit versions for installation on either Windows 3x or Windows 95. These two programs are discussed in more detail in separate chapters later in this book.

You find as you surf the chat channels that there are many different kinds of chat software available. Following are some of these other chat software clients with a brief description of each. These are covered in more detail in Chapter 12.

Alpha World™ and its Active Worlds software is a virtual reality chat program populated by real people. In Alpha World you become one of its citizens and help to shape it. You acquire and develop property, assume an online persona, and interact in and with a living, breathing, multi-user community. It is not some preprogrammed simulation—it is as unpredictable and unique as the individual users who help create it.

Alpha World is a chat 3-D multi-user community. You are no longer interacting *with* your computer, but rather *through* your computer. You are represented by your own online avatar, or personification, letting you see and interact with the avatars of other people. With this software you build your dream house, create a new world, and experience not only by sight but by sound too.

This software lets you claim land, build on it, create commerce applications, and explore ever-changing online environments. You can become part of an online virtual community with this freeware. See Figure I-c for an example of one of Alpha World's environments with avatars.

Figure I-c. Alpha World community

Internet TeleCafé is an IRC software program that works in conjunction with a membership-based group of users. There are three levels of users with this program: Trial member, Regular member, and VIP member. There is no fee for the Trial or Regular members, however there is for the VIP member.

With the various memberships come certain limitations or privileges. Regular members can move freely through most of the rooms and options of the TeleCafé. As a VIP member you get the following:

- Access to the entire TeleCafé (including access to the VIP Lounge)
- Access to set up a total of five custom actions for yourself
- Custom Entrance and Exit messages.

The Palace is kind of like a cross between IRC and hypercard, yet completely unique in many respects. You can create and run your own social online environment on your server or visit other people's servers. Using a scripting language, you can create any visual look you want.

LOLChat, formerly called Cyberbabble, is a chat software package that offers many unique and exciting features. It includes rich text formatting; an answering machine; unlimited connections; macros for text, format changes, sounds, or any combination of the three; synchronized sounds that let you send all the sound files you have but that other users don't; and the capability of letting you surf the web with multiple leaders and followers. See Figure I-d on the following page for an example of LOLChat's chat screen and font examples.

LOLChat is freeware, however, the user can register it. When the program is registered the user gets the following:

- Free maintenance
- Password-protected nickname
- The ability to enter an e-mail address, home page, and a picture for others to see while chatting with them.
- All macros, sound lists, and address book entries are saved to disk.
- A User Info page, like a mini web page.
- The ability to post to the Message Board with a password.

■ Priority tech support

The registration fee is $20 and includes activation of all the above features.

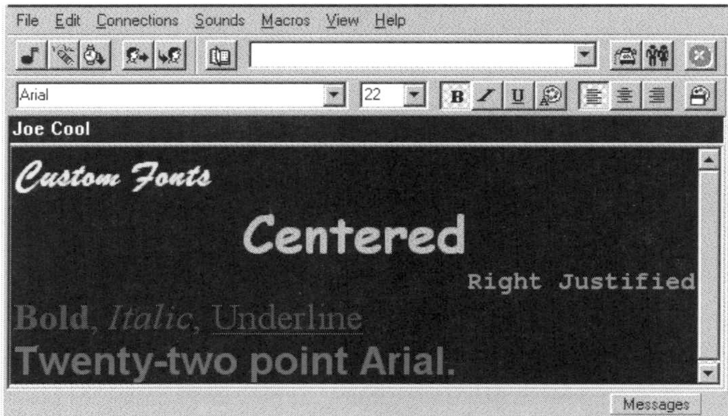

Figure I-d. LOLChat chat screen

OrbitIRC is another of the newer chat clients available. It is designed for Windows 95 users and gives you easy point-and-click control over all aspects of chat. There are no windows hiding other windows—everything is in the open for you to monitor your IRC sessions. It allows users to keep track of their public, private, and DCC chats. OrbitIRC has DCC Draw which lets you activate a picture box and doodle back and forth with other chatters. This chat client also lets you create a bot called OrBOT to handle some of the more mundane IRC tasks for you. See Figure I-e for a view of a chat session with OrbitIRC.

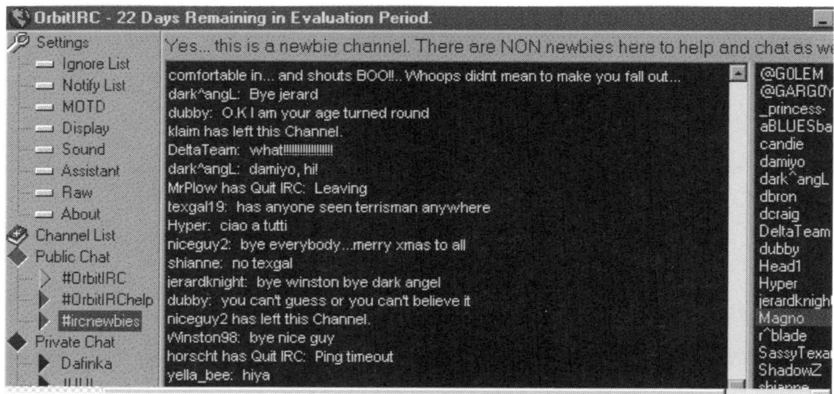

Figure I-e. OrbitIRC chat screen

VIRC lets you format your text with bold, underline, and italics and allows for seamless integration with your web browser just like mIRC and Pirch. It also lets you conduct real-time audio chat with other users and lets you establish video conferencing supporting any Windows-compatible video camera. See Figure I-f for an example of a login window for VIRC.

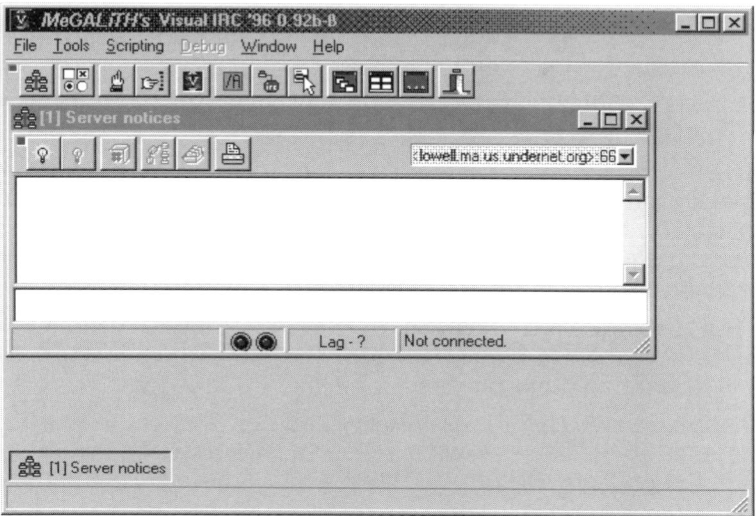

Figure I-f. VIRC login window

Westwood Chat is an IRC client that lets you start or arrange a game of Monopoly CD-ROM or Command & Conquer, discuss strategies, or even talk with tech support and guest speakers. This program is also freeware.

Microsoft's Comic Chat is a new kind of graphical chat program that lets you choose a comic strip character as your avatar. You type your messages or text into Comic Chat and a comic strip unfolds showing the various participants in the conversation as comic strip characters with their utterances in word balloons. This program is shareware and works with Microsoft's servers and net (see Figure I-g).

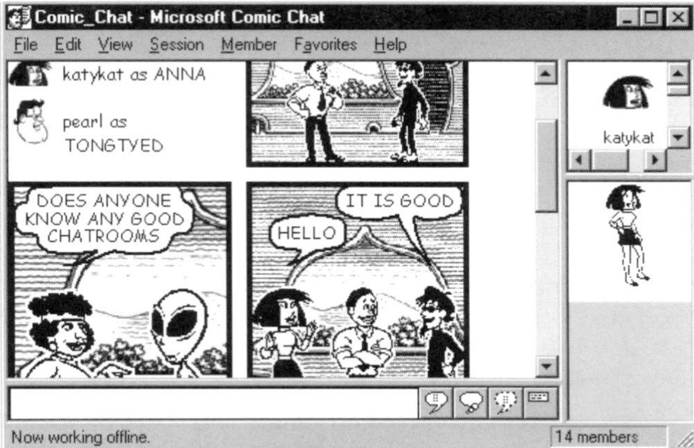

Figure I-g. Comic Chat window

Mimix is a freeware chat program where you can chat with a remote partner using a large collection of gestures performed by different characters. You are able to add additional gestures to existing characters and even generate new characters. This program, like Microsoft's Comic Chat and Active Worlds, requires that you use it with their servers on their net. I have tried several times to use this software and found no one available to chat with. This may change as the Internet community learns about this program.

Speak Freely is a chat client that lets you chat with real voice to users over a network. Speak Freely supports Internet RTP protocol which lets it communicate with other Internet voice programs that use that protocol. It also communicates with programs that support VAT (Visual Audio Tool) protocol. It is a freeware client available at http://www.download.com.

EZ-IRC is a shareware chat client that's easy to use. It also includes an ice-breaker—the Chinese Go-Moku (five in a row) game which includes a waiting room to help you find other players.

Chat-Man! Shareware client is easy to use and says that you won't have to write any commands at all. All commands are just a click away. You can also access global chat networks by clicking on WWW links.

OnLive Traveler is a freeware 3D virtual world client that gives you an entertaining live community by letting you talk with other users with your own voice through expressive, animated avatars. The avatars which represent users can be customized to lip-synch what the user is saying in real-time. This client works as a stand-alone application or as a web browser helper application.

Winsock IRC is a freeware chat client designed specifically for the novice user. Firc is another freeware chat client designed for the beginner, and advanced users may find it lacking. Netscape also has its own chat client for use with Netscape Navigator.

These are just some of the chat software programs that are available. There are others out there as well as new ones being developed on an ongoing basis. Test some of these for yourself and talk to friends or people you meet on IRC. Find out what they are using and how they like what they have. Choose a software program based on what you hear and what works best with you and your system. Or play around with others from time to time.

Nets

Within the Internet there are many different nets. Some of these are furnished or sponsored by local providers, some by BBSs (bulletin board systems), and some by university systems or other organizations or individuals. IRC is comprised of four major nets and several smaller nets. The major nets are called the EfNet, the UnderNet, DALnet, and SuperChat (formerly SuperLink). These and the other, smaller nets are explained in more detail in this section.

The EfNet was the first net that was formed and is the largest of the nets. EfNet has no central authority and no particular structure. If you find yourself on IRC and are not sure what net you're on, chances are it's this net.

The EfNet can be very slow and unreliable. It often splits into more than one network when the links between servers go down. There may be times when a message you send either does not reach its destination or does not reach it for several minutes. The EfNet is also prone to hacking and offers no protection from those hacking attempts.

Its size is one of the reasons for the problems with this net. At any given time of the day or night you can find more than 20,000 people connected to this net. There are more than 100 servers available for the EfNet. However, with the massive number of people logging on or trying to log on, this is often not enough. The more users these servers have to handle and process information for, the slower they become and the more problems they experience.

The EfNet has its own unique society of people. Explore it to find out what it has to offer. Who knows, this net may be the one where you find a long-lost friend or even make a new friend you would not have met anywhere else.

The UnderNet evolved out of the EfNet. It began its existence on the Internet in 1992. It was formed when a group of users decided to form a new net after they grew discontented with what they perceived as excessive problems with the EfNet. Since it began it has grown from 1,000 users in February of 1995 to over 18,000 users at the end of the first quarter of 1997. By the time you read this book, that number may be closer to 20,000 or more users.

This group of rebels set about to make this new net more organized. The UnderNet operators agreed to cooperate with each other to get the best links to servers and to make your time on their net more pleasant. The UnderNet has grown to almost match the size and scope of the EfNet and is experiencing many of the same problems that caused its founders to create it. It now experiences the same problems with hackers, netsplits, lags, and takeovers that the EfNet experienced before the UnderNet was formed.

When the UnderNet was formed, the founders made some changes over the tried-and-true EfNet way of doing things. One of the changes was adding features to the servers that assist operators and users. The UnderNet also strives to get the best route to its servers.

They also established a channel service to help make the UnderNet a happier place to be. This service functions to help preserve channels, prevent hostile takeovers, and register channels. To this end the UnderNet formed several committees to assist users. These committees have mailing lists you can subscribe to so you can keep up to date on the latest UnderNet happenings.

The UnderNet also gives its users news and newsletters with information in them to help users and keep them up to date on happenings on their net. Its newsletter is touted as a fun yet informative publication of the UnderNet Public Relations Committee. For a peek, go to the UnderNet web site at: http://www.undernet.org/.

So, if you need more organization, this net is for you. You find many of the same channel names here as you find on the EfNet. You may see some of the same characters from time to time on both nets. You may even notice these people on both nets at the same time.

One of the smaller nets of the "Big Four" is DALnet. This net started as a role-playing-game alternative network with a rather cultish group of users. Originally you could find an average of 130 users on this net. However, with the recent growth of the Internet and IRC usage, this net has grown to well over 8,000 users during peak hours.

DALnet prides itself as being the friendliest IRC network. It recognizes the fact that without its users, IRC would be nothing. DALnet's policy is to be as friendly and open to its users as possible. It, too, has made changes to its servers, making them as user friendly as possible. DALnet servers are also designed to minimize your harassment from other users.

DALnet allows users to have longer nicknames and to register those nicknames. It is the only one of the Big Four nets that lets you register a nickname. At one time you were able to register a nickname on the EfNet; however, that service was discontinued in 1994. There are just too many users on the other two nets for nickname registration to be feasible.

If you are looking for a quieter place to go, try DALnet. If you need to carry on an intense conversation with someone without worrying about being interrupted, this net is the ideal spot.

The last and smallest of the major nets is SuperChat. SuperChat is also the youngest of the four nets, formed in early 1995. Originally it was called SuperLink net. It began as a very elite net. Since changing to SuperChat it has opened its doors and allows as many people on as can get a connection. At any given time you can see no more than 500 users. As the Internet continues to grow and more and more people go online, figures for users on each net grows proportionately.

SuperChat's organization is very similar to the UnderNet's. It allows you to register channels. It also strives to keep the servers functioning at optimal levels. Its community is growing. As the other three bigger nets become overcrowded, you will see more and more users switching over to SuperChat. So, if you like the idea of being part of a much smaller group that is growing, this net is the one for you.

There are a dozen or more other nets out there on the Internet. New nets are being added constantly. As more and more people get connected to the Internet, the older nets will not be able to handle all the traffic.

Already, the UnderNet is undergoing many of the same problems that drove its founders to establish it. As more and more people get frustrated, the demand creates the supply.

Here are several other nets I have found:

- OuterNet or Starlink Italia—a very small net that caters to users from Italy. This net has ten servers and had less than ten users on during the morning hours U.S. time. It was created around August of 1996. I found no sex or warez (hacker) channels on this net the few times I was there.
- UpperNet—came online in January of 1996. It has 15 servers and very few users online. During the morning hours U.S. time, I logged about 45 users. I didn't find any sex or warez channels the few times I logged onto this net.
- WarpedNet—is another new net that was created in the fall of 1996. The few times I was on this net, there were approximately 100 users online. It has ten servers and allows users to have bots but not register channels. I did not notice any sex or warez channels, but I also did not note any overt denial of these kinds of channels from any of the IRCops or administrators.

- ChatNet—has grown since its inception in March of 1996. It claims it was born out of the ashes of an older network (SuperChat, formerly SuperLink). This network, like the UnderNet, also offers channel bots and registration. It is a midsized network with a loyal user base and friendly hosts. This network does **not** allow sex or warez channels. It has 13 servers you can use to access the net. It averages around 600 to 700 users during peak periods.
- GalaxyNet—began May 20, 1996. It offers a net bot that lets you register your nickname and your channel. This is very similar to what DALnet uses. It has 22 servers and averages around 500 to 600 users. This net does allow sex and warez channels and I noticed several of these were there.
- StarLink—is a fairly new net which came online in July of 1996. It refuses to host sex or hacker channels. It claims to have the best server administrators, friendly IRCops who actually talk, and a great Cservice staff. This network offers channel bot and channel registration just like the UnderNet does. It has 14 servers and approximately 150 to 250 users on at any given time.
- PrimegateNet—is a new net which began in January of 1997. It is still very small and averages around 10 to 20 users. It has four servers. Its server software (conference room) allows users to register nicknames and channels.
- NewNet—is another of the newer midsized nets. It averages between 700 to 900 users and has 48 servers. This net is another net that allows sex and warez channels and I noticed there were several of these kinds of channels.
- MicrosoftNet—is the Comic Chat network. You can use the Comic Chat software you read about in Chapter 12 on this net. It averages around 1,500 to 2,000 users on three servers. This net allows any type of channels so you can find sex and warez channels here.
- Kidlink—is a private net for participants in KIDLINK: Global Networking for Youth 10-15. It requires registration for use of this net.
- WorldWide Free-Net—is a chain of Free-Nets linked around the world. Free-Nets are exactly as they sound. They are free to their users. They ask for donations of time or money to offset expenses. These Free-Nets are linked by their own servers. They allow no pornography and provide a clean, enjoyable place to exchange cultural information and ideas from around the world. This net includes the following Free-nets: Alachua Free-net, Prairienet Free-Net, LA Free-Net, FEN Free-net, Omnifest Free-Net, Greater Detroit Free-Net, Grand Rapids Free-net, and Chester Community Interlink.

I know there are probably more nets than this, but this list gives you an idea of what is out there. Visit them and see what they have to offer. They may become the new alternatives to the other four mentioned previously. The Internet is growing so fast, anything is possible.

As mentioned before, the nets are networks of servers. Servers are what you use to connect to these nets. Each net has its own group of servers to let you connect to it. In this section I give you three servers for each net.

Following are lists of servers for most of the nets we have talked about in this chapter. Add any or all of these to your server lists in your chat software. Explore the different nets to see which one feels right for you. Remember that the Internet is growing so fast that it evolves faster than most people can keep up with it. These lists should give you a basis with which to start exploring IRC.

EfNet Servers

Address	Location
irc.cris.com	Canada
irc.colorado.edu	Colorado
piglet.cc.utexas.edu	Texas

UnderNet Servers

Address	Location
lowell.ma.us.undernet.org	Massachusetts
manhattan.ks.us.undernet.org	Kansas
norman.ok.us.undernet.org	Oklahoma

DALnet Servers

Address	Location
irc.dal.net	Server pool
irc.services.dal.net	Server pool
glass.oh.us.dal.net	Ohio

SuperChat Servers

Address	Location
irc.superlink.net	Server pool
Dallas.TX.US.SuperChat.Org	Dallas
mars.superlink.net	unknown

OuterNet Servers

Address	Location
SaltLake.UT.US.OuterNet.Org	Utah
channels.OuterNet.Org	Server pool
Uworld.OuterNet.Org	Server pool

UpperNet Servers

Address	Location
irc.uar.net	unknown
irc.speed.net	unknown
irc.cps.k12.ny.us	New York

WarpedNet Servers

Address	Location
Boston.MA.US.warped.net	Boston
osu.us.warped.net	Oklahoma
warped.us.warped.net	unknown

ChatNet Servers

Address	Location
Portland.OR.US.Chatnet.Org	Oregon
SF.CA.US.Chatnet.Org	California
Pensacola.FL.US.Chatnet.Org	Florida
Stillwater.OK.US.Chatnet.Org	Oklahoma

GalaxyNet Servers

Address	Location
washington.us.galaxynet.org	Washington
irc.telluric.com	unknown
Sedona.AZ.US.galaxynet.org	Arizona

StarLink Servers	
irc.cinti.net	Ohio
Roseburg.OR.US.StarLink.Org	Oregon
Rochester.MI.US.StarLink.Org	Michigan

PrimegateNet Servers	
primegate.com	Server pool
wbolsove.campus.vt.edu	Virginia
apocalypse.ml.org	unknown

NewNet Servers	
irc.nycmetro.com	New York
irc.gaianet.net	California
irc.chelmsford.com	Massachusetts

MicrosoftNet Servers	
MIC1.microsoft.com	unknown
comicserv1.microsoft.com	unknown
comicserv2.microsoft.com	unknown

While these lists are far from complete, they give you a base on which to start your travels in IRC land. I cannot guarantee that you will be able to connect to all of these servers. You find as you use IRC more and more that you get proficient at learning which are the best servers for you and your area.

When you are trying to connect to servers, you are often asked which port you wish to connect to. A port is like a line into the server. Ports come in numbers. Almost all of the servers let you connect to the universal port of 6667.

Most of the EfNet servers have additional ports you can use. If you are having a hard time getting connected to a server on the 6667 port, then try one of the alternate ports. For the EfNet servers the ports range from 6660 to 6670.

The UnderNet servers also use the universal, or default, port of 6667. However, you may be able to get a better or faster connection by using one of the alternate ports of 6660 through 6669.

Since the other nets are much smaller than the other two, the default port of 6667 is probably all you need. However, as these nets grow, you may need to try different ports. These ports should be consistent with the other nets, so try using any one in the range from 6660 through 6669.

With the information in this chapter on software, nets, and their servers, you are able to get to IRC and anywhere you want to go there. In the first chapter, we begin by covering aliases. We show you how to create aliases in Pirch and mIRC.

Chapter 1
Aliases

In this chapter you learn:

- ☑ *What are Aliases?*
- ☑ *How to Create Aliases*
- ☑ *Exercises*

If you have been using IRC for several months or longer, you probably already have several aliases set up. More than likely these are some of the easier and more common aliases, like for joins and parts and things of that sort. You may even have some aliases or macros set up to respond to various questions or statements on your channels.

Now that you have a taste for what these aliases can do, you hunger for a challenge, for something more. This chapter teaches you how to create some of the more complicated aliases in mIRC and Pirch.

Some of the more advanced aliases can use scripts as part of their make-up. This chapter does not deal with those types of aliases. Scripts in aliases are covered in Chapter 13 and are brought together for you in Chapter 19.

What are Aliases?

Aliases are custom commands or macros you set up in an IRC client, like mIRC or Pirch. You use common IRC commands and shortcut keys to set up these aliases. Along with these commands you also use identifiers, variables, If-then-else statements, and Goto commands to define your aliases.

Identifiers return the value of a built-in variable. For example, the identifier $time returns the current time. When mIRC locates an identifier in your command, it replaces the identifier with the current value of that identifier. Some identifiers can also perform functions on information that you give and then return a result. Variables are identifiers you can alter and use later in aliases and remotes. If-then-else statements let you compare values and execute different parts of a script or alias. Goto commands jump to different points in your alias or script.

Following is a list of the common identifiers or variables you can use for each of the two clients—mIRC and Pirch. The identifiers or variables are listed under each client.

mIRC

- $asctime(N) — converts time values returned by $ctime and ping replies into full date in text format.
- $ctime — returns total number of seconds elapsed since 00:00:00 GMT (Greenwich Mean Time), January 1, 1970.
- $date — gives the current date in day/month/year format.
- $adate — U.S. format of current date.
- $day — returns the name of the current day.
- $duration(N) — gives the specified number of seconds in a week/day/hour/minute/second format.
- $fulldate — gives the current date in day/date/time/year format.
- $idle — returns your current idle time.
- $time — returns the current time in hour:minute:second format.
- $timestamp — gives the current time in [00:00] format.
- $abs(N) — returns the absolute value of the number N, i.e., $abs(5) returns 5.
- $lower(text) — returns text in lowercase, i.e., $lower(GOODBYE) returns goodbye.
- $rand(v1,v2) — returns a random number between v1 and v2 when you supply it with numbers for v1 and v2 or it returns letters when you substitute letters for v1 and v2, i.e., $rand(a,d) returns a letter in the range from a through d.
- $str(N,text) — returns text repeated N times, i.e., $str(3,ha) returns hahaha.
- $strip(text) — returns text with all bold, underline, reverse, and color codes stripped out.
- $upper(text) — returns text in uppercase, i.e., $upper(goodbye) returns GOODBYE.
- $dir — lets you select a filename which is inserted in an alias. This identifier pops up a full directory and file dialog box.
- $file — does the same as $dir but pops up a quick file dialog box.
- $hfile — does the same as $file but lists files horizontally.

Note: Do not use $file or $dir with the /dcc send command because this command has its own built-in DCC Send dialog box.

- $findfile(dir,filename) — searches the specified directory and its subdirectories for the filename and returns the full path and filename if it is found.
- $getdir — returns the DCC Get directory specified in the DCC Options dialog box.
- $lines(filename) — returns the total number of lines in the specified text file.
- $logdir — returns the Logs directory as specified in the Logging section of the Options dialog box.
- $nofile(filename) — returns the path in filename without the actual filename.
- $read — reads a line from a file and inserts it into the current position in an alias command. The format is $read [-nl# -stext] <filename>. This command inserts any text and works like normal commands. For instance, you can create

an alias that reads a random line from a text file and inserts it at that position in the command. The command looks like this: /say $read c:\<filename.ext>.

- $readini — reads information from an INI file and inserts it into the current position in the alias command. The format is $readini <filename> <section><item>.
- $wavedir — returns the waves directory specified in the Sound Requests Options dialog box.
- $address(nickname,type) — searches the Internal Address List for the address associated with the specified nickname.
- $level(address) — finds a matching address in the remote users list and returns its corresponding levels list.
- $mask(address,type) — returns an address with a mask specified by type. Standard masks are:
  - 0: *!user@host.domain
  - 1: *!*user@host.domain
  - 2: *!*@host.domain
  - 3: *!*user@*.domain
  - 4: *!*@*.domain
  - 5: nick!user@host.domain
  - 6: nick!*user@host.domain
  - 7: nick!*@host.domain
  - 8: nick!*user@*.domain
  - 9: nick!*@*.domain
- $me — returns your current nickname.
- $snicks — returns a string of currently selected nicknames in the active channel listbox.
- $active — returns the full name of the currently active window.
- $chan(N/#) — returns information on channels that you are currently on. For example, you can use this command to get the topic, mode, key, or limit on channels you specify.
- $cb — returns the first 256 characters of the clipboard contents.
- $host — returns your local host name.
- $ip — returns your local IP address.
- $port — returns the port number of the server you are connected to.
- $server — returns the name of the server you are connected to.
- $url — returns the currently active URL in your web browser.
- $usermode — returns your current usermode on the IRC server you are connected to.

Technique: You can use $$?1 or $?1 which tells mIRC to try to fill in the value with a parameter if one exists and to ask for it if it doesn't exist.

Pirch

- $me — returns your current nickname.
- # — current channel or nickname.
- $+ — trims extra space from between parameters.
- $activeurl — returns the active URL in your web browser.
- $day — returns current day of the week.
- $date — returns current date.
- $host — returns your local host name.
- $ip — returns your local IP number.
- $logpath — your log file directory.
- $member — returns the number of people in a channel.
- $sendpath — the default DCC upload path.
- $server — the name of the server you are connected to.
- $soundpath — the default sound file path.
- $time — the current time.
- $usermode — your personal user mode.
- $url — the currently highlighted URL in the WWW window.
- $read — reads a line from a text file. The format is $read [-L<#>] <filename>.
- $readini — reads a line from an INI file.
- $file — pops up a file dialog box letting you select a filename to use. The format is $file <caption> <filename>.
- $addrmask — for private message windows only; contains the address mask for the user of that message window.
- $cliptext — returns text from the system clipboard.
- $activewin — returns the name of the active window.
- $mode — returns the channel mode.
- $topic — returns the channel topic.

Tip: Pirch allows you to add a Run PIL script command to the Alias window. This functions essentially the same as a /runscript command.

This covers many of the identifiers and variables for these two IRC software clients. Now let's move on and learn how to create some aliases using some of these identifiers.

How to Create Aliases

In this section we show you how to create aliases. I know you already know how to create some of the simpler aliases. Here, we show you how to create more advanced aliases using the identifiers and variables we listed in the previous section. You learn step by step and through examples how to create these more complicated aliases to automate several of your activities. This section is broken down into steps for creating aliases in each of the two IRC clients—mIRC and Pirch.

The If-then-else statements and Goto commands are covered in Chapter 13 about scripts. These are statements and commands you use in scripts and are better dealt with in that chapter. However, in Chapter 19 all these commands, scripts, and aliases are brought together for you in step-by-step learning activities.

Let's begin learning how to create advanced aliases. We begin with aliases in mIRC, then we move on to aliases in Pirch.

mIRC

From time to time you might upset someone who in turn is vengeful and wants to exact their revenge on you by trying to flood you off IRC. You can counteract this by setting up an alias with a hot key you can press when you notice someone trying to flood you.

Flood Protection

Activate your alias edit box and type in this command: /F12 /ignore -tiu120 *!*@* | /speak <your message>. Then when someone is trying to send you floods, either CTCP or otherwise, you simply press the F12 key and they are put on ignore for two minutes. You do not receive any more messages or CTCPs from them for that length of time.

Tip: Aliases can also be called from popups, remotes, and timer, play, or other identifiers.

If you have been on IRC recently, you have noticed users sending colorful hugs and such things to people on the channels. mIRC added colorized text to its new version which allows you to create all kinds of wonderful colorful text and ASCII art. Aliases also let you utilize those color codes in creating macros.

When creating these aliases using these color codes or special formats like bold, underline, italics, and reversed text, you do have to type in the codes as you would if you were typing them into a channel. The nice thing about aliases is that once you get them set up, you only need to type the shortcut and the alias pops up on the channel, saving you time and strain on your fingers and wrists.

Tip: You can also create aliases with more than one command on one line by separating them with the pipe character — |.

Fancy Aliases

Here are a few examples of some colorized aliases you can add to your alias edit box (in all of these examples, press Ctrl+k (press and hold Ctrl and type k) to activate the color codes; the Ctrl key is represented here by the ^ character):

- /greet /say_0,1^k1^k^k2^k^k5^k^k6^k^k3^k^k7^k^k14 ^k^k10^k^k12^k^k4^k^k13^k^k9^k^k11^k^k8^k^k0,1 $1 ^k0,1^k8^k^k11^k^k9^k^k13^k^k0,1^k4^k^k12^k^k10^k^k 14^k^k7^k^k3^k^k6^k^k5^k^k2^k^k1-^k

Tip: Aliases can call other aliases or call themselves recursively, however, calling aliases from within aliases uses a lot of memory and might cause problems when memory is low.

When you type this in yourself, replace the ^ character with the Ctrl key. Once you add this to your alias edit box and click on OK, this alias shows up on channel as colored boxes around the specified person's nickname when you use it. (Remember to type these all on one line.)

Tip: As a safeguard against infinite loops in aliases, mIRC has set a default maximum recurse depth of 10. You can change this with the /maxdepth command. The minimum allowed is 1, which means that aliases can't call other aliases, and the maximum is 100.

- /ball /me gives a bunch of balloons to ya :) ^k3~O**~ O**~ O**~ ^k4¸ ,ø¤°\` ^k10 $$1 ^k4\`°¤ø,¸ ^k13~O**~ O**~ O**~\` ^k4°¤ø,¸ ^k10 $$1 ^k4¸,ø¤° ^k14~O** O**~ O**~ ^k4¸,ø¤°\` ^k10 $$1 ^k4\`°¤ø,¸ ^k6~O**~ O**~ O**~ ^k4\`°¤ø,¸ ^k10 $$1 ^k4¸,ø¤°\` ^k8~O**~O**~O**~ ^k4¸,ø¤°\` ^k10 $$1 ^k4\`°¤ø,¸ ^k9~O**~O* ~O**~ ^k4\`°¤ø,¸ ^k10 $$1 ^k4¸,ø¤° ^k2~O**~ O**~O**~ ^k4¸,ø¤°\` ^k10 $$1 ^k4\`°¤ø,¸ ^k11~O**~ O**~O**~~

This alias displays in channel with this ASCII art of ballons in color around the person's nickname.

- /b1 /say ^k ^k2,2 *1 $+ ! | /say ^k ^k0,2 *1 ^k1,1! | /say ^k ^k2,2 *1 ^k1,1! | /say ^k ^k0,0 ^k1,1 *1 $+ !

This alias displays on channel as a blue box taking up several lines with a nick or a word in white type in the center. Try your hand at creating this alias using any of the color codes available from 0 through 15.

Tip: If you find your alias performing an infinite loop, you can stop it by pressing Ctrl+Break.

Read Alias

When you create a text file, you can set up aliases to read the file to a channel. Type the command as follows: /<shortcut> /say $read <directory\path\filename>. For example, I set up a text file for rules for a channel called #writers. I named the file writers.txt and put it in my mirc\text directory. So, my alias looks like this: /rules /$read c:\mirc\text\writers.txt. When I type /rules on the #writers channel, mIRC reads one line of the text. The next time I type /rules in the channel, mIRC reads the next line of the text file, and so on.

One command that you see used often in these aliases is /echo. This /echo command prints text to a specified window. mIRC also lets you force it to evaluate identifiers within commands or to perform quietly rather than to a channel or status window. When you prefix commands with two forward slashes //, it forces mIRC to evaluate identifiers following it when you execute commands from a command line. For instance, if part of your alias included /echo My nickname is $me, mIRC displays this as My nickname is $me. With the double forward slashes — //echo My nickname is $me — mIRC displays this as My nickname is <your current nickname>. To force a command to perform quietly, simply place a period or dot in front of the command. Therefore, if you want to ignore someone but not openly, you can type /.ignore <nickname>.

Timer Alias

With mIRC you can set up a timer in your alias that lets you perform commands at specified times, on a regular basis, or a preset number of times. The identifier you use is /timer. For instance, you can create a text file with actions or statements in it and use the timer to send random statements from the file at preset intervals. For example, the alias could look like this: /test /timer1 0 180 /describe $chan $!read <directory and file name>.

In this alias /test is your shortcut, the command you type to activate it; the /timer1 0 180 is the command it performs and the times to perform it, every 180 seconds; the /describe $chan tells the program to send this information to the channel; $!read tells it to re-evaluate the file each time the timer hits it and read a line from the file; and the <directory and file name> is the path where the text file can be found on your hard drive. Now that you have this set up, you want to also be able to stop it once it becomes tiresome or annoying. The command you can use to stop this alias is /timer1 off.

Taking this a step further, you can combine this alias with syntax to select random nicks and use these actions to interact with others on your channel. As an example, this new alias could look something like this: /test1 /timer2 0 180 /describe $chan !read <directory and file name> <your message> $nick($rand(1,$nick(0,#)),#). This alias will choose a nick at random from the channel names list and send a line from your text periodically. To make it really interesting, you can add the color codes to the text or to your alias.

Technique: When you use the $$ parameter type, the parameter must be filled in or the command is not executed.

If you would rather only send these random messages to certain people in your channel, like only the ones with ops or only the ones without ops, then you can also create an alias just for that. It would look something like this:
/test4 timer 5 0 180 /describe $chan !read <directory and file name> <your message> $opnick($rand(1,$nick(0,#)),#) or
/test4 timer 5 0 180 /describe $chan !read <directory and file name> <your message> $nopnick($rand(1,$nick(0,#)),#) or
/test4 timer 5 0 180 /describe $chan !read <directory and file name> <your message> $spnick($rand(1,$nick(0,#)),#).
The $opnick tells the program to only look for nicks with ops, the $nopnick tells it to only look for nicks without ops, and the $snick tells it to only address this message to those nicks you have selected from the channel names list.

Along these same lines you can create an alias that posts a certain message to the channel at a specified time. For instance, you could create an alias to send a message to the channel at 10 p.m. Here is what your alias would look like: /test 3 /timer3 10:00 1 1 /notice $chan <your message>.

Through the course of your time online, channels change. They grow or deplete in members. If you would like to keep up to date on the changes in channels while you're on, you can set up a timer alias to perform a channels list at specified times. This is called a channel refresh and the alias looks like this: /test3 /timer4 0 7200 /list -min 20. Remember that some servers boot you off if you try to do a whole list, therefore, you need to set a limit to the list command, in this case we used -min 20 which gives us a list of all channels that have a minimum of 20 people on them. See Figure 1-a for an example of the mIRC alias edit box with these aliases in it.

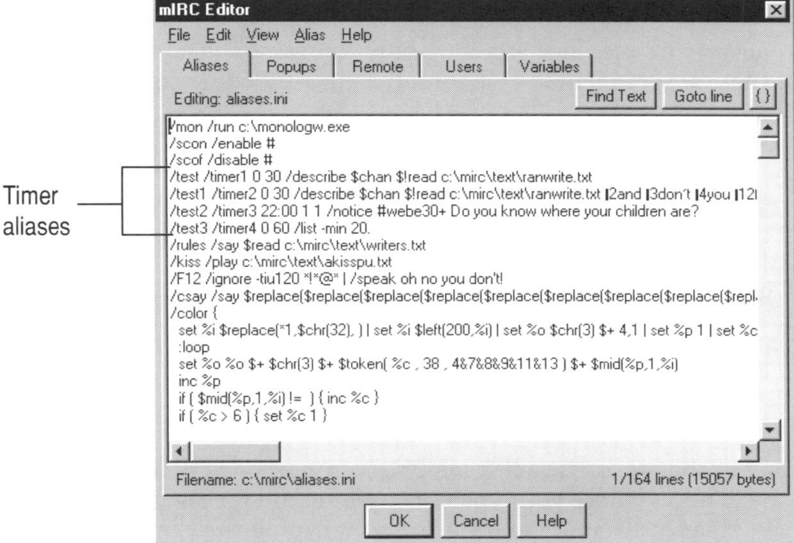

Figure 1-a. mIRC Alias edit box

These give you an idea of how you can use these identifiers in aliases. Try a few on your own. Also, try the exercises at the end of this chapter. They help you learn how to use some of the other identifiers.

Pirch

Pirch handles its aliases a little different than mIRC. In Pirch you type the shortcut in a dialog box and it appears in the Alias box on the right-hand side of the Alias editor box, then you type the alias command in the Command Definition area of the alias edit box. Pirch also does not use some of the commands and identifiers that mIRC does like /say, /describe, /$parmn and $chan. The /speak command in both mIRC and Pirch lets you initiate voice chat via Monologue. The /describe identifier is replaced by the /me, the /$parmn is replaced by $n, and the $chan is replaced with # in Pirch.

> **Note:** Never create a shortcut for an alias using the same name as an existing IRC command. Pirch and mIRC always use the IRC command over the alias command.

In order for some alias identifiers to work in Pirch, make note of the following:

- $activeurl — returns the active URL in your web browser. ($activeurl <type in the URL address>)
- $+ — trims extra space from between parameters. Example: $+ $snick $+.
- $readini — reads a line from an INI file. Example: Track alias /$readini c:\pirch32\tracking.ini # *2 L3.
- $addrmask — for private message windows only; contains the address mask for the user of that message window. (Useful for /ignore $addrmask.)
- $server — the name of the server you are connected to. Caution: Do not make an alias called Server.
- $members — returns the number of people in a channel.

Let's take some of the aliases we used for mIRC and make them Pirch aliases. I'll also show you a few unique aliases you can create in Pirch. To begin, open your Alias editor box. Then click on the Add button. In the dialog box that appears type in the shortcut for your alias. The first alias we work with is an alias to read a file or lines in a file. We are using the text file we created for mIRC and the shortcut for it.

Read a File

Once you have typed in that shortcut, click on OK. Your cursor moves to the Command Definition box. This is where you type in the command for the alias. For the read command, type $read <directory and filename>. Typing the command this way causes Pirch to read a random line in the file. If you want to specify lines for it to read, type the command using the -L parameter with a line number specification. For instance if you want the command to read line two, type $read -L2 <directory and filename> in the Command Definition pane of the Pirch Alias edit box (see Figure 1-b).

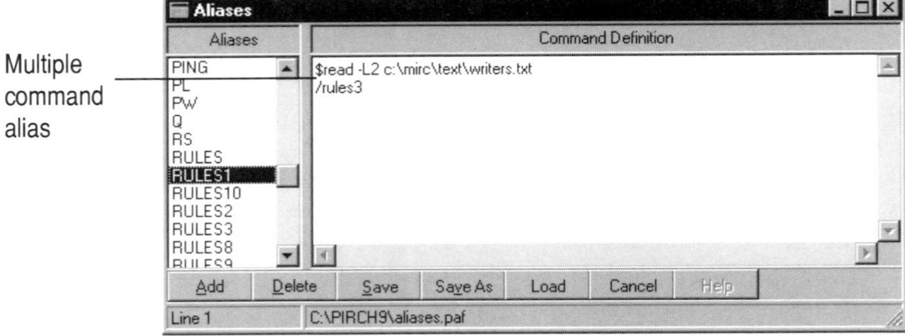

Figure 1-b. Pirch Alias edit box

Tip: In Pirch the Alias edit box can be kept open while you test aliases in your chat windows.

Fancy Aliases

In Pirch you can also create fancy and colorized text and ASCII art aliases. Remember to use Ctrl+k preceding any color changes when creating these aliases, just as you would if you were typing them into the channel each time. Here are a few examples you can add to your aliases.

Type DOZ in the Alias dialog box, then type the following in the Command Definition pane:

/me gives $$1 a dozen beautiful roses
^k^k4,1@^k3}-`-,-`-- ^k^k4,1@^k3}-`-,-`-- ^k^k4,1@^k3}-`-,-`--
^k^k4,1@^k3}-`-,-`-- ^k^k4,1@^k3}-`-,-`-- ^k^k4,1@^k3}-`-,-`--
^k^k4,1@^k3}-`-,-`-- ^k^k4,1@^k3}-`-,-`-- ^k^k4,1@^k3}-`-,-`--
^k^k4,1@^k3}-`-,-`-- ^k^k4,1@^k3}-`-,-`-- ^k^k4,1@^k3}-`-,-`-- .

When you type /doz <nickname> into the channel command line, this alias displays your message to the nick followed by a dozen ASCII art red roses on a black background. Very pretty!

For the next alias, type BALLOONS in the Alias dialog box after you click on the Add button. Then type the following into the Command Definition pane:

/me gives a bunch of balloons to ya :)
^k3~O**~ O**~ O**~^k4¸,ø¤º°` ^k10 $$1 ^k4`°º¤ø,¸
^k13~O**~ O**~ O**~`^k4°º¤ø,¸ ^k10 $$1 ^k4¸,ø¤º°
^k14~O** O**~ O**~^k4¸,ø¤º°` ^k10 $$1 ^k4`°º¤ø,¸
^k6~O**~ O**~ O**~^k4`°º¤ø,¸ ^k10 $$1 ^k4¸,ø¤º°`
^k8~O**~O**~O**~^k4¸,ø¤º°` ^k10 $$1 ^k4`°º¤ø,¸
^k9~O**~O*~ O**~^k4`°º¤ø,¸ ^k10 $$1 ^k4¸,ø¤º°
^k2~O**~ O**~O**~^k4¸,ø¤º°` ^k10 $$1 ^k4`°º¤ø,¸
^k11~O**~ O**~O**~~ .

When you type /balloons, this alias appears on the channel as your message followed by various ASCII art balloons (see Figure 1-c).

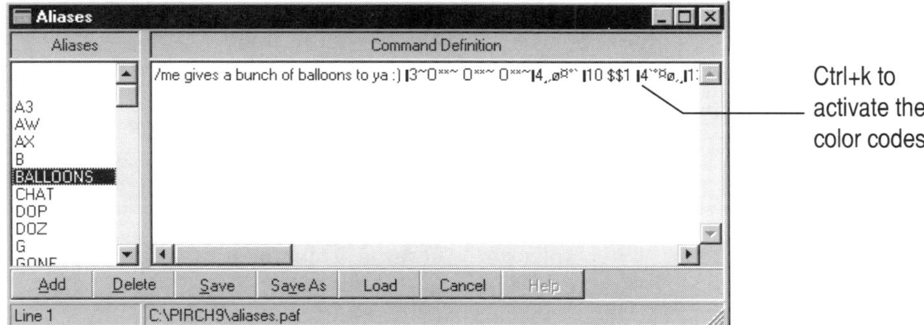

Figure 1-c. Pirch Alias edit box

The color codes for Pirch are the same as they are for mIRC. Use Ctrl+k with the numbers or combination of numbers from 0 through 15. Be sure to separate number combinations with a comma.

With Pirch you can also create linking aliases. These are aliases that you create that link to other aliases. If, for instance, you set up some rules for your channel, you can create linking aliases that will display your rules to the channel. Let's take the $read command from before and create linking aliases.

Make the first alias a shortcut called Rules, then type in the Command Definition pane: /notice $nick The following is a list of rules for #<channelname>... | /rules1. Next create a second shortcut alias of Rules1 with the command $read -L1 <directory and file name> | /rules2 and so forth until you have all your rules linked. Make sure that each rule includes a different line parameter for the read command. Now when you are in a channel and you want to display these rules to a newcomer to your channel, you simply type /rules <nickname> and all your rules display one by one.

Timer Alias

In Pirch, the /timer identifier command is used to automatically execute a command at specific time intervals. This command contains several sections—/timer <timername> <iterations> <interval> <command>. Timername is any name or number you want to give it, but do not use spaces. Iterations is the maximum number of times you want to have the command executed. After this command has performed the last iteration, the timer is deactivated and destroyed. To have a timer iterate indefinitely, use -1 as the iteration Pirch or IRC command.

Pirch lets you monitor your timers in several ways:

- view status of all timers by typing /timer with no parameters
- view status of an individual timer by typing /timer <timername>
- enable/disable a timer by typing /timer <timername> <on|off>
- remove a timer by typing /timer <timername> die

The alias to read a random line from a file at intervals looks like this: /timer <name> -1 30 $read <directory and file name>.

In Pirch you have to write a PIL script to get it to select random nicks to get these actions to interact with others on your channel. Pirch uses $members as the identifier to identify members of your channel. You need to write a PIL script to look at each $member and check if they are an op or not to select only ops or nonops for these messages to be addressed to. Other than very simple aliases, many aliases require a PIL script in Pirch. You can find many PIL scripts on the web if you do a search on Pirch aliases or Pirch. In Chapter 13, I cover scripts and give you some you can use for some of these aliases.

Tip: The /addpil <scriptname> command forms a disk file, letting you share or install PIL scripts easier.

In order to create a timer alias that would post a certain message at a specified time, you have to do two things. First, you have to create a PIL script. Then for this script to work, you have to figure the difference, in seconds, between the time you start or set the alias and the time you want it to go off, and set the timer for that many seconds. I don't know about you, but that's entirely too much work. I'd rather just forgo creating this alias in Pirch.

Through the course of your time online, channels change. They grow or deplete in members. If you would like to keep up to date on the changes in channels while you're on, you can set up a timer alias to perform a channels list at specified times. This is called a channel refresh and the alias looks like this: /test3 /timer4 0 7200 /list -min 20. Remember that some servers boot you off if you try to do a whole list; therefore, you need to set a limit to the list command. In this case we used -min 20, which gives us a list of all channels that have a minimum of 20 people on them.

You can set up a timer alias in Pirch that displays an away message every few minutes. Once you set yourself away you can activate this alias by typing the shortcut name. This is the alias command you type in the Alias edit box. I give this one the shortcut name of Page. Enter this information: Page in the Alias pane then /timer 20 100 180 /me <your message> \-2 /ctcp $me PAGE \-2 in the Command Definition pane. This alias then activates a timer that displays your message every 180 seconds, or 3 minutes, letting everyone know you are away but can be reached through the CTCP Page command. You can adjust the time in seconds and the number of times it displays to reflect how you want this command to respond. The number of times it displays is the second number here, the 100.

If you find yourself away very often, you want to create a shortcut key to change your nick so that others will know at a glance that you're not really with them. Pick an F key you want to be your away nick change key. Then click on the Add key in the Alias edit box and type that key number in the Alias entry box and click on OK. In the Command Definition pane, type /nick <shortnickaway>. For instance, mine is /nick katyaway. Now when I set myself away I can also press my shortcut key and set my nick with away at the end. You can also set up a shortcut key to change your nick back to what you normally use.

This gives you a good base to work from in creating some of the more complicated Pirch aliases. Add these to your Alias edit box and play around with a few on your own. Use the exercises here to learn how to create other aliases in Pirch.

Exercises

mIRC

1. Create a flood protection alias. Use the directions under mIRC aliases to help you.
2. Create a timer alias. Use the directions under Timer Aliases to help you. Create any type of timer alias you want.
3. Create a read alias. Set the command up to read a random line at time intervals.

Pirch

1. Create a timer alias.
2. Create a color-coded alias with ASCII art.
3. Create a read alias and link it to other aliases.

With all of these exercises, refer back to the instructions in the chapter and read the help files for the IRC client.

Chapter 2

Popups

In this chapter you learn:

- ☑ *What are Popups in mIRC and Pirch?*
- ☑ *How to Create Popups in mIRC and Pirch*
- ☑ *Exercises*

What are Popups in mIRC and Pirch?

Outside of aliases, popups are the most popular feature of these IRC clients. They let you point and click to perform actions or send messages to a channel. Popups are similar to aliases in how they are created, but they function differently. To activate aliases, you have to type a shortcut command. With popups, you simply click on the channel names list or a nickname in that list and then right-click to bring up the popup menu. Next you select the action from that menu that you want to perform.

With aliases you have to remember all the shortcuts you set up. But with popups, you get a menu listing all the items you can choose from. This makes it much easier to decide what action or message you want to send to your channel or about a certain nick.

Let's take a look at some of the popups you can create and add to your Popups menu. Just as we did in the last chapter, we cover popups for each of the IRC clients—mIRC and Pirch.

How to Create Popups in mIRC and Pirch

This section is designed to help you learn how to create popups in these two popular IRC clients. For each client I give you examples of popups you can add to your clients and from those you can learn to create others on your own. We begin with learning popups in mIRC and then go on to learn about popups in Pirch.

mIRC

You have probably already experimented and added a few of your own popups. If you have, then you're one step ahead in learning some of these more complicated popups. To begin, click on the Popups menu icon in the tool bar to open up the Popups edit box. Next click on Status and add some useful popup commands there. Notice there are already a few commands preset for you. These commands are automatically included with the mIRC program.

Tip: mIRC has increased the maximum number of items it allows in popup menus from 300 to 600.

The commands we add here automate some of the functions you can do before you join a channel but after you log onto an IRC net. One of the commands you can add here lets you set yourself away, puts your away message on a timer, or even speaks your message out loud. The first step we take here is to create the basic away command and message. In the edit box first create a menu. Remember, to do this you type the name you want to give your menu. You can type this any way you want—all caps or normal. I gave my menu the name Away. Under this menu name type a period and then type your command as follows: .Away:/away <your message>. Now if we want to make that away message appear on the channel at specified intervals, you add a timer to the command. If you want the away message to let people who message you speak to you via the /ctcp command, you add /ctcp instructions. You can even set up your away message with multiple command syntax. These commands are entered like this:

- Away with timer: .Awaytime:/ame is Away ($+$?=<give reason> $+) | /away <your message> |/timer{#} 10 900 /ame is away <your message>, then to set yourself back the command is: .Setback:/ame is back <your message> |/away | /timer{#} off (notice in this command the {#} after timer. In place of this {#} type in a number for your timer. Choose a number that you have not used before.)
- Away with speak: .Awayspeak:/away <your message> /ctcp $me speak [phrase]

Notice that the Away with timer command includes multiple commands and that they are separated by the pipe character (|). Now when you want to set yourself away, you can click on your Popups menu and select the command from there. When you right-click in a channel or status window, this Status popup menu opens and you select one of these menu items. See Figure 2-a on the following page for an example of the mIRC edit box for the status window popup menus and commands.

The next item in this Popup edit box is the Query/Chat option. In this option you set up menu items to handle CTCP functions, DCC Sends and Chats, and other activities of this sort. Let's begin with the DCC Send menu and add a popup to it.

If you often find yourself sending your picture out to friends you meet online, you can create a popup to let you do this quickly and easily. The command is: .Picture:/dcc send $$1 <directory and file name>. This command only works and shows in the menus when you right-click on a private or query window.

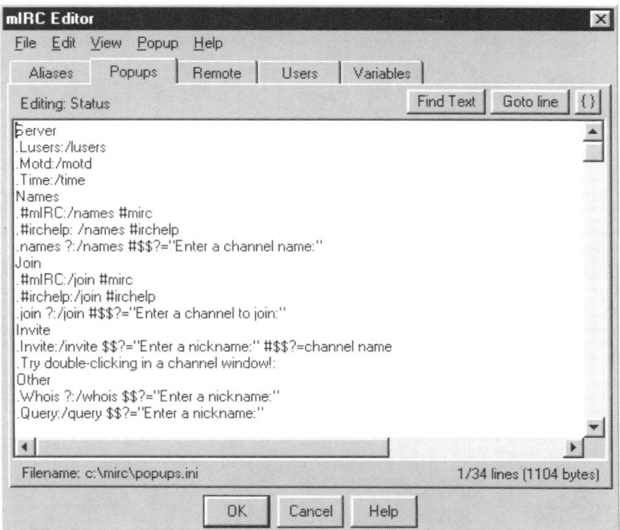

Figure 2-a. mIRC Popup status edit box

In this section you can also set up how you want to ignore certain people who are messaging you. Again, this only works in private message or query windows. If you want to ignore someone and tell him or her why, the command under the menu item Ignore is: .Ignore Completely:/ignore $$1 3 | /notice $$1 <your message> | /close -m $$1. If you only want to ignore a user for a specified time period, say an hour, the command is: .Ignore one hour:/ignore -pcntiu3600 $$1 3 | /notice $$1 <your message> | /close -m $$1. And if you want to only ignore a user in private messages and not in the channel for a time, the command is: .Ignore one hour except channel: /ignore -pcntiu3600 $$1 3 | /notice $$1 <your message> | /close -m $$1.

Tip: Invalid CTCP messages are not replied to.

In these commands you already know what the /ignore, the $$1, and the /notice mean. The -pcntiu3600 tells mIRC to ignore this nick for 3,600 seconds (one hour) and the -m tells mIRC to close the message window for that nick. See Figure 2-b on the following page for an example of the Popup Query/Chat option and these commands.

The next option in the Popups edit box is Channel. In this option, you set up Channel popup menu items. These are activities and actions you can perform on or to a channel. These type of activities and actions include phrases you say a lot, commands you use most often, and so forth.

Tip: Although the maximum number of items for menus in popups has increased, you can still only have 300 menu items for each popup menu.

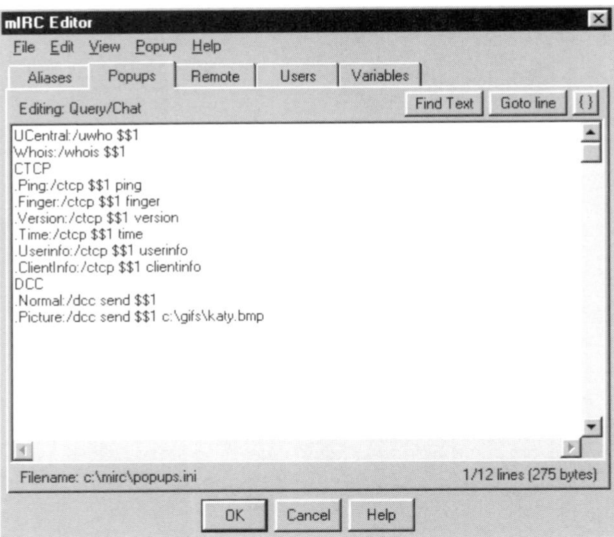

Figure 2-b. mIRC Popup query/chat edit box

Begin by creating a menu item called Commands. Under this menu item add some of your most often used commands. Here are a few examples of some you can use:

- .Action:/action $$?="enter action:" — pops up a dialog box and lets you enter your action statement
- .Invite:/invite $$?="enter nick:" $$?="enter #channel:" — lets you invite a nick to your channel by specifying a nick in the dialog box that appears
- .List of channels w/keywords:/list$$?=only channels with over ? odd people:" $$?=List only upto ? channels on list:" $$?="Find Channels with words like:" — performs a list of channels for you per the minimum/maximum and keyword settings you specify in the dialog boxes that appear
- .Msg:/msg $$nick?="enter #channel or |nickname:" $$?="enter message:" — lets you private message someone
- .Notice:/notice $$?="enter nick:" $$?="enter message:" — lets you send a notice to someone

You can use these command parameters to set up other similar channel commands, such as notifies, notices to all channel ops, or messages to all channel ops. You can also use this section to set up menu items for other commands like /say, /logging, /ulist, /flood, /fsend, /fserve, /perform, /quit, /flush, and others. Following are some of the commands you can create popups for:

- .Say:/say $$?="enter what you want to say:" — lets you say something on a channel
- .Play:/sound $$?="enter nickname or #channel:" $$?="enter sound file:" or .Play .wav or .mid files:/splay $$?="enter filename:" — lets you enter the name of the sound file and the channel to play wave or midi files
- .Logging:/log $$?="on or off:" $$?="enter channel or window name to log:" — lets you start a log
- .User list:/ulist | $$?="enter level:" — lists all users in your remotes users list

- .Flood control:/flood $$?="enter number of lines:" $$?="enter seconds:" $$?="enter pausetime:" — lets you set up a crude flood protection
- .Fsend:/fsend $$?="set to on or off:" — lets you turn your file send on and off
- .Fserve:/fserve $$?="enter nickname:" $$?="enter maxgets:" $$?="enter home-directory:" — lets you set up a user to access your file server
- .Quit:/quit $$?="enter message:" — lets you enter a parting message before you quit IRC
- .Add/Remove Ignores:/ignore -rpcntik $$?="enter on or off:" $$?="enter nick-name or address:" — lets you turn ignore on and off for specified users

Use these as examples and set up a few of your own. Next we look at the Nicknames options in this edit box. This Nicknames option lets you set up popup menus that interact with nicknames. You can add kick and/or ban commands, op and deop commands, and CTCP commands. mIRC has given you some to start with, but you can also add some of your own custom commands. I do not cover any of these here because they are pretty basic commands you can learn by copying what mIRC has already given you. See Figure 2-c for an example of the Popup Channel option and these commands.

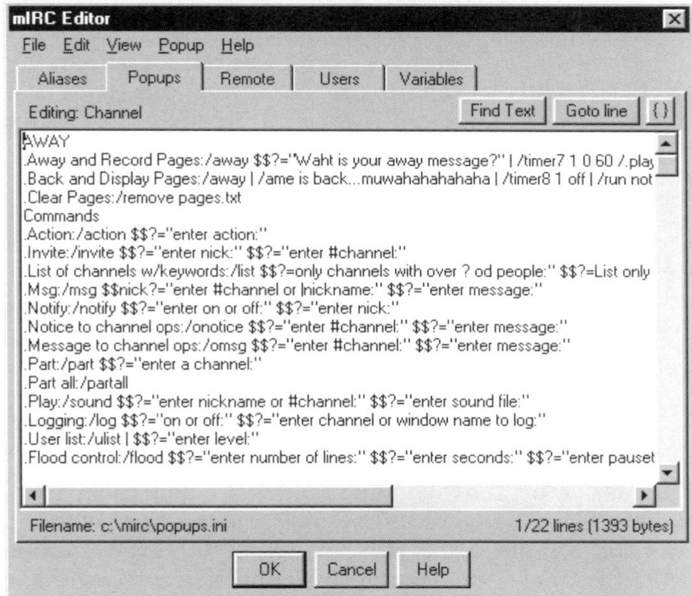

Figure 2-c. mIRC Popup channel edit box

Technique: mIRC has improved this new 5.11 version to let you build as many levels of popup menus as you need.

This area is where you can add some of those fancy hugs and other actions as well as text files. Remember to type these commands all on one line and to use Ctrl+k before entering any color codes. You can also set up the same ignore, send, and chat commands you set up under Query/Chat. Refer back to that section and copy those commands here if you want to be able to use them with nicknames in channels or with the channel names list.

Technique: You can cause mIRC to perform a /whois on people in your notify list when they log into IRC by placing a + sign before their nickname or address in your notify list.

Occasionally you see people display panes full of ASCII art. What they are doing is telling mIRC to display the contents of a text file. You can create popups to read or play text files when you click on them. I made a menu called Text and then submenus for the type of text files I have, for instance, .Cats, .Bunny, .Flag, etc. The command to initiate a text file to a channel is: .<submenu name>:/play <directory and file name>. Therefore if you have a text file of ASCII art of cats the popup command looks like this: .Cats:/play c:\mirc\text\cats.txt.

Then there are all those fancy greetings and hugs you see people use on channels. You can create popups for them just like you did for aliases. Here are a few you can add and use as examples to learn how to do some on your own:

- .RRoses:/say ^k9^~+*<^k3{^k4@ ^k9^~+*<^k3{^k4@^k^k1 $$1 ^k^k4@^k3}^k9>*+~^ ^k4@^k3}^k9>*+~^ (The ^ character after the numbers is the ^ character you use in this popup; it is not the Ctrl key. The Ctrl key is only used with k to insert the color codes that follow it and the k.) — This popup displays red roses with the nick you selected onto the channel.
- .Smiles:/me ^k1,14:) ^k1,8:) ^k1,4:) ^k1,5:) ^k1,6:) ^k1,8:) ^k1,6:) ^k1,9 $$1 ^k1,11(: ^k1,12(: ^k1,7(: ^k1,9(: ^k1,10(: ^k1,9(:^k1,8(: — This popup displays smiley faces in different colors around the nick you selected.
- .Big Hug!:/me hugs ^k10,15 (¯`'·.¸(¯`'·.¸ $$1 ¸.·'´¯)¸.·'´¯) /me hugs ^k10,15 (_¸.·'´(_¸.·'´ $$1 `'·.¸_)`'·.¸_) — This popup displays wavy hearts around the nick you selected.

See Figure 2-d on the following page for an example of this Nicknames option in the Popups edit box and the commands covered in this section.

The Popup Menu option for the menu bar works the same as for the Channel Popup menu option. The $1 always refers to the nickname of the user you have selected. You can add popups in this edit box option. I, however, choose to leave it blank because the Channel and Nicknames List options are easier to access and display for me to see anytime I right-click.

There are several different types of popups in this section. Several of the identifiers were used in creating these popups. Use this section to practice creating popups in mIRC and learn how to create custom aliases for your needs.

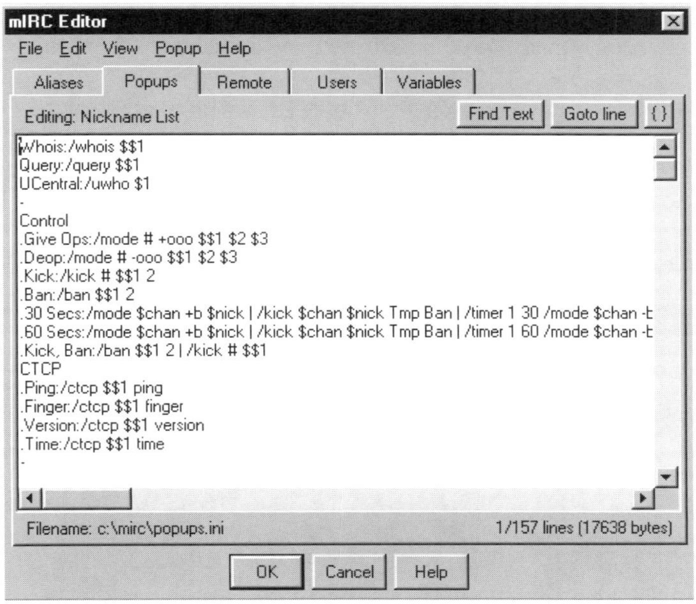

```
mIRC Editor
File Edit View Popup Help
Aliases Popups Remote Users Variables
Editing: Nickname List                         Find Text  Goto line  { }
Whois:/whois $$1
Query:/query $$1
UCentral:/uwho $1
-
Control
.Give Ops:/mode # +ooo $$1 $2 $3
.Deop:/mode # -ooo $$1 $2 $3
.Kick:/kick # $$1 2
.Ban:/ban $$1 2
.30 Secs:/mode $chan +b $nick | /kick $chan $nick Tmp Ban | /timer 1 30 /mode $chan -b
.60 Secs:/mode $chan +b $nick | /kick $chan $nick Tmp Ban | /timer 1 60 /mode $chan -b
.Kick, Ban:/ban $$1 2 | /kick # $$1
CTCP
.Ping:/ctcp $$1 ping
.Finger:/ctcp $$1 finger
.Version:/ctcp $$1 version
.Time:/ctcp $$1 time
-
Filename: c:\mirc\popups.ini                   1/157 lines (17638 bytes)
OK  Cancel  Help
```

Figure 2-d. mIRC Popup nicknames list edit box

Pirch

Pirch differs a little in how its commands are handled in popups just as it does for aliases. Not all the commands and identifiers are the same between these two programs. Also, Pirch has its Popups editor window set up similar but slightly different than it is in mIRC. Pirch breaks its popups into four groups—Server Window, Channels (Names List), Channel (Main Pane), and Private Msg/DCC Chat.

To start creating popups, select Popups from the toolbar and start with Status Window. In this window we can create some popups like we did in mIRC that work when you right-click on the Status Window. Many of the popups you create in Pirch to work like the ones we covered in mIRC require you use PIL scripts with them. The Away with Timer is one of those. These type of popups are discussed in detail in Chapter 13.

Pirch already has a Set Away and Cancel Away popup setup for the Status Window. You do not find this in the list of commands when you click on the Status Window option in the Popup edit box. But, when you right-click on the Status Window, Away is the first menu item you get. Under Away is Set Away and Cancel Away. These are simple away commands that let you type in the message you want to leave and click to cancel the away.

The next option in this Popups edit box is the Channel (Names List). In this section you set up popups to interact with the other members on the channel. Of course Pirch already has some set up for you to handle CTCP commands as well as mode changes and kick/bans.

Following are some fancy popups and text file commands you can set up under the Channel (Names List) option of this edit box to interact with users on your channel:

- .HUGS1:/me ^k^k13,1gives a ^k^k8,1R^k^k9,1a^k^k10,1I^k^k11,1n^k^k12,1b^k^k13,1o^k^k4,1w ^k^k13,1hug to ^k^k^k8,1{^k^k9,1{^k^k10,1{^k^k11,1{^k^k12,1{^k^k13,1{^k8,4 $1 ^k8,1}^k^k9,1}^k^k10,1^k^k11,1}^k^k12,1}^k^k13,1}^k — this popup displays a rainbow of colors around the nick you select.
- .Hearts:/me ^k3 (¯`'·.¸(¯`'·.¸ $$1 (_¸.·'´(_¸.·'´ $$1 `'·.¸_)`'·.¸_) ^k9 (¯`'·.¸(¯`'·.¸ $$1 ¸.·'´¯)¸.·'´¯) ^k11 (_¸.·'´(_¸.·'´ $$1 `'·.¸_)`'·.¸_) ^k12 (¯`'·.¸(¯`'·.¸ $$1 ¸.·'´¯)¸.·'´¯) ^k13 (_¸.·'´(_¸.·'´ $$1 `'·.¸_)`'·.¸_) ^k14 (¯`'·.¸(¯`'·.¸ $$1 ¸.·'´¯)¸.·'´¯) ^k3 (_¸.·'´(_¸.·'´ $$1 `'·.¸_)`'·.¸_) ^k4 (¯`'·.¸(¯`'·.¸ $$1 ¸.·'´¯)¸.·'´¯) ^k9 (_¸.·'´(_¸.·'´ $$1 `'·.¸_)`'·.¸_) ^k11 (¯`'·.¸(¯`'·.¸ $$1 ¸.·'´¯)¸.·'´¯) ^k12 (_¸.·'´(_ — this popup displays wavy hearts around the nick you select.
- .TXrose:/me ^k^k^k4hands $1 a dozen TEXAS Roses, 1 YELLOW and 11 RED! ^k^k8,1{@}^k^k3,1-}--}--- ^k^k4,1{@}^k^k3,1-}--}--- ^k^k4,1{@}^k^k3,1-}--}--- ^k^k4,1{@}^k^k3,1-}--}--- ^k^k4,1{@}^k^k3,1-}--}--- ^k^k4,1{@}^k^k3,1-}--}--- ^k^k4,1{@}^k^k3,1-}--}--- ^k^k4,1{@}^k^k3,1-}--}--- ^k^k4,1{@}^k^k3,1-}--}--- ^k^k4,1{@}^k^k3,1-}--}--- ^k^k4,1{@}^k^k3,1-}--}--- ^k^k4,1{@}^k^k3,1-}--}--- ^k^k4 cuz you're the best!! — this popup displays colored ASCII art roses around the nick you select.
- .Bunny:/playfile # c:\mirc\text\bunny.txt — this popup displays the contents of a text file to the channel. Notice that in mIRC the command was /play and here in Pirch it's /playfile.

You can also set up a popup to introduce and play a text file with the fancy popups. Here are a few that I have:

- .Rabbit:/me hands \-2 \-22 $$1 \-22 \-2 | /playfile # c:\pirch\text\bunny.txt 1
- .Rose:/me hands $$1 | /playfile # c:\pirch\text\rosepu.txt

You can find numerous sites on the web that have text or ASCII art files you can use in the popups and aliases. One site that I recommend is http://home.sol.no/kseide/Ascii/index.html. This site has several links for sources of ASCII art.

Also under this Popups option, you can create actions and other interactive popups. Pirch has already created popups for some of the commonly used commands you can use with other users like ignore, notify, protect, add users, and so forth. However, you can add others to this option to create custom popups with more functionality.

Begin by creating a menu item for each type of command you want to create. For the first menu, create one called Commands. Under this menu item let's add some commands you use most often. Here are a few examples of some you can use:

- .Action:/action $$?="enter action:" — pops up a dialog box and lets you enter your action statement
- .Invite:/invite $$?="enter nick:" $$?="enter #channel:" — lets you invite a nick to your channel that you specify in the dialog box that appears
- .List of channels w/keywords:/list $$?=only channels with over ? odd people:"

$$?=List only upto ? channels on list:" $$?="Find channels with words like:" — performs a list of channels for you per the minimum/maximum and keyword settings you specify in the dialog box that appears

- .Msg:/msg $$?="enter nickname:" $$?="enter message:" — lets you private message someone
- .Notice:/notice $$?="enter nick:" $$?="enter message:" — lets you send a notice to someone
- .Request Bio:/notice $$1 !BIOSEND — sends a notice to the highlighted user that you want their bio
- .Send Bio:/bio send $$1 — sends your bio to the highlighted nick
- .View the Bio:/bioview $$1 — lets you view a bio

You can use these command parameters to set up other similar channel commands like for notifies, notices to all channel ops or messages to all channel ops. You can also use this section to set up menu items for other commands like /say, /logging, /ulist, /flood, /fsend, /fserve, /perform, /quit, /flush, and others. Following are some of the commands you can create popups with:

- .Say:/say $$?="enter what you want to say:"
- .Play:/sound $$?="enter nickname or #channel:" $$?="enter sound file — lets you enter the name of the sound file and the channel to play wave or midi files.
- .Quit:/quit $$?="enter message:" — lets you enter a parting message before you quit IRC.
- .Picture:/dcc send $$1 <directory and file name> — lets you send your picture to a nick you select

These will get you started and help you learn to create others on your own. Pirch commands for these aliases and popups are a little more difficult to learn, but given time and practice, you can master it. See Figure 2-e for an example of the Channel (Names List) option and the commands covered here.

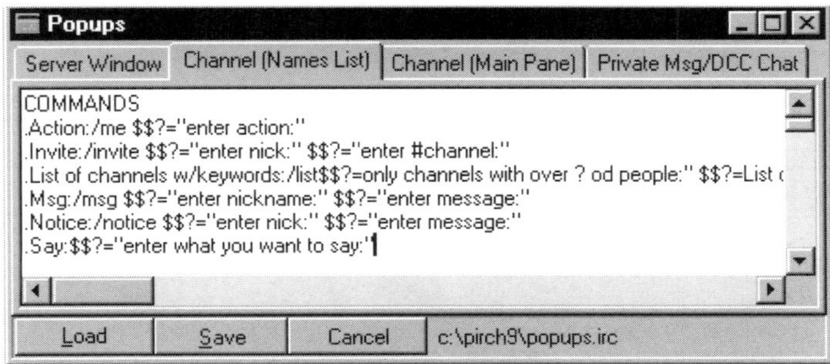

Figure 2-e. Pirch Popup Channel (Names List) edit box

The next option in the Popups edit box is Channel (Main Pane). Pirch has already established several popups that pertain to the main window panes. You can add to these if you like. The only things I added to mine were some text files to play on channel when I select them. Refer to the Channel (Names List) for an example of the command to use (see Figure 2-f).

Figure 2-f. Pirch Popup Channel (Main Pane) edit box

The last item in this Popups edit box is the Private Msg/DCC Chat option. In this option you set up menu items to handle CTCP functions, DCC Sends and Chats handled with private messages, and DCC Chats. You can also add the DCC Send of your picture to this section. See the previous section for the command to use. Then when you right-click in a message or query window, you can select this menu item to send your picture.

In this section you can also add an ignore command. Unless you create a PIL, you cannot just create the basic commands for ignoring someone for a set amount of time like you can with mIRC. Again, these commands only work in private message or query windows. If you want to ignore someone and tell them why, the command under menu item Ignore is: .Ignore Completely:/ignore $$1 3 | /notice $$1 <your message> | /close -m $$1 (see Figure 2-g).

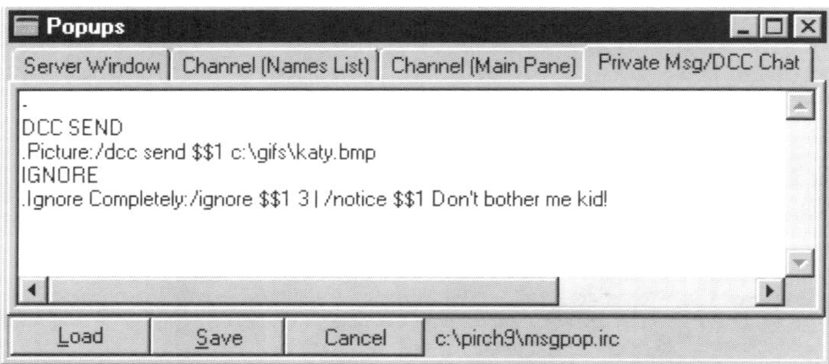

Figure 2-g. Pirch Popup Private Msg/DCC Chat edit box

The commands and popups we created here give you a good base to start with. Use them, copy them into your popups, and alter them to fit your needs. The exercises here also help you to learn how to do some of these on your own. Soon you'll be a popup master and your online friends will look at you with awe!

Exercises

Refer back to the chapters and use the help files for the IRC clients to help you with these exercises.

mIRC

1. Create an away popup with a timer and a message.
2. Create a DCC Send popup to automatically send your picture to a user.
3. Create a fancy color-coded popup.

Pirch

1. Create a Send Bio popup.
2. Create a fancy color-coded popup.
3. Create a text file popup.

Chapter 3

Remotes and Events

In this chapter you learn:

- ☑ *What are Remotes and Events?*
- ☑ *How to Create Events and Commands, etc. in mIRC*
- ☑ *How to Create Events and Controls in Pirch*
- ☑ *Exercises*

What are Remotes and Events?

The Remote tool in mIRC and the Events tool in Pirch let you specify how you want the programs to react or reply to CTCP messages or IRC events by or from other users. These tools let you set up their programs to respond to almost any remote command you can think of. Almost any command you can type can be executed remotely with these tools. Setting up remote events and commands frees you up to participate more in the actual chatting on IRC channels and forces the programs to handle the commands for you.

This chapter discusses the two most popular IRC clients—mIRC and Pirch—and how you can create remotes or events in them. You learn some of the most common remotes and events you can create and how to create and customize some of your own.

Remotes and events are some of the more complex of the two IRC clients' functions to master. You need a good understanding of aliases and IRC commands in order to master this area of these programs. In this chapter I give some remotes for various situations and in the exercises you learn to create some of your own. Between examining how the examples are created and work and the exercises, you learn how to create some of the more complicated and complex remotes and events to automate some of your most common commands.

How to Create Events, Commands, etc. in mIRC

To begin, select the Remotes toolbar icon. Notice this Remote edit box has five options—Users, Variables, Commands, Events, and Raw. The Users option is where mIRC keeps a list of all authorized users and their access levels. Variables contains a list of all your currently defined variables. Commands is where you set up a list of CTCP commands that mIRC is to react to. Events keeps a list of events to which mIRC should react. Raw contains a list of raw numeric server messages that mIRC is to respond to.

Tip: mIRC shows the User mode in the status window title bar.

Users

Let's take these options one by one in the order they appear in the Remote edit box. The first option is Users. Click on it to display the Users edit box. In this section of remotes, you assign various user levels to your friends and potential enemies. This option is important to the other options in these remotes. Many of the events and commands you set up rely on your users lists to respond correctly. They allow you to control how mIRC reacts to certain users.

Technique: Using the /flush <level> command clears the users lists of nicknames that are no longer valid. mIRC checks these users lists for nicks that match the specified level and if the nick is not currently on a channel you're on, it removes them from the list. If you don't specify a level, mIRC clears all nicks from the users list that aren't on channels you're on.

For instance, if you want to kick people from your channel when they use certain words, you can set up a remote to do that. But if you only want to kick certain people or not kick your channel ops, your closest friends, you can do this too with these remotes, and this is where the user lists and levels come into play.

Tip: Users in your users list can have more than one access level.

What numbers you choose for user levels is entirely up to you. However, by default, mIRC assigns anyone not specified as a user the level of 1. Whatever level you choose for friends and enemies determines how you set up many of the commands and events in this Remote tool.

See Figure 3-a for an example of user lists and commands.

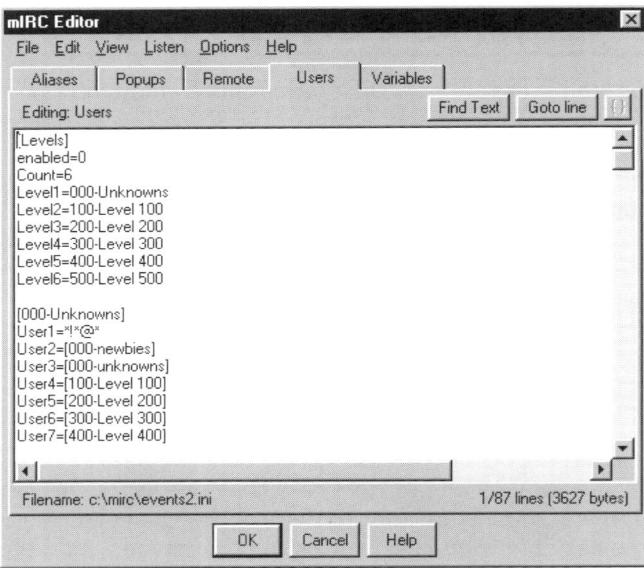

Figure 3-a. mIRC Remote/Users edit box

As a review, the command line for adding users is: /auser <level> <nick or address>. Using this command, mIRC adds the nick or address you specified to the level you specified without checking the validity of the address. It is added exactly as you typed it. You can of course use the /guser <level> <nick> [type] command which adds a nick to your user list. With this command, mIRC performs a /whois on the nick you indicated and adds the returned address to the user list level you specified. Using [type] as part of the command tells mIRC to add the nick with several types of wild card addresses.

Tip: The /auser, /guser and /ruser commands can handle multiple levels. The /auser and /guser, by default, replace existing users with the specified level unless you use -a in the command to add specified levels to existing users. The /ruser command removes the specified level and if all levels are removed, the user is removed.

Along with these adduser and getuser commands you can also remove users with the /ruser <nick or nick! or address [type]>. To use this command you must know exactly how the nick or address is listed in your user list.

Tip: If a user is listed in your user list as nick!username@host.net, you can use the /ruser nick! to remove the entire line.

mIRC recognizes several different types [type] of user addresses. They are as follows:

- Type 0 — *!username@host.net

- Type 1 — *!*username@host.net
- Type 2 — *!*@host.net
- Type 3 — *!*username@*.host.net
- Type 4 — *!*@*.host.net
- Type 5 — nickname!username@host.net
- Type 6 — nickname!*username@host.net
- Type 7 — nickname!*@host.net
- Type 8 — nickname!*username@*.host.net
- Type 9 — nickname!*@*.host.net

Technique: mIRC extended the /rlevel command to include an option -r. When the -r is used in the command with a level, the specified level(s) are removed from users that have them; if it's not used, the command works as usual.

If you don't specify a type, then mIRC removes the indicated nick from the user list. However, if you do specify a type, mIRC looks up the user's address and removes that address from the list. The stars and exclamation points in these addresses are wild cards. You can use these wild card type addresses to indicate users with changing IP addresses.

Tip: Type 6 is the default type for users lists.

These users lists you create are stored in an internal database in mIRC. They help speed up the performance of commands like /ban, /guser, and /ruser. These commands automatically perform a /whois on the nick the command is issued on and the database stores their address information. Then when commands are performed that need this information, mIRC does an internal list search to match the nick address to its list of addresses.

Another user command you may have need for is the /flush command. This command removes all users who are listed by their nicks and not currently in any channels that you are in. It does not remove any users you added using the /guser command. To perform a flush of your user list type /flush <level>. <Level> is the level of users you want flushed from the user list. Along these same lines you can also use the /rlevel command to do essentially the same thing. Typing /rlevel <level> removes all users with that level setting from your user list.

Technique: mIRC maintains an internal list of nick!user@address for all users that are in the same channel(s) you're in, and uses that list search and find user address for your users lists.

If you want to change the level of a user on your list, use the /auser -a <level> or /guser -a <level> command. For instance, if you have a friend whose nick is johnd and has a level 100 and you want to increase him to a level 300, you can type this command as /auser -a 300 johnd. Now johnd is a level 100 and a level 300.

To find out who is on your user list for a certain level without having to open up the Remote tool, type /ulist <level>. This gives you a list of everyone on that level in your user list. You can also use the greater than and less than characters to list users on levels higher or lower than the level you indicate. The command looks like this: /ulist >100 and lists all users with a level of 100 or higher.

You can prevent users from accessing certain levels by beginning their level with an equal sign. Their level would look like this: =150:nickname!username@host.net. This nick only has access to level 150 commands you program into commands or events. You can also use the = prefix to give a user access to several levels. For instance you can give johnd access to levels 100, 200, 300, and 400 by typing 100=200=300=400:nickname!johnd@host.net. Each level following the equal signs is treated as equal and this user can access any commands equal to or lower than 100. This user also has access specifically to levels 200, 300, and 400 commands.

Once you get your users lists set up, they work interactively with commands and events to react to those users. This is discussed with the exact commands under these two sections.

Variables

The Variables option lets you save information you use often and also information that you want to be able to edit. Variables always start with the % character and can have names of any length that contain numbers, words, or lines of text. With variables using numbers you can use mathematical manipulations to increase, decrease, add, and subtract variables with given values to or from each other.

Variables may seem to be difficult to use or understand. However, they are relatively easy to use and can be helpful in script writing. In this section we only cover some of the simpler variables. The more complex variable are covered in the scripting chapter, Chapter 13.

One of the easiest variables you can set up is one that counts for you. For instance, if you want to know how many people access your fserve during an IRC session, you can count them yourself or you can set up a variable to count for you. The basic command for a variable is: /set [%variable][value]. The %variable is the way variables are listed; remember they always have the % preceding them. The [value] is what the variable will be.

For a variable to count the number of times your fserve is accessed, you need to begin with the command you have in your remote events option that activates your fserve. That command looks like this: 1:ON TEXT:*!fserve*:#:/fserve $nick 5 <directory and path>. Next you want to alter this command to not only let users access your fserver but to also count those accesses. To begin with you set your variable to 1 with this command: /set %fserve 1. In order for this variable to count the number of accesses to your fserve you must tell it to increase or decrease the variable by using the /inc or /dec commands. Therefore, if we want this variable to count up the number of users who access our fserve we need to type the command as: /inc %fserve 1. Now we add this to our existing fserve ON TEXT command line separated by the pipe character. The command now looks like this: 1:ON TEXT:*!fserve*:#:/fserve $nick 5 <directory and path> | /inc %fserve 1. With this command, mIRC counts each time a user types !fserve. See Figure 3-b for an example of this variable.

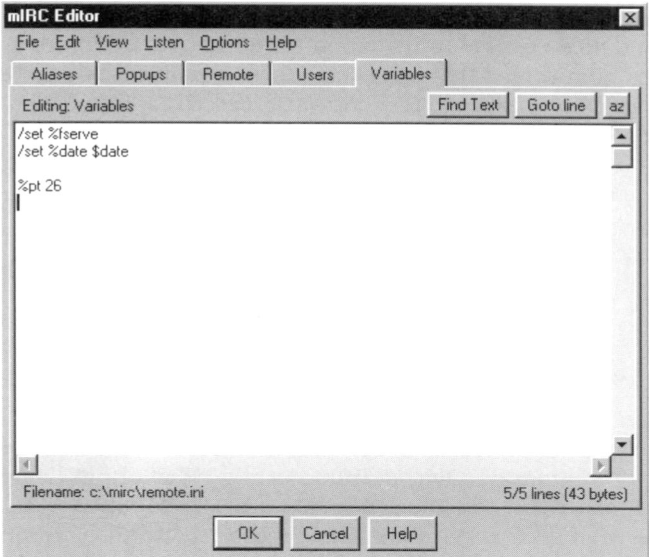

Figure 3-b. mIRC Remote/Variables edit box

Following are some available variable commands you can use:

- /set — sets the variable
- /unset — unsets the variable
- /unsetall — deletes all variables
- /inc — increases a variable by a number or variable
- /dec — decreases a variable by a number or variable

Since variables are used mostly with scripts and scripting, it is covered in more detail in that chapter. Variables as used in aliases, popups, remotes, events, and commands are given detailed coverage in Chapter 13.

Commands

The Commands option in mIRC Remotes is for specific commands—CTCP commands. This option lets you do only one thing—force mIRC to respond to CTCP commands sent by other users. The normal CTCP commands you can respond to are Version, Ping, Time, Userinfo, Clientinfo, and Finger. Normally, mIRC responds in a standard format when one of these commands is sent to it. In this option, you can set up customized responses to any of these CTCP command requests.

For instance when someone does a CTCP Ping on you, the normal response back to them is [yournick PING replay]: pingtime or [katykat PING reply]: 1 second. When you set up a CTCP Ping command reply in this Command option, the user gets a different response. He gets your reply notice and the standard reply. For example, -katykat- and you thought I was sleeping....LOL :> - [katykat PING reply]: 1 second. You can also set this command response so that it does not give the standard ping reply in addition to your custom ping reply.

Remember that one of the words in IRC is Relay. Relay means that your messages to other people and vice versa pass from one server to other servers until they reach their target. Sometimes this can take a few seconds or less and sometimes longer. For this reason the command /ping was created. Along these same lines /version, /userinfo, /time, /finger, and /clientinfo were created. All these commands give you some kind of information about the user you perform them on. Let's take a look at how you can use this Command option to set up custom responses to the command requests for information.

With pings you can determine not only how mIRC responds to other users performing them on you, but how it responds to you when they do. To begin, we start with a reply that is sent when someone pings you. In this command edit box type the following: 1:PING:/notice $nick <your message>. Then when someone pings you he gets your message in response.

Notice that these commands are made up of three sections separated by colons. This is how this command breaks down: <command level>:<ctcp command>:<triggered command(s) with parameter(s)>. Command Level is the level of users this command responds to—remember 1 is the default level for all users. Ctcp Command is the CTCP command mIRC is to respond to. Triggered Command(s) with Parameter(s) is where you define the trigger command—how mIRC is to respond. In this area there are specific identifiers and commands that are recognized. They are as follows:

Note: The $chan is not recognized or defined in mIRC's Remote commands.

Identifiers

- $nick — the nick of the person who sent the command
- $address — the full address of the person who sent the command
- $site — the site of the person who sent the command
- $level — the user's remote level
- $parms — any text the person sent including ! the command
- $parm1 — lets you break down $parms into individual words
- $parm2* — has the second word in the command and all after it
- $parm3* — has the third word in the command and all after it

Warning: Improper settings can crash mIRC with a GPF (general protection fault).

Commands

- ping — gives the lag time of a user
- version — gives the version of the software the user is using
- userinfo — gives you information on the user similar to /whois information
- clientinfo — gives the type and version of IRC program the user is using
- time — gives the user's current time

- finger — gives the user's finger info, usually an e-mail address unless he or she specifies otherwise with finger text file
- whois — gives current status of user—ID info, idle time, who and where the user is, and what server he or she is on
- whowas — gives status info on a user that just left IRC, such as ID info and what server he or she was on

Other identifiers and commands recognized

- notice — send notice to user
- dcc send — send files to user
- fserve — activates the file server
- wavplay — plays a sound
- splay — plays a sound
- speak — activates Monologue speak utility

The CTCP command can be named anything you want. You can use the standard CTCP commands or you can create some of your own, like OPME, Leave, XDCC List, etc. You can also, as in aliases and popups, have multiple commands as long as you use the pipe character (|) to separate them.

Now that you have some commands and identifiers to work with, let's create some other commands for this option. Previously I told you that you could use this option to set up commands that react to users performing these CTCP commands on you and also to respond to you when this happens. You learned how to set up a custom response to a CTCP Ping request. Now let's see how to set up replies to users with different user levels. The commands look like this:

<user level>:ping:/notice $nick <your message>, example, 1:ping:/notice $nick and you thought I was sleeping:)

<different user level>:ping:/notice $nick <different message>, example, 2:ping:/notice $nick ewwww......that tickles.....hahahahaha

<different user level>:ping:/notice $nick <different message>, example, 3:ping:/notice $nick any my current time is----→ LOL

When users with these different user levels ping you, they get the response that matches their user level. Make sure your user levels here match the user levels in your users lists.

Now if you want to be notified with a sound when someone pings you, or you want to send a wave file to the sender when you are pinged, the command is as follows: 1:PING:/splay <soundfile> |/notice $nick <your message>. Of course you can set these up for different responses and waves for different levels of users.

If you want to also ping the person back who has pinged you and give that person either your custom response or your custom response and play a sound, the commands are as follows:

- Ping back with response only — 1:PING:/notice $nick <your message> |/ping $nick
- Ping back with response and sound — 1:PING:/splay <sound file> |/notice $nick <your message> |/ping $nick

When the person pings you, your sound plays, he gets your custom message, and he gets pinged back by you. Or, if you chose not to use the sound command, he just gets pinged back and receives your message. Customizing responses to the other commands works much the same way.

If you use this /ping nick back command, do *not* ping yourself. When you ping yourself with this command line in your remotes, you get into a continuous loop of pinging yourself again and again. The only way to stop this is to disconnect from the server and relog.

Following are some examples of commands you can include in this Command option to respond to the other CTCP command requests you might get from other users:

Tip: You can also use /play as a command in Remote commands.

- Finger — 1:FINGER:/notice $nick <your e-mail and home page address>. You can add the sound command and finger back command separated by the | and you can customize these to different user levels. Example, 1:FINGER:/notice $nick tokat@flash.net and http://www.flash.net/~tokat | /finger $nick |/halt
- Version — 1:VERSION:/splay <sound file> | /notice $nick <your message> |/version $nick. Example, 1:VERSION:/splay crazy.wav |/notice $nick I am using mIRC version 4.72, how about you? |/version $nick
- Time — 1:TIME:/notice $nick <your message> $time. Example, 1:TIME:/notice $nick My time is $time
- Userinfo — 1:USERINFO:/notice $nick <your message> |/halt. Example, 1:USERINFO:/notice $nick why not just ask..I'll be glad to tell you:) |/halt

Technique: With this new version of mIRC you can use 1:PING:/notice $nick <your message> or the old format 1:PING:/notice *1:$nick <your message>. However, the first command processes faster.

These give you a few examples of some CTCP command responses you can use to customize the replies mIRC sends. Notice in the Finger and the Userinfo commands the /halt command at the end. This prevents the normal reply to this CTCP request from being sent. See Figure 3-c on the following page for an example of these commands. Try these out and create some of your own to customize your replies.

You can use this Command edit box to add any number of different commands to interact with users and CTCP queries. You can create a command that lets high level users send you /ctcp commands to have you kick people—500:KICK:/kick $parm2* which takes everything after the word kick and sends it to the kick command. For instance if someone sent you this: /ctcp <your nick> kick #<channel name> <nick to kick> <their message>, it would activate the kick command through you and kick the indicated nick from your channel. You can set up OPME, DEOPME, and other such commands here. Play around with this and see what you can create on your own.

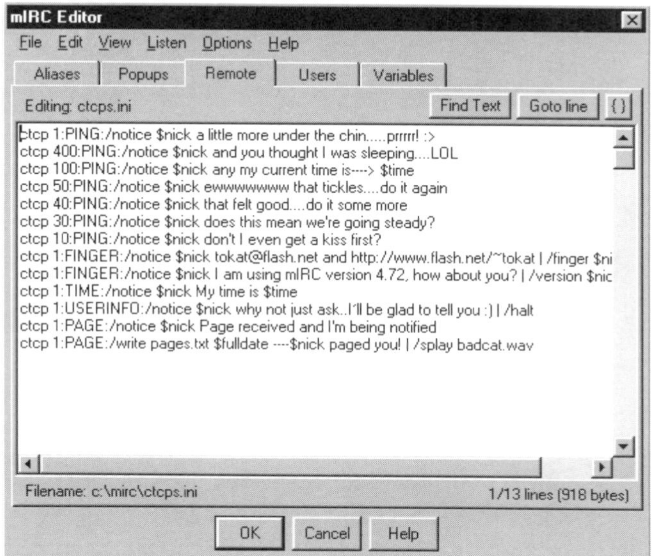

Figure 3-c. mIRC Remote/Command edit box

Events

Events is where you can have a lot of fun and create many different commands to interact with users. These Remote/Events deal with just about anything else that can happen on IRC. These events respond to certain events as follows:

- ON TEXT — happens when specified words or phrases are found in channels or private messages
- ON JOIN — occurs when a user joins a channel

Tip: Adding a + sign before the user level in an Event command limits this command to only that level user.

- ON PART — happens when a user leaves a channel
- ON KICK — occurs when a user is kicked from a channel
- ON OP — happens when a user is opped

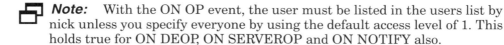

Note: With the ON OP event, the user must be listed in the users list by nick unless you specify everyone by using the default access level of 1. This holds true for ON DEOP, ON SERVEROP and ON NOTIFY also.

- ON DEOP — happens when a user is deopped
- ON BAN/ON UNBAN — works on users that are banned or unbanned
- ON INVITE — happens when you are invited to a channel
- ON NICK — occurs when a user changes his nick

- ON QUIT — works when a user quits IRC
- ON TOPIC — happens when the channel topic is changed
- ON SERVEROP — occurs when a server gives ops status to a user on a channel
- ON NOTIFY — works when people on your notify list join IRC
- ON MODE — forces a certain set of channel modes
- ON SERVERMODE — same as ON MODE
- ON VOICE/ON DEVOICE — reacts to people getting or losing voice on channels
- ON ACTION — occurs when specified words or phrases are used in action statements
- ON NOTICE — works the same as ON TEXT and ON ACTION
- ON SNOTICE — listens for server notices and lets you filter, display or react to them
- ON CHAT — happens when specified words are used in DCC Chats
- ON SERV — works like ON CHAT but listens to DCC Fileserver text
- ON FILESENT — reacts to all successful DCC Send file transfers
- ON FILERCVD — reacts to all successful DCC Get file transfers
- ON CTCPREPLY — listens for replies to CTCPs

Technique: The ON TEXT event searches for keywords according to how you specify using wild card definitions, e.g., =text recognizes the exact word, text* recognizes the start word, *text recognizes this word as the end of a line, and *text* recognizes the word used anywhere.

Along with these events, this option also uses special identifiers. Here are a few you use most often:

- $nick — the nick of the person who activated the event
- $address — the full address of the person who sent the command
- $site — the site of the person who sent the command
- $level — the user's remote level
- $chan — the channel where the event triggered the command
- $parms — any text in the line that triggered the event
- $parm1 — lets you break down $parms into individual words
- $parm3* — contains the third word and all after ($parm2* contains the second word and all after, etc.)

Tip: You can use $snick to return a list of selected nicks from the channel names list and this identifier can be used in commands that take multiple nicks.

Along with creating events you can also create groups of Commands or Events. You separate these groups by placing a # symbol in front of the group name. For example: #GroupA Start, #GroupB Start, etc., with command lines under them.

Then you end them with #GroupA End, #GroupB End, etc. You can also enable and disable groups by using the /enable #<groupname> or /disable #<groupname>. Then a group that is disabled is ignored by the remote when processing these events. You can have many different groups, but you cannot have groups within groups.

Technique: When you use /echo -a in a command, the event results are displayed in your active window. If your active window isn't a status, channel, or query/chat window, it displays in the status window.

You can use the events to handle a number of things for you. They can automatically send sound files to users, activate your file server, send e-mail or phone number information about people on your users list to others on that list, and auto respond to any number of words or phrases you set up. Using any of the events covered previously, you can set up events to automatically handle almost any command you can type manually. Let's take a look at some of the commands mIRC recognizes that you can set up using these events.

Tip: When the $chan identifier is used in a command, it refers to the channel where both you and the user that triggered the event are and on which you are an op.

ON TEXT

If you have a steady group of regular users that often ask for e-mail addresses or phone numbers, you can set up an automatic response to send them this information when they use a keyword. The command looks like this: <user level>:ON TEXT:!<keyword or nick>:# or #<channelname>:/notice $nick <keyword or nick> <e-mail or phone number>, example, 400:ON TEXT:!kirkw:#:/notice $nick kirkw - kirkw@host.com. When a user types !<keyword or nick> the information displays as a notice to them. You can set up one of these for each person for your channel.

Technique: You can use the @ symbol before user levels in event command lines to indicate these users must be a channel operator. However, these events will still work in private messages.

When you want to set up an event to automatically send sounds to people on your channel when they request them, type the following into the Events edit box: <user level>:ON TEXT:!<keyword or nick>*.*:/dcc send $nick <directory and path> $+ $parm2. My command line looks like this: 1:ON TEXT:!katy*.*:/dcc send $nick c:\mirc\waves $+ $parm2. Be sure to put all your waves in their own directory.

Technique: You can also use the * sign to indicate commands that can only be performed by those with ops status.

If you have a tendency to remain logged onto IRC while you do other things, like cook dinner, wash the dishes, do the laundry, watch your favorite television program, or some other real life activity, and want to be alerted when someone in channel is talking to or about you, you can set up an event for just that. The command line looks like this: <user level>:ON TEXT:*<your nick>*:#:/splay <soundfile> or <user level>:ON ACTION:*<your nick>*:#:/splay <soundfile>. Now whenever someone on channel mentions your nick, that sound will play, alerting you.

Tip: When you use the /sound or /wavplay commands, the wave directory and all its subdirectories are searched for the specified wave filename. Therefore you can organize your waves into subdirectories and be confident that mIRC will find the right wave to play.

When you want to warn people that offensive language is not acceptable on your channel, you can set up this command line: 1:ON TEXT:*<offensive word>*:#<channel name>:/notice $nick <your message>. Then when someone uses this offensive word they get this notice sent to them. If you would rather forgo the warning and kick anyone who uses such language, the command line is: 1:ON TEXT:*<offensive word>*:#<channel name>:/notice $nick <your message> | /kick $chan $nick <your message>. You can use these command lines and alter them to include any word you deem should send a warning notice to a user or kick them.

Technique: When you use the /echo command in Event/Commands, it displays text in the specified window.

These give you an idea about what you can do with the ON TEXT event. Add the ones I've given you here and use them as a base to create some of your own. ON NOTICE and ON ACTION do the same thing as ON TEXT but they react to Notices and Actions.

ON JOIN

Of course you can set up auto greets to send greeting messages to users as they join your channel. But there are other things you can do when people join like a /whois on them, /kick, or /splay a sound. Here are how these commands look:

Tip: The /play command can be used with Remote/Events also.

- Whois — 1:ON JOIN:#:/whois $nick
- Kick — 25:ON JOIN:#:/kick $chan $nick <your message> — kicks any level 25 user who joins your channel and sends him your message
- Splay — *+3:ON JOIN:#:/splay <sound file>

Technique: When using the $read or the /play commands in these events, you do not need to specify the number of lines in a file on the first line of the file. mIRC counts the lines itself. However, it does work faster if you include the number of lines.

You can also alter and add to these commands. Use the pipe character (|) to separate commands and add any other commands to these to expand them and have them perform multiple commands. For instance, you can have a sound play when someone joins and also send a greeting or play the sound and then kick him from your channel if that is what you want to do.

Tip: You can use "me" as a user level when creating events. This limits the command to only those events caused by you and your client. This is useful when you have bots with the same address as you have.

ON PART

ON PART is similar to ON JOIN, except it works when someone leaves your channel. You can send a notice or message, send a message to the channel, or invite that person back. Some examples of ON PART commands are: 1:ON PART:#:/notice $nick <your message>, 1:ON PART:/invite $nick $chan or 1:ON PART:#:/msg $nick <your message>.

Tip: The $read identifier picks a line randomly from a file and reads and inserts any text, even commands with identifiers which is the same word as normal commands.

ON KICK

The ON KICK event lets you send a message to the kickee or the kicker or to send a sound file to either party. Here are some examples of ON KICK command lines: 1:ON KICK:#:/splay <sound file>, 1:ON KICK:#:/notice $nick <your message>, or 100:ON KICK:#:/kick $chan $nick | /invite $knick $chan | /notice $nick <your message>. This last command activates when any 100 level user is kicked from your channel and causes you to kick the kicker, invite the 100 level kicked person back, and send the kicker a message.

Tip: The /play command plays single lines randomly picked from a file or you can specify a line. Using -r with this command picks a random line and using -l picks a specified line. You cannot use *1, $1, etc. in the played line.

ON OP and ON DEOP, ON BAN, and ON UNBAN

These ON OP and ON DEOP and ON BAN and ON UNBAN events let you send notices or messages to other users when they have been opped or deopped, banned or unbanned. Here are some examples: 1:ON OP:#:/notice $opnick <your message> or 1:ON DEOP:#:/msg $opnick <your message>. The ON UNBAN with the

ON BAN can easily auto-unban your friends and ban other users.

ON INVITE

With this ON INVITE event you can send messages back to the person inviting you or put him on ignore for a certain period of time. Examples are: 1:ON INVITE:#:/notice <your message> or to ignore 1:ON INVITE:#:/ignore -iu15 $nick 3.

ON NICK

This ON NICK event automatically sends a message to a user when he changes his nick. The commands looks like this: 1:ON NICK:/notice $newnick <your message about> $nick. $nick is the identifier for the old nick and $newnick is the identifier for the new nick. Notice the where portion, the :#: area, of the command line is not used with this event.

ON QUIT

ON QUIT lets you send messages to yourself, the channel, or other users when someone quits your channel. Here is an example of a command you can use: 1:ON QUIT:/notice $me <your message>. Notice again that with this command you do not need the where portion. This event only activates when someone quits IRC altogether.

ON TOPIC

This event lets you send messages when a topic is changed. You can also set up a command to change the topic to one you like and send a message to the channel and/or kick the user that changed the topic. This is especially useful if you have one person who is changing the topic and putting up topics you don't like. The command is as follows: +<userlevel>:ON TOPIC:#<channelname>:/describe $chan <your message> | /topic $chan <your new topic> | /kick $chan $nick <your message>. Then when someone with the user level you specified changes the topic, the channel gets your message, the topic changes to the one you specified, and the user that changed the topic is kicked and gets your kick message.

ON SERVEROP

From time to time the net splits and servers split off from each other. When this happens and the servers rejoin each other, they give ops to those returning to the channel. This is called serverops. Some people know when these splits happen and ride these servers back in to get server ops and then go about disrupting channels by deopping and/or kicking and banning the regular users. You can prevent this from happening by using this ON SERVEROP event. The command is: *1:ON SERVEROP:# or #<channelname>:/mode $chan -o $opnick. You can also add a message to the end that is sent to the person or persons being deopped why you are doing this. Be sure to separate the message command with the pipe character (|).

ON MODE and ON SERVERMODE

The ON MODE and ON SERVERMODE events let you use mIRC to enforce modes you want when someone or the servers change channel modes. A couple of commands you can use for these events are: <user level>:ON MODE:# <channelname>:-<channel modes>+<channel modes>:/notice $nick <your message> and/or: <user level>:ON SERVERMODE:#<channel name>:-<channel modes>+<channel modes>:/notice $me <your message>. This is not a perfect system to react to mode changes. It reacts to any channel mode change and there is no way to make it react to specific mode changes. Even though it's not perfect, it does work if you want to try it out. Also, bear in mind that if you let a higher level person change the modes without you reacting, when a lower level person changes the modes, mIRC resets all the modes, even those set by the higher level person.

ON VOICE and ON DEVOICE

This event reacts to users getting or losing voice on moderated channels. Some examples of this command are: 1:ON VOICE:/notice $nick <your message> or 1:ON DEVOICE:/notice $vnick <your message>. Unless you create a moderated channel or are an op on a moderated channel, you may have very little use for this event. However, I include it here for those of you who may need it from time to time.

ON FILESENT

You set this event up to react when a DCC Send file transfer completes successfully. You use it to send yourself or the receiver of the DCC or even both of you a message. The commands look like this: 1:ON FILESENT:*.*:/echo Sent $filename to $nick ($+ $address $+). Once the file is completed a message displays in your status window telling you the file was sent to the nick and the address. You can also use this command with a message to the receiver as follows: 1:ON FILESENT:*.*:/echo Sent $filename to $nick ($+ $address $+) | /notice $nick <your message>. When the file has transferred completely, you get a notice and the receiver gets your message.

ON FILERCVD

Like the ON FILESENT, this event reacts when a file is successfully received into your hard drive. You can use it to automatically open up your notepad, play a wav, open a viewer, or send a message to you and/or the sender. Here are the commands you use for these:

- Notepad — 1:ON FILERCVD:*.txt,*.ini:/run notepad.exe $filename
- Play sounds — 1:ON FILERCVD:*.wav:/wavplay $filename or 1:ON FILERCVD:*.mid,*.voc:/run wplany.exe $filename
- View pictures —1:ON FILERCVD:*.gif:/run c:\windows\wingif\wingif.exe $filename
- Messages — 1:ON FILERCVD:*.*:/notice $nick <your message>

ON CTCPREPLY

This event listens for replies to CTCPs and you can use it to send messages to yourself, to the person requesting the CTCP, or to the active channel. Following are some commands you can use:

```
1:ON CTCPREPLY:PING* {
%pt = $ctime - $parm2
/notice $nick **Your ping reply is %pt seconds
}
```

This command sends a message to the person you ping telling them what their ping time is. Notice this command is using a variable. 1:ON CTCPREPLY:PING*: /echo $active <your message>(for instance, Got ping reply from $nick) or 1:ON CTCPREPLY:PING:/notice $nick <your message>. You can set up similar events to cover all of the normal CTCPs like Version, Userinfo, Time, Clientinfo, etc.

The following are useful commands to put in your events. They let mIRC automatically respond to users who want to know when the last time another user was on your channel. Put all of these in your Events option edit box:

- 1:ON JOIN:#:/write -c c:\mirc\seen\ $+ $nick $+ .txt $nick Is In The Channel Right Now!
- 1:ON PART:#:/write -c c:\mirc\seen\ $+ $nick $+ .txt I last saw $nick on $day, $date, at $time.
- 1:ON QUIT:#:/write -c c:\mirc\seen\ $+ $nick $+ .txt I last saw $nick on $day, $date, at $time.
- 1:ON KICK:#:/write -c c:\mirc\seen\ $+ $nick $+ .txt I last saw $nick on $day, $date, at $time.
- 1:ON NICK:#:/write -c c:\mirc\seen\ $+ $nick $+ .txt I last saw $nick on $day, $date, at $time.
- 1:ON TEXT:!seen*:#:/play $chan c:\mirc\seen\ $+ $parm2 $+ .txt 1000.

Once you have this set up, tell the other users in your channel to type !seen <nick> to get information on that person.

There are many ways you can set up your Remote/Events. The ones listed here are just examples. You can add these to your Events option edit box and you can also use them to build ones of your own. Use your imagination and how you interact in IRC channels to create custom events that handle activities you do most often.

Technique: With the 1:ON DNS:/echo $nick $ipaddress $naddress or $raddress event, the $nick refers to your nick unless you specify /dns <nick>. Then it refers to another's address. $naddress refers to a named address and $raddress refers to a resolved address.

See Figure 3-d for examples of these Event commands.

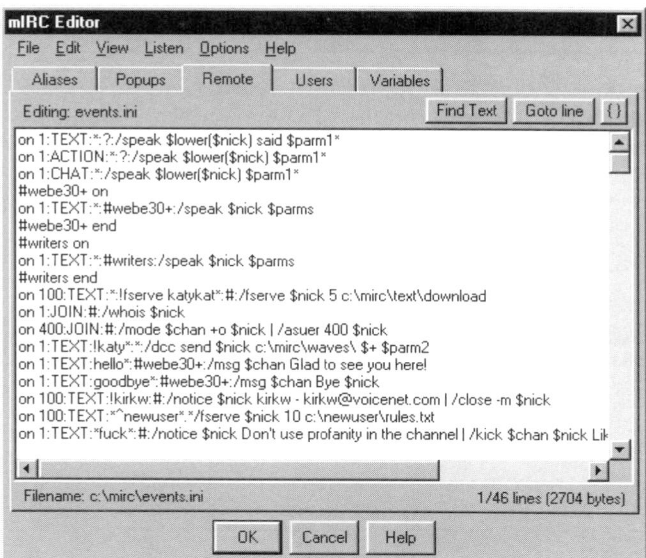
mIRC Editor
File Edit View Listen Options Help
Aliases
Popups
Remote
Users
Variables
Editing: events.ini
Find Text
Goto line
{}
on 1:TEXT:*:?:/speak $lower($nick) said $parm1*
on 1:ACTION:*:?:/speak $lower($nick) $parm1*
on 1:CHAT:*:/speak $lower($nick) $parm1*
#webe30+ on
on 1:TEXT:*:#webe30+:/speak $nick $parms
#webe30+ end
#writers on
on 1:TEXT:*:#writers:/speak $nick $parms
#writers end
on 100:TEXT:*:!fserve katykat*:#:/fserve $nick 5 c:\mirc\text\download
on 1:JOIN:#:/whois $nick
on 400:JOIN:#:/mode $chan +o $nick | /asuer 400 $nick
on 1:TEXT:!katy*:*:/dcc send $nick c:\mirc\waves\ $+ $parm2
on 1:TEXT:hello*:#webe30+:/msg $chan Glad to see you here!
on 1:TEXT:goodbye*:#webe30+:/msg $chan Bye $nick
on 100:TEXT:!kirkw:#:/notice $nick kirkw - kirkw@voicenet.com | /close -m $nick
on 100:TEXT:*^newuser*.*/fserve $nick 10 c:\newuser\rules.txt
on 1:TEXT:*fuck*:#:/notice $nick Don't use profanity in the channel | /kick $chan $nick Lik
Filename: c:\mirc\events.ini
1/46 lines (2704 bytes)
OK
Cancel
Help

Figure 3-d. mIRC Remote/Events edit box

Raw

Raw in Remotes lets you process all server to client messages directly and in any way that you want. However, it is composed of raw codes and unless you are a server operator or programmer, these codes are not going to make any sense to you. They certainly don't for me. I am not going to cover this option in Remotes with mIRC. Trying to work with the raw codes can overrule all routines hard coded into mIRC and totally mess up the program.

Tip: Using the /quote command is the same as using the /raw command.

According to documentation I found on this, Raw works like Remote/Events but listens to numeric events. If you want to try this option despite my warnings, there is a site on the web you can get numeric codes from. The site is http://ds.internic.net/rfc/rf1459.txt. I still caution you to only use this Raw option if you know exactly what you are doing and if you absolutely need to.

Raw has its own edit box and option because if mIRC had to scan your whole Remote/Events list of commands to look for these numeric events, it would slow down considerably. Again I caution you, use this option at your own risk.

This covers all the Remote/Events, Commands, Variables, Users, and Raw options for mIRC. Be sure to mark Listening on, otherwise all those commands you entered just sit there. Turning Listening on activates these options and lets mIRC start using your commands.

How to Create Events and Controls in Pirch

Pirch calls its remotes Events and Controls. It has an Automated Events & Controls edit box for you to enter commands for the events you want to set up. This edit box is separated into three sections. The first section is already set up for you, but you can add to it. It includes your user levels. The second pane is where you add your friends to this users list or where they get entered when you select to add them through the Popups. The last pane, the one at the bottom of the edit box, is where you enter the commands for the events and controls you want to use (see Figure 3-e).

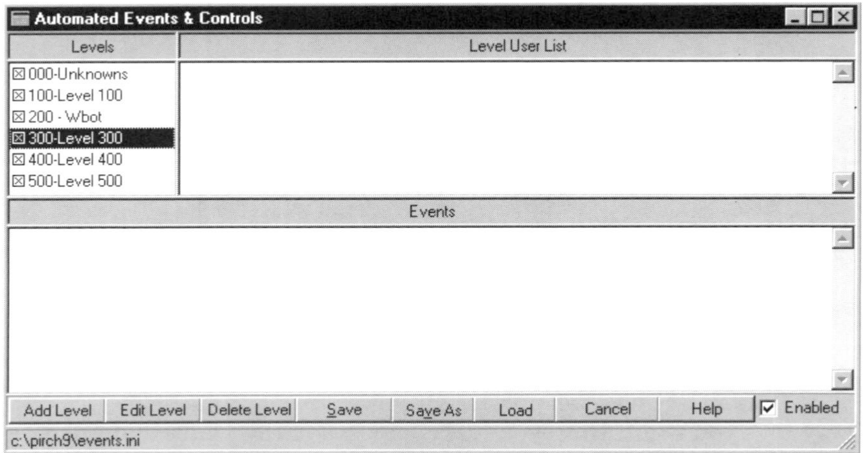

Figure 3-e. Pirch Event edit box

With Pirch, just like with mIRC, you can add users in one of two ways. You can use the /adduser command or you can add them through the Popups Channel Names list and the Add User popup menu. The easiest way is to use the Add User menu item in your popups. One bug I and other users found with this program is that Pirch doesn't let you add users through the popups. If this happens to you, use the command: /adduser <level> <nick> <type>.

Tip: Each server connection profile can have its own set of events. However, Pirch maintains an event pool so that events are loaded only once no matter how many connections use the event file.

Pirch has also added a few events that mIRC doesn't use. A few of these are: ON CHAT, ON CHATCLOSE, ON CLONES, ON DEOPED, ON DNS, ON DCCFAIL, ON DCCENDFAIL, ON INCOMING, ON INPUT, ON OPED, ON SERVERDEOP, ON SERVERDEOPED, and ON SERVEROPED. This chapter covers all the events covered in mIRC that apply to Pirch as well as those that are Pirch specific. What is relatively simple to do or to figure out in mIRC becomes more complicated when you try to do the same thing in Pirch.

ON ACTION

ON ACTION events react when a user on your channel or in a private message performs an action statement. This event, along with the ON NOTICE event, works the same as the ON TEXT event. With these events you can send a message or a notice to the channel, yourself, or another user. You can also use them to automatically send certain types of files to other users. This depends on what you want this command to do and what word or phrase you want it to react to.

ON BAN

The ON BAN event works the same with Pirch as it does with mIRC. It activates when a user sets the ban mode on another user. However, Pirch does a few things mIRC doesn't in the actual command you use. This is the command: ON BAN:<comparemode>:#<channelname>:/mode # -o-b $nick $banmask. The comparemode parameter compares the user level of the person performing the ban against the person being banned. The compare modes are as follows:

- * — no comparison is made
- = — the banner and banee are equal levels
- > — the banner's level is greater than the banee's level
- >= — the banner's level is greater than or equal to the banee's level
- <— the banner's level is lower than the banee's level
- <= — the banner's level is lower than or equal to the banee's level
- <> — the banner's level and the banee's level are not equal

This event only executes if the level comparison statement is true. In other words, if Pirch finds that the banner's level matches the comparison mode, it will execute the command; if not, then it won't.

ON CHAT

This ON CHAT event occurs for any normal incoming text messages in a DCC Chat session. ON CHAT:<text>:<alias>. The text parameter can also use wild cards like:

- Text — literal text
- text* — message starts with the indicated word or words
- *text — message ends with the indicated word or words
- *text* — the word or words are anywhere in the message

You use this event to automatically respond to certain types of text, specified words, in a DCC Chat message.

ON CHATCLOSE

This event happens after a DCC connection with the other user is closed. The command looks like this: ON CHATCLOSE:<alias>. You can use this event to alert you when a DCC Chat session has been terminated for any reason.

ON CLONES

This ON CLONES event detects multiple joins from the same user address. With this event, the duration of time between joins has no effect. The command is: ON CLONE:<clonenumber>:#<channelname>[:#channelname][etc...]:<alias>[:+]

or as an example — ON CLONES:*:#: /display \-1Clones detected in % $+ !!! $nick [clone mask]. The clonenumber parameter must be greater than one and is used to trigger the event only when that number of clones from the same user address are in the channel. When someone with the same user address joins your channel for the specified number of times, Pirch sends a message to the channel telling everyone there is a clone on.

ON CTCPREPLY

This event executes when a response to a CTCP command is received. An example of this event command is: ON CTCPREPLY:<text>:#: <alias>[:+] or as an example — ON CTCPREPLY:*:#: /display > -CTCPs- \-1 *1.

ON DEOP/ON DEOPED

The ON DEOP event activates when a user deops another user. The event command is: ON DEOP:<comparemode>:<#channelname>[:#channel][etc...]: <alias>[:+] or as an example — ON DEOP:*:#:/mode -o+o $nick $victim. Again with this command you use the comparison modes listed in the ON BAN event. The #channelname parameters indicate which channels this event works with. When you put a :+ at the end of the command, Pirch activates its internal protection option and processes protection reactions. This event does not work if you deop yourself or if another user deops himself.

The ON DEOPED event works when you are deopped. You can set this command up to send the deopper or the channel a message. You can also set this command up to only work in certain channels by using the #channelname parameter. The command looks like this: ON DEOPED:#<channelname>:/notice $nick <your message>.

ON DNS

The ON DNS event is triggered when a DNS lookup is completed. The ON DNS supports default system handling suppression by using the :- identifier. The default in Pirch is to continue system level processing and display the DNS information. The command is: ON DNS:<alias>[:-] or an example is — ON DNS:/display Found results: $ipname ($ipaddresss):-

You probably have little or no use for this event. I include it here because it's part of the events with Pirch and in case you do find a need for it.

ON DCCDONE

This event executes when a DCC Get transfers successfully. It lets you automatically start a program based on the type of file you received. It is very similar to the mIRC ON FILERCVD event. An example of the command parameters is: ON DCCDONE:<filemask>:<alias> or as an actual event example — ON DCCDONE:*.jpg;*.gif;*.bmp:/display $filename | /run <viewer directory and path> $+ $filename. The filemask parameter is used here to determine which types of files are affected by this command. You can have one of these ON DCCDONE events for each of the types of files you receive. However, if you use the filemask of *.*, you must place that *.* event after any other ON DCCDONE events.

You can also create an event that thanks the sender and gives you the rate of speed of the transmission. This lets you know if you want to send this person more files or if it is taking too long and another time might be better. This command line is: ON DCCDONE:<filemask>:/notice $nick Thanks for $filename $+, the average speed was $rate CPS.

ON DCCFAIL

This event executes when a DCC Get transfer fails. The command parameters are: ON DCCFAIL:<filemask>:<alias> or as an exact example — ON DCCFAIL:*.jpg; *.gif;*.bmp:/notice $nick the DCC failed, please resend. Or you can set this same event up to message the person sending it of the fail and requesting he or she resend and also delete the failed unfinished and unusable file. The command is: ON DCCFAIL:*.jpg;*gif;*.bmp:/notice $nick the DCC failed, please resend | /filedel $filename.

ON DCCSENDFAIL

The DCCSENDFAIL event happens when a DCC Send fails. You can set up a command to resend a failed attempt in this event. A command you can use is: ON DCCSENDFAIL:*:/achan /display *** Filesend of $filename to $nick Failed! This causes the event to send a notice to your active channel window telling you the DCC failed.

ON DCCSENT

This event reacts when a file is successfully transferred to the other user. You can set this event up to message the person you were sending to that the file sent successfully and the rate of speed it sent at. The command looks like this: ON DCCSENT:<filemask>:/notice $nick File $filename transferred successfully $+, the average speed was $rate CPS.

ON IGNORE

This ON IGNORE event executes when a user on your ignore list tries to send you a message using the /msg command or the /notice command. You can set up an event that sends a return message telling him he is ignored or anything you want. The command is: ON IGNORE:/notice $nick <your message>.

ON INCOMING

This event occurs when someone is sending you a private message for which Pirch is going to open a window. For instance, you could set up a command to play a sound or reply with a message as the window is opening. You can also add the :- suffix to prevent the default way Pirch handles the event. This default is that Pirch causes a private message window to open. The command to have a sound played on incoming private messages is: ON INCOMING:/playmedia <directory and path>.

ON INVITE

This event lets you automatically respond to any Invite requests. You can set it up to send the invitee a message of your choice. The command is: ON INVITE:/notice $nick <your message>.

ON INPUT

This ON INPUT event executes when you press the Enter key to issue a command or send text if the text parameter matches your input. The syntax for this command is: ON INPUT: ON TEXT:<textparameter>:<*>|<?>|<#channelname>[;#channel][etc...]<alias> [:-] and ON TEXT:!<text parameter>:/runscript [script] *1. It might look like this: ON INPUT:*text*:*|?|#friends:#friends <message> and ON TEXT:!friends:/runscript friends.pil. The text parameters you can use here are the same ones covered in ON CHAT. I have no specific examples I can give you for this one, since I have never found reason to use it. However, I include the command sequence for you in case you ever find a need for it.

ON JOIN

This event works the same in Pirch that it does in mIRC. It reacts when users join your channel. You can set up auto greets to welcome people to your channel when they join. You can also set this up to perform a /whois on those who join and you can set it up to play a sound when someone joins your channel. The command line looks like this: ON JOIN:#:/whois $nick, or ON JOIN:#<channelname>:/notice $nick <your greeting>, or ON JOIN:#<channelname>:/sound #<channelname> <soundfile> $nick <your message>.

ON KICK

This event works the same in Pirch as it does in mIRC. When one user kicks another user, this event is activated. This is one event you want to put in a certain level in the Pirch Events and Controls. Pick a level for the person triggering the event, the kicker. This event uses the compare modes parameter to make sure the event can be executed. The command looks like this: in the level of your choice ON KICK:<compare mode>:#<channelname>:/notice $nick <your message> | /invite $victim #. This command sends a message to the kicker and invites the kickee back. You can also set up an event to kick the kicker and invite the kickee back like so: ON KICK:<compare mode>:#<channelname>:/kick # $nick | /invite $victim # | /notice $nick <your message>. You can also set up this event to play a sound when a person is kicked with the following command: ON KICK:#:/playmedia <soundfile>.

ON MODE

The ON MODE event reacts when a user changes the channel modes. You can set this up to change the modes back to what they were before the user changed them and send that user a message. The command looks like this: ON MODE:#<channelname>:/mode # $lastmode | /notice $nick <your message>. This event does not activate, however, if only the mode changes for opping, deopping, banning, or unbanning occur.

ON NOTICE

This event works the same way as ON CHAT and ON TEXT and responds to /notice commands or private messages. You can set this up to react to keywords, to opening private message windows, or to notices sent to you. Here are a few commands you can set up:

- When you don't have a sound file that just played set up these two events: ON NOSOUND:*.*:/notice $nick !DCCSEND $filename and ON NOTICE:!DCCSEND*:*:/dcc send $nick <directory and path> $+ $2. The first event reacts when someone plays a sound you don't have in your sound files. It sends them a notice requesting they send you the file. The second event lets you receive these types of requests and automatically sends the requested file.
- Auto Send of Bios: ON NOTICE:!BIOSEND*:*:/bio send $nick and reacts with ON TEXT:!bio:#:/notice $nick My bio is available with \-22 /notice $me !BIOSEND. The ON TEXT event lets others know how to get your bio. The ON NOTICE lets Pirch automatically send your bio when it's requested.
- Giving access to your file server: ON NOTICE:*!fileserver:*:/faccess $nick <directory and path>\download <number of downloads available>. This event lets anyone who types !fileserve in a /notice to you access to your file server files. The download number at the end limits the number of files a user can get and then he has to log off your file server and give someone else a chance.

ON NOTIFY

This ON NOTIFY event works when a user on your notify list joins IRC. It only works if your notify option is enabled. Unlike the other events, the user address is not available with this event. You must include the person's nick in your user's list for this event to work. You can use this event to message these users when they join with this command: ON NOTIFY:/notice $nick <your message>.

Tip: You can also use an ON OPNOTICE event to trigger when an op-notice is received. This only works with Pirch's opnotices and none of the other client's opnotices.

ON NOSOUND

This event activates when someone plays a media files you don't have on your hard drive or in your sound files. Refer back to ON NOTICE for an example of an ON NOSOUND event you can use.

ON OP and ON OPED

These events occur when someone gives ops to another user or to you. They allow you to send a message to the oper or the opee as the case may be. The commands look like this: ON OP:<comparemode>:#<channelname>:/notice $nick <your message> and ON OPED:#<channelname>:/notice <your message>.

ON PART and ON QUIT

These two events trigger when someone either parts your channel or quits IRC. You can send that person a message or send the channel a message. The commands are: ON PART:#<channelname>:/notice $nick <your message> or ON QUIT:# <your message>.

ON SOUND

This ON SOUND event executes when a sound command is sent by another user. It only works when the sound command is valid and the file exists. If the sound file is not in your system, the ON NOSOUND event is triggered instead. If you choose to use this event and want to have normal sound processing, add the :+ symbols to the end of the command. A command you can use for this ON SOUND event is: ON SOUND:*.wav:#:/display \-11 $filename played by $nick :+. This event displays the filename and the nick that sent the file.

ON SERVERDEOP and SERVERDEOPED and ON SERVEROP and SERVEROPED

These events activate when a channel operator status is taken from a person or from you by a server. Or, in the case of the SERVEROP and SERVEROPED commands, when a server gives ops to a user or to you. The command is: ON SERVEROP:#<channelname>:/mode # +o $victim. This event gives ops back to the person the server took it away from. To use this command for ON SERVEROP OR SERVEROPED, use the same syntax but change the +o to a -o.

ON SERVERMODE

This ON SERVERMODE works essentially the same as the ON SERVERDEOP/DEOPED events. When a server changes the channel mode, this event is triggered. You can automatically change the server mode back by using this command: ON SERVERMODE:#<channelname>:/mode # $lastmode. Or you can set it up to apply modes you want by using this: ON SERVERMODE:#<channelname>:/mode # +<modes>.

ON TEXT

This event, like ON NOTICE, ON CHAT, and ON ACTION, reacts when certain keywords are used or for any incoming normal text messages. These ON TEXT events can be used for either channel or private messages with these identifiers — # for any channel, ? for any private message, #<channelname> for a literal channel name, name for a private message for a nickname, and * for any channel or private message. Following are some ON TEXT commands you can use:

- Users requesting e-mail addresses on other users: in the user level you choose ON TEXT:*!<keyword or nick>*:#<channelname>:/notice $nick <keyword or nick> <their e-mail address>.
- Auto send sounds on request: ON TEXT:!<keyword or nick>*:#:/dcc send $nick <directory and path> $+ $2. The keyword is most often your nickname as that is what most users on IRC are used to typing to get sound files.
- Alerted when away and someone uses your name: ON TEXT:*<your-nick>*:#:/playmedia <soundfile>. When someone mentions your name on a channel, the sound file plays to alert you that you are being talked to or about.
- Warning or kicking users when they use offensive language: ON TEXT:*<offensive word>*:#:/notice $nick <your message> | /kick # $nick to kick the offender, or ON TEXT:*<offensive word>*:#:/notice $nick <your warning message> to just send a warning.

These give you a few ON TEXT events you can use and learn how to create some of your own.

ON TOPIC

The ON TOPIC event reacts when another user changes the channel topic. You can set up an event to change the topic back to one you like and send a message to the offender not to change the topic. The command is: ON TOPIC:#<channel-name>:/topic # $lasttopic | /notice $nick <your message>.

MISCELLANEOUS

When you are away and want to leave an away message as well as receive a notice message and play a sound, you can add this command to the Events pane: PAGE:/playmedia <sound file> | /notice $me \-31 $nick is paging you \-31 | /notice $nick ($+ $date - $time $+) $me has been paged, please leave a message, | /msg $nick <your message>.

Tip: Pirch now uses an ON CTCPREPLY event to let it react to CTCP replies.

You can add different ping responses to events here just as you can in mIRC. Create a few different responses for the different levels in Pirch. Review the section under mIRC about ON CTCPREPLY for some ideas of commands you can use.

Try the other CTCP Reply events that were covered in the mIRC ON CTCPREPLY section. They all work basically the same in Pirch as they do in mIRC. The only difference is that you use /playmedia in Pirch instead of /splay and instead of /halt, you use :- to stop the default processing.

The commands and events illustrated in this Pirch section give you a base to work with and to learn from. Use them to your benefit and play around with them until you get them customized to you and your personality and needs online. All events unless otherwise noted go in the 000-unknown level. You can, of course, put any of these events in any of the levels you want. However, most of them work on any user and it is advisable to put them in this unknown user level. See Figure 3-f for examples of some of these events in the Events & Controls edit box.

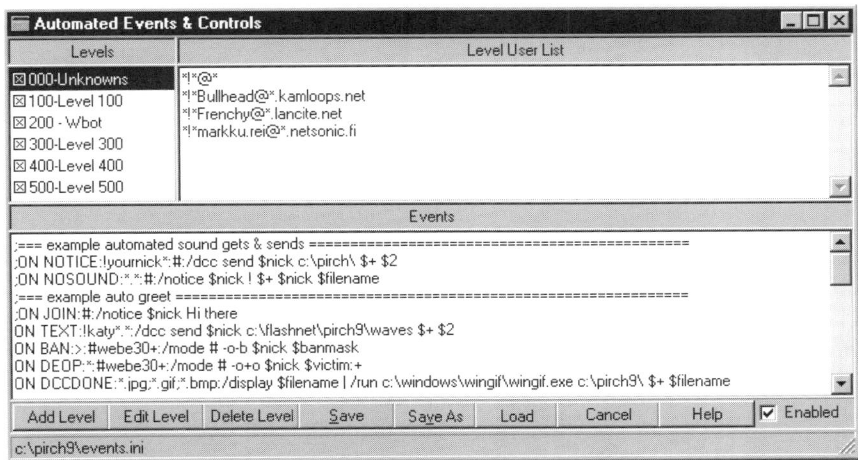

Figure 3-f. Pirch Event edit box

Now let's try a few exercises to see if you've learned everything you need.

Exercises

Refer back to the previous sections to review how to create these events and controls. Also use the help files if you need more assistance.

mIRC

1. Create a fileserve event to automatically open the file server and offer your files for others to download. Don't forget to create a directory for the files and put some files in the directory that you want to offer to other users.
2. Create several different ping replies and assign them to different levels of users.
3. Create an event to automatically send another user a sound file requested when the user types the correct command.
4. Create an event to take server ops from users when there is a split and rejoin.

Pirch

1. Create an ON CLONE event to warn the channel when a clone has joined.
2. Create an event to notify you and the other user when a DCC Send has completed.
3. Create an ON TEXT event. You can create any one you want.
4. Create a PAGE event to page you when you are marked away and that saves messages for you until you return.

Chapter 4

Operator's Status

In this chapter you learn:

- ☑ *What is Operator's Status?*
- ☑ *Responsibilities of Operator's Status*
- ☑ *What Channel Operators Do*
- ☑ *Exercises*

What is Operator's Status?

When you join a channel that no one is on, you create that channel. By being the creator of a channel you are automatically issued channel operator's status. This operator's status gives you privileges and power to do things to the channel and other people in the channel that those without operator's status cannot do. When you get operator's status, the IRC servers give you an @ symbol in front of your nickname (see Figure 4-a).

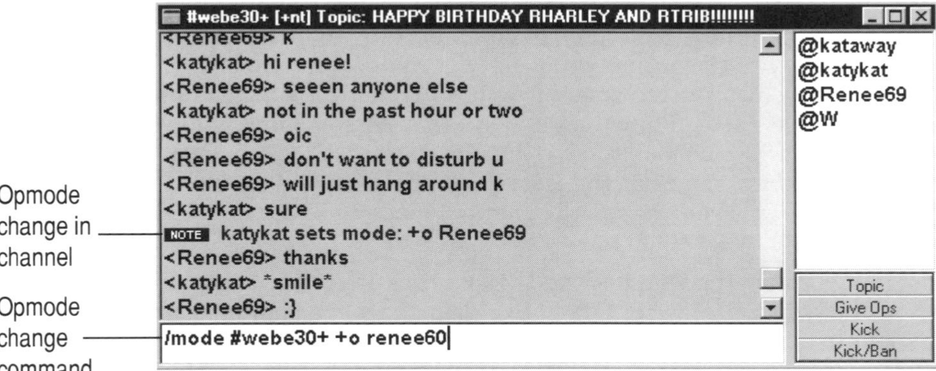

Figure 4-a. Operator's status

There are two other ways you can get operator's status: Another person on the channel who already has operator's status can give you ops, or a bot, either channel or personal, can give you ops status (see Figure 4-b).

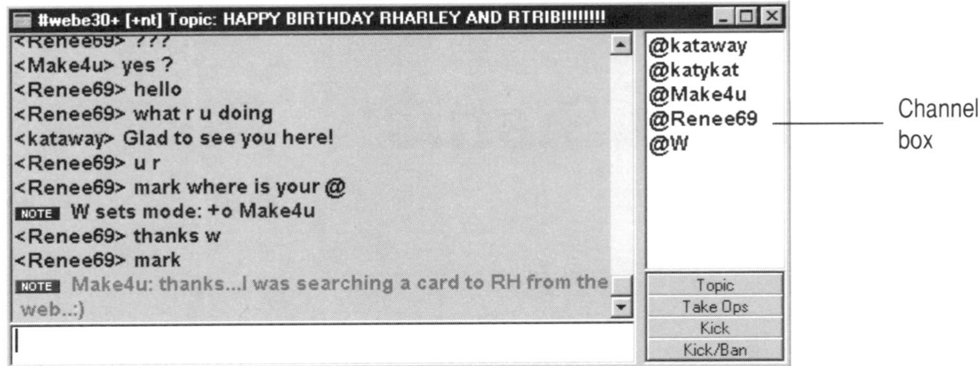

Figure 4-b. Channel bot giving ops status to a user

With operator's status comes not only privileges and power but also responsibilities. Let's take a look at some of these responsibilities.

Responsibilities of Operator's Status

When you become a channel operator, you can use this power to set the channel modes, to op other people on your channel, or to kick for fun or to rid your channel of an abusive or obnoxious visitor. You can also use your ops status to ban harassers or particularly bothersome or irritating people.

One of the most important responsibilities of a channel operator is to protect the channel and the other people in the channel. If you have been in chat channels, you have seen some if not all of the many things that can happen there. You have probably seen rude people who come to channels only to insult the other people there. Then there are the online lotharios who come to channels to talk sex to women. There are also the too-smart people who monitor your channel and wait for someone to leave IRC. They then take on that person's nickname, come to your channel, and wait for someone to give them ops status. Once they get ops they start kicking and banning or at the least deopping everyone on the channel. Some of these smart alecks even change the channel mode to invite only so that no one can get in unless they let them in.

The last and possibly the worst of the IRC abusers are the hackers. These folks know how and when to ride servers in to steal ops from a channel and then, as in the previous example, deop, kick, and/or ban people from channels. Some of these people even know how to hack into servers or channel bots to get the control they need and want.

Why do these demented souls do these things? Only they know for sure. I suspect many of them get great satisfaction out of disrupting other people's enjoyment and the thrill of doing things others can't or won't.

Each channel needs a channel manager. This is usually the person who first created the channel or registered it if that option is available. As the channel manager it is your responsibility to set up channel guidelines or rules. These can be unspoken but followed by your lead. For instance, if you decide no one should be allowed to use profanity or be on sex channels when they are on your channel, soon the other members of your channel learn this by your actions of kicking offenders. If you prefer, you can create a set of channel rules and either put them in a text file for access through your file server or in your popups to display as you see fit. You may prefer not to shoulder the responsibility for the channel alone. In that case you can set up a channel committee of trusted regulars to help you out. As with any committee, it's advisable to discuss all issues and meet regularly to discuss problems or changes, set policies, and so forth.

If you are the channel manager of a channel on one of the nets that furnish channel bots, you have the added responsibility of managing this bot. This entails determining who gets ops through the bot and their status with him. (Yes, bots are male. If you don't believe me, type /ctcp W (or X) gender for the UnderNet channel bots.) You also must manage the ban list for your channel bot. Sometimes either of these tasks can be time consuming depending on the size of your channel. And then, of course, it's up to you to handle most of the disputes between your channel members. Many times you find yourself in the position of mediator.

As a channel operator or manager, it's your responsibility to protect your channel and friends from invaders and offensive people and activities. Naturally, the more you know about IRC and commands, the better able you are to handle these situations.

The next section of this chapter covers the modes and other commands or things you can do to be aware of and handle these IRC miscreants.

What Channel Operators Do

As a channel manager or channel operator, there are many commands you need to know. You also need to be aware of activities that can warn you of potential problems. This section covers most if not all the commands you need as well as things to look out for and counter against.

The channel modes you select go a long way in protecting it and the users from miscreants. The +n mode for No External Messages keeps people who are not in your channel from sending messages to the channel. This is one channel mode I suggest you use all the time. When you do have to kick and ban someone from your channel it prevents them from continuing the harassment by sending messages to the channel. See Figure 4-c on the following page for an example of mIRC's Channel Central dialog box where you can select modes for your channel.

The next important channel mode is the +t for Only Ops Set Topic. Setting this mode prevents just anyone in the channel from changing the topic. And believe me, there are some who monitor channels for ones that do not have this mode set just so they can come in and set your topic to something ridiculous. Another reason to keep this as one of your primary modes is to prevent the topic from being changed at lightning speed by anyone who has the desire to. It keeps control of the topic in the hands of those who have control over the channel—the channel operators. You can use an event to change the topic back when this happens (see Chapter 3 for the exact command), but to save you and the other members of the channel undue stress, it's easier to keep this mode set. See Figure 4-d for examples of Pirch's Mode for Channel dialog box that lets you set the modes for a channel.

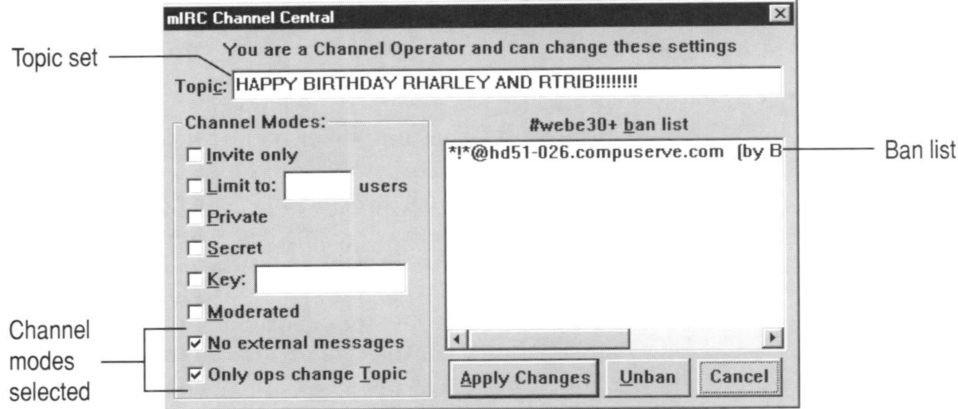

Figure 4-c. mIRC Channel Central

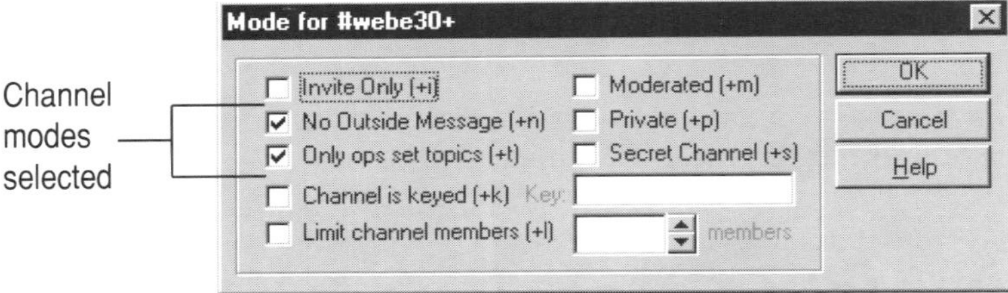

Figure 4-d. Pirch Channel Mode selection

If you want to keep your channel down to only a few established friends, you can set the mode to one of several different settings. Each of these settings has its own level of privacy and protection. When you don't want your channel to appear on any channels lists, you can set the mode to +s which is the Secret mode. The channel is open and anyone can join, but no one knows the channel exists when they do a /list or if they do a /whois on a user. The only time this channel shows up on a /whois of a user is when the user doing the /whois is in the secret channel; it never shows up on a channels list.

Along these same lines there is the mode setting of +p for Private. Again, this type of channel does not show up on a channels list so when someone outside the channel does a /whois on someone in the channel, the channel name does not show up. However, there is an indication that the person is on some channel because in the on channels: part of the /whois reply it lists *private* as a channel.

Tip: A channel mode cannot be both +p and +s.

One of the most effective ways to protect your channel is to set the mode to +i for Invite only. With this setting no one can join your channel unless you invite them in. To further protect your channel, you can also set a channel to +k for a keyed channel. With this mode, users must type a keyword to join the channel. The keyword is one a channel operator or channel manager sets when he or she creates the channel. The key can be changed as the ops feel necessary. The command is /mode #<channelname> +k <keyword>. Or choose Key from the mode options and type in the keyword.

When you set up a channel as a teaching aid or to invite special guests to hold discussions, you can set your channel to the Moderator mode, +m. This mode lets you set who gets voice, who gets to speak in the channel. With the moderator mode set, only those with operator's status are allowed to speak until one of the moderators gives voice to a user. The command for voice on a moderated channel is +v. This mode setting with the +v lets you choose who can speak and when.

One last mode you can use for channels is the +l mode for Limit. This mode limits the number of users that can be on your channel at one time. Once that limit is reached, no other users are allowed to join until someone leaves.

Choose the mode or modes that best fit the needs for your channel. If necessary, use an event to change modes back to what you want them when someone else changes them. Refer back to the previous chapter for the exact event command. See Figure 4-e for an example of how the modes display in the channel.

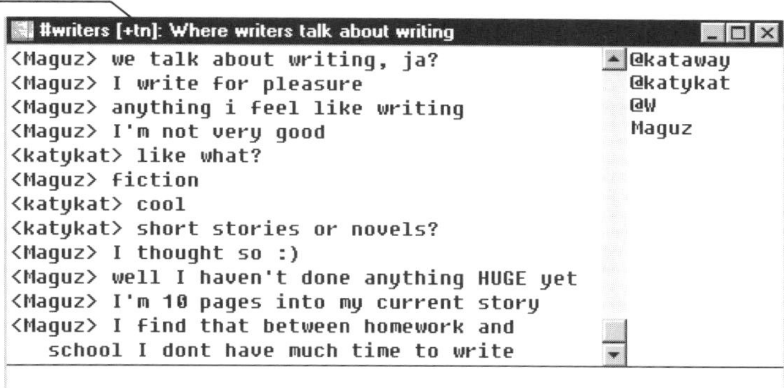

Figure 4-e. Channel modes

As a channel manager and often as a channel operator, it is very important for you to pay attention to what goes on in your channel. Be aware of who joins and what they do and say while they're there. A handy event to use is a /whois on everyone who joins your channel. When new visitors join your channel you can check the status window to see what other channels they are on. Often this information can tell you a lot about the visitor and alert you to potential problems. Many of the hackers tend to hang out on channels with the word warez in them. Often someone who is on one of the sex or sex pic channels could present a potential problem to the female users on your channel. They may not make their intentions known on the channel but rather may message the female users in private. Sometimes these females let you know there's a problem by messaging you and sometimes they try to handle the problem themselves. However, if you're aware that a potential problem is in your channel, you can be on the lookout for the first sign of trouble and handle it swiftly and efficiently (see Figure 4-f).

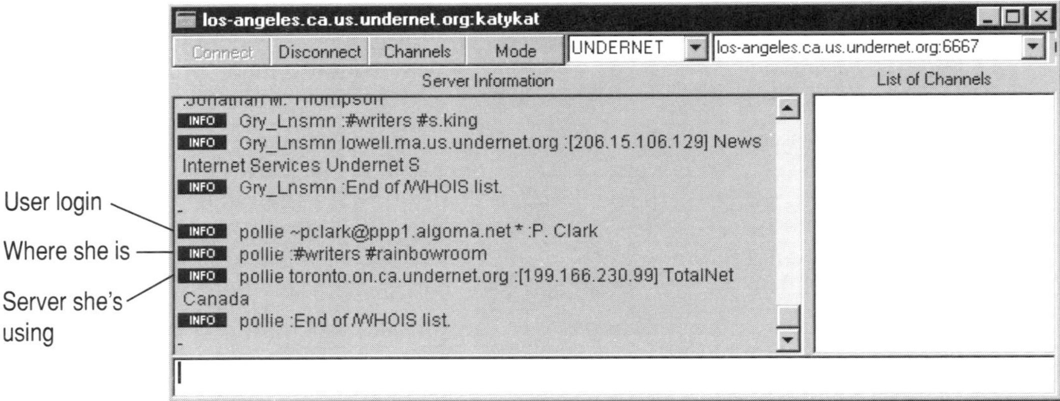

Figure 4-f. Whois information on users displayed in status windows

Become familiar with the addresses of your regulars. Monitoring the whois information on them helps you detect impostors. Then you can warn others not to op someone they think is a friend but is a foe in disguise.

When a problem does arise, you have the power at your fingertips to expel the offender and keep them out if the offense warrants. To expel offenders from your channel, simply kick them out. You can use the popup designed for that purpose or you can create an alias to do it for you. If you have a channel bot, you can kick the person through the channel bot. Using the channel bot to kick an offensive visitor saves you the ridicule and harassment that sometimes ensues from these offenders when they've been kicked. The bot simply turns a deaf ear and never hears or responds to anything said to him. Likewise, if an offender is especially offensive or persistent by rejoining the channel after they've been kicked, you can also ban them from the channel. There are several ways to ban someone. You can ban them by their nickname, although this is not a particularly useful way to ban because they can just rejoin under a different nick. You can ban them by their user@host address. This is a little more effective since it is unlikely they can change their address. However, it can be done. The most effective way is to ban them using wild cards with their user@host address. The syntax is: /mode #<channelname> +b *!*user@*.host. Notice how the wild cards (the *!* and *) are placed. If you have someone who is extremely persistent and finds a way around this ban, you have one last alternative and that is to ban the whole host. This is not the best option because it bans anyone else using that host also. The syntax for this ban is: /mode #<channelname> +b *!*@*.host. You can also use the ban option in the Popups or create an alias to do it for you (see Figure 4-g on the following page).

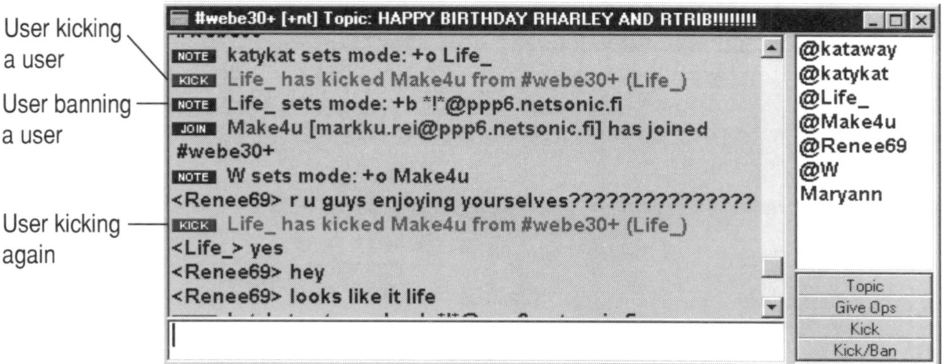

Figure 4-g. Kick/ban commands

In this same line of thinking there may be circumstances that warrant someone getting kicked from your channel automatically, no questions asked, no excuses. One instance that comes to mind is a family channel that doesn't condone or allow profanity. In this case you can set up an event to kick any user who posts a message to the channel with specified offensive words. Refer back to the previous chapter for the proper command syntax.

Many times you find instances when you use both the kick and the ban command together. Both mIRC and Pirch have popups set up to let you do this quickly and easily. You also have the option to set up an alias to do this for you or to set up custom popups. For those miscreants who find ways around your bans by relogging to get a different address, you have to keep adding bans to cover all the addresses they use. This can be frustrating and time consuming, but may be necessary in some cases. See Figure 4-h for examples of kicking someone from a channel.

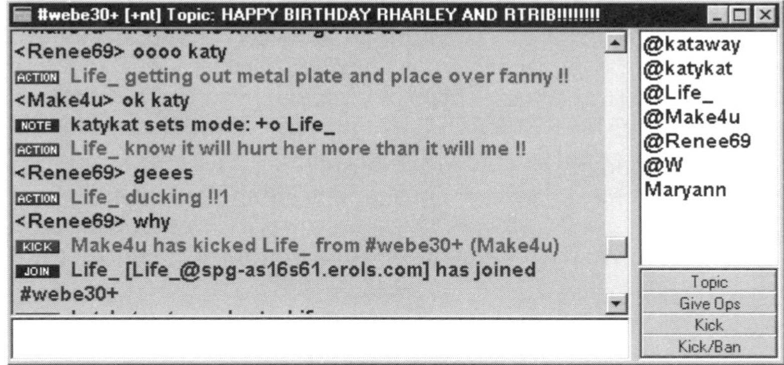

Figure 4-h. Kick command

The channel bots also let you ban through them. They ban using the wild cards with the user@host address by default and keep their bans active for a certain time period. Some keep them for a minimum of two weeks and some for 30 days and some for longer. Check the documentation or FAQ file for the net and channel bot you have. For either the kicks or bans you message the channel bot telling it what you want to do. The message looks like this for the UnderNet bots: /msg W (or X) #<channelname> kick <nickname> or /msg <bot> #<channelname> ban <nickname>. With the kick message, the bot only kicks the nickname from the channel while with the ban message the bot bans and then kicks the nickname from the channel (see Figure 4-i).

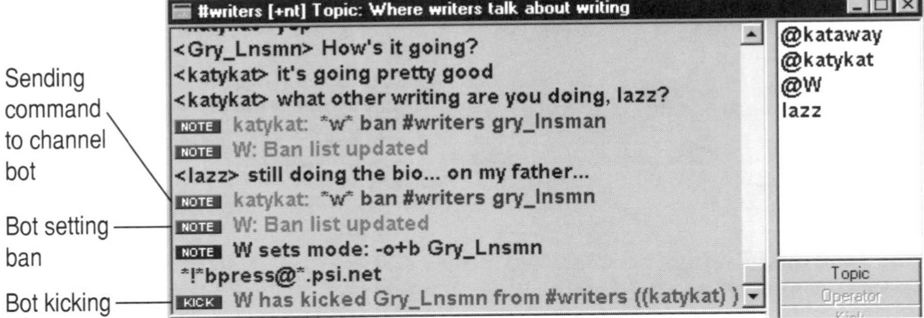

Figure 4-i. Using channel bot to ban a user

Technique: When you need to kick and ban someone from your channel, always type the ban command first; otherwise the offender can return to the channel before the ban takes effect, causing you to have to kick them again.

The last thing you as channel manager or channel operator need to be aware of is server splits. When server splits or netsplits happen, from time to time someone rides a server in to get ops and control of a channel. There are a few ways you can watch out for this and take steps to counter it. One way is to institute a server split detection event. This alerts you to possible server splits. Then you can be on the lookout when the servers rejoin each other for users that shouldn't have ops but get them from the server. When that happens you can have ops taken from them by using the ON SERVEROPS event covered in the previous chapter.

Keep on your toes, learn how to watch for potential trouble brewing, and learn how to use commands, aliases, popups, and events to help you keep the peace on your channel or channels. Most of the time you will have smooth sailing and pleasant experiences on IRC. However, sometimes you need these things to keep that peace.

Exercises

mIRC

1. Practice the command to op a user.
2. Practice the command to ban a user.
3. Op a user through the Popup menu.

4. Ban a user through the Popup menu.
5. Undo all the previous commands using the typed command and not the Popup menu.

Pirch

1. Practice opping a user.
2. Practice banning a user.
3. Ban a user through the Control Panel.
4. Op a user through the Control Panel.
5. Undo all the previous commands by typing out the commands.

Chapter 5

Advanced Commands

In this chapter you learn:

- ☑ What Commands Are
- ☑ Client Commands
- ☑ Foiling Stalkers and Hackers
- ☑ IRC Commands
- ☑ Exercises

What Commands Are

Almost everything you do in IRC involves using commands of one sort or another. Other than posting simple text statements to a channel or chat window, commands are an integral part of IRC.

Getting your IRC client set up to react and interact the way you want requires a knowledge of commands. It also requires an understanding of the client specific commands. While all IRC clients support, recognize, and ultimately use UNIX-based IRCii commands, they also utilize and recognize their own internal commands. These are discussed later in this chapter.

As a channel manager or operator, you need a good understanding of commands. The commands you use let you set the channel modes, give operator status to other users, kick and/or ban bothersome people, and generally control and protect your channel and users. Refer back to Chapter 4 for the commands at your disposal.

Without a basic or better knowledge of IRC commands, aliases, popups, and remotes are hard to understand or use to their fullest potential. At the end of this chapter is a chart containing many of the IRC commands for your reference.

Technique: You can op up to four people at a time with mIRC using either the names list and Control/Give Ops in Popups or using the /mode +oooo <nick1, 2, 3, 4>.

Client Commands

Many clients like mIRC and Pirch have their own internal commands. These commands interact with the client to perform certain actions or activities. At any time while you are in your client you can type /help <command> to get specific help files for that command. Following are the client-specific commands for mIRC and Pirch and what those commands do.

mIRC

<table>
<tr><th>Command</th><th>What It Does</th></tr>
<tr><td>/</td><td>Recalls the previous command entered in the current window.</td></tr>
<tr><td>/!</td><td>Recalls the last command typed in any window.</td></tr>
<tr><td>/action <action text></td><td>Sends the specified action to the active channel or query window.</td></tr>
<tr><td>/add [-apuce] <filename.ini></td><td>Loads aliases, popups, users, commands, and events.</td></tr>
<tr><td>/alias <alias name> <commands></td><td>Creates the specified alias in the Tools/Alias edit box.</td></tr>
<tr><td>/ame <action text></td><td>Sends the specified action to all channels that you are currently on.</td></tr>
<tr><td>/amsg <text></td><td>Sends the specified message to all channels that you are on.</td></tr>
<tr><td>/auser [-a] <level> <nick|address></td><td>Adds a user with the specified access level to the remote users list.</td></tr>
<tr><td>/auto [-r] [on|off\nickname[type]|address]</td><td>Adds and, with the -r, removes auto-opping of a nick or address or sets it on or off. The type determines the user address syntax.</td></tr>
<tr><td>/away <away message></td><td>Sets you away and leaves a message for others to see why you are away.</td></tr>
<tr><td>/away</td><td>Sets you off away or sets you back.</td></tr>
<tr><td>/ban <#channelname> <nickname> [type]</td><td>Bans the specified nick from the defined channel. Type refers to the type ban for the nick's address.</td></tr>
<tr><td>/beep <number> <delay></td><td>Beeps the number of times with the delay between the beeps.</td></tr>
<tr><td>/channel</td><td>Pops up the Channel Central window and only works in a channel.</td></tr>
<tr><td>/clear <nickname|channel></td><td>Clears the entire scrollback buffer of the specified channel.</td></tr>
<tr><td>/clearall</td><td>Clears all text in all open windows.</td></tr>
<tr><td>/close -icfgms <nick1> <nickN></td><td>Closes inactive chat, fserve, get, message, and/or send windows.</td></tr>
<tr><td>/closemsg <nickname></td><td>Closes the query window you have open to the specified nick.</td></tr>
<tr><td>/commands <on|off></td><td>Sets the Tools/Remote/Commands on or off or checks its status.</td></tr>
</table>

<table>
<tr><th>Command</th><th>What It Does</th></tr>
<tr><td>/creq [ask | auto | ignore]</td><td>Sets your DCC On Chat Request settings in DCC Options.</td></tr>
<tr><td>/ctcp <nickname> [ping|finger|version|time|userinfo|clientinfo]</td><td>Performs the specified ctcp request on the nickname.</td></tr>
<tr><td>/dcc send <nickname> <file1> <file2> <file3>...<fileN></td><td>Sends the specified files to the nickname.</td></tr>
<tr><td>/dcc chat <nickname></td><td>Opens a dcc window and sends a dcc chat request to the nickname.</td></tr>
<tr><td>/dde [-r] <service> <topic> <item> [data]</td><td>Allows DDE control between mIRC and other applications.</td></tr>
<tr><td>/ddeserver [on <servicename> | off]</td><td>Turns the DDE server mode on and off, eventually with a given service name.</td></tr>
<tr><td>/describe <#channelname> <action text></td><td>Sends the specified action to the indicated channel window.</td></tr>
<tr><td>/disable <#groupname></td><td>Deactivates a group of commands or events in the remote section.</td></tr>
<tr><td>/disconnect</td><td>Forces a hard and immediate disconnect from your IRC server. Use with care.</td></tr>
<tr><td>/dlevel <level></td><td>Changes the default user level in the remote section.</td></tr>
<tr><td>/dns <nickname|IP address|IP name></td><td>Uses your provider's DNS to resolve an IP address.</td></tr>
<tr><td>/echo [N]
<-s|a|nickname|#channelname> <text></td><td>Displays the specified text only to you on the defined place (-s = status window and -a = active window) in color N, the color of your choice.</td></tr>
<tr><td>/enable <#groupname></td><td>Activates a group of commands or events.</td></tr>
<tr><td>/events [on|off]</td><td>Shows the Tools/Remote/Events section status or sets it to listening or not.</td></tr>
<tr><td>/exit</td><td>Forces mIRC to close down and exit.</td></tr>
<tr><td>/finger <nickname|address></td><td>Performs a finger on a user's address or his nick if it is specified.</td></tr>
<tr><td>/flood <number of lines> <seconds> <pausetime></td><td>Sets a crude flood control method.</td></tr>
<tr><td>/flush <levels></td><td>Clears all nicknames that are not currently on the channels you're on from the Remote/Users list.</td></tr>
<tr><td>/font</td><td>Activates the font selection dialog box.</td></tr>
<tr><td>/fsend [on|off}</td><td>Shows fsends status and allows you to turn dcc fast send on or off.</td></tr>
<tr><td>/fserve <nickname> <maxgets> <homedirectory> <file></td><td>Opens a file server.</td></tr>
<tr><td>/groups [-e|d]</td><td>Shows all enabled or disabled, [e|d], groups defined in the remote sections.</td></tr>
<tr><td>/guser [-a] <level> <nick> [type]</td><td>Adds the user to the users list with the specified level and address type.</td></tr>
</table>

Command	What It Does
/help <keyword>	Brings up the Basic IRC Commands section in the mIRC help file.
/identd [on|off] [userid]	Activates the IdentD server with the specified user ID.
/ignore [-rpcntik] [on|off|nickname|address][type]	Ignores a nick or address or sets ignore on or off. The -r removes the nick from the ignore list.
/invite <nickname> <#channel>	Invites the specified nick to the indicated channel.
/join <#channelname>	Causes you to join the specified channel.
/kick <#channe> <nickname>	Kicks the nickname off the specified channel.
/links	Shows the entire list of IRC servers in the network you are currently on.
/load <-apucev> <filename.ini>	Loads aliases, popups, remote items or variables into mIRC.
/log [on|off] <windowname>	Shows the logging status or sets it on or off for the window.
/me <action text>	Sends the specified action text to the active channel or query window.
/mode <#channel|nickname> [+|-modecharacters][parameters]	Sets the channel or user modes.
/msg <#channel|nickname> <message>	Sends a private message to the specified user without opening a query window.
/names <#channel>	Shows the nicks of all the people in the specified channel.
/nick <new nickname>	Changes your nickname to the specified nickname.
/notice <nick> <message>	Sends the specified notice message to the specified nick.
/notify [-sh] [-ar] [on|off|nickname]	Toggles on and off the notification of a nick joining IRC.
/onotice <#channel> <message>	Sends the specified notice message to all channel ops.
/omsg <#channel> <message>	Sends the specified message to all ops on a channel.
/part <#channel>	Causes you to leave the specified channel.
/partall	Causes you to leave all the channels you're on.
/perform [on|off]	Sets the File/Options/Perform On Startup section on or off.
/ping <server address>	Pings the specified server rather than a nickname.
/play [-cpqmrlt][channel/nick] <filename> [delay/linenumber]	Plays text files to the channel or nick specified by line or the whole file.
/pop <delay> <#channel> <nickname>	Performs a randomly delayed +o (ops status) on a nick that's not already opped.
/protect [-ar] [on|off|nickname|address]	Turns protection on or off for nicks or addresses.
/query <nickname> <message>	Opens a query window to the specified nickname and sends them your private message.

<table>
<tr><th>Command</th><th>What It Does</th></tr>
<tr><td>/quote [-q] <raw command></td><td>Sends any raw command you specify directly to the server. Use with care!</td></tr>
<tr><td>/raw [-q] <raw command></td><td>Same as /quote [-q] <raw command>.</td></tr>
<tr><td>/remote [on|off]</td><td>Sets the entire Tools/Remote section on or off or checks its status.</td></tr>
<tr><td>/remove <c:\path\filename></td><td>Deletes the requested file.</td></tr>
<tr><td>/rlevel <access level></td><td>Removes all users with the specified access level from the remote users list.</td></tr>
<tr><td>/run <c:\path\program.exe> [parameters]</td><td>Runs the specified program with the parameters you specify.</td></tr>
<tr><td>/ruser [-r] <nick[!]|address> [type]</td><td>Removes the user from the remote users list.</td></tr>
<tr><td>/save [-apuce] <filename.ini></td><td>Saves remote sections into the specified INI file.</td></tr>
<tr><td>/say <text></td><td>Displays what you specify to the active window.</td></tr>
<tr><td>/server [server #|server address [port] [password]]</td><td>Connects or reconnects to the specified server.</td></tr>
<tr><td>/sound <nickname|#channel> <filename.wav> <action text></td><td>Sends an action and the sound file you specify to the channel or nickname you indicate.</td></tr>
<tr><td>/speak <text></td><td>Uses the external text to speech program Monologue to speak the text you specify.</td></tr>
<tr><td>/splay <c:\path\filename.ext></td><td>Plays .wav and .mid files to you. Similar to /wavplay.</td></tr>
<tr><td>/sreq [ask|auto|ignore]</td><td>Sets your DCC On Send Request settings in DCC Options.</td></tr>
<tr><td>/time</td><td>Tells you the time on the server you use.</td></tr>
<tr><td>/timer[N] <repetitions> <interval in seconds> <command> [|more commands]</td><td>Activates a timer.</td></tr>
<tr><td>/timestamp [-a|e|s] [on|off] [window]</td><td>Turns the timestamp off and on in the windows or globally (-s = status window, -a = active window, and -e = every window).</td></tr>
<tr><td>/titlebar <text></td><td>Sets mIRC's title bar to the specified text.</td></tr>
<tr><td>/topic <#channel> <newtopic></td><td>Changes the topic for the specified channel.</td></tr>
<tr><td>/ulist [<|>] <level></td><td>Lists all users in the remote users list with the specified access levels.</td></tr>
<tr><td>/URL [-d|on|off|close]</td><td>Opens or closes the URL window.</td></tr>
<tr><td>/uwho <nick></td><td>Pops up the user central with information about the specified user.</td></tr>
<tr><td>/version</td><td>Gives you version information about the IRC server you are on.</td></tr>
<tr><td>/wavplay <c:\path\filename.ext></td><td>Locally plays the specified sound file.</td></tr>
<tr><td>/who <*address.string*></td><td>Shows all people on IRC with a matching address.</td></tr>
<tr><td>/whois <nickname></td><td>Gives you information in the status window about the specified nick.</td></tr>
</table>

Command	What It Does
/whowas <nickname>	Gives information about the specified nick who just left IRC.
/whois <*nickname*>	Gives information on all forms of the nickname you specified that are on IRC. This information shows in the status window.
/whois <*IP address*>	Searches for the user by the IP address and gives information about him or her in the status window.
/write [-cidl] <filename> <text>	Writes the specified text to a .txt file.
/writeini <inifile> <section> <item> <value>	Writes to an .ini file.

Tip: The /ignore command ignores all notices, which means you can't perform a ctcp request on anyone in your ignore list.

Many of these commands can be used from a status line as well as part of aliases, popups, and remote commands or events. Following is a list of the various syntaxes that are included in these commands:

- [-a] — adds an item to a list
- [-r] — removes an item from a list
- [-q] — causes the operation to perform quietly—no report in any window

Several of these commands are universal to both mIRC and to IRC. As you work with some more advanced aliases, popups, and remote events and commands, you use many of the mIRC specific commands. You use these commands to perform many operations and activities while you're on IRC and it's to your benefit to at least understand what these commands are and what they do.

Pirch

Commands	What They Do
/? <topic|who|, etc>	Lets you quickly locate a help topic on the text you specified.
/achan <command>	Sends text or issues a command on all the channels you have joined.
/addpil <drive:\path\script.pil>	Adds the specified PIL script to aliases.
/adduser [-q] <level,[[level],...]> <nick[!user@host]> <maskmode>	Adds a user to the user list of an event level. The -q parameter indicates the command should be done without displaying the change in the server/status window. MaskMode is the address masking/wild carding options which should be applied to the person's address prior to adding to the list.
/admin	Retrieves administration information from the IRC server you are currently connected to.
/aserv <command>	Issues the specified command to each server to which you are connected.

Commands	What They Do
/autoop [-d] <nick[!user@host]> <maskmode>	Adds or removes a user to or from your autoop list. If the -d parameter is supplied, the user will be removed; otherwise he will be added.
/away <message> /away	Marks you as being away from your computer and sends the message you specified to anyone who sends you a private message. To clear the away, use /away again with no message or /unaway.
/awin <command>	Sends text or issues a command for each channel or message window you have open.
/ban <#channel> <nick[!user@host]>	Bans a particular nick and prevents that nick from joining the specified channel.
/beep	Causes a simple audio beep sound.
/bio send <nickname> <biofilename>	Sends your personal bio information to another person. Note that personal bios are Pirch-specific features and both you and the person you are sending to must be using Pirch.
/bioview <nickname|filename>	Open the personal bio viewer.
/callback [-d] <server reply code> <PIL script name>	Installs a callback script to handle a particular server reply code. /callback is probably the most advanced and unfortunately, most complicated command to understand and master. Basically /callback allows you to install a script to handle a variety of incoming server messages.
/cascade	Arranges the windows on the desktop in an overlapping fashion.
/clear	Clears all the text from the active window.
/clearcache <scriptname|uwho>	Forces PIL script's compiled binary image to be removed from Pirch's internal script cache and free the associated memory.
/close <windowname>	Closes the specified window or the active window if no window is specified.
/compile <scriptname|uwho>	Forces a PIL script to be compiled to a binary image and stored in Pirch's script cache without actually running the script or passing parameters to it.
/ctcp <nickname> clientinfo	Retrieves the name and version of the IRC client the specified nickname is using.
/ctcp <nickname> version	Retrieves the version number of the client used by the specified nickname.
/ctcp <nickname> finger	Retrieves the finger information from another client.
/ctcp <nickname> userinfo	Retrieves some information about the user of another client.
/ctcp <nickname> time	Retrieves the time of day information from the client of the specified nickname.
/dcc tsend <nickname> <filename>	Transfers files through a DCC connection using the TDCC protocol, which is faster than standard DCC protocol, to another user on IRC.

Commands	What They Do
/dcc video <nickname>	Sends a live video to the specified nickname. You must have a camera and PIRCHVDO running at the time you send this command.
/dccmsg <nickname> <message>	Sends a text message to the nick you have an established DCC chat connection with. This command is generally useful only for ON CHAT events.
/ddepoke <topic> <service> <item> <data>	Performs a DDE client transaction of XTYP_POKE to the topic and service.
/define <variable>=<value>	Creates and sets user-defined variables.
/describe <#channel> <message>	Describes an action.
/disable [-q] <eventlevel>	Disables an event level. The level name may be a partial name or wild card in which case all matching levels are affected.
/display <>windowname> <text>	Displays information to yourself in the server status window. This command does not generate an IRC message and no one but you will be able to see this message.
/dns <nick|[user@]host>	Looks up an Internet protocol address or domain name. The results of the DNS will show the name and IP number as reported by the domain name server.
/enable [-q] [eventlevel]	Enables an event level.
/execread [-L#] <filename>	Reads and executes a line read from a file composed of aliases. If the -L parameter is not supplied, Pirch reads a random line.
/execute [-oep] <drive:\path|drive:\path\filename>	Launches an executable file or document files.
/faccess <nickname> <homedirectory> <maxgets>	Gives a user access to your file server.
/fetch [url]	Fetches HTML web pages. Also, by default, use of /fetch without any parameters will retrieve a channel MOTD (Message of the Day) for the active channel from a default WWW server. Not all channels have MOTDs.
/filecopy <sourcefile> <targetfile>	Copies a file to another file.
/filedel <filename>	Erases a file. You must specify the exact filename.
/filemove <sourcefile> <targetdirectory>	Moves a file from a source to a target directory.
/flush	Flushes any pending messages from Pirch's internal flood control queue, and can only be used if your flood control option is enabled.
/help	Retrieves a list of valid commands from the server to which you are connected and displays them in the server/status window.
/info	Shows basic information about the server you are connected to.
/ison <nickname [nickname]...>	Lets you check whether one or more nicknames entered are currently on IRC. Separate each nickname with a space.

Commands	What They Do
/links [-s] <servername>	Shows other IRC servers connected to the network.
/loadurl <url>	Loads the specified URL address into your web browser.
/login [-a] <profile>	Creates a new server connection. Profile is the name of the profile you want the new connection to use.
/lusers	Lists the users currently on the network.
/map	Displays a map of the IRC network layout showing how each server is connected to the network.
/max <windowname>	Maximizes a window.
/min <windowname>	Minimizes a window.
/motd <servername>	Retrieves and displays the "Message of the Day" for the server that you are connected to.
/newwindow <windowname>	Creates a new child window on the Pirch desktop. The caption of the window will display the window name. Windows created with this command do not have a command/edit line, but are useful for redirecting particular text using events.
/note	Lets you leave notes for people on an IRC server, which get delivered to them when they sign on. However, this command is server specific, which means it may work on some servers and may not on others.
/opmsg <#channel> <message>	Sends a private message to all channel operators for the indicated channel.
/opnotice <#channel> <message>	Sends a notice to all channel operators for the indicated channel.
/playfile <nickname|channel> <filename>	Displays the contents of a text file in either a channel, private message, or dcc chat window.
/playmedia <filename>	Plays a multimedia file residing on your computer system.
/playpause	Temporarily stops the displaying of text started by the /playfile command.
/playresume	Restarts the displaying of text which had been previously paused with the /playpause command.
/playstop	Stops the displaying of text which had been previously started with the /playfile command.
/quote or /verbose <text>	Sends text directly to the server without any modification by Pirch.
/remuser [-q] <level,[[level],...]>	Removes a user from the user list of an event level.
/restore <windowname>	Restores a window's size and position from a minimized or maximized state.
/runscript <scriptname> <parameters>	Runs a PIL script.
/save	Saves all profile options.
/savebuffer <filename.txt>	Saves the current window's text buffer into a text file.
/set <option> <value>	Sets a variety of options from the command line or within aliases.

Commands	What They Do
/silence [+l-] <nick!user@hostlmask>	Stops private message flooding at the server of the flooder. You can use "/silence nickname" to get a list of the silence masks of the specified nickname.
/stats <servername>	Gives the statistics for a particular server.
/tile	Arranges the windows on the desktop in a non-overlapping fashion.
/time [servername]	Gives the time according to the server you specified.
/timer <timername> <iterations> <interval>	Automatically executes a command at specific time intervals.
/trace	Shows the network route taken for message delivery to a particular user.
/undefine <variable>	Undefines and frees the memory associated with a user-defined variable created with the /define command.
/userhost <nickname> [nickname]...	Returns a list of information about up to five nicknames.
/write [-CDIR#] <filename> <text>	Stores a line of text to a text file and with -C clears the text file removing all lines; -D# deletes line # from the file; -I# inserts text at line #; R# replaces line # in the file.
/writeini <filename> <section> <key>	Writes to an .ini file.
/version <servername>	Queries a server and has it report back the server software version.

These encompass most of the Pirch-specific commands. There are some here that are also common commands for IRC. As with mIRC, these Pirch commands can be used either from a command line or as part of aliases, popups, and events. All of these commands for both mIRC and Pirch help you to create operations and perform activities on IRC. Learn them or keep these pages bookmarked for future reference. You will use these pages a lot.

Foiling Stalkers and Hackers

As much as we would love IRC to be all sunshine and roses, it's not. It is populated by real people. It is its own society or groups of societies. When you get a group of people together, whether it be a relatively small group or a very large group, you get a diversity of personalities. The larger the group, the more diverse those personalities are and the greater the chance that you are going to have more of the shadier characters in that group.

IRC is a very large group made up of many different societies it calls channels. Since most of the channels are open, anyone can come and go as they please between these channels. When that happens, from time to time you are going to get some of the shady characters coming to your channel. Sometimes they present only a nuisance factor and sometimes they manage to disrupt your whole channel or upset some in your group. There are even times when some of these miscreants come to your channel to create nothing but havoc and to even take your channel away from you.

This section covers how you can foil these IRC delinquents and maintain or re-establish peace in your small part of this huge online world. I teach you how to foil stalkers, hackers, and harassers. Let's begin with stalkers and harassers.

Your client gives you one way to foil these sources of potential heartache to you. When you set up your client, one of the first steps to consider is the space that asks for your Real Name. The wise thing to do here is to put a nickname, an alias, or a quote you admire. Avoid using your real name on IRC if at all possible.

The second field in your setup asks for your e-mail address. Here you can enter your valid e-mail address or an e-mail alias. Some Internet service providers allow you to have a secondary e-mail address called an alias that forwards mail to your account. This is common where service providers create your account with your name as the account ID.

If your e-mail address contains your name, consider using a mask. A mask can be anything you want to set—a group of characters, a different login name, a nickname. While on the one hand it can be handy to be able to point to your login ID and say "that's my e-mail," it can cause problems if someone should decide to deluge you with harassing behavior. Sometimes an e-mail mask is a wise choice. If you do decide to mask, and it doesn't change your /whois information once you connect to IRC, check your setup. You may also have to change the information in the IdentD or firewall sections.

When chatting online, be wary of giving out personal information. Don't casually give out your name, address, phone number, or even e-mail address to just anyone. A little bit of caution can save much heartache later.

There are several ways that you can find people online or people can find you. If you are searching for a friend online, you can use a variety of commands to find the person. The most versatile is the /who command. By using the * wild card you can define a search that gives information on any user that matches the text. For example, if you are looking for a friend whose user@host id is gremlin@hubble.com, you can type: /who *gremlin*. This returns any user with the word and/or letters "gremlin" in his or her ID. The /who *hubble.com* returns any users who are hubble.com subscribers and are currently connected to IRC. The /who *gremlin@*.hubble.com* narrows your search by searching for gremlin and hubble.com, but the * in the middle would mask out the slip address, which often changes when people connect. These commands can also be used to find you or others online.

If, at times, you want to hide out, you can use the command: /mode <yournick> +i. This sets your personal user mode to invisible. This means that you do not show up in /who or /names listings. If someone knows your nickname, however, you still show up in a /whois command or in the notify list of a person who has you in notify.

By setting your mode invisible, you also lessen your chances of getting mass-invites or mass-messages that are sent by people at random to promote products, to invite people to channels or nets, etc.

The next thing you need to do is protect yourself from flooders. Flooding on IRC simply means overloading another person's computer. This can be done with dccs, pings or other ctcp commands, or even normal text if it comes to your connection too quickly.

Tip: The /flood command inhibits only specific types of replies to the server; usually these are events triggered by other users.

It is wise to program a script that ignores ctcp requests if you find yourself a victim of intentional flooding. One of the most effective ways to do this in mIRC is to set up a "gfp" (global flood protect) alias. The command looks like this: /gfp /ignore -tu60 *!*@*,private,notice,ctcp,invite. This ignores every private message, notice, ctcp command, or invitation to a channel from everyone for a period of 60 seconds. At that point you have time to enable a more permanent /ignore command without getting flooded off the server. In order to set this same kind of alias up in Pirch you need to program a PIL script. Refer back to Chapter 2 and also to Chapter 13 for instructions on how to do this.

Tip: The crude flood control command you set up in events prevents mIRC from sending any lines to the server if it has sent too many lines in the specified number of seconds and they are not stored.

If you find yourself the victim of harassment or flooding, you can use the /ignore command. This can be done with a nickname or with a user@host mask. For example: /ignore gremlin or /ignore *!*gremlin@*.hubble.com. The first example ignores the nickname gremlin. The second example ignores anyone with the user@host id of gremlin@hubble.com. The first wild card * tells the client to look for any nickname the person may be using, while the ! is a separator character.

A stronger command is the /raw silence command. This command sends a message directly to the server so the messages are ignored from there and never make it to your machine. The syntax is the same, with the same wild card masks, but the command is /raw silence. Raw is a mIRC override command that tells the program to send the command directly to the server. The silence command is one that the server recognizes.

What if this doesn't work? Then it's time to resort to more drastic measures. One of these is to e-mail the administrator of the harasser's Internet service provider, detailing the incidents. Attach logs if you can. Logs give you more credibility and also provide the system administrators with the ammunition and proof they need to do their jobs.

Another option is to contact an IRCop. This can be done by typing /who 0 o (zero lowercase o). It provides you with a list of IRCops currently logged in.

If you don't know the user@host of the person (if their login ID is represented as a group of numbers), you can use the following command to get the name of their service provider: /dns <nickname>. This takes the IP (Internet Protocol) number and resolves it to an address. The other way to use this /dns command is to paste or type in the series of numbers (i.e., /dns 111.111.111.111) in a person's IRC login address, which also furnishes the ISP (Internet service provider). You can do this if the person has disconnected or changed nicknames.

It's a good idea to keep a pad and paper beside your computer. If you cannot resolve the host, you can record the IP number and report it to an IRCop. The op can take measures to investigate the incident and suspend the service for that address.

These are some measures you can take to protect yourself and to get the information you need to stop harassment once it has started. If you have proof, contacting a user's provider is as effective a means of stopping this kind of behavior as any. Keep in mind that anytime you feel your life is in danger or you are threatened with bodily harm by a user on IRC, you do have the recourse of going to the authorities, whether that be the FBI or the local police.

The next group of IRC miscreants is possibly the nastiest. They are the IRC hackers. Hackers are people on IRC who are likely bored and have entirely too much time on their hands. They are generally just looking for a thrill, and a thrill to them is taking over a channel. Sometimes they choose a channel because someone in the channel annoyed them, and sometimes they do it just to see if they can or just because they can.

You have one of three options in countering these banes of IRC existence—try to appease them, ignore them, or try to defend the channel. Trying to appease them often doesn't work. It tends to only boost their egos especially if they feel they can intimidate or manipulate you. Trying to appease these IRC delinquents often results in continued harassment and attempts to take over your channel.

Ignoring these hackers is a better way to handle them. Simply make a new channel and wait them out. When they are no longer getting the attention they crave, albeit negative, they give up and move on to more fertile ground. While you're at it, put them in your ignore list and instruct the other users in your channel to do the same. If necessary, set the channel mode to secret and/or invite only. The only problem with this option is that it's inconvenient and hackers know this. Therefore they have reached their goal—they have taken over your channel, chased you away, and caused you at the least an inconvenience and probably a good deal of stress. Once they know they can get to you, they continue to find you and harass you and your friends.

The last option—defending your channel—means you need an arsenal. Your arsenal is composed of a strong knowledge of IRC, commands, your IRC client, some programming ability, good bots, and a lot of time.

Along with your arsenal, you and your regulars need to follow some general rules like:

- Use your judgment and be very careful about what you do.
- Never op anyone unless you are sure they are who they are supposed to be and you know them.
- Always deop anyone who comes in from splits with ops. You can always op your regulars later.
- When your channel is under attack, have all the ops mark themselves invisible and change their nicks.
- Ban any nicks and their addresses or accounts that are known troublemakers. When your channel is under attack, either change the channel mode to invite only or kick and ban any accounts you think are dangerous or suspicious.

Follow your instincts and trust your judgment. If someone comes to your channel and you suspect trouble, don't be afraid to take cautionary measures. It's better to err on the side of caution than lose your channel or suffer the stress and aggravation of a hostile takeover. The same holds true for opping people. Never op anyone you don't know and be very aware of who you are giving ops to. A channel takeover cannot happen if the hacker doesn't have ops status.

Following the rule to always deop anyone who returns from a split with ops prevents a hacker from slipping in with server ops and taking over the channel. Explain to the other members of your channel why you are doing this—make it a channel policy—and that they get ops back once you make sure everyone is who they are supposed to be. It's a good idea to not shoulder this responsibility alone. Set up two or three trusted regulars to help you with this. Make sure you and your trusted ops are not all on the same servers. That way if a split does happen you all won't split off together. Train them in how to protect the channel and make sure they know as much as you do. Use the clients you connect with to assist you in foiling these hackers. You and your trusted ops need to program events to automatically deop anyone coming in with server ops. Refer back to Chapter 3 for instructions on how to set up this event.

Having your channel ops change their nicknames and banning anyone you think is dangerous or suspicious prevents these hackers from finding you and your regulars and also prevents nick collisions. These nick collisions often happen during net splits and rejoins. Be sure to have everyone change their nicks after the banning and when these hackers are no longer in your channel.

On the nets that let you register channels and give you channel bots, you get some of the best protection for your channel and members. These channel bots are set up to not only keep the channel open round the clock but to also protect it and its members. If you choose not to register a channel on one of these nets or prefer to have your channel on a net that doesn't offer channel bots, you can use a personal bot instead. Be sure to get permission from servers if required before putting your own bot up. There are several protection and war bots you can download from the web. These are discussing in more detail in Chapter 14. If you have time and the programming knowledge, you can create your own bot to protect your channel.

Be aware of everything that goes on in your channel. Be prepared to take defensive actions when necessary. Search the web for bots and information about hackers and how to protect yourself against them. Learn all that you can about IRC, your client, and commands. Start here with this chapter and the rest of this book to learn how to protect yourself, your channel, and channel members from any contingency.

IRC Commands

As promised, here is the chart of all the IRC commands. Use it to find the command you need to perform a certain action or operation.

Commands	What They Do
/nick <nickname>	lets you give yourself a nickname
/join #<channel name>	lets you join a channel
/topic #<channel name>	gives you the topic that is set for the channel you indicated
/list	lists all the channels on the net you are connected to
/list <parameters>	lets you set parameters for the list — limit the size of the list
/names	does the same as the /list command but gives you a list of nicks that are in each channel
/server <server address>	connects you to a server
/links	lists all the servers that have links to the server you log onto
/time	gives you the time for the server you are connected to
/time <nickname>	gives you the time for the server of the nick you specified
/whois <nickname>	tells you if that nickname is on, its address, and where it is on the net
/whowas <nickname>	tells you where that nick was just before it left IRC
/who #<channel name>	tells you who is on the channel you specify
/msg <nickname> your message	sends a private message to the nickname you specify
/query <nickname>	does the same thing as the /msg command
/ping <nickname>	tells you how long it takes that user's response or message to get to the channel and be seen by you or the other users
/invite <nickname> #<channel name>	invites the nick to the channel you indicate
/me your message	lets you type action type messages
/notify <nickname>	notifies you as soon as the nick you specified joins IRC
/ignore <nickname>	lets you type in the nicks of people you wish to ignore
/away <message>	marks you as being away
/help	brings up a list of commands in the help file
/leave #<channel name>	takes you out of the channel you are in
/part #<channel name>	takes you out of the channel you are in
/exit	takes you out of IRC completely
/signoff	also takes you completely out of IRC
/quit	does the same thing as /exit
/bye	also takes you completely out of IRC
/bye <comments>	leaves your parting comments with the channel and takes you out of IRC

Commands	What They Do
/set hold_mode on	pauses your screen once one screen full of messages has accumulated
/dcc send <nickname> <file name>	lets you send a file from your computer to another person on IRC
/dcc get <nickname> <file name>	the command the person receiving the file needs to type in order to start the send/receive process
/dcc chat <nickname>	lets you establish a private chat conversation with another nick
/ctcp <nickname> finger	gives you idle time information on the nick you specified
/ctcp <nickname> ping	gives you lag information on the nick you specified
/ctcp <nickname> clientinfo	gives you a master index on the user's client information
/ctcp <nickname> userinfo	gives you information about the user
/ctcp <nickname> version	gives you information about the IRC software the user has installed
/mode #<channel name> +o <nickname>	bestows channel operator's status on the nick you specified
/mode #<channel name> -o <nickname>	takes ops status away
/topic #<channel name> <topic>	allows you to set the topic for your channel
/mode #<channel name> [+t,n,s,p,I,m,k,l]	changes the mode of a channel
/mode #<channel name> +v <nickname>	this command gives a user without ops on a moderated channel voice
/kick #<channel name> <nickname>	this command kicks someone off the channel you are in
/mode #<channel name> +b <nickname>	bans a user from your channel
/mode #<channel name> -b <nickname>	removes the ban from the channel

Between the client-specific commands and these IRC commands, you have a pretty extensive list of commands you can use to accomplish anything you want to do in IRC. Study these, get familiar with them, and refer back to this chapter as often as you need to.

Exercises

1. Perform a search for a particular nickname.
2. Perform a search for a particular address. Use any address you can think of.
3. Perform a search for a particular provider.
4. Perform a search for a dns on a particular nickname.
5. Create an ignore alias to use if someone is stalking you.

Chapter 6
Splits and Lags

In this chapter you learn:

- ☑ *What is Lag?*
- ☑ *What are Splits?*
- ☑ *How to Alleviate Lag*
- ☑ *What to Do About Splits*

If you spend any amount of time on IRC and in one of the big three nets, you have experienced lag and splits. Most of the midsize to smaller nets have very little problem with these. However, it does happen on these smaller nets too. You probably won't see splits happening very often—they just don't have the traffic or the number of servers the larger nets do.

Lags and splits are a fact of life if you frequent the EfNet, UnderNet, or DALnet. They can create frustration and anxiety to you and others on the net. Sometimes either or both are so bad that chatting in channels, private messages, or DCC Chats or trying to send files through DCC Send are virtually impossible.

Let's take a look at each of these scourges of IRC and some steps you can take to alleviate your frustration, anxiety, and stress when you find yourself experiencing them.

What is Lag?

On IRC you have various nets. Each of these nets is made up of networks of servers. Servers are pieces of hardware and programs located at a site somewhere. The two most common residences for these servers are universities and service providers.

These servers are IRC-specific servers and are typically UNIX servers. They are interconnected to each other via the Internet. A few of these servers are the hub servers—the main servers. All others are connected or routed through to each other via one or more of these hub servers and other servers. This is similar to how phone lines are routed to and through each other to let you talk long distance to friends and family.

These servers then process your messages, the channels, DCC Chats and Sends, and everything that goes on in IRC. When you type a message to a channel, a private message or otherwise, it is sent first to the server you're on and then from server to server until it reaches its intended destination.

These net servers are routed generally through telephone lines. Telephone lines send their signals through satellites and/or fiber optic lines. Many different factors can affect the transmission of signals and therefore these IRC servers.

Because these servers are hardware and programs, the number of users that are connected or trying to connect to the net can affect how they perform. If a server has to be routed through too many routes or through other servers that are having problems, this can slow them down. Sometimes the weather affects how these servers perform by the way it affects telephone transmissions and connections.

Any one of these factors can cause servers to perform poorly. This is what sometimes causes lag. And lag in essence is how long it takes from the time you type your message or command and press Enter until that message or command reaches its destination—the channel, a private message, or a DCC Chat window.

Sometimes lag can be a matter of only a few seconds to half a minute or so. Sometimes lag can run on for minutes. Most of the time only a few servers are affected. However, on occasion, most if not all the servers are affected.

When lag happens it can be very frustrating. You begin to feel like everyone is ignoring you. It seems as though you are talking to yourself. Often you see people put up messages like "Hello?" or "Can you see me?" or "Is anyone here or am I lagged??" Sometimes you experience what is called screen freeze. Your screen doesn't move for several long seconds or even minutes, then it scrolls through a screen or two or even several. This is also called lag/scroll on IRC.

If you are the only one experiencing either of these problems, then chances are it's the server you are on that's having the problem. But if most or everyone else is also having the same problems, then the cause is likely a universal net problem.

No matter whether the problem is isolated to one server or affects many or all servers, you can rest assured the system operators and IRCops are doing their best to rectify it. They are scrambling to find better routes when possible or trying other methods to increase the performance of their servers. Later in this chapter we discuss ways you can get around or solve this problem with lag.

What are Splits?

As mentioned before, servers link to each other via the Internet. When the traffic gets heavy on the Internet—all the Internet, not just IRC—then the links and routes get overloaded and some of the links break. Sometimes hackers take down a server and cause a break in the routes and a strain on the other servers.

When these links break it's called a netsplit. To give you an idea of how this might work, imagine a spider web. In the center of this web is the mother spider—the Internet. Each strand of that web represents a server. Then imagine there are hundreds of baby spiders on each of these strands. These baby spiders are us, the users (see Figure 6-a).

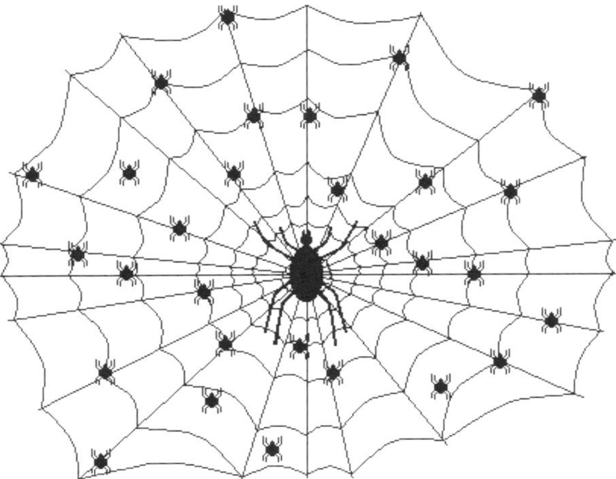

Figure 6-a. Spider web example of nets

If a strong wind, a human hand, or even too many babies on one or more strands causes one or more of those strands to break, those babies lose contact with the rest of the web. This is similar to what happens on the Internet and IRC when netsplits happen (see Figure 6-b).

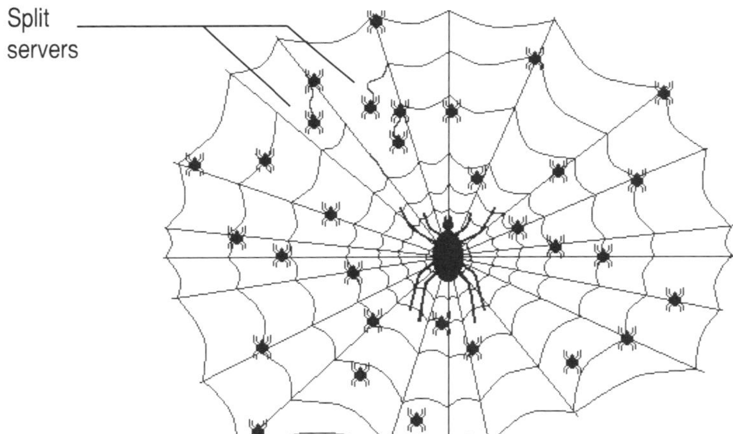

Figure 6-b. Spider web example of a split

When you are on IRC you can tell when a netsplit happens when you see several or all of the other people leave your channel. When they leave it looks like this: W has quit IRC (Chicago-R.IL.US.Undernet.org ann-arbor.mi.us.undernet.org). This shows that the connection between the two servers broke down. This does not necessarily mean that the person that split is on that particular server or that you are the one split. It merely means that one of you was on the side where the server connections broke down. See Figure 6-c for examples of a person leaving IRC normally and a netsplit.

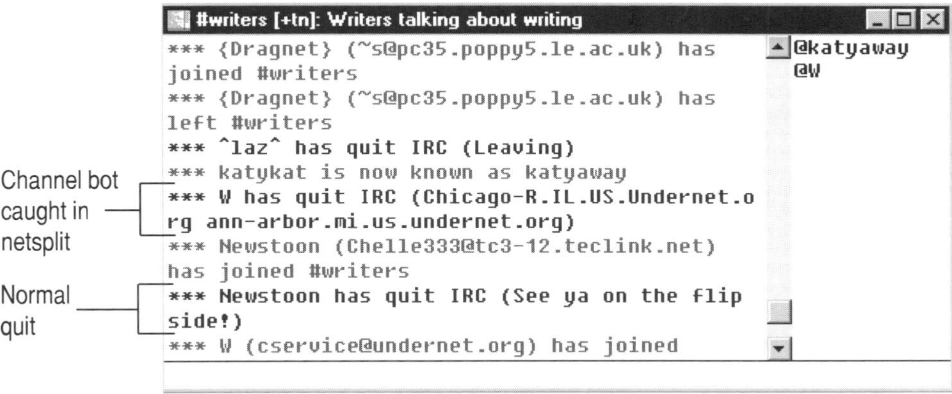

Figure 6-c. Netsplit and normal IRC quit

When these netsplits happen messages aren't relayed to the split servers and vice versa. You can communicate with other users on the same server you're on or on servers linked to the one you're on. When the connections repair themselves you are able to carry on normal chats again. However, just because you see those split servers returning doesn't mean the split is completely repaired. Sometimes it takes several more seconds before the split is completely repaired and normal conversations can resume. Sometimes the repair is temporary and you see those same people split again before conversations can begin again. This happens during particularly bad times on the nets and you can see these splits happen repeatedly in just a few hours online.

When these server splits or netsplits happen, these servers don't know what the other servers are doing and often don't know they are split. The split servers carry on as through it's business as usual—channels form, people get ops, and other usual IRC activities carry on. As the servers come back together, they update each other on what has been going on. This is called synching info. You see the splitters rejoining the channel and then you see the server give ops to some of the returning users.

Sometimes these netsplits and split servers act in a bit more subtle fashion. You can be on a channel and see several nicks in the channel names list but only see posts from one or two other users actually chatting. When you do a /whois on the users in the channel, you notice the only ones you can see are the ones on the same server that you're on. In this situation, you're on a split server. You can't see what most of the others in the channel are posting but they can see you and all you are posting. They probably even respond to you until they figure out that you can't see them even though they can see you.

These are the various scenarios and symptoms of splits and lags. Now let's look at some ways you can work around them or get past these scourges of IRC.

How to Alleviate Lag

When you find yourself on a lagged server, you have a few options. You can stay with the server you're on to see if it catches up to the other servers. Sometimes this is advisable especially when it's evident that the lag you're experiencing is a netwide occurrence. One trick you can try to bring your lag time down is to ping yourself several times. Many times pinging yourself repeatedly lessens your lag. I have never seen or heard of an explanation or even acknowledgment of this; I just know from experience that it often works. There are times, however, when this won't work.

If lag is affecting your DCC Sends or Chats, you can try pinging yourself and the other user. Ping each other every few seconds. This sometimes help keep you two from lagging which can cause the DCC to fail.

You can check to see what server most of the other users on your channel are connecting to. Then you can change over to that server. However, if the lag is a net problem—evident usually by a universal lag/scroll—this probably won't do much to alleviate your problem.

If you frequent the same channel or channels, it's a good idea to coordinate with the other regulars there. Agree on a server you all can connect with. When all or most of the users in a channel use the same server they are less likely to experience lag to each other. Also when splits occur, they all stay together and don't miss out on any chatting.

Sometimes the lag is caused by your provider. It has equipment problems or overloads and that affects the speed at which you can connect or slows you down. There's not much you can do other than try to relog with your provider. Or you can just ride out the storm and hope the problem is corrected soon.

The last and probably the most undesirable action you can take is to give up and log off. During times when a net is experiencing an excess of trouble with lag, this may be your best option. Of course, logging off doesn't necessarily mean logging off IRC completely. You can choose to try one of the other nets. Beware that if one of the big three nets is having problems, then either of the other two nets could be also. If you must get your IRC fix, then try one of the smaller or midsize nets.

What to Do About Splits

When you frequent any of the big three nets, splits are often a natural occurrence. You do have a few options to get around splits.

If you find yourself on a server that keeps splitting off from the others, it is advisable to just change servers. Sometimes splits are isolated to only one or two servers and finding a better server is the best option.

There is a way to detect when possible splits are happening. You can put a command in your Remote/Events in mIRC or Events and Controls in Pirch to scan quit messages to check for splits. The command for mIRC is as follows and needs to be typed in exactly as it appears here:

```
1:ON QUIT:#:{
IF (irc* ISIN $parms) {
echo 4 *** Possible Split: $parms
{
{
```

You can create a similar event for Pirch by creating a PIL script. This is covered in Chapter 13.

If the splits look to be a netwide problem, your best option may be to just ride out the storm. Changing servers in this instance isn't going to do you much good. When various servers and their links are breaking connections, you can't guarantee you can find a stable server.

As mentioned with lag, agree with the other regulars on your favorite channels on a universal server for you all to use. At least when you are all on the same server, you stay together when there are netsplits.

The last and least favorite option is to leave or quit the net that's having the problem or to leave IRC altogether. On particularly horrendous times in IRC, this may be the only thing that saves your sanity and doesn't spoil you on chat completely. One of the other nets might prove much more conducive to uninterrupted chatting.

Apply these techniques to your chatting to overcome some of the inconveniences of IRC life. Lag and splits need not turn you into a babbling fool or stress you to the point of hospitalization. There are ways to combat them.

Chapter 7

DCC and Sound

In this chapter you learn:

- ☑ What is DCC?
- ☑ Sounds
- ☑ Exercises

What is DCC?

DCC lets you send files to or chat in private with other users on IRC. DCC is short for Direct Client to Client protocol. It allows you to communicate directly—provider to provider—with other users. Although you are connecting directly to each other, you must be connected to IRC before you can initiate the DCCs.

Using DCC you can establish direct connections with other users and then send files from your computer to theirs, receive files from other users, or chat in private. These DCCs are referred to as DCC Sends, DCC Gets, and DCC Chats.

Tip: The nickname in the DCC send dialog box defaults to the last nickname that a file was sent to.

There are three ways you can establish these DCCs. You can type out the commands — /dcc send <nickname> <filename>, /dcc get <nickname> <filename>, or /dcc chat <nickname>. You can use the easy way and click on a name in the channel names list and then select DCC from the Popups menu. Next you simply choose Send or Chat from the selections that appear. To receive a file from another user, just click on OK in the DCC Get dialog box that appears. The last option is to left-click in your file manager or in the DCC Send dialog box listing of files on the file you want to send. While holding down the left mouse button, drag it over to a nickname in the channel names list, to a channel window, or to a private or chat window. This drag and drop feature is new to both mIRC and Pirch (see Figure 7-a).

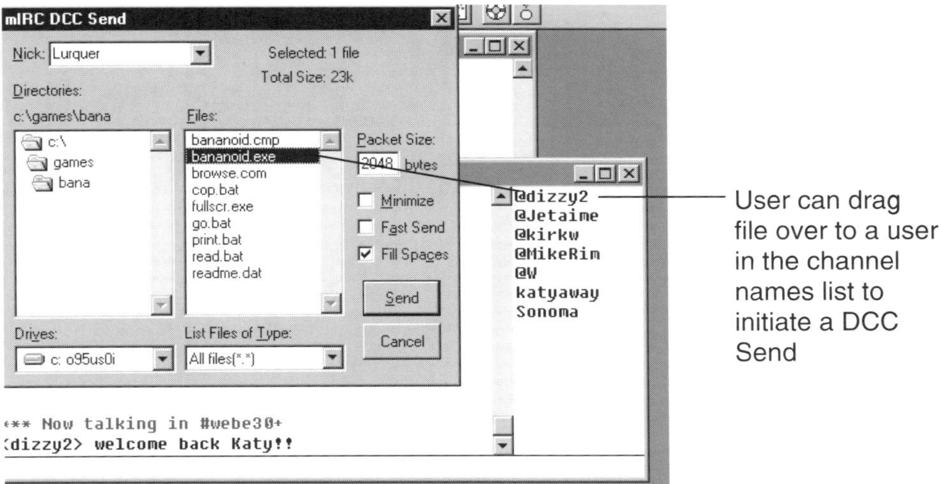

Figure 7-a. Drag and drop DCC box in mIRC

Technique: Drag and drop lets you drag files onto channels, to nicknames in channel names lists, to queries, and DCC Chat windows.

When you use this drag and drop feature you can also set up aliases to associate with the different kinds of files you choose rather than just send the files. For instance, you can have mIRC or Pirch read a text file to another user by creating an alias for it. The alias is: *.txt:/play $1 $2 for mIRC and *.txt:/splay $nick # $filename for Pirch. In miRC the $1 is for the user or channel where the file is dropped and $2 is for the name of the file. The /play command sends each line of the file to the user or channel.

Technique: The DCC Get dialog lets you choose a different directory for the incoming file.

In mIRC you can also let different aliases execute for the same file type by holding down the Shift key when you drop a file. The default settings without the Shift key are: *.wav:/sound $1 $2 and *.*:/dcc send $1 $2. Therefore, when you drop a wave file it plays where you dropped it. The *.* indicates that mIRC is to treat all other files as DCC Sends. The default setting for dropping files while holding down the Shift key is: *.*:/dcc send $1 $2 (see Figure 7-b on the following page).

Tip: When a user tries to initiate a DCC Chat request with you at the same time you are initiating one with him, mIRC treats this as an acceptance.

These same aliases in Pirch are: *.wav:/playmedia $nick $filename and *.*:/dcc send $nick $filename. There are no Shift key alternatives (see Figure 7-c).

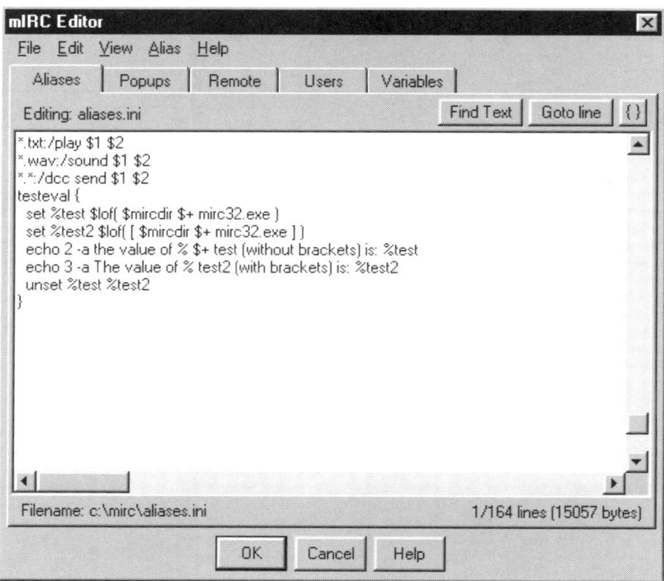

Figure 7-b. Drag and drop aliases in mIRC

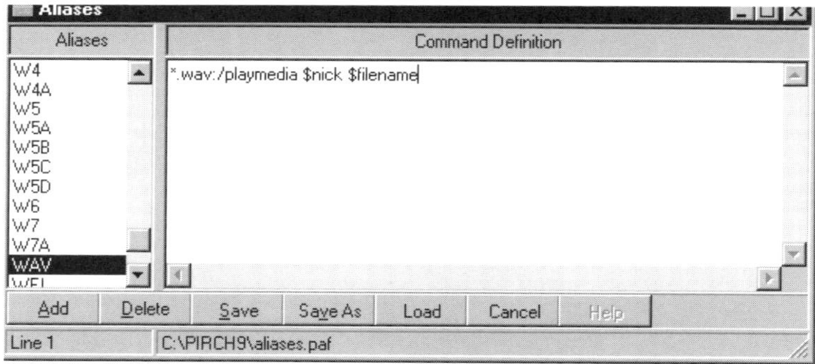

Figure 7-c. Drag and drop alias in Pirch

Tip: Remote DCCs close windows automatically when finished.

With mIRC you can also set up Remote/Events to automatically send files to users. You can set these up to send to anyone or only to specified user levels. Following are some user level commands to handle these automated functions for you:

- <user level>:XDCC LIST:/notice $nick Files offered: #1<filename>(size) ; #2<filename>(size), etc.
- <user level>:XDCC SEND #1:/dcc send $nick <directory and path for file #1>
- <user level>:XDCC SEND #2:/dcc send $nick <file #2 directory and path> (and so on for as many files as you want to offer)
- <user level>:XDCC SEND:/notice $nick You must specify file #1 or #2, etc.

- <user level>:XDCC:/notice $nick Try XDCC LIST
- <user level>:MYLEVEL:/notice $nick You have access level <user level you set for that user>

Use these as examples to set up user level XDCC options for the different files you want to offer different level users. Notice with these options you set your Remote/Events to react to the varying needs of your users. Set these up for a group of files you want to offer to one level of user—level 50, for example. Then change the level and set them up again for this different level and the files you want to offer them. You can do this for as many levels and files as you want (see Figure 7-d).

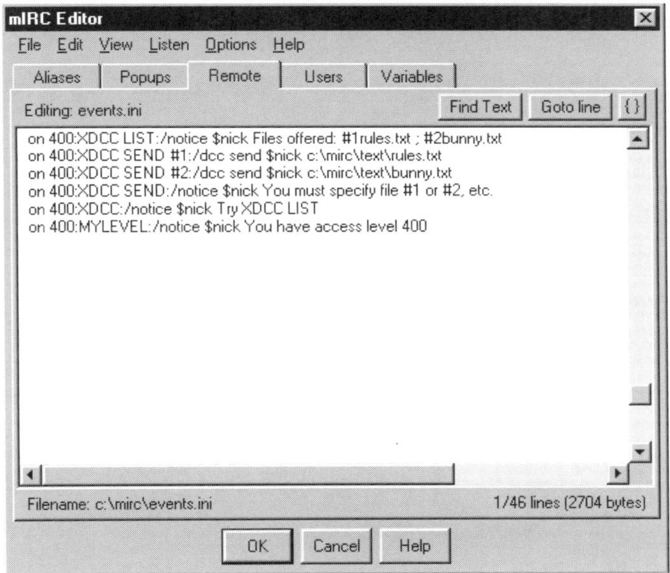

Figure 7-d. XDCC events in mIRC

Tip: Pirch added a TDCC send which is a faster DCC file transfer protocol and mIRC added a Fast send to its DCC options to let you send files faster.

By changing the identifiers and placing these in the user level panes you want in Pirch, you can do essentially the same thing. Next all you have to do is let your friends know you have this automated. The easiest way is to set up an ON TEXT event to trigger for the keywords DCC SEND. Refer back to Chapter 3 for the command syntax to create an ON TEXT event for this (see Figure 7-e).

Technique: When users change nicks while in a DCC Chat with you, the chat window updates with the user's new nick.

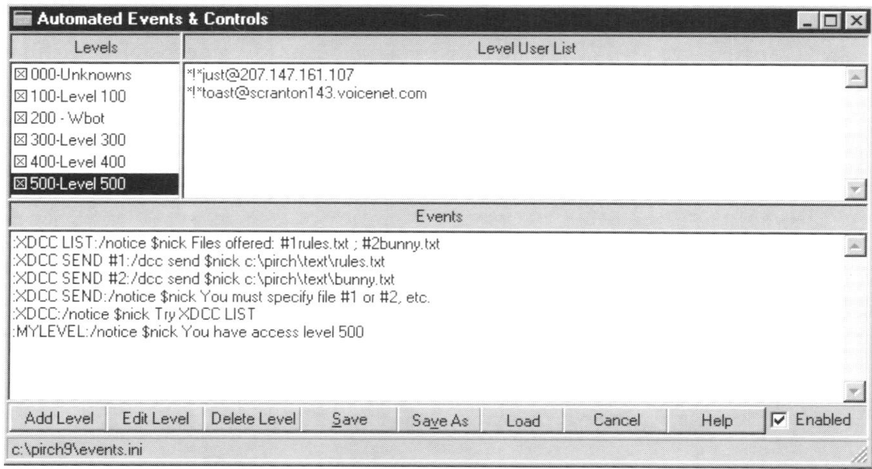

Figure 7-e. XDCC events in Pirch

Before you do all this and begin letting others access your files, you need to make sure your DCC Options are set up correctly for your client. In mIRC select DCC from the toolbar. In the DCC Options dialog box set the Send/Get Transfer Time Out for the number of seconds you want it to wait before it times out due to no response from the other user. You also need to set the time for the Fileserver Time Out for when a user is idle for a specified number of seconds. Then set limits for the number of simultaneous remote DCC Sends (Max. DCC Send) and for the file-server (Max. Fileservers). Experiment with them to see what works best for you or you can use the defaults already set up by mIRC. All of these keep mIRC from getting tied up with idle users or gluttons (see Figure 7-f).

Figure 7-f. DCC options in mIRC

Technique: The remote DCC window automatically closes when the other user crashes or cancels the DCC Get.

With Pirch select DCC Options from the Pref toolbar item. The options you can set are basically the same as those in mIRC. With Pirch you have one other option you can use with DCCs. It is the DCC Extension Map. This is a new option to this newer version of Pirch.

The DCC Extension Map lets you specify where to store DCC Gets according to the type of file downloaded. It lets you store different file types to different directories based on the file extension. Extension types that aren't found in this extension map are stored in the default DCC Download directory you specified in the DCC Options (see Figure 7-g).

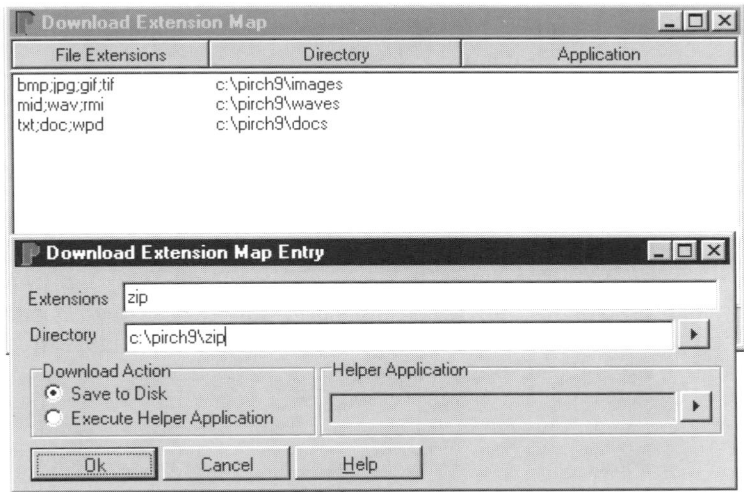

Figure 7-g. DCC Extension Map in Pirch

When specifying similar files with different extensions, be sure to separate the extensions with semicolons. Following are the types of files you can specify in this DCC Extension Map:

- bmp;gif;tif;jpg — c:\pirch\images
- mid;rmi;wav — c:\pirch\sounds
- txt;doc;wpd — c:\pirch\docs
- zip — c:\pirch\zip

Use the options and activities covered in this section to handle and process DCC functions. DCC no longer needs to interfere with your chat time.

Sounds

Sounds come in three file types—waves, MIDIs, and RMIs. Waves with the extension of .wav are waveform audio files and the most common type of sound files you run across in IRC. MIDIs with the extension of .mid are Musical Instrument Digital Interface audio files. RMIs with the extension of .rmi are a variation of MIDI files and AVI—a video file.

Most of the sounds you hear and exchange with other users are wave files. They are the most prolific and popular of all the sound files. There are channels on many of the IRC nets where you can go to exchange sound files. There are also sites on the web where you can download sound files. If you do a search for waves, sounds, or IRC, you should be able to find any number of these sites.

Refer back to Chapter 3 and this chapter for instructions on how to set up remotes, events, and auto DCC Sends to exchange sound files with your friends and other users. Save yourself the distraction and time spent trying to send these through popups or commands. Do it the automated way!

If you have a sound card, which you need in order to hear sounds, and a microphone, you can create your own sounds. Record parts of your favorite songs. I advise you not to try to record whole songs. These become quite large files and can take a long time to send to others. Many users even record their own voices saying or singing something. Windows 95 and many of the newer computer systems have a built-in feature that lets you record your own sounds. Once you create these files, exchange them with your IRC friends.

Learn to use DCC to send and receive files and how to set up your client to take care of those sends automatically for you. Spend more time chatting and let your program do the work it was designed for.

Exercises

Refer back to the chapter for instructions on how to do the following exercises. In addition use the help files for the IRC clients to assist you if you need to.

mIRC

1. Create a split detector event to let you know when a split is in progress.
2. Create a DCC Send alias.
3. Create an XDCC event.

Pirch

1. Create a playmedia alias.
2. Create an XDCC event.
3. Create extensions in the Extension Map.

Chapter 8

Advanced Pirch

In this chapter you learn:

- ☑ *Autoexec Commands*
- ☑ *Colors*
- ☑ *File Servers*
- ☑ *Video*
- ☑ *Text to Speech*
- ☑ *Miscellaneous*
- ☑ *Exercises*

Pirch is one of two of the best IRC clients available. It has many features to enhance your time in chat. Many of these were covered in the previous chapters on aliases, popups, and events. This chapter covers other aspects of Pirch that enhance or help you in your online chat activities.

This chapter covers how to set up and use autoexec commands—commands that automatically execute when you open Pirch. We also discuss colors, how to use them in text, and how to use them to change the appearance of your chat windows and lines of text generated by Pirch and IRC. Next we cover how to use File Server and then the video part of Pirch. With most newer computers, you get a program called Monologue. This program converts text to a form of speech. It's not a perfect speech quality—it's a little stilted—but it can be amusing to play with. Pirch utilizes this program to let you hear some messages spoken rather than just displayed to your screen. Lastly we combine a few of the other features and some commands to help you master them. Some of these include the IdentD Server, DCC Extension Map with Helper Applications, the Verbose command for lists, and the Fetch command.

Technique: When you use multiple connections and use the same primary profile or .ini file, you can load new alias, popup, and event files or do a save as, and all connections that use that profile also recognize any changes and use these same alias, popup, and event files.

Autoexec Commands

These autoexec commands are activities you want to happen each time you connect to an IRC server or open up Pirch. For instance, you can set this up to automatically join your favorite channel and get a channel names list. In the Auto Load Profile option you can have Pirch automatically load your profile when you start up.

Using these features particular to Pirch frees up more of your time and handles some of the more mundane functions for you. To use these features, first select the option you want to use. Auto Load Profile is under IRC in the menu bar and Auto Connect Setup option and Autoexec Commands are under Options in the menu bar. Following are some autoexec commands and the Auto Load profile:

- Auto Load Profile — from the Auto Connect Setup option under IRC in the menu bar, click on Add in the Auto-Connections Setup dialog box. Then select your profile from the Pirch directory in the Auto Profile to Start dialog box. Of course, you must save your profile first. If you have more than one member of your family who uses Pirch, let each one set up a profile using his or her name or nick for the name of the file (see Figure 8-a).

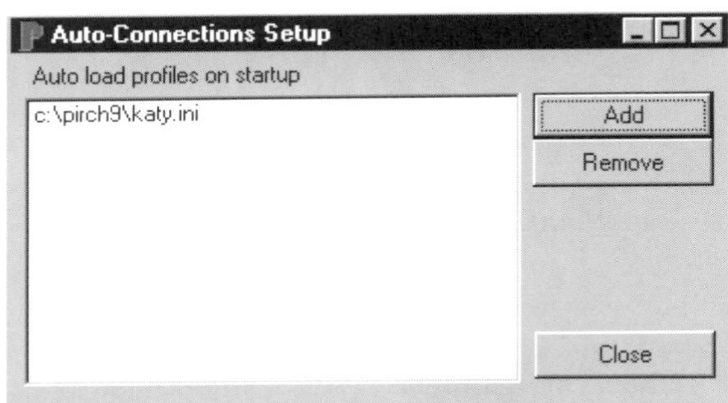

Figure 8-a. Auto-Connections Setup dialog box

- Auto Join a Channel — from the Autoexec Command option under Options in the menu bar, type /join #<channelname> in the IRC Autoexec dialog box.
- Auto /who a Channel — in this same IRC Autoexec dialog box on a separate line type /who #<channelname>. Do this for as many autoexec commands as you want as long as you put each one on a separate line (see Figure 8-b).

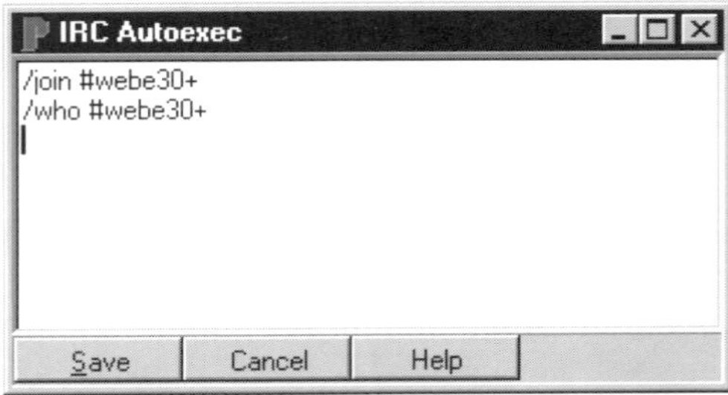

Figure 8-b. Autoexec commands dialog box

You can use these autoexec commands to perform almost any function automatically for you when you connect to a server. I always check to see who is on my favorite channels or the competing channels. I am also in the autoops database for two channels. To get those ops I have to message the bot with my passwords. If you're on a channel bot for ops, you can set this autoexec command up to message the bot for you when you connect to a server. Test out a few of the commands you do when you first connect to IRC and let the autoexec commands handle them for you.

Colors

Pirch gives you two ways you can work or play with colors. The first is used to change your window background colors as well as the various colors of lines of special text that display in your windows. These special lines of text include notes, notices, actions, ctcp responses, wallops, server messages, ops notices, part and join messages, and so forth. The second way to work with colors is to add colors to the text you type.

To manipulate the colors of your windows, etc., click on Options in the menu bar and then choose Colors from the menu. A Color Setup dialog box pops up with the options you can change, a color chart, and a pane showing how the colors you change actually look. Click on various options and select a few different colors to test how this works. Now choose options one by one and choose a color you like for each. When you have everything the way you want it, click on OK to exit and save your changes. Next join a channel and see how your changes affect the way the channel window looks. See Figure 8-c for an example of what this Color Setup dialog box looks like.

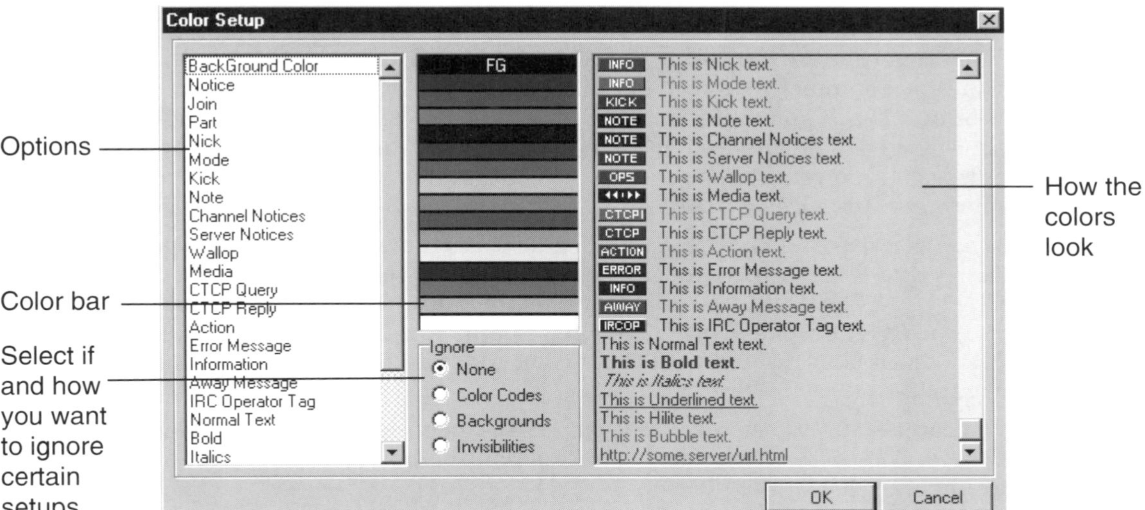

Figure 8-c. Color Setup dialog box

While you are changing line text colors, look at the various options you have for backgrounds. Select Options from the menu bar and then choose Desktop Options. In the Desktop Options dialog box choose a background you like best from the options Pirch gives you or choose one from your hard drive if you have any (see Figure 8-d).

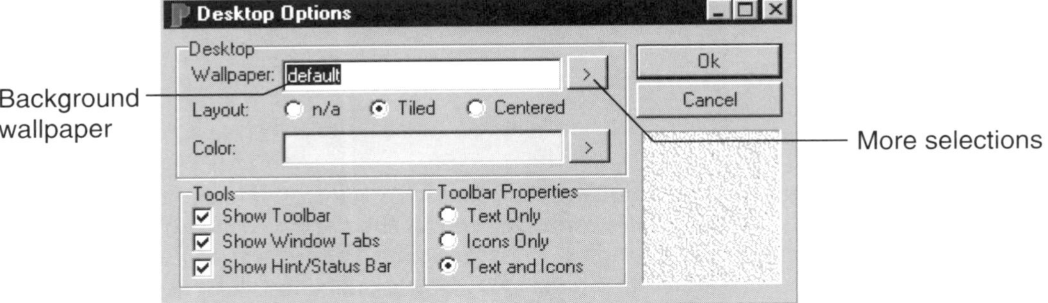

Figure 8-d. Desktop Options dialog box

Now that you have your background and line text colors set up, let's look at what you can do to add color to the text you type. Pirch lets you change or add color to text by using color codes. These color codes are activated by pressing Ctrl+k (press and hold Ctrl and type k). Pirch gives you sixteen different colors to work with. They are:

* 0 — White	* 1 — Black	* 2 — Navy	* 3 — Green
* 4 — Red	* 5 — Maroon	* 6 — Purple	* 7 — Olive
* 8 — Yellow	* 9 — Lime Green	* 10 — Teal	* 11 — Aqua
* 12 — Blue	* 13 — Fuchsia	* 14 — Gray	* 15 — Silver

Each time you use Ctrl+k it activates or deactivates the color code option. When you type a number following Ctrl+k, you activate the color that corresponds to that number. If you prefer a different way to activate color coding, right-click in the edit line of a window and click on Color from the menu you get. You must do this each time you want to change a color. I prefer to use the Ctrl+k method since my fingers are already there.

When you use Ctrl+k with a number, all text following the code appears on channel as that color. If you use Ctrl+k with two numbers separated by a comma, e.g., Ctrl+k 2,4, the first number you type is the text color and the second number is the background color. Try typing a few simple words using a combination of two color codes. Play around with these color codes and see what you can do (see Figure 8-e on the following page).

You can also use these color codes in aliases, popups, and events. Refer back to the chapters on these operations for instructions on how to do this and to get some examples.

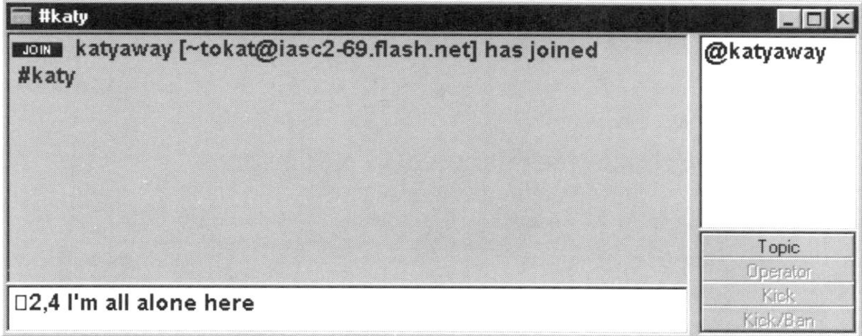

Figure 8-e. Color code command — the box is what appears when you press Ctrl+k.

On the web and in some Pirch channels, you can get PIL scripts to add to your aliases and create various color schemes and text for aliases and popups. More is covered about the scripts in Chapter 13. Do a search on the web for Pirch Aliases or Pirch PILs and I'm sure you'll find more PILs than you could ever want.

Play around with these color codes. Test them out and create a few aliases and popups with them. Take some of your existing aliases and popups and add a few colors to them. If you need help with creating fancy text in aliases or popups, refer back to the chapters on these two subjects.

File Servers

The File Server option in Pirch lets you set up a way for others to automatically download files from you. It is advisable to set up a special directory or directories with only the files in them you want to offer your IRC friends.

Tip: Server windows have drop-down menus for networks and servers to let you find servers and networks easier.

Let's set up a file server now. First create a home directory. For simplicity's sake, set it up in your Pirch directory and name it Text. For example, it might look like this: c:\pirch\text\download. Be sure to add the \download at the end. In other words, you need to make Download a subdirectory of Text. Put a few of your ASCII art text files in it. Next go to Tools in the menu bar and select File Server from the options. In the dialog box that appears, select Server Setup. You then get a File Server Options dialog box. In this box you enter the values you want for each option. Pirch already has this set up with default options. These are the suggested options but you can select your own or leave these as they are. The options you can set up are:

- Idle Disconnect — the amount of time a user can be idle in your file server before he is automatically disconnected.
- Default Max Gets — the maximum number of files a user can download during a single file server session. User is disconnected when the maximum number of downloads is achieved.

- Default Home Dir — is the root directory and its subdirectories users can access.
- Sign-on Msg File — a standard text file that is displayed to a user when he or she logs into the file server.

See Figure 8-f for an example of how these options look.

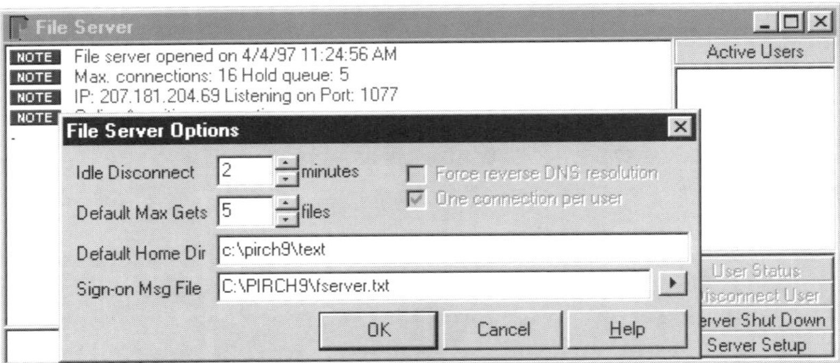

Figure 8-f. File Server setup boxes

Once you have your file server options set, you're ready to let your friends start using it. Before anyone can access your file server you have to give them permission by using the /faccess command: /faccess <nickname> <directory> <number of files they can get>. When a file server connection is established and a file or files are requested, the requested files are sent to that user via DCC Send.

You can type this command each time someone wants to access your file server or you can automate the command. Select Events from the Toolbar menu and choose a level of users. In the Events pane type the following command: ON NOTICE:*!fileserver:*:/faccess $nick <your directory> <number of gets>. Then your friends only have to type /notice <yournick> !fileserver to gain access to your file server.

Technique: Only one file server window can be created, but the server supports multiple connections.

Once you have all this set up and a user sends you a notice that he wants to access your file server, Pirch tries to establish a DCC connection with the user via DCC Chat. Then the user can issue certain commands to get certain kinds of information from your file server or to get files. These commands are:

- Help — the user types Help to get a list of available commands or to get specific help on a command.
- Get — the user types the Get command with a filename to retrieve files from your file server.
- Tget — the user types Tget to retrieve files via a TDCC connection; the user's client must have TDCC capability.
- Read — lets the user issue this command to view the contents of a text file while online with the file server.

- CD — lets the user change directories to retrieve files from.
- Exit or Bye — closes the file server connection.

Get your file server set up. Then create an event to automatically give permission to your friends to access it. Test it out on a few of your friends to see how much easier it is and how much time it saves you. See Figure 8-g for an example of the file server window you get when someone accesses your file server.

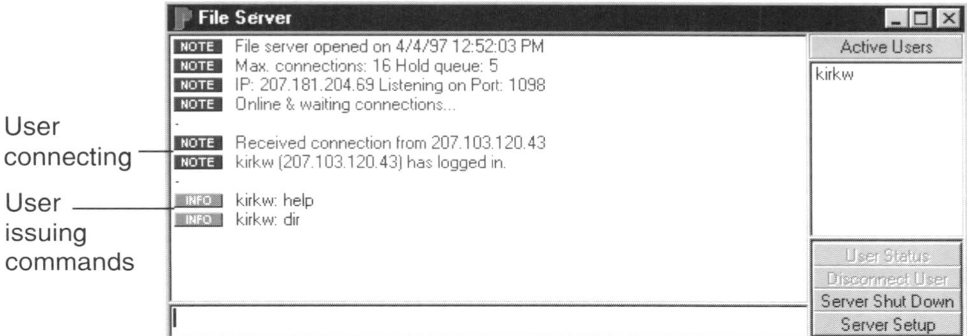

Figure 8-g. Active file server

Video

With the video option in Pirch you can do two things—receive live video feeds or send live video feeds. To receive these video feeds, there is no special hardware or software you need other than Pirch.

However, to send a live video feed to another user, you do need special hardware and/or software. You need a digital video camera or a camera and a video capture board. The camera you use must be compatible with Microsoft Video for Windows.

Technique: Server entries let you add a series of port numbers separated by a comma.

Pirch versions .90 and higher come with a pirchvdo.exe program. This is a video server. If you have the camera and so forth you can open this pirchvdo.exe file through Tools in the menu bar and select the Video Server option.

When you're ready to let someone on IRC see a live video of you, type /dcc video <nickname>. Of course the person on the receiving end must have a means to view your video—either Pirch or some other video viewer program.

If you have the right equipment and know others who do also, give this a try. If not, do like the rest of us and IRC in ignorant bliss.

Text to Speech

Pirch supports Text to Speech applications. There are two external programs that convert text to speech and are compatible with Pirch—Monologue and Text Assist.

To activate Monologue, run monologw.exe, select the DDE Server option, and minimize the Monologue window. To use the Text Assist program you need an additional application—tasdde.exe. Execute this tasdde.exe file which is self-extracting. Next run TASSDDE. In order for Pirch to work with either of these external programs you must select Text to Speech from the Options menu. In the dialog box type insert the full path name of your external program in the Text to Speech Application box. Next, in the Service/Topic box type MONOLOGUE|TALK for Monologue and TASSDDE|TALK for Text Assist. You must enter the appropriate information in these boxes. You can leave the DDE Item Format box blank (see Figure 8-h).

When you are ready to use this Text to Speech option you must tell Pirch what you want to do. The command you use is /speak. This command sends information to the Text to Speech utility like Monologue. Then when you or a user uses the /speak command followed by text, the utility says the words audibly through your sound system.

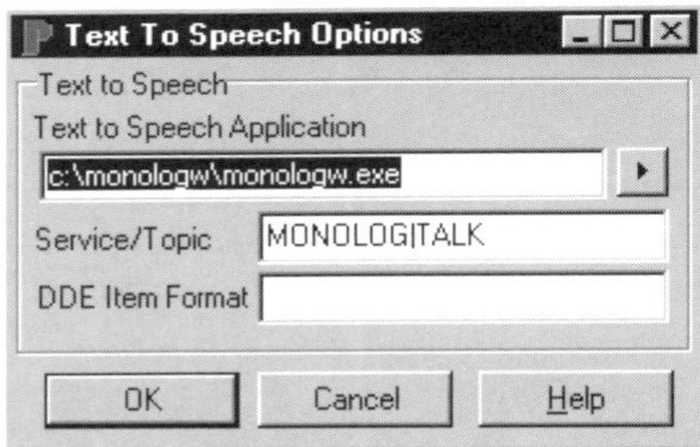

Figure 8-h. Setting up text to speech

If you want to automate certain events or activities associated with this /speak command you can. You can create ON TEXT events to speak words of text like: ON TEXT:*:#:/speak *1. This particular event converts all text in channels to speech. This is helpful if you like to multitask and still want to know what's going on in your channels. Refer back to the chapters on aliases and popups for examples of some other things you can do using Text to Speech.

Miscellaneous

Pirch lets you do any number of things that assist you or make things easier for you while you're in IRC. One of these things is the DCC Extension Map. This feature was discussed in the previous chapter. However this option has an added feature not covered there. It has a Helper application. These applications assist Pirch in performing certain functions. This option lets you add these helper applications like Real Audio or an image viewer to certain types of files you download.

When you want to add a helper application to perform with certain file extensions, first select Download Extension Map from the Options menu. When the dialog box appears, click on the Add button. Enter the extensions and the directory you want to send the files with those extensions to. Choose Execute Helper Application in the Download Action section of this dialog box and enter the directory and path of the application in the Helper Application box. When you click on the OK button this information appears in the extension map. Click on OK again to save your changes and exit. The next time you receive a file with one of the extensions you entered here, the helper application is used with the file. If that helper application is Real Audio, for instance, it plays .ra or .ram files (if you used those extensions with this helper application) when you download them. See Figure 8-i for an example of what the helper application part of the DCC Extension Map looks like.

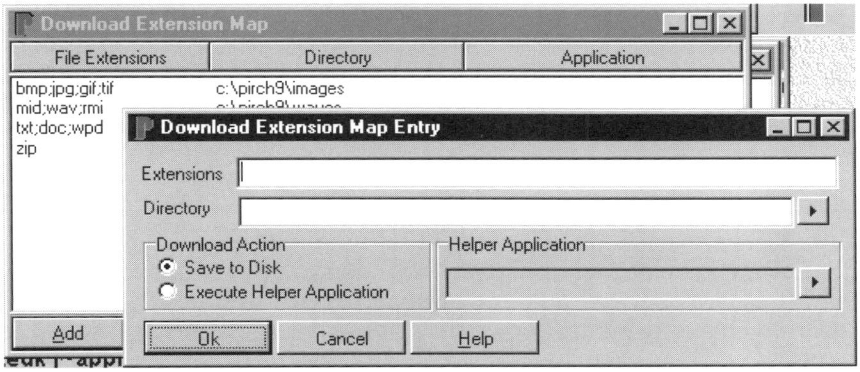

Figure 8-i. Download Extension Map helper application

Many servers on the UnderNet no longer let you perform a complete channel listing. When you type the /list command they dump you off the server for excess flood or max send req. The server administrators decided to stop allowing users to get complete channel lists because they put a strain on the servers, especially on this busy net. However, with Pirch, you can use the /verbose List <quantifier> <number of users on a channel> to get past this problem. There are several quantifiers you can use. When used with the number of users on a channel these limit the results of a /verbose list. Following are your options:

- < max users — returns a list of channels with a total number of users less than you indicated.
- > min users — returns a list with a total number of users in a channel with more than the number you indicated.
- C< max minutes — shows channels that exist less than the max minutes.
- C> min minutes — shows channels that exist more than the min minutes.
- T<max minutes — shows channels with a topic last set less than max minutes ago.
- T>min minutes — shows channels with a topic last set more than min minutes ago.

Use the /verbose list command with these quantifiers to get lists of channels with these specifications and get around the server dumps when you try to do a complete channel listing. You won't get a full list with these commands, but you will get something to work with.

The /fetch command lets you retrieve information and files from World Wide Web servers or channel MOTDs if they have one. Issuing a /fetch command for a channel's MOTD causes Pirch to try to load the channel's MOTD and display it in a scrolling display bar.

You can create a MOTD file for your channel by creating a file, either a text file or an HTML file, containing the information you want for your channel MOTD. Then you copy the file to a web server, like your account, and name the file after your channel name with an .motd extension. The last thing you do is enter the base URL anywhere in your channel's topic. Then you can use the /fetch command to retrieve this channel MOTD.

You may or may not ever find a need for this. Not many channels use the MOTD yet. However, that could change in the near future when the word gets out that this is an option.

If your scrolling display bar is scrolling too slow you can speed it up. Right-click over the scrolling panel and then select Options. Next change the delay and step rate to suit your preferences and system capabilities.

The IdentD server is a way to perform identification required by a few IRC servers. It causes your computer to respond to other systems that request your identification and returns the information you enter in the fields for the IdentD server.

When you log onto IRC, Pirch uses the identification from the e-mail address information you entered in the Connection dialog box. Then the server combines this information with your IP address to identify you on the net. With an Ident server, the server uses the Identifier supplied by the Ident server instead of this other information. When the Ident server is used, your identification is preceded by the tilde symbol (~) on the net.

Use the topics covered in the chapter to help you learn how to use Pirch to its fullest. Learn how to let Pirch work for you as it was designed to do. Free up more of your time so that you can spend more of it chatting and less of it handling mundane or administrative type tasks.

Exercises

1. Set up some autoexec commands for activities you frequently perform when you connect to IRC.
2. Change the background colors for your windows and the colors for the various types of text you see on the channels and in the status window.
3. Set up a file server.
4. Set up a Text to Speech option.
5. Retrieve a MOTD.

Chapter 9

Advanced mIRC

In this chapter you learn:

- ☑ *Colors*
- ☑ *Address Book*
- ☑ *File Servers*
- ☑ *Text to Speech*
- ☑ *On Connect Perform*
- ☑ *Exercises*

mIRC is one of the better IRC clients available. It is possibly the most popular and widely used. Of the two clients—Pirch and mIRC—mIRC is easier to use when getting into implementing some of the more advanced activities. For the average user with no programming experience, mIRC is by far much easier to get acquainted with and master. Pirch is still an excellent client and a challenge. Both clients are comparable in sophistication and features for IRC programs. Pirch does offer a few things mIRC does not, but for the features that most chatters use, they both run head to head in what they offer the user. In past versions this wasn't always true. If you have a programming background, Pirch may be the ideal program for you but for those of us who are programming handicapped, mIRC is the best alternative.

Technique: You can press Ctrl+Enter and the text is sent as plain text even if it begins with a command slash (/) symbol.

In previous chapters we covered many of the features of mIRC like aliases, popups, and remotes. This chapter covers some of the other features of this excellent program. In this chapter you learn how to use colors with text, file servers, and text to speech.

Tip: You can use either an IP address or the hostname to connect to IRC servers.

Colors

With mIRC as with Pirch you can add color to the text you type for a channel or message window. To do this you use special color codes. As with Pirch the color codes are preceded with Ctrl+k (press and hold Ctrl and type k). When you want to add color to your text you begin by pressing Ctrl+k. Then you follow this with the color code number for the color you want the text to appear in. Following are the color codes:

* 0 — White	* 1 — Black	* 2 — Navy	* 3 — Green
* 4 — Red	* 5 — Maroon	* 6 — Purple	* 7 — Olive
* 8 — Yellow	* 9 — Lime Green	* 10 — Teal	* 11 — Aqua
* 12 — Blue	* 13 — Fuchsia	* 14 — Gray	* 15 — Silver

Technique: Using * with a color code number selects the default text and background. Using *<color code number> selects the color code you indicated for text and the default as the background, and using *<color code, color code> selects the first color for the text and the second color for the background.

If you want to type your messages in the color maroon, you first press Ctrl+k, 5 (press and hold Ctrl and type k, release Ctrl, then type 5), then you type your message. When you want to type text with a background you use Ctrl+k and the two color codes you want to use, separated by commas. The first color code number is the text color and the second is the background color. So if you want to have yellow text on a black background you would press Ctrl+k, then type 8,1 <your text>. You can also combine these color codes with special text formatting like bold, underline, and reverse. To use these special formats with text, press Ctrl+B for bold, U for underline, and R for reverse text (see Figure 9-a).

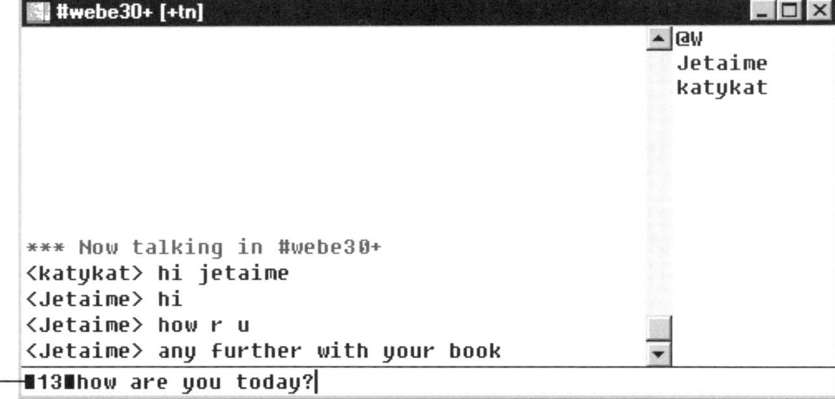

Figure 9-a. Color coding text

If you prefer not to use these colors and not to see them either, mIRC gives you an option to turn them off or strip them out. mIRC gives you two ways to do this. You can type /strip <-b, -r, -u, -c> to strip the special formatting you want or <-burc> to strip all the special formatting codes. The second option is to go to IRC Switches under General Options and under Strip Codes choose the codes you want mIRC to strip out.

Tip: These color codes also work in DCC Chats.

Play around with the codes and the text you type. See what you can do with the colors and your text. Also try them out with your aliases and popups; you might even want to try them with a few of your remotes. If you need help or some suggestions or examples, refer back to the chapters on aliases, popups, and remotes.

In addition to the color-coded text you can create, you can also change the color of your background and IRC text colors within the channel and status windows. In the toolbar at the top of your mIRC window, there is an icon that looks like red, green, and blue crayons stacked side by side.

When you click on this icon, you get a dialog box that lets you select the color you want for your background. You can also indicate which colors you want for the various types of text that appear on your channel or status windows while you're in IRC. See Figure 9-b for an example of this mIRC Colors dialog box.

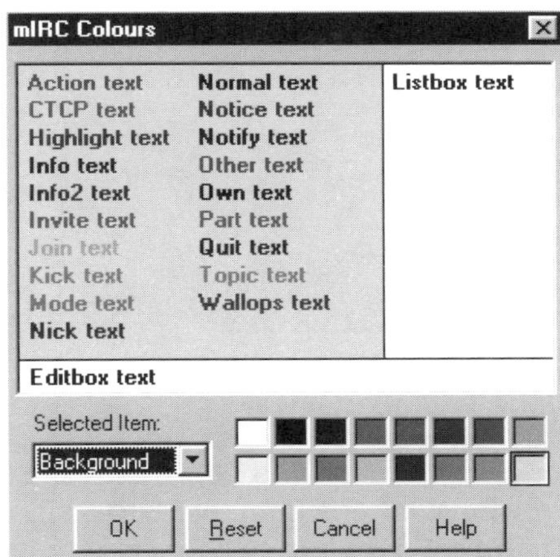

Figure 9-b. Colors dialog box

Simply select the option you want to change from the Select Item drop-down box and then choose a color from the palette. Play around with these colors to get the variations of text and background colors you want for your windows and text.

Address Book

Another excellent feature was added to this new version of mIRC. It is the Address Book. The Address Book lets you add your friends to an address book feature that lets you keep track of important information like e-mail address, web page address, IP address, and notes, as well as perform a whois on a nickname. See Figure 9-c for an example of the Address Book.

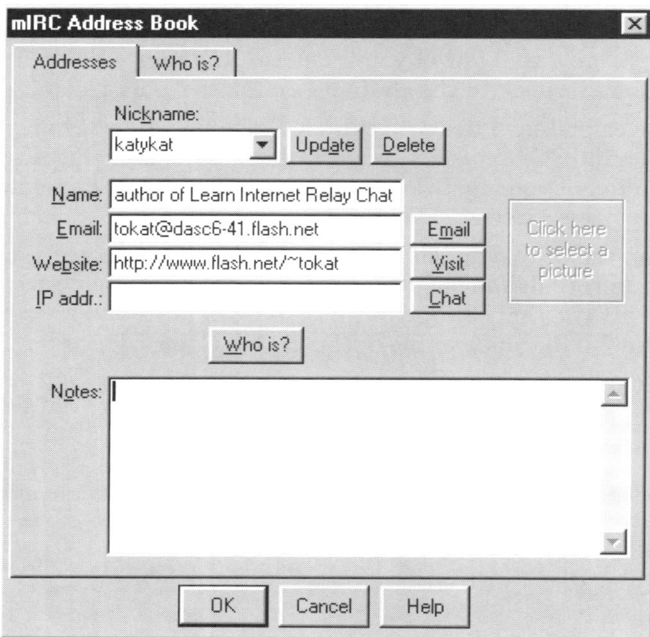

Figure 9-c. Address Book feature

In the Address Book there is a second tab named Who is? When you click on this tab, you can ask mIRC to perform a whois on a nickname. MIRC will then perform the whois and give you all the pertinent information of the nickname, such as the person's name or tag line, address, the channels that person is on, how long the person has been idle, any away information, what server the person is on, and the status of that person.

With this Who is? section of Address Book you can also add the person to the listing, find the person's profile, and perform a ping, time, version, or finger on the screen. The Who is? gives you the answer to the CTCP Reply line part of that window. See Figure 9-d for an example of this Who is? section of Address Book.

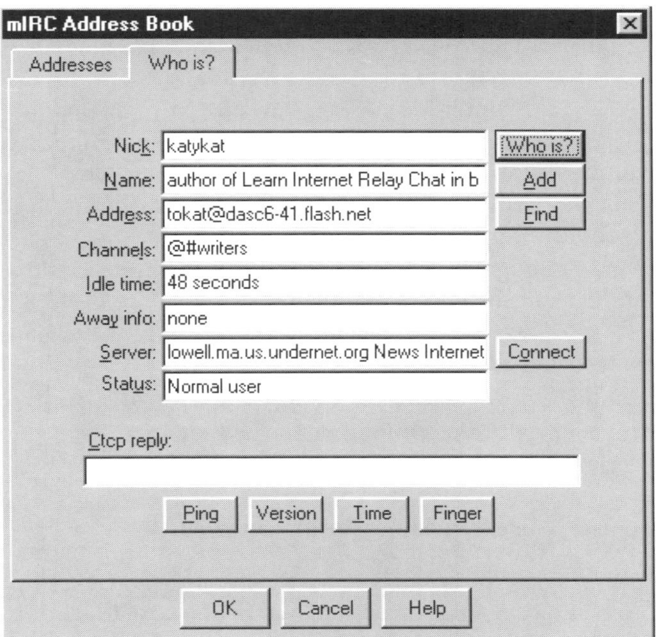

Figure 9-d. Address Book Who is? tab

File Servers

File servers let you choose which files you want to make available to other users. Through a file server you can let other users download files from you. Users are able to search your files for the ones they want and then request those files be downloaded to them.

When you set up your file server you designate only the files you want other users to have access to by creating a home directory and/or subdirectories. You can also limit the number of files these other users can transfer at a time and therefore prevent them from overloading you and flooding you off IRC.

The nice thing about setting up a file server is that the user gets to pick and choose which files of yours they want to download. You also don't have to spend your time manually sending files to them because this is an automatic function.

Technique: Users can use the read command to page and prompt them whether to continue listing or to stop.

When a user requests a file server transfer from you, a DCC Chat session is set up between him and your file server. In that chat window, he can type commands to get help, to search your files, and to choose the files to download. All this is done between the user and your file server and you don't have to do a thing once you get it set up initially. In Pirch, you don't see this DCC Chat window. You get the file server connection box instead. With mIRC you get the DCC Chat window and can observe what the user is doing there.

Once he or she connects to your file server, a directory line is displayed. This is the directory you make available to users. Following are the commands your friends use in the DCC Chat window to access and use your file server:

- dir — this gives users the directory and/or subdirectories you have available to them through the file server.
- cd — lets the user change directories. With dir and cd, once the user types these commands he or she gets a list of files in those directories. After typing cd to change directories, the user needs to type dir again to get this list of files.
- get — lets the user get files in your directories.
- read — lets the user view the file before he or she downloads it.
- help — lets the user get help while in your file server.
- quit — causes the user to quit the file server session. Exit or bye works here also.
- ls — gives the user a list of files in your directories.

Setting up your own file server is fairly easy. First you need to set up a home directory. To make it easy let's set up a directory with some text files in it. Name that directory Text. To give someone access to your file server you can do it manually or you can set up an event or a popup to handle it automatically for you. The manual command is: /fserve <nick> <max number of gets they can perform> <directory>, for example /fserve lucy 5 c:\mirc\text.

Technique: If you have a large directory, one with a lot of files in it, split it up and create subdirectories. This improves the performance of the file server connections and transfers.

Creating a popup to handle this automatically for you is fairly easy and faster for you. In the Channel Names section of the Popups edit box, type in this command: Fserve:/fserve $1 <max gets> <directory>, for example, Fserve:/fserve $1 5 c:\mirc\text. When you're ready to give a user access to your file server you simply highlight his name in the channel names list, right-click to bring up the Popup menu, and select Fserve (see Figure 9-e on the following page).

To totally automate this function, you can create an event to handle it for you. In Events in the Remotes edit box type the following command: <user level>:ON TEXT:*!fserve*:#:/fserve $nick <max gets> <directory>, or 1:ON TEXT:*!fserve*:#:/fserve $nick 5 c:\mirc\text. Of course you can set this event to only work with a certain user level or to work for any user level. That option is up to you. With this event set up, anytime a user in a channel you're on types !fserve he or she gets automatic access to your file server. To cut down on confusion if there are several people in your channel who use file servers, you may want to change the ON TEXT activator word to *!fserve <yournick>*. Doing it this way prevents a user from getting file server connections from several different people at the same time (see Figure 9-f).

File server command

```
mIRC Popups: Channel
File Edit View Popup Options Help
AWAY
.Away and Record Pages:/away $$?="Waht is your away message?" | /timer7 1 0 60 /.play -
.Back and Display Pages:/away | /ame is back...muwahahahahaha | /timer8 1 off | /run notep
.Clear Pages:/remove pages.txt
Commands
.Action:/action $$?="enter action:"
.Invite:/invite $$?="enter nick:" $$?="enter #channel:"
.List of channels w/keywords:/list $$?=only channels with over ? od people:" $$?=List only u
.Msg:/msg $$nick?="enter #channel or |nickname:" $$?="enter message:"
.Notify:/notify $$?="enter on or off:" $$?="enter nick:"
.Notice to channel ops:/onotice $$?="enter #channel:" $$?="enter message:"
.Message to channel ops:/omsg $$?="enter #channel:" $$?="enter message:"
.Part:/part $$?="enter a channel:"
.Part all:/partall
.Play:/sound $$?="enter nickname or #channel:" $$?="enter sound file:"
.Logging:/log $$?="on or off:" $$?="enter channel or window name to log:"
.User list:/ulist | $$?="enter level:"
.Flood control:/flood $$?="enter number of lines:" $$?="enter seconds:" $$?="enter pausetir
.Fsend:/fsend $$?="set to on or off:"
.Fserve:/fserve $$?="enter nickname:" $$?="enter maxgets:" $$?="enter homedirectory:"
.Quit:/quit $$?="enter message:"
.Add/Remove Ignores:/ignore -rpcntik $$?="enter on or off:" $$?="enter nickname or addres:
Editing: c:\mirc\popups.ini    1/22 lines (1393 bytes)
OK  Cancel  Help
```

Figure 9-e. Popup nicknames list edit box with file server command

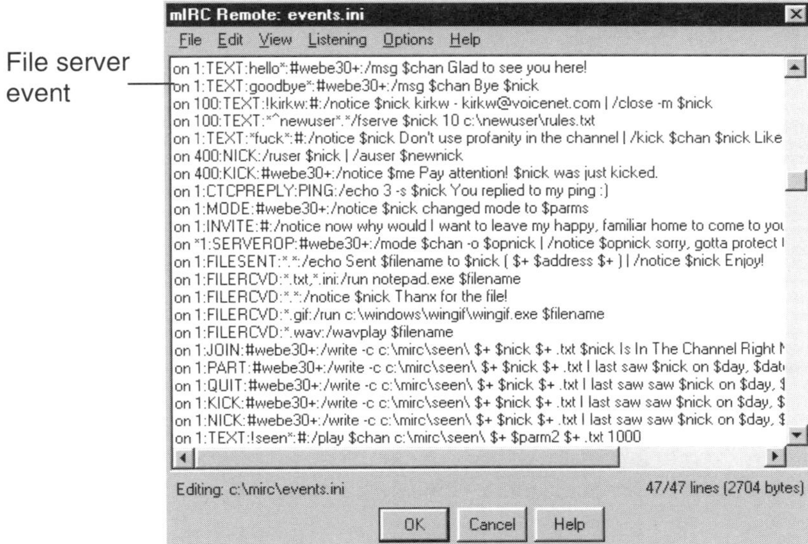

Figure 9-f. Event edit box with file server command

If you plan to use your file server a lot, you need to make some adjustments in the settings. Select DCC Options from the toolbar. Set a number of Max Fserves to one that is reasonable. This only allows the number of file server connections you specified. When you have met that number of file server connections, the next person who tries to access your file server gets a message telling him to try again later. Then you need to check the Auto Close options for send, get, and chat. This causes the windows to automatically close when a session is completed. Lastly in these DCC Options, set the Fserve Time Out at 180. The timeout is the number of seconds the file server waits on an idle user before it shuts down.

Tip: The file server sends a 30-second timeout warning to an idle user.

If you use the event to automate your file server, set a number of max gets that is manageable. A number between 2 and 5 is manageable and won't allow users to hog your file server, bog you down, or flood you off IRC. They can always access your file server again to get more files if they need to. See Figure 9-g for an example of the DCC Options dialog box and file server settings.

Figure 9-g. DCC Options dialog box

If you are concerned about the security of your hard drive when you use this file server option, you can use it with the SUBST'd drive. The cd command in the DCC Chat window is not able to let the users change drives. Using this SUBST'd drive, therefore, limits them to only a portion of your hard drive. See Figure 9-h for an example of what the file server connection looks like for you.

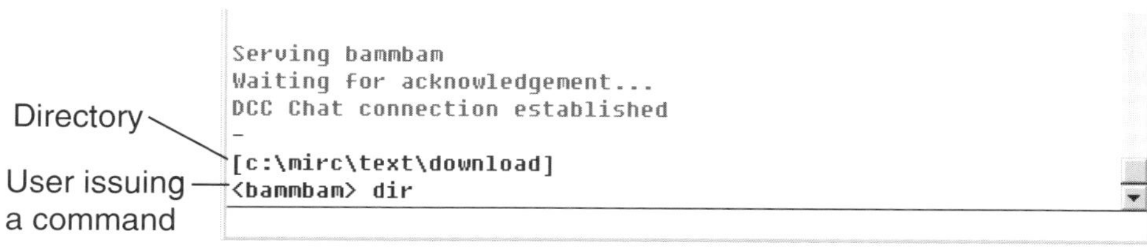

Figure 9-h. File server connection in mIRC

Text to Speech

The Text to Speech option in mIRC converts text to spoken words through your computer and your sound system. You need an external program for this to work. The program that works best with mIRC is Monologue.

Monologue for Windows is commonly found on old Soundblaster setup disks and comes with most of the newer computers (two years or younger) as part of the multimedia package. In mIRC Monologue speaks the name of the person along with the text the user typed.

To use Monologue with mIRC, run or execute Monologue for Windows and make sure it's functioning in the DDE option. In mIRC you can test it by typing the command /speak followed by a few words. Anytime you want to use this to convert text to speech, type /speak and the text you want converted. You can set up aliases, popups, or events to activate this for you. A couple of aliases you can set up to turn the speak on and off are: Speak on:/scon /enable # and Speak off:/scof /disable #. Before these aliases can work you first need to start up Monologue from mIRC. You can create an alias for this also as follows: /mon /run c:<directory and path for your Monologue.exe program> (see Figure 9-i).

Activating Monologue aliases

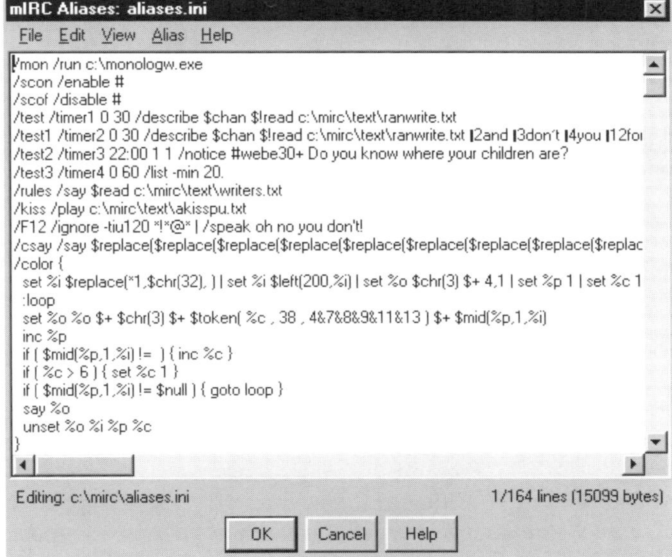

Figure 9-i. Alias edit box with text to speech commands

Tip: Save all aliases, popups, and remotes in their own .ini file separate from the main mirc.ini file. The mirc.ini file cannot handle the storage of these larger files.

Along with these aliases for Monologue, you can also set up an event that you can enable and disable through these aliases to automate the text to speech. In events type these lines:

```
#<channel name> disabled
1:ON TEXT:*:#<channel name>:/speak $nick $parms
#<channel name> end
```

The two aliases enable and disable the event and let you control when you want to use the text to speech conversions. Remember that Monologue is a simple program. It does not work well in busy channels. It stops when another user enters text and tries to speak out what they say without completing what the first user said. However, there are good uses for this function (see Figure 9-j).

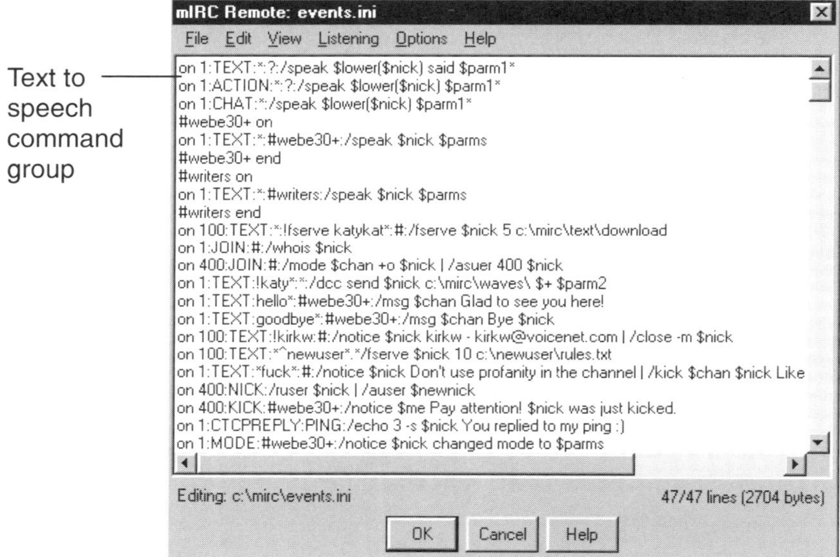
Text to speech command group
mIRC Remote: events.ini
File Edit View Listening Options Help
on 1:TEXT:*:?:/speak $lower($nick) said $parm1*
on 1:ACTION:*:?:/speak $lower($nick) $parm1*
on 1:CHAT:*:/speak $lower($nick) $parm1*
#webe30+ on
on 1:TEXT:*:#webe30+:/speak $nick $parms
#webe30+ end
#writers on
on 1:TEXT:*:#writers:/speak $nick $parms
#writers end
on 100:TEXT:*!fserve katykat*:#:/fserve $nick 5 c:\mirc\text\download
on 1:JOIN:#:/whois $nick
on 400:JOIN:#:/mode $chan +o $nick | /asuer 400 $nick
on 1:TEXT:!katy*:*:/dcc send $nick c:\mirc\waves\ $+ $parm2
on 1:TEXT:hello*:#webe30+:/msg $chan Glad to see you here!
on 1:TEXT:goodbye*:#webe30+:/msg $chan Bye $nick
on 100:TEXT:!kirkw:#:/notice $nick kirkw - kirkw@voicenet.com | /close -m $nick
on 100:TEXT:*^newuser*:*/fserve $nick 10 c:\newuser\rules.txt
on 1:TEXT:*fuck*:#:/notice $nick Don't use profanity in the channel | /kick $chan $nick Like
on 400:NICK:/ruser $nick | /auser $newnick
on 400:KICK:#webe30+:/notice $me Pay attention! $nick was just kicked.
on 1:CTCPREPLY:PING:/echo 3 -s $nick You replied to my ping :)
on 1:MODE:#webe30+:/notice $nick changed mode to $parms
Editing: c:\mirc\events.ini
47/47 lines (2704 bytes)
OK
Cancel
Help

Figure 9-j. Events edit box with text to speech command group

You can use this with the CTCP commands to speak messages to you when you're marked as away. Remember in Chapter 2 you created this popup: Awayspeak:/away <your message> /ctcp $me speak [phrase]. When another user types /ctcp <your nick> and then their message, you hear the words they typed spoken. This is a nice feature to use if you multitask and want to be alerted when someone is looking for you.

You can have all your private messages or only action statements spoken by creating an event to automate it for you. Of course you have to activate Monologue and have it running in the background before any of these work. The event commands are: <user level>:ON TEXT:*:?:/speak $lower($nick) said $parm1* or <user level>:ON ACTION:*:?:/speak $lower($nick) $parm1* (see Figure 9-k).

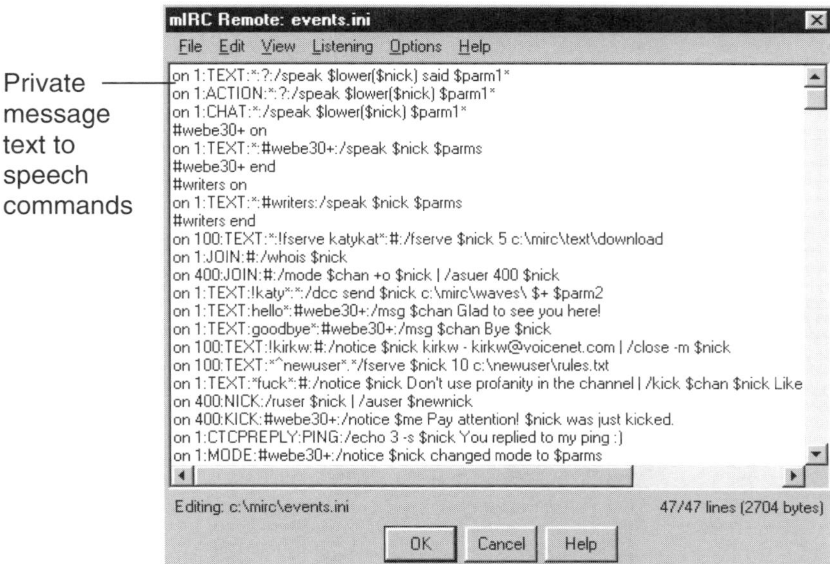
Private message text to speech commands
mIRC Remote: events.ini
File Edit View Listening Options Help
on 1:TEXT:*:?:/speak $lower($nick) said $parm1*
on 1:ACTION:*:?:/speak $lower($nick) $parm1*
on 1:CHAT:*:/speak $lower($nick) $parm1*
#webe30+ on
on 1:TEXT:*:#webe30+:/speak $nick $parms
#webe30+ end
#writers on
on 1:TEXT:*:#writers:/speak $nick $parms
#writers end
on 100:TEXT:*:!fserve katykat*:#:/fserve $nick 5 c:\mirc\text\download
on 1:JOIN:#:/whois $nick
on 400:JOIN:#:/mode $chan +o $nick | /asuer 400 $nick
on 1:TEXT:!katy*:*:/dcc send $nick c:\mirc\waves\ $+ $parm2
on 1:TEXT:hello*:#webe30+:/msg $chan Glad to see you here!
on 1:TEXT:goodbye*:#webe30+:/msg $chan Bye $nick
on 100:TEXT:!kirkw:#:/notice $nick kirkw - kirkw@voicenet.com | /close -m $nick
on 100:TEXT:*^newuser*.*/fserve $nick 10 c:\newuser\rules.txt
on 1:TEXT:*fuck*:#:/notice $nick Don't use profanity in the channel | /kick $chan $nick Like
on 400:NICK:/ruser $nick | /auser $newnick
on 400:KICK:#webe30+:/notice $me Pay attention! $nick was just kicked.
on 1:CTCPREPLY:PING:/echo 3 -s $nick You replied to my ping :)
on 1:MODE:#webe30+:/notice $nick changed mode to $parms
Editing: c:\mirc\events.ini
47/47 lines (2704 bytes)
OK
Cancel
Help

Figure 9-k. Events edit box with ON TEXT commands for the text to speech for private messages

When someone types a message to you or an action statement in a private message window, Monologue prefaces the messages with <nick> said. This makes it easy for you to know what was said where. However, it is still jerky and when another user enters text while Monologue is speaking, it stops the first user's text and starts the second. However, there are versions of Monologue that don't do that.

These are a few examples of how you can set mIRC up to convert text to speech. I'm sure you can find other ways to use this feature. Test some of these out to see how you like them. This is not a perfect form of hearing words on your computer. After all it comes out in a robot-like voice and the words are rather stilted. If you have someone who doesn't spell well or type well, those words are virtually unrecognizable. The abbreviations we use in IRC and the emoticons as well as the way some users type their messages can make for some entertaining text-to-speech conversions.

On Connect Perform

mIRC lets you set up functions that are performed when you start up the program and get connected to an IRC server. Take some of the commands you normally type each time you connect to IRC and make them automated functions. This is similar to the autoexec commands in Pirch.

Tip: Aliases, Remote Users, Remote Commands, and Remote Events are unlimited, meaning you can have as many as you want. However, you are limited by the size of the edit boxes for each of these.

Go to the General Options setup dialog box and choose the Perform tab. Then check the On connect, perform these commands: box to activate this function. Now type in a few of the common commands you use when you connect to an IRC server. You can include the command to join your favorite channel, perform a names list on your favorite channel, send the password message to the channel bot if you are on its ops list, and any other commands you typically type when you join IRC. Before these work the first time, you have to log off IRC and reconnect. See Figure 9-l for examples of some commands you can use here. Be sure to put each command on a separate line.

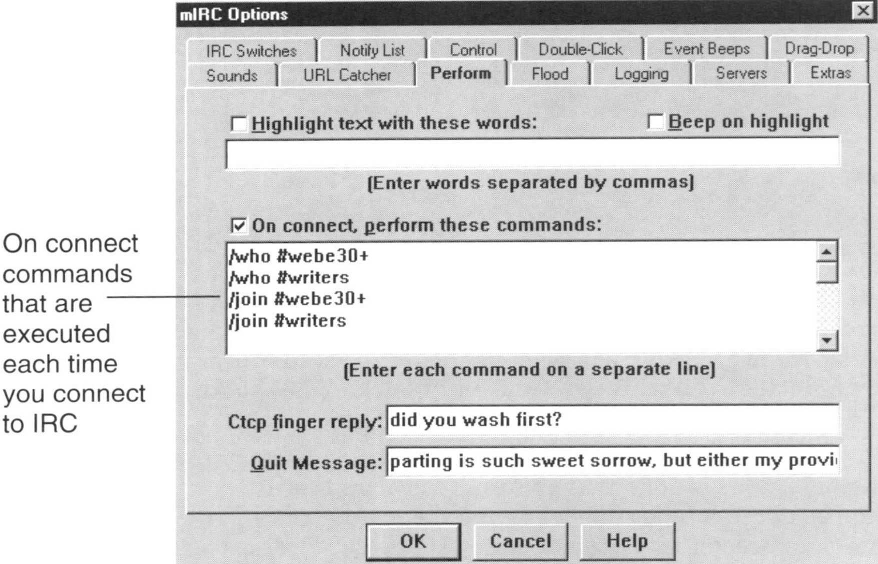

Figure 9-l. On connect perform in mIRC

This chapter gives you a few more things you can do and use mIRC for and with to make your online experience more enjoyable and automated. Use them to free up more of your time for the serious stuff like chatting!

Exercises

1. Set up a file server and create events to activate it automatically.
2. Create text to speech aliases and events.
3. Set up the activities you normally perform when you connect to IRC in the On Connect option.

Chapter 10
VIRC

In this chapter you learn:

- ☑ *What is VIRC?*
- ☑ *How to Use VIRC*
- ☑ *Exercises*

There are many different IRC clients available to let you access IRC. Some of those are covered in Chapter 12. Each of these IRC clients has its own unique features and handles certain activities differently. They also have a distinct look to them.

Some of these clients are better than others. This becomes obvious by the number of users for them. For instance, mIRC and Pirch are the two most popular IRC clients in use. mIRC probably has the most users with Pirch a close second place. They are popular because of their ease of use and the enhanced features they offer.

While mIRC and Pirch are the two most popular IRC clients that are available, there are other clients that have a following also. VIRC is one of those clients. VIRC has many of the same types of features of mIRC and Pirch. It allows you to conduct many of the universal activities with ease as do the other two.

What is VIRC?

VIRC is an IRC client similar to mIRC and Pirch. It has its own enhanced features and uses its own language designed by its developer, Adrian Cable. It supports all the universal IRC commands and activities as well as some of the special formatting and other features you find in other chat clients.

VIRC combines the best of all the chat programs into one program. It contains the hyperlink support like mIRC and Pirch does. VIRC also supports the colored text, formatting features, and font selection of these two programs. In addition, it uses the TDCC protocol for sending DCCs just like Pirch does and the XDCC of both Pirch and mIRC. Many of VIRC's features are very similar to those in either mIRC or Pirch or both.

VIRC does have some additional features that make it different from these other two programs. One of these added features is Audio Chat. Another is a DCC Whiteboard. The third added feature of this program is Video Conferencing. These three enhancements add features none of the other IRC programs have.

With Audio Chat you can carry on a real-time voice conversation with another VIRC user. This feature lets you talk to other users rather than rely on straight text chat. The DCC Whiteboard lets you and the other user you are in a DCC Chat session with draw on a paint-like whiteboard surface. The Video Conferencing lets you view other VIRC users and vice versa as you are chatting with them.

Tip: Before you voice chat with another user, you both must be using VIRC.

Along with these unique features, VIRC also allows you to create aliases, macros, and events. VIRC uses its own programming language for these shortcut features. Once you learn the language and how to set up these aliases, macros, and events, you can eliminate typing command strings to do mundane tasks.

For simple IRC activities, this program is easy and fun to use. It has a nice interface that makes it easy to keep track of your channels and private conversations. The screen setup for the channels makes it easy to keep track of who is typing messages and the activities that are going on in your channels. See Figure 10-a for an example of a VIRC channel window.

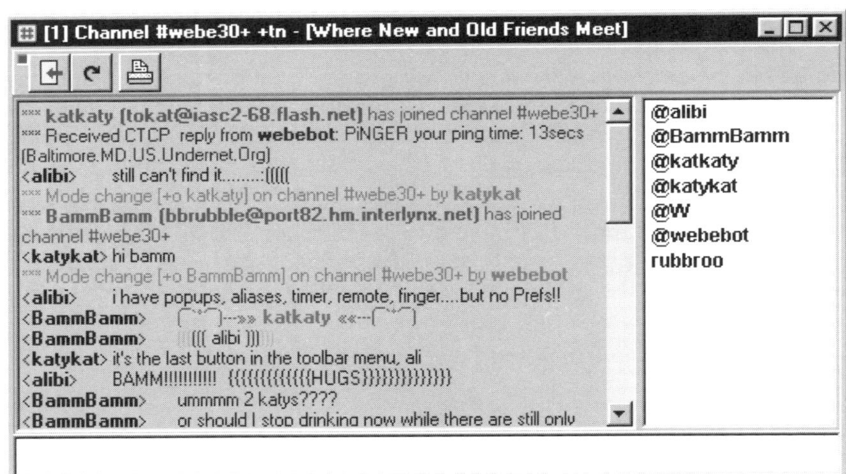

Figure 10-a. Channel in VIRC

In order to experience all that VIRC has to offer you need to learn how to use it. The next section covers how to use this unique IRC client.

How to use VIRC

Before you can begin to enjoy the benefits of VIRC, you need to configure the program to your preferences. You can do this one of two ways: You can select File and Client Setup from the menu or you can click on the Client Setup icon in the toolbar. This icon is the second from the left and has two boxes and two circles in it.

One box has an x in it and one circle has a dot in it.

After you select Client Setup, you get a dialog box with several tabs in it for the different areas you can configure to your preferences. Figure 10-b shows this Client Setup dialog box and all the various tabs you can configure. Many of them look very similar to the ones you find in mIRC and Pirch. VIRC has added a few that are unique to its program.

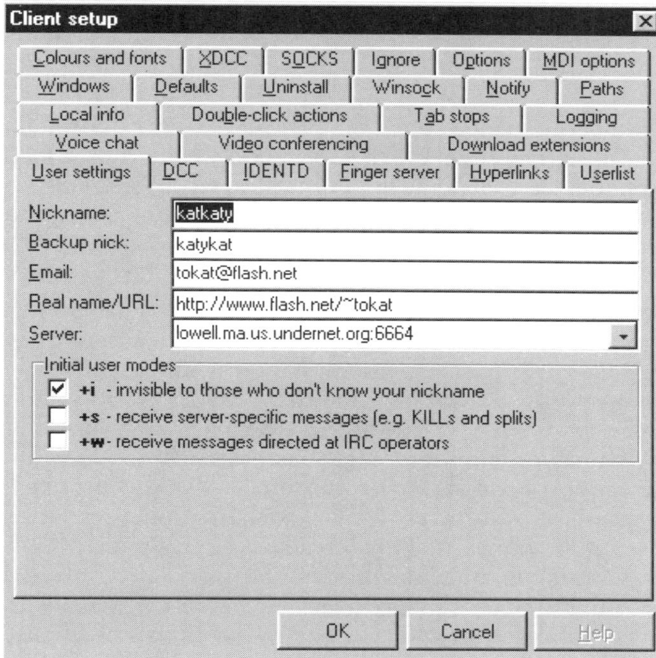

Figure 10-b. Client setup dialog box

In the User settings tab you set up all your user information. This includes your primary nickname, backup nickname, e-mail address, URL for your web page, the server you want to connect to, and whether you want to be marked invisible and receive server and wallops messages. In the server box, there is a down arrow. When you click on that down arrow you get an IRC Server dialog box. In this dialog box you can add and remove servers to a servers list. You can also choose a server from this list for the one you want to connect to when you open VIRC.

The DCC tab lets you configure the VIRC client for how you want DCC Sends and receives handled. In this tab you can select the packet size, or block size as VIRC refers to it. You also choose how you want DCCs accepted—automatically or not—by checking boxes. Then you select if you want the DCC window to be minimized when sending or receiving DCCs. Lastly, in this box you can choose to have the windows for all DCCs close when they are completed or when they fail.

Under the IDENTD tab you can manually type in your provider's address for server identification or you can let VIRC search for the information and send it to the server on its own. This is the preferable method. With the Finger server tab, you can designate how you want the Finger server handled and enter a message that is sent to anyone performing a finger on you.

The Hyperlinks tab lets you choose which browser you want as your default browser. It lists the three most common browsers—Netscape Navigator, Microsoft Internet Explorer, and Enhanced Mosaic.

The Userlist tab lets you set up a list of users you want to protect and assign levels to.

The next section of tabs deals with voice, video, and download extensions. Under the Voice chat tab, VIRC looks for your sound card and initializes it for you and the program. This tab lets you set up the incoming call buffer. The Video conferencing tab tells you if your video capture hardware was configured for the program, if you have that type of hardware. If you don't have the video capture hardware, you are able to receive videos from other users but can't send videos in return. You can use this tab to establish settings for your video capture hardware. If you don't have this hardware, skip this tab. The Download extensions tab lets you set up where you want downloaded files to go when they are received.

The next set of tabs lets you configure your windows, set your defaults, uninstall VIRC, and set up your winsock, your notify list, and your paths. Under the Windows tab you establish your preferences for Window Adjustments and choose a background for your main application window. VIRC gives you a choice of three backgrounds. If you don't care for any of those backgrounds you can select one from your hard drive. The Defaults tab lets you choose how you want VIRC to respond to CTCP requests and set up an automatic kick and quit message as well as your title bar message. VIRC provides you with an Uninstall tab that lets you uninstall the program if you want. This tab also includes a warning in case you accidentally click on this tab and the Uninstall button. VIRC automatically configures Winsock for you, but you can change any of the settings you want in this Winsock tab. The Notify tab lets you add and remove users to a notify list. When you click on this tab, VIRC lets you know if anyone on this list is connected to the same net you are on. The Paths tab lets you designate where you want uploads and downloads to be stored.

The last set of tabs includes the Colours and fonts, XDCC, SOCKS, Ignore, Options, and MDI options tabs. With the Colours and fonts tab, you can select background colors for your various windows in VIRC as well as colors for your text in these windows. See Figure 10-c for an example of what the windows look like when you configure colors for the background and the text. The XDCC tab lets you set up how you want XDCC requests handled. Under the SOCKS tab, you can configure VIRC to work around or with a firewall. The Ignore tab lets you add and remover users from your ignore list. Under the Options tab you can select options for Server Options, Aesthetic Options, and Miscellaneous. This Options tab has the three subtabs that let you select options for each one. The MDI options tab lets you choose which windows you want to make desktop windows so that you can drag them to your desktop and multitask in other applications while still being able to keep up with your chat windows.

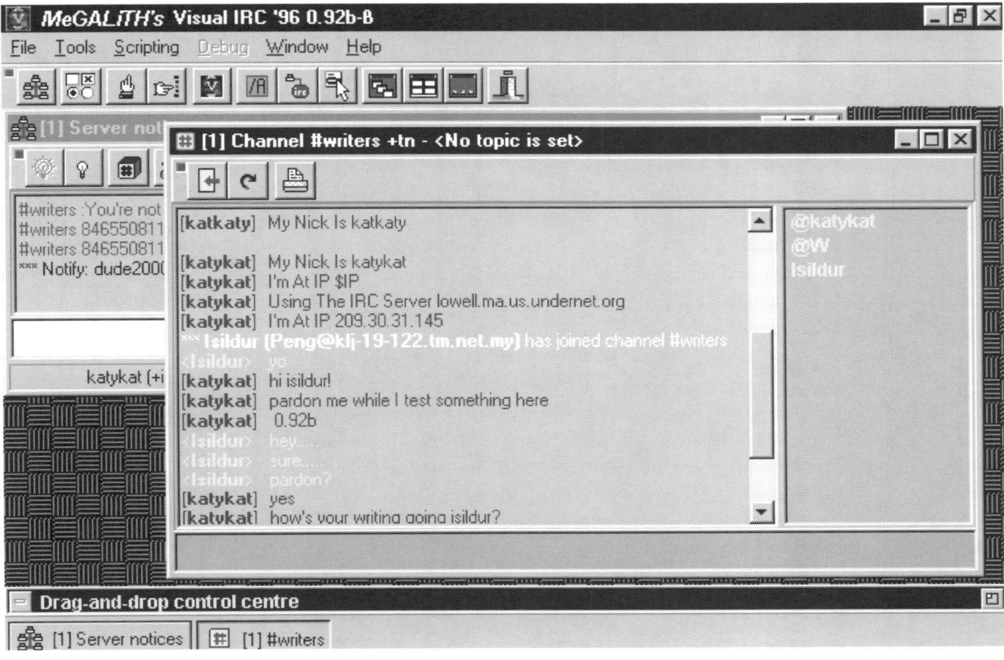

Figure 10-c. VIRC with background

After you have VIRC configured to your preferences, click on the OK button to save your selections and exit the Client Setup dialog box. Now you are ready to join a channel or two. You can join a channel by typing the command or you can create an alias to use for that purpose. To create aliases in VIRC, you can click on the /A icon in the toolbar or you can select Scripting from the menu bar and then choose Aliases.

Creating aliases in VIRC is a little different from creating aliases in either mIRC or Pirch. VIRC uses a different set of identifiers and its own programming language. Some of the simpler aliases can be set up the same way as in mIRC and Pirch. For instance, you can designate a shortcut and then the command /join #channel to set up a join channel alias.

Tip: Study VIRC's help files to learn how to use its identifiers.

When you get into more complicated commands you must learn the identifiers that are specific to VIRC. VIRC is set up so that it doesn't matter if you use the forward slash to precede commands. It recognizes commands you set up in its alias section as commands and automatically inserts the forward slash when it executes the command after you type your shortcut.

The Edit aliases dialog box looks different from the ones you see in mIRC and Pirch. When you create aliases here, you click on the Add button at the bottom of the window. An Add Alias dialog box pops up and you type in the shortcut you want to use and click on the OK button. Your shortcut now appears beside a ball.

You then type the alias command you want to use in the right-hand pane of the Edit aliases dialog box. Figure 10-d is an example of the Edit aliases dialog box.

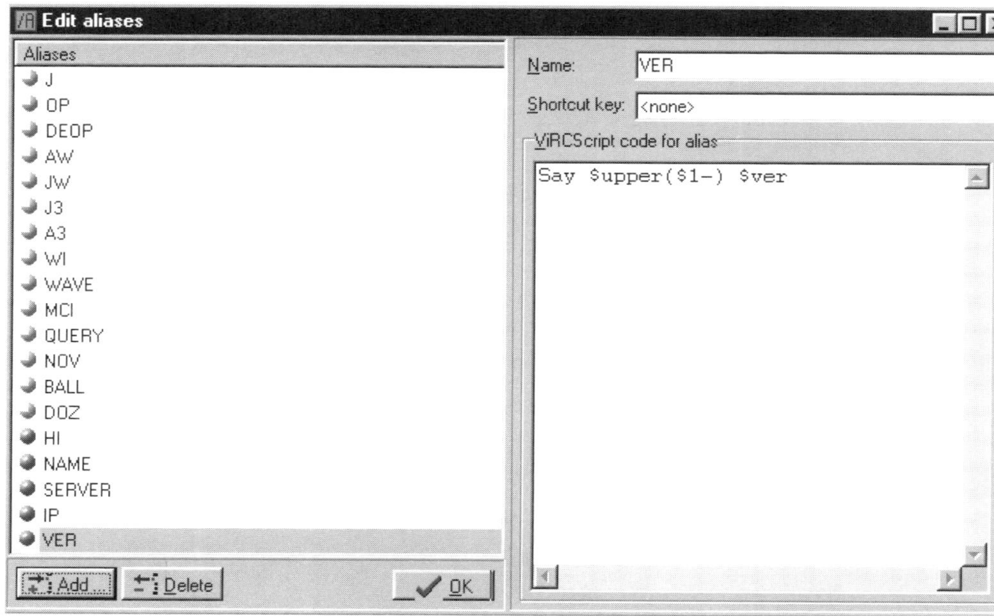

Figure 10-d. VIRC Edit aliases dialog box

All identifiers in VIRC are preceded by the $ sign. VIRC doesn't recognize many of the identifiers you use with mIRC and Pirch. It has its own set of identifiers. Some changes in identifiers for VIRC are as follows:

- $C is the identifier you use to represent the channel you are in when you type the shortcut to execute the alias. For example, a command in VIRC to say hello to the channel could look like this: Say $C Hello everyone!!
- $N is the identifier for nicknames. Therefore, if you wanted to create an alias that calls up a nickname, you use the $N identifier in the alias. For example, if you want to create an alias to say your nick in a channel, you can type the following command into the Aliases dialog box: Say My Nick Is $N.
- $server is the identifier for a server. You can create an alias to give the name of the server you're on when you type an alias shortcut. The command looks like this: Say Using The IRC Server $server.
- $upper indicates that anything following it is typed in uppercase. You use this command to create aliases in uppercase text. For example, you could type the following command into an alias: Say $upper($1-) $ver.
- $ip indicates the IP address of a user. You can create an alias to display your IP address when you type the alias shortcut. The command looks like this: Say I'm At IP $ip.
- $ver is the identifier for version and displays the version of software a user is using.
- $1 and other numbers are command line parameters and sorted in sequence

like $0 $1 $2 $3 $4, etc. $0 is the name of the alias. Therefore, in the Say $upper($1-) $ver alias above, the $0 equals getver $1 = this $2 = is, and so forth. The $1- means all the values from $1 to the end of the command line parameters.

These are a few of the identifiers you can use with VIRC. Try to add a few of your own. You are not limited to just these few identifiers. However, the documentation for this client is not as thorough as it is for mIRC and Pirch. A search of the web turned up very little information on this product and very little to help with setting up alias, events, and popups.

Technique: When you perform a whois on a user, the information appears in its own window, not in the status window.

Next you may want to create a few events for VIRC. You can access the Event Manager for VIRC either through the toolbar icon or through the menu item Scripting|Events. The toolbar icon looks like a computer connected to the letters IRC in a red circle.

The Event manager dialog box is broken into two panes. In the left pane you add the event type you want to use—ON JOIN, ON PART, etc. In the right pane you type the event command. To add events you click on the Add button and type in the Event Identifier—ON JOIN, etc. Then you click on the OK button and type the Event command in the right pane. Figure 10-e is an example of the Event manager.

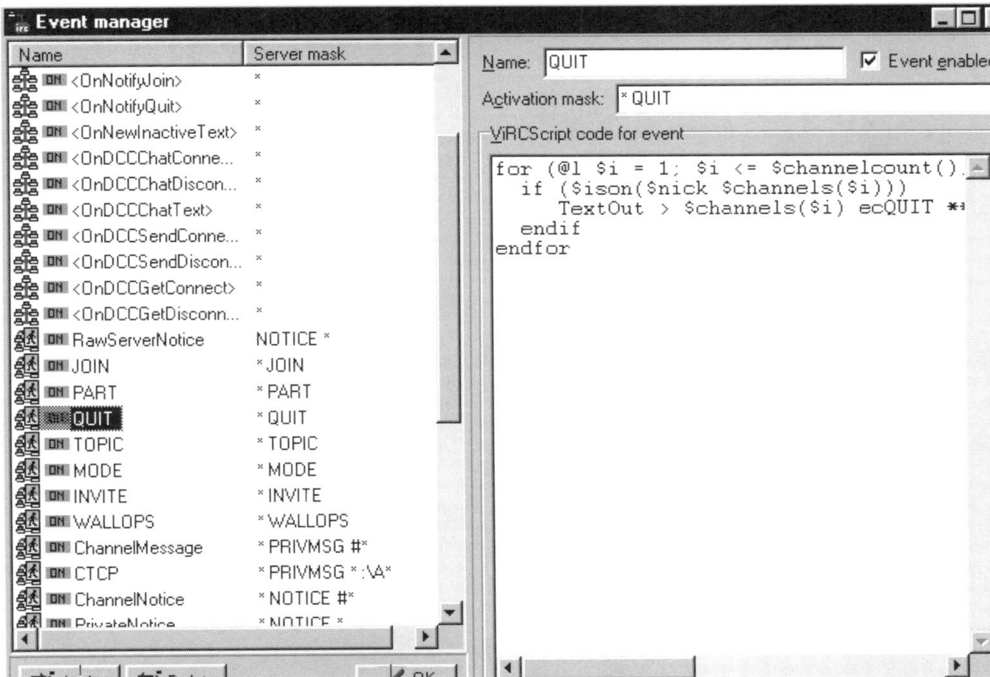

Figure 10-e. VIRC Event manager

VIRC has several sample events set up in the Event manager. Remember that with VIRC you do not need to use the forward slash as part of commands in aliases, events, and popups. You can create many of the same events you created in mIRC and Pirch here in VIRC. Just remember to use the identifiers and variables specific to VIRC when you do.

Just like the other sections of VIRC the Menu/popup editor dialog box is set up different from either mIRC or Pirch. Like the Event manager and the Aliases editor, this Menu/popup editor is broken into two main sections. The left-hand section lets you define the type of popup you want to create and the right-hand section lets you create the popup.

You can set up popups for the four main sections of VIRC. These are Main menu, Server popup, Channel nicks popup, and Channel text popup. For each of these sections of popups you click on the Add button. Then you get a dialog box that asks you to provide a name for the menu. Once you enter that name, which must start with an M_, and click on the Enter button, you are given another dialog box asking you to provide a name for the file. Then you can enter the popup you want to associate with the menu item and file. Figure 10-f is an example of the Menu/popup editor with popups entered.

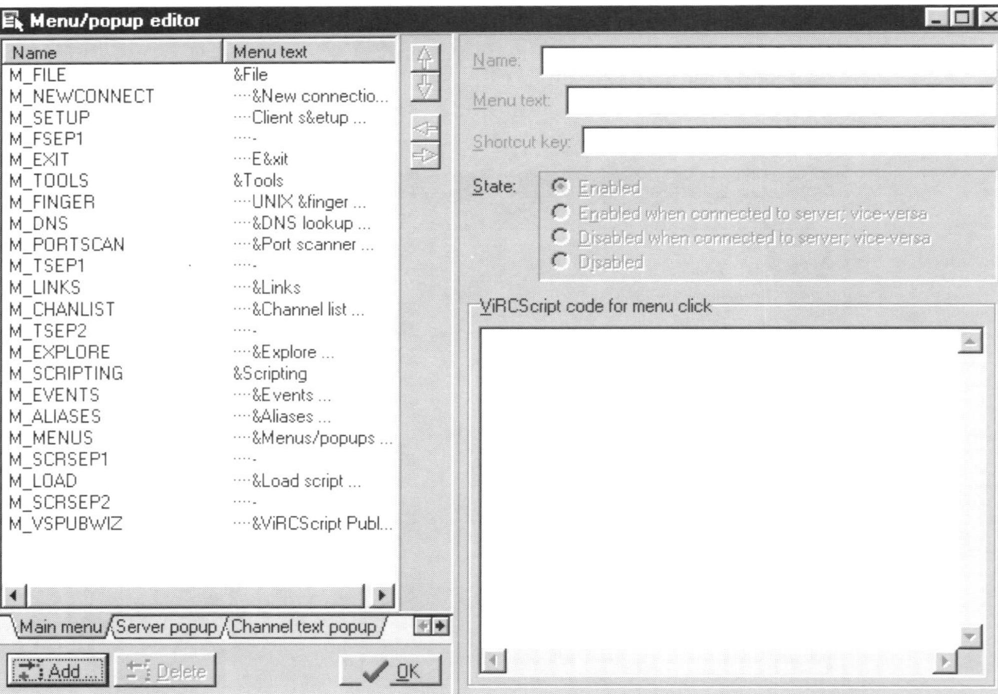

Figure 10-f. VIRC Popups editor

Look at some of the popups that VIRC already has set up for you to get an idea of how this client handles popups. Try to add a few of your own and remember to use the identifiers that are specific to VIRC. Then use these aliases, events, and popups just like you do with mIRC and Pirch.

DCC with VIRC gives you several options. You can do the normal DCC Sends and Chats. You can also do the fast DCC Sends with TDCC. In addition to these typical DCCs you can also establish TDCC Video and Voice Chats with other users. You must both have VIRC to accomplish this. When you try to initiate a voice chat with another VIRC user, click on his or her nickname in the channel user list and then left-click to bring up the popup menu. From the popup menu select TCC Voice. A dialog box appears that tells you it is trying to connect to the user. Once a connection is established you can talk to the other user by clicking on the Push to Talk button in this dialog box. Each time you want to speak, you must click on the Push to Talk button. Figure 10-g is an example of this TDCC Voice Chat dialog box.

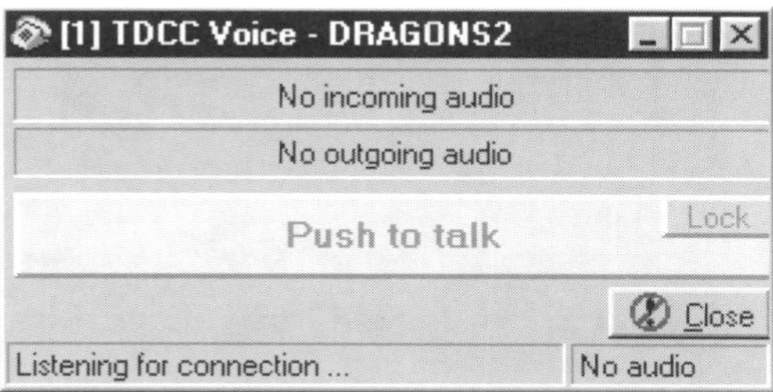

Figure 10-g. Voice Chat initiator

If you have the video capture hardware and/or someone else does who wants to send you live video and vice versa, you can click on that person's name and access the popup menu. Then choose TDCC Video to establish a video connection between the two of you. Once that has been established you can send live video back and forth to each other as long as you both have the video capture hardware. You both also have to be VIRC users. If either of you do not have the video capture hardware, you are only able to receive video. This feature only works in black and white, however. Figure 10-h is an example of the dialog box you get when you try to establish a TDCC Video connection with another user.

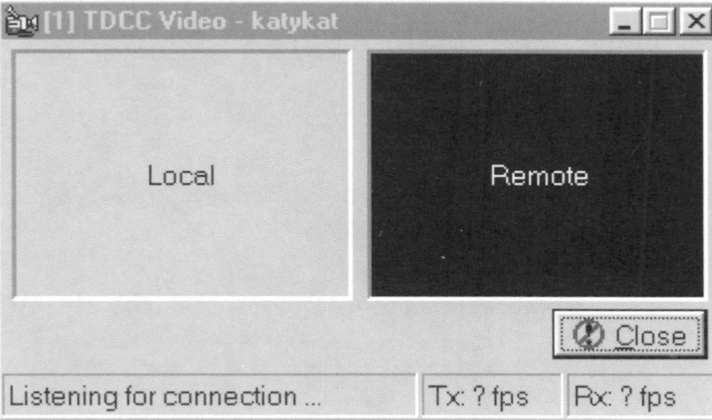

Figure 10-h. Video dialog box

VIRC has a few other features that make your activities in IRC and the program easier and faster. One is the Drag-and-Drop Control Center and the other is the Tasktray Watchdog. The Drag-and-Drop Control Center is displayed at the bottom of your VIRC application window. When you double-click on the blue Drag-and-Drop Control Center bar, a window opens up. In this window are icons for DCC Chat, DCC Send, TDCC Send, and TDCC Voice. You can drag a nick from the channel list to any of these icons to start a session with someone. The Tasktray Watchdog lets you minimize VIRC down to an icon in your Windows task bar. When you get a private message, VIRC sends you a message box and asks you if you want to bring VIRC back up again.

VIRC is a very nice IRC client. It has several combined features that no other IRC client has all in one package. It allows you to do much more than any other IRC client. However, most of these features are only compatible with other VIRC users. With all these added and enhanced features, VIRC can be a fun and worthwhile IRC client to use.

Exercises

1. Set up VIRC the way you want it configured for your preferences.
2. Perform a whois on a user.
3. Create a join alias.
4. Create an ON TEXT event.
5. Create a simple popup.

Chapter 11

Multiple Channels and Nets

In this chapter you learn:

- ☑ How to Manage Multiple Channels in mIRC
- ☑ How to Manage Multiple Channels in Pirch
- ☑ How to Manage Multiple Nets in mIRC
- ☑ How to Manage Multiple Nets in Pirch
- ☑ Exercises

Any one of the nets on IRC offers you a number of channels to choose from. Sometimes you may find that it's very hard to choose which channels you want to join. There also may come a time in your IRC adventures when you find there are two or more channels that you like.

As you venture around IRC and experiment with different nets, you make friends with people on those nets. From time to time you may want to be on more than one net at a time so that you can talk with all your friends.

Now that you've become more proficient at using IRC and your client, you are ready to try your hand at multiple channels and nets. Although this isn't the most complicated activity you can do in IRC, it does take some finesse. Keeping up with the conversations in these channels and nets takes a certain talent and the ability to not only concentrate but also a good deal of dexterity.

You can find some people in IRC who are in several channels at the same time. I have seen some people in nine or ten channels at once. This is not something I recommend you try in the beginning. Try just a couple at first until you get the hang of it. Once you master switching from channel window to channel window, then you can add more channels.

To be in two or more channels at the same time, simply join your first channel, get it set up the way you like, and then join the second channel. You get two separate windows, one for each chat channel. You can now tile, cascade, or arrange them any way that you prefer. In mIRC and Pirch the windows cascade automatically.

Keep in mind that these channel windows aren't the only windows you can have conversations in. Some people in IRC prefer to talk to others in private messages or DCC Chats. Therefore, in addition to the channel windows you have open, you can also have any number of private chat windows to deal with. The balancing act to keep up with all the conversations in all your windows can be quite daunting. I find that quite often I have to scroll back through individual window buffers to catch up on parts of conversations I've missed while involved in another channel or swamped with private messages.

When you add other nets and channels to the equation, you increase your need for more concentration and dexterity. Not only this, but you have to keep track of which nets people are on. You also have to keep track of which net which channel belongs to, especially when you join channels with the same name on different nets. It can become quite confusing if you're not paying attention.

The IRC clients have features that are designed to help you manage multiple channels and nets. Let's take a look at how mIRC and Pirch assist you in these activities.

How to Manage Multiple Channels in mIRC

After you have requested a channels list, you may find that there are a couple of channels that you would like to join. You can now join as many channels as you want. It is like having two files open in a Windows package. You get a window for each channel you join. As with your other Windows applications, you can tile or cascade these windows. You can also resize them and rearrange them.

Versions 4.7 and higher of mIRC have a tab feature. What this does is place tabs at the bottom of your application window for each channel, status, and private/DCC Chat window you have open. Then when someone in any one of those windows posts a message, the color of the tab changes from blue to red. This lets you know when activity is happening in a window that's hidden behind another window or buried under other windows. Then you simply click on the tab to bring that window forward. See Figure 11-a for an example of mIRC's channel tabs.

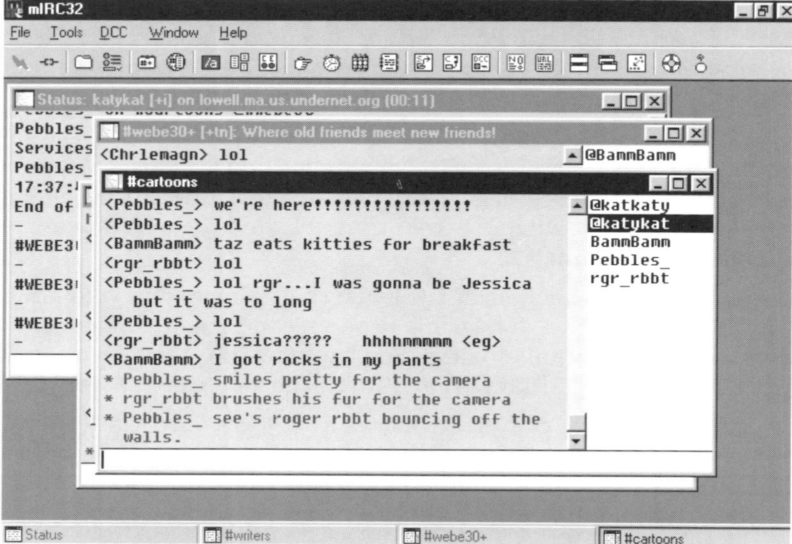

Figure 11-a. Window tabs in mIRC

When you learn to watch these tabs for changes, you are better able to keep up with the conversations in all your windows. You're less likely to miss too much of the conversations, unless you choose really busy, active channels. A channel that has more than fifteen to twenty people on it at a given time is hard enough to keep up with. When you combine one busy channel with several other channels or other busy channels, you set yourself up for a speed race to keep up.

Another option in mIRC that helps you manage all these windows is the Beep feature. When you turn beeps on, every time someone posts a message to one of your inactive windows, you hear a beep. These beeps can be activated by clicking in the upper left-hand corner of each of your chat windows and selecting Beeps from the drop-down menu.

With the tabs and the beeps to help you, soon you can master almost any number of chat windows simultaneously. This gives you the opportunity to meet more people and add to your list of IRC friends.

How to Manage Multiple Channels in Pirch

Pirch also gives you the same tabs for each window you have open in the application. Pirch, after all, was the first to implement these tabs as part of its client. The tabs in Pirch function the same way they do in mIRC—the color changes when someone posts to a chat window. See Figure 11-b for an example of Pirch's window tabs.

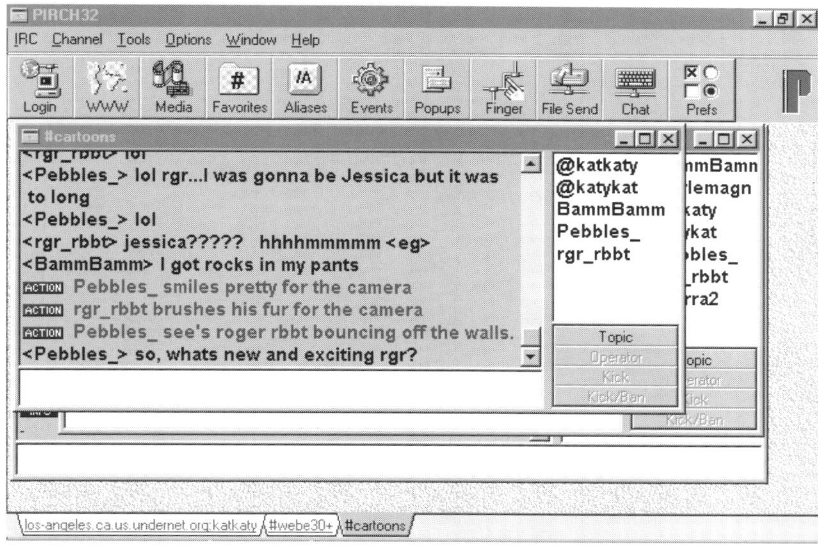

Figure 11-b. Window tabs in Pirch

With Pirch you can also activate beeps to alert you when activity is happening in chat windows that are inactive. To turn this option on, select Pref from the toolbar menu. Then under the General tab, check Beep on Private Notices and Beep on Inactive Msgs.

How to Manage Multiple Nets in mIRC

Once you master joining and managing multiple channels, you may want to try your hand at joining channels in more than one net. This isn't much more complicated than joining multiple channels on the same net.

To connect to more than one net at a time with mIRC, you need to have a second copy of mIRC open. To be in two or more nets at one time, you begin by opening mIRC and select the server to connect you to the first net. Then you join the channel or channels you wish to be on. To get to the second net, you open mIRC a second time and select the server for the second net, then join the channels you want to be on. Repeat this process for each of the nets and channels you want to be on.

If you leave things as they are, you have two or more application windows open for your nets and channels. Then you have to tile or cascade those windows and toggle between them to keep up with all the conversations and windows. This can get very frustrating and is rather difficult to manage effectively.

mIRC, however, has a solution to this problem. When you click on the upper left-hand corner of your chat windows you get a drop-down menu. One of the menu items there is Desktop. When you select this item, you can then move that chat window to your desktop. Do this for each of your chat windows in all of your nets. Then you can arrange them on your desktop so that they are easier to manage and follow conversations. See Figure 11-c.

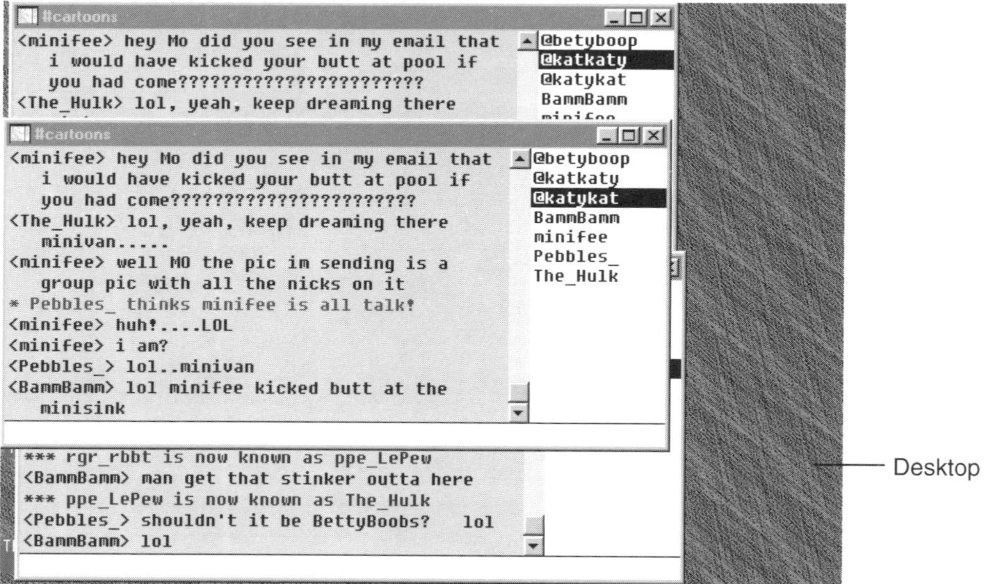

Figure 11-c. Two nets in mIRC

When you move these chat windows and your status windows to your desktop, tabs for each one are placed at the bottom of your desktop screen. When activity happens in one of these windows, the tab lights up to let you know. You can also use the beep function to alert you when activity is taking place, just as you do for multiple channels in a single net.

How to Manage Multiple Nets in Pirch

Pirch gives you an easier way to connect to multiple nets. It allows you to join more than one server, no matter which net that server belongs to. It keeps all your windows in one application window with tabs at the bottom of the window to help you keep track.

With Pirch, you simply log onto each of the servers for the nets you wish to be on. When you join multiple nets using Pirch, each server and each channel is displayed as a separate window within the Pirch application window. The tabs at the bottom of the application window help you to keep track of all the channels and nets you connect to. As with multiple channels in one net, you can also turn beeps on so that you're alerted when activity is happening in a channel that is inactive. See Figure 11-d.

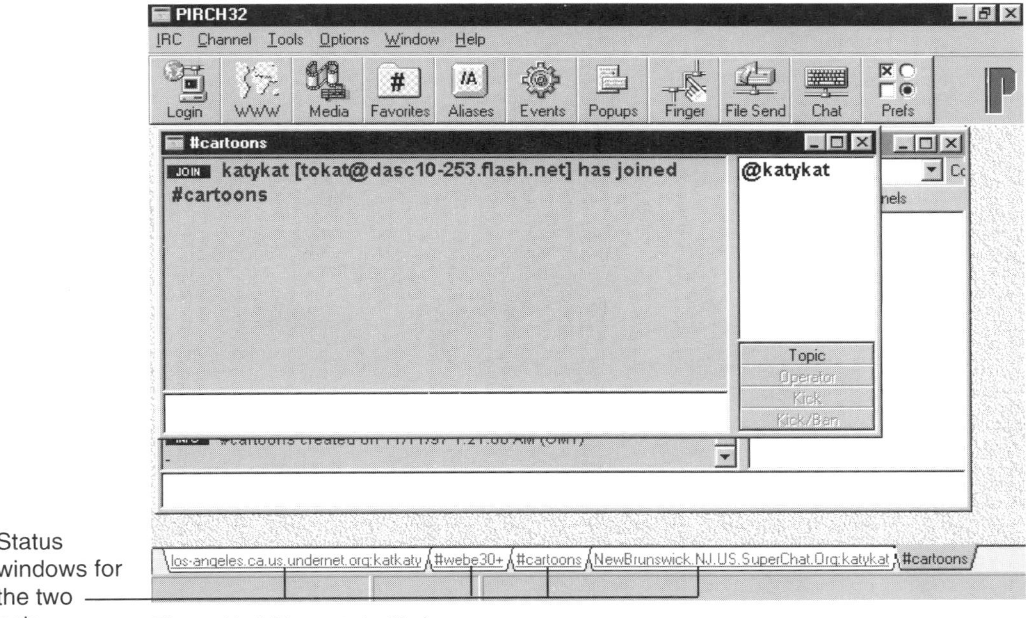

Figure 11-d. Two nets in Pirch

As you can see, connecting to multiple nets with Pirch is easier. It's easier to connect and it's easier to manage all the different nets and channels you choose to be on. However, with practice, you can learn to manage this same task using mIRC and your desktop.

Exercises

mIRC

1. Join two or more channels.
2. Join two different nets.

Pirch

1. Join two or more channels.
2. Join two different nets.

Chapter 12

Web Chat and Other Chat Programs

In this chapter you learn:

- ☑ *Web Chat Programs*
- ☑ *3-D Chat Programs*
- ☑ *Other Chat Programs*

Chatting isn't limited to using the Internet and IRC. There are several other ways you can chat with people via the Internet. Many web sites let you chat via their sites. There are also web-based chat programs. In addition to these web-based chats there are other fun chat programs available to use or play around with.

Each of the various programs has its own unique capabilities and unique look. Most of these programs use their own servers and most don't even use the same servers you use for IRC.

These are all text-based chat programs. They differ from other chat programs we have discussed because they either are accessed through the web or they use some sort of avatar to represent users. In the other chat programs section of this chapter, there are a couple of text-based chat programs included that don't use avatars or the web. These either use their own servers or can be used with IRC. They are included here because of the uniqueness of their features.

In this chapter we discuss web chat, the 3-D chat programs, and several other chat programs. We cover them in some detail but not to the extent that mIRC and Pirch are covered. Let's start with web chat.

Web Chat Programs

There are a number of web sites that offer chat as part of their site. Some are family oriented, some are professionally oriented and, of course, there are sexually oriented sites that offer chat.

The web chats you run across come in a few different varieties. All the web chats I found were text based like they are in regular IRC. Most require that you download a Java applet or script before you can begin to use the chat part of the web site. This is generally done automatically for you and can be used universally throughout any of the other web chat sites you access. If a different helper application is needed, the site will let you download the helper while you are there.

With some of these web chats, the screens look similar to IRC chat screens. However, the conversations don't move as fast. Another thing you notice is the user level is very low. There are usually as few as four to as many as fifty people on these chats. There are some web chat sites that boast over 2,500 users. But this is the exception rather than the rule in web chats. With IRC and the busier nets you see thousands of users, or hundreds with the smaller nets.

In some of the web chats you are required to update or refresh the chat every few seconds. Some programs can be set up to do this automatically for you and others require you to do the refreshing manually. You do not see any new conversations from the other users until you refresh or update.

Tip: The chat in web chat may be slower than in IRC.

If you're concerned about what your children might see on regular IRC, then web chat is an excellent alternative. There are several good web chats that are designed exclusively for families and children. These chats do not allow pornography or profanity of any kind. In these chats you find support channels or rooms for parents, religious rooms, and rooms specifically for different age groups of children.

There are several professionally oriented web sites that offer chat as part of their site. The Writers Bulletin Board is one example. IDG Books also has a chat room where you can discuss their books with others. In Figure 12-wc-1 you see an example of the text-based chat for the Writers Bulletin Board. This particular chat is free flowing. In other words, you don't have to refresh the screen every few seconds to see what the other person is saying to you.

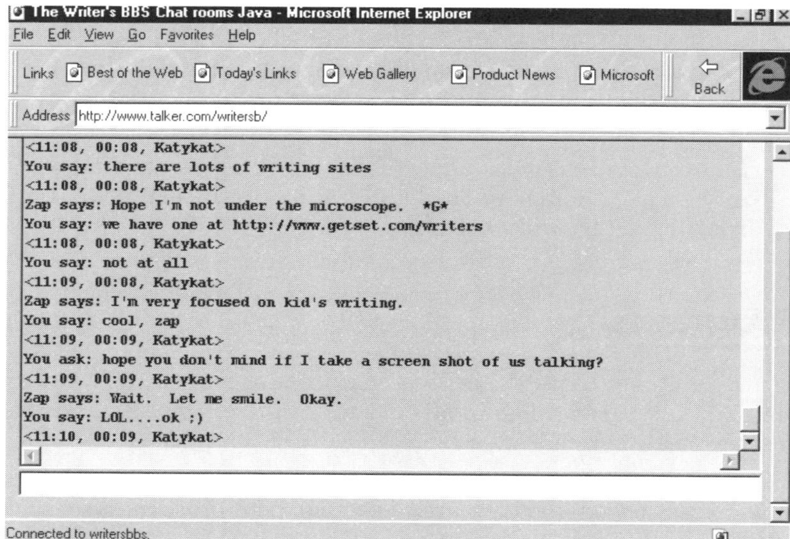

Figure 12-wc-1. Professional web chat site

This web site has three different types of chat rooms you can select from. Figure 12-wc-1 shows the Talker chat. The other chats available on this site are the types that have to be refreshed every few seconds. This site offers writers a chance to chat with other writers in various genres and fields.

Tip: The Java applets and plug-ins some of these web chats use can malfunction and cause you to lose your web page and your chat.

As you surf the web you find many sites that are family or children oriented. Several of these offer chat on their sites. One such site is World Village. This site was set up for families and offers many activities and chats for the whole family. It even offers a weekly e-mail newsletter for anyone who wants it. In Figure 12-wc-2 you see an example of the entry page. This lists the various chat rooms World Village has to offer.

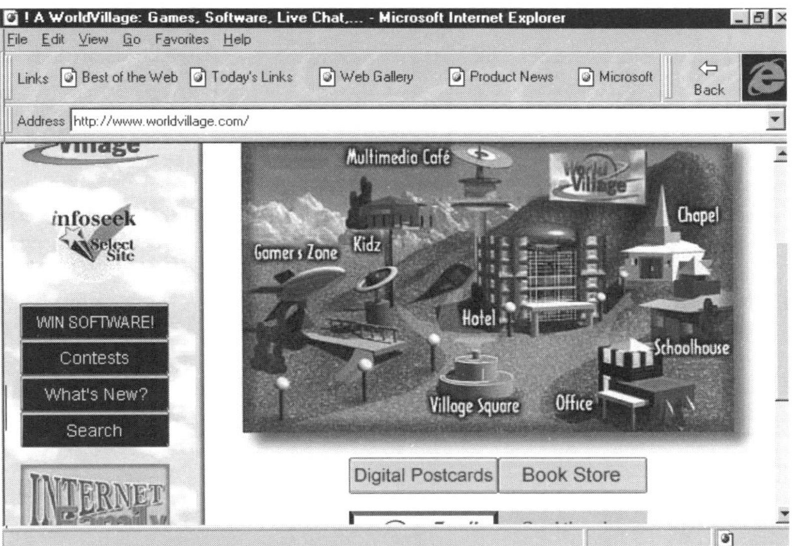

Figure 12-wc-2. Family web chat site

When you click on any of the areas on this web page you are taken to a chat room for that area. In these chat rooms you can chat with others just like you do on IRC. The chats are in real time and there is no need to refresh every few seconds in these chat rooms. Figure 12-wc-3 is an example of what the chat looks like for this web chat.

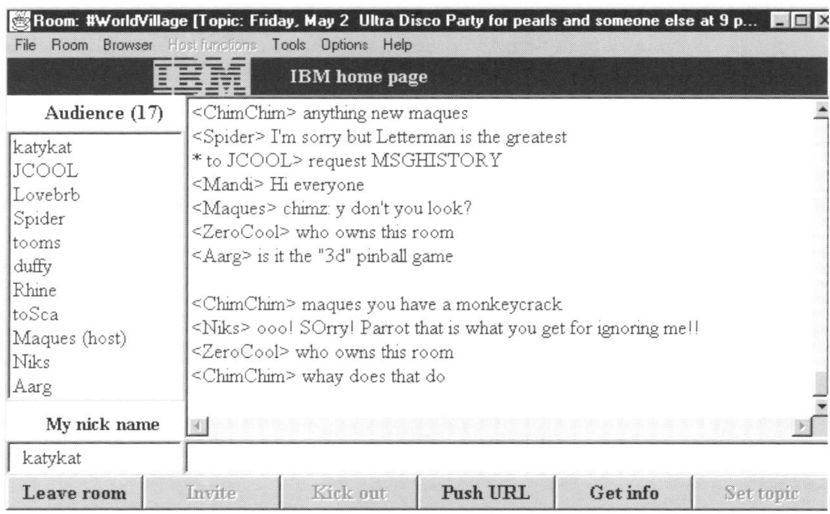

Figure 12-wc-3. Family chat room

Zia Chat is another Java/web chat site. This site also offers many family oriented chat rooms. There are rooms for adults and parents to socialize or to get support. There are also rooms for various age groups of children. These rooms are designed to let the children talk about what interests them. In Figure 12-wc-4 you see an example of one of the chat rooms on the Zia Chat site. With this chat you do have to refresh every few seconds in order to keep up with the conversations.

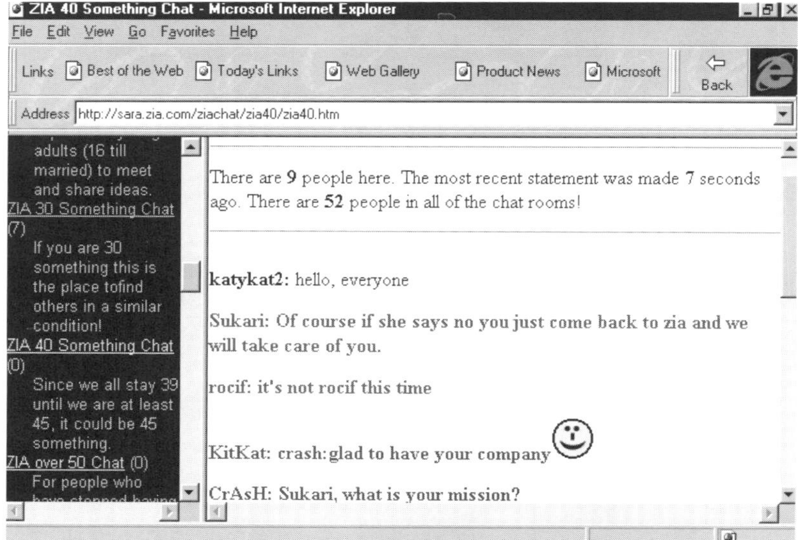

Figure 12-wc-4. Zia 4D Something Chat room

Figure 12-wc-5 shows you how another web chat site handles its chat rooms. This is another of the web chats that requires you to refresh every few seconds to keep up with the conversation. When you do a search for web chats on the search engines for the web you find many listings for chat sites. One such site is The Web Chat Broadcasting System. Use the search engines to help you find web chat rooms that fit your interests.

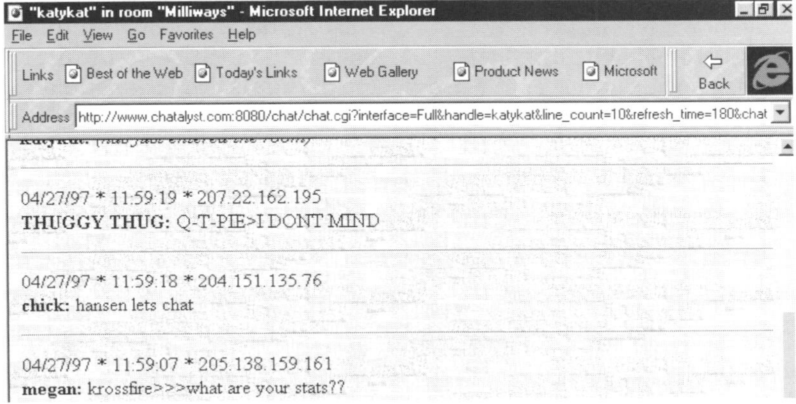

Figure 12-wc-5. Another web chat example

The Globe chat is a site on the web that caters to generation Xers. On this site you find chat rooms that are rather eclectic and art or music oriented. In Figure 12-wc-6 you can see some of the rooms The Globe chat site offers its visitors. To participate in these chats you have to become a member of The Globe. Membership is free and it only takes a few moments to register. Along with the chat rooms this site offers other areas of interest to generation Xers.

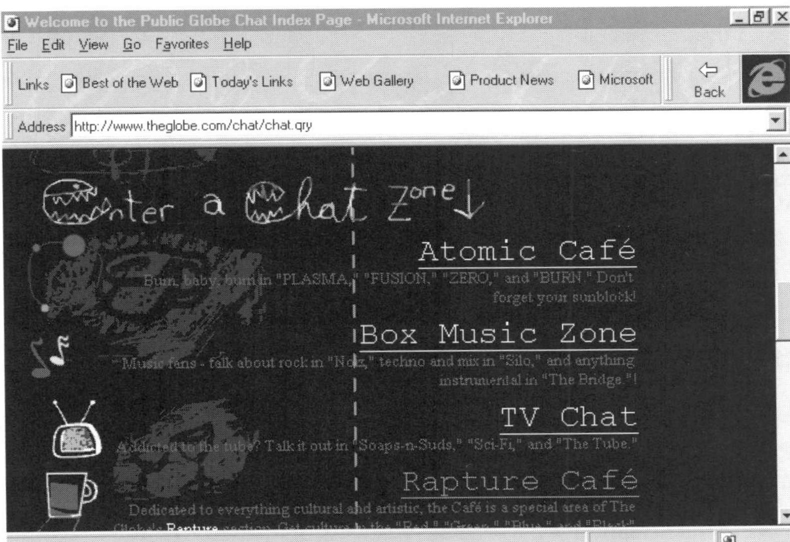

Figure 12-wc-6. The Globe chat site

As you enter a web chat room you see something similar to one of the earlier figures shown in this chapter or the one in Figure 12-wc-7. When you are ready to receive the latest message you click on the Refresh or Chat button on the page. All new information is entered at the top of the screen. If there is no new conversation since you last clicked on the refresh, the browser tells you this also. When you are ready to send a message to the room, you simply type it in the text box provided and click on the Chat button. Some of these programs also let you display a picture of yourself or anything you like. For the programs that allow this feature, you fill in the Picture box with the http:// address for the picture you want to use. Be courteous to the other users: Don't use a picture that is too large and also think about the sensibilities of others. In other words, don't use a picture that is offensive to others.

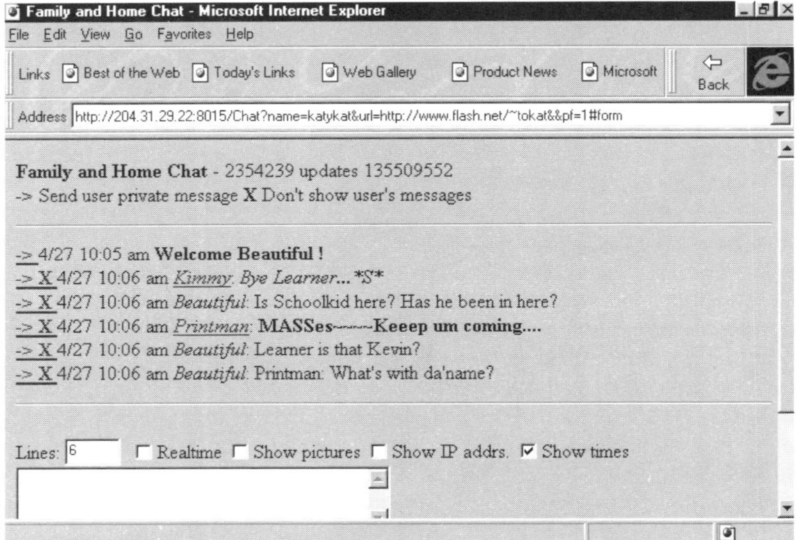

Figure 12-wc-7. Another type web chat

Web chat is fairly easy to use. Most of the sites give you instructions on how to use their chat. Those that don't are so similar to IRC chat that you should have no problems mastering them. Just remember that the IRC commands do not work in web chat. Each web chat has its own set of commands. Check out the help files for specific commands.

3-D Chat Programs

Other than the chat you can participate in as part of individual web sites, there are a few web-based chat programs. These are all 3-D chat programs. These 3-D chat programs let you either select an avatar from their group of avatars or create your own avatar or representation of yourself.

These avatars can be humanlike figures, pictures of yourself, or anything you choose. In one of these programs—Active Worlds—you can select from its group of avatars. With OnLive Traveler and The Palace you can create your own avatars.

With The Palace you are initially given a ball as your avatar. At any point you can change this ball to the avatar of your own design. You can also keep the ball and add accessories to it to dress it up and personalize it.

In each of these programs, you can wander through various worlds. Each one of these worlds has its own scenery or background. With Active Worlds you can build your own property in designated areas. You can create a building or house and invite others in. In The Palace, you just enter different rooms or worlds by entering doors. Microsoft V-Chat lets you create your own avatars or use one of theirs. You can gesture when communicating with these V-Chat avatars.

Each one of these programs also has its own servers. These are web servers, therefore, before you can use them, you must have one of the two major browsers installed—Microsoft Internet Explorer or Netscape Navigator. Let's take a closer look at these 3-D chat programs.

The Palace

The Palace gives unregistered or guest users three free hours to use with the program. With these three free hours you can do everything a registered user can. You can give yourself a name, create avatars, wear accessories, run scripts, and so forth. However, other than the main server, you will not be able to change the guest login name The Palace gives you.

When you click on The Palace in your Start menu, you are connected to a special Palace server. With this program, everything users type as conversation appears in balloons. There are a few different types of balloons you can use—thought balloons, spiky balloons, and rectangular balloons. In Figure 12-3d-1 notice the background and the conversation displayed in a balloon.

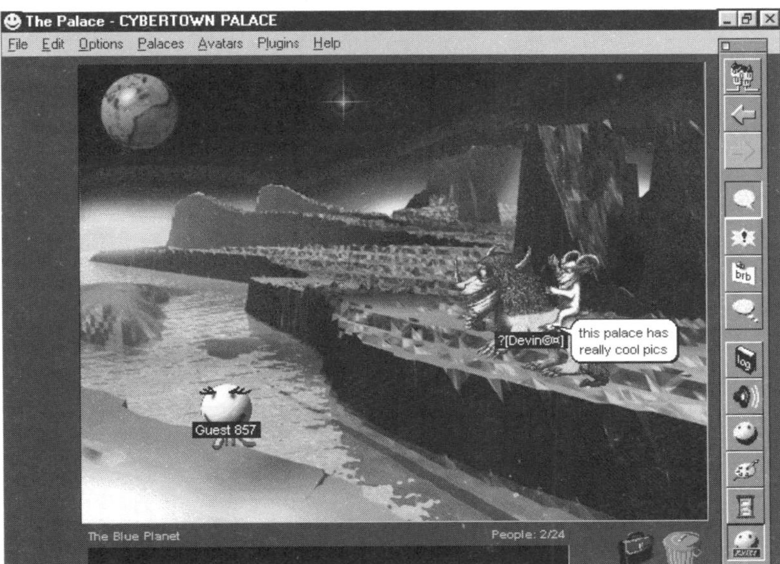

Figure 12-3d-1. The Palace environment

This program also gives you several preformatted, special sound files you can play while you're in The Palace. You can choose from sounds like Amen, Applause, Belch, Boom, Crunch, Debut, Fazein, Guffaw, Kiss, No, Ow, Pop, TeeHee, Wet1, Wind, and Yes. You play these sounds by clicking on the speaker icon in the toolbar menu that runs down the right-hand side of your window. Then you select the sound you want to play.

Your first time in The Palace you are given a Palace-specific avatar. These avatars are referred to as round heads. You can change the facial features of these round heads from normal to smile, frown, wink, or angry. To change the features, click on the round head avatar icon in the toolbar and select the feature you want. See Figure 12-3d-2 for an example of round heads, guest logins, and the features icon.

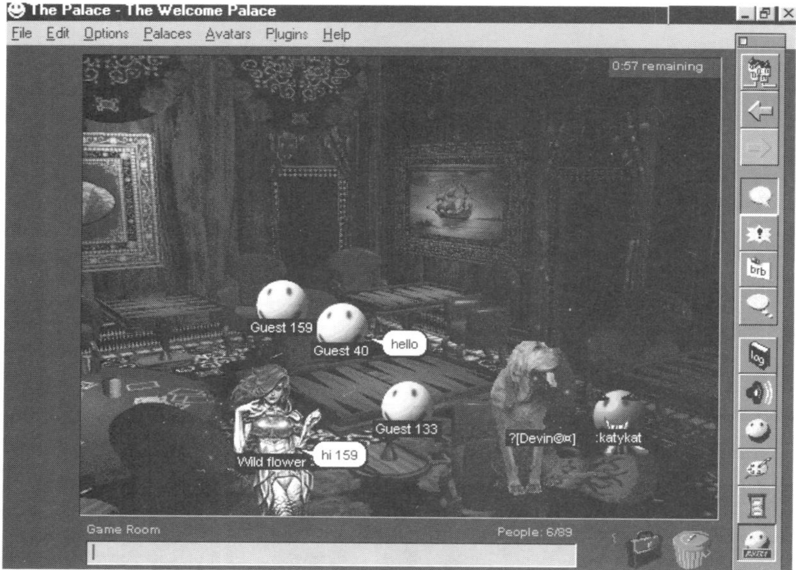

Figure 12-3d-2. Round head avatars

When you enter The Palace you are in a courtyard. This is the initial gathering place. In the background is a mansion. You enter this mansion by clicking on one of the doors or windows. Anytime you want to leave a specific area or room you click on a door or window. If none are visible, you can click on the Door icon in the toolbar to display where the exits are. Each one of the rectangular or triangular boxes indicates an exit. Click on any of those boxes and you go to another area or room on that Palace server. See Figure 12-3d-3 for an example of how the exits are marked when you click on the Door icon to display exits.

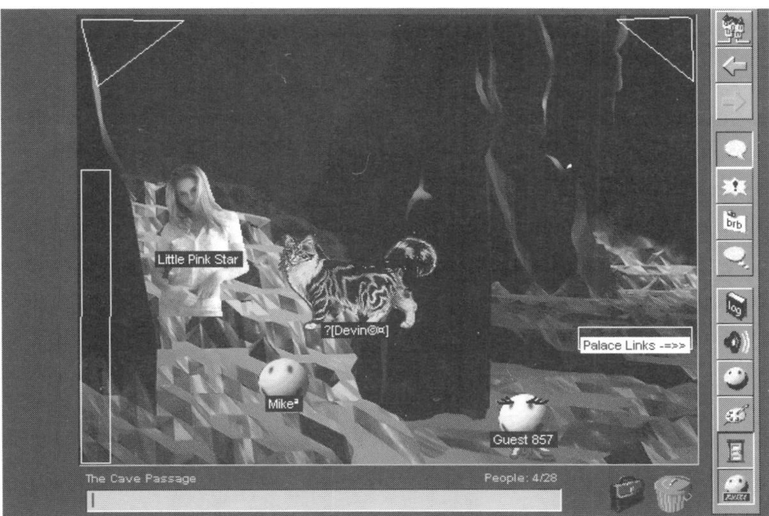

Figure 12-3d-3. Doors displayed in The Palace

There are also numerous other areas in The Palace you can explore. In the menu bar select Options and then Rooms to see a menu of the various other areas that are available as shown in Figure 12-3d-4. Select any one of these and double-click on it to take you there. When you choose Palaces from the menu bar you get a list of the other Palace servers available. You can also look for your friends using the Options menu item. When you select users from the Options item, you get a list of all the users on the server you're on along with what areas or rooms they are in. You can then select a user and double-click to take you to that area.

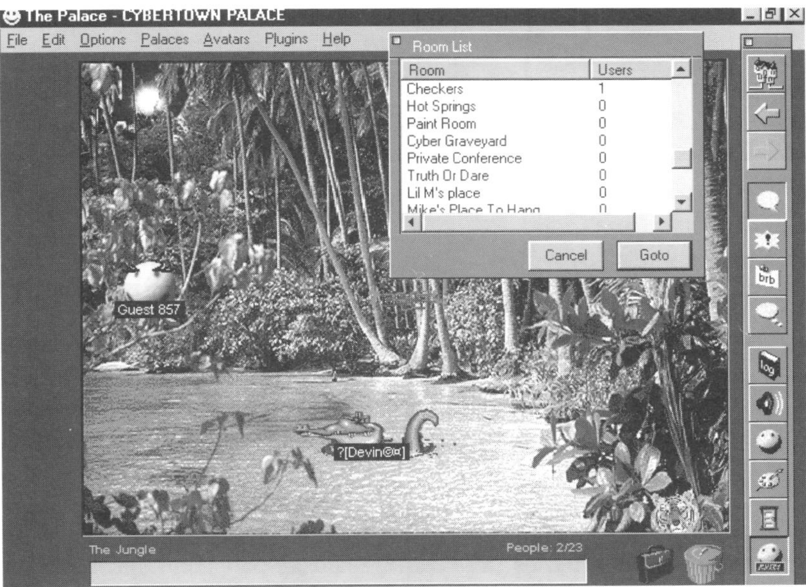

Figure 12-3d-4. The Palace chat rooms

As you join different rooms or areas in The Palace for the first time, the background for that area loads for you. The Palace has several different servers. On each of these servers there are dozens of rooms or areas you can explore. When you are on a guest account there are certain rooms and areas that you are unable to access. These are restricted to members only. Each of the figures in this section, including Figure 12-3d-5, were taken in different areas in The Palace. Leaving one area to get to another area or room is a simple matter of clicking on an exit or choosing a room or area from the Options/Rooms menu. There are an abundance of rooms you can explore as well as servers with their own unique areas.

Tip: Some of these graphic files take a long time to load onto your hard drive.

Figure 12-3d-5. Another The Palace environment

With the main server for The Palace and your guest account, you can change your name and your avatar. With the other servers, you're stuck with guest and the number The Palace gives you until you purchase and register as a member. You can, however, add props to the round head avatar the program gives you. To add these accessories, click on the round head avatar icon in the bottom right-hand corner of the toolbar. A group of accessories appears with options. Select the ones you want and press the Wear button to add these accessories to your avatar. These can be added to the round head avatars or to your custom avatar.

On many of the servers there are prop rooms. You can go to any of these prop rooms and copy props from them. When you do this the program requests that you leave a prop from your files in exchange. These prop rooms contain props that are specific to the theme of the rooms and areas specific to that server. You can find quite a few interesting props in these rooms. Use the accessories to add a little spice and creativity to your avatars whether they be round heads or ones you create yourself.

The Palace can be a fun and interesting chat environment to play and explore in. Once you've tried it out and decide you like it, you can register for the membership. This membership is only $25 and gives you unlimited use of the program and all its features, rooms, areas, and servers.

Microsoft V-Chat

This 3-D chat software gives you several different rooms you can go to. You can select from the avatars Microsoft makes available to you or you can create your own avatar. You find with this program that most people use the avatars that the program has to offer.

In order to run this software you must also download Microsoft's DirectX helper application. If you have already downloaded the DirectX application to play some of Microsoft's games you do not have to download it again.

When you first open the V-Chat program, you are asked to give yourself a handle or nickname. Then you get a screen that is a quick guide to the features of the program and things you can do. Once you click on the OK button for this screen, the program pops up another screen that asks you if you want to connect to a V-Chat environment or Show all available environments as shown in Figure 12-3d-6.

Figure 12-3d-6. V-Chat environment selection box

After you select the option you want, the program connects you to a server. If you selected a specific V-Chat environment, the program takes you to that environment. If you select Show all available environments, then the program connects you and takes you to a screen so that you can choose which environment you want to go to. Once you make your selection, click on the Go To button and you are taken to that environment. See Figure 12-3d-7 for an example of the dialog box for environment selections.

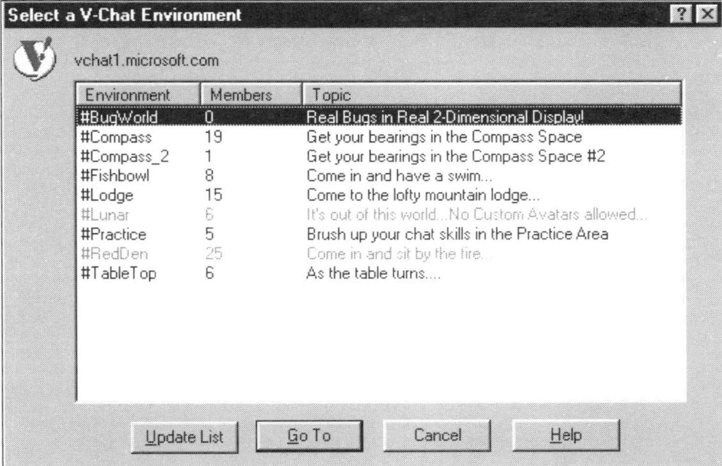

Figure 12-3d-7. Selecting a V-Chat environment

Each of the environments has its own unique background. The Compass environment is a general gathering place and the default when you initially open the program. After you select another environment it becomes the default when you close the program. See Figure 12-3d-8 for an example of the Lodge environment.

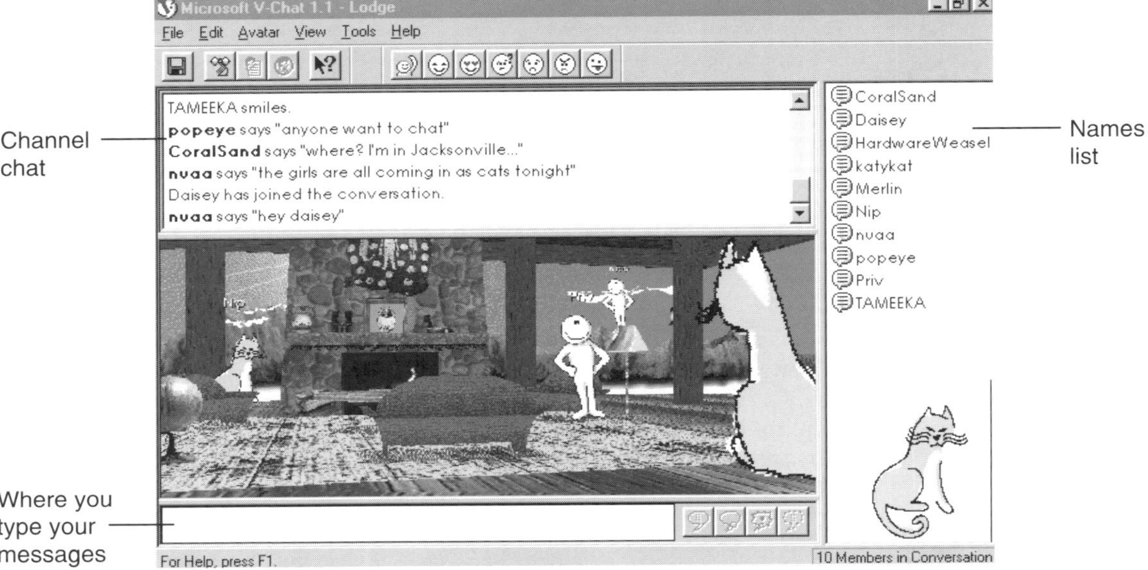

Figure 12-3d-8. Lodge environment in V-Chat

The chat is visible in a box at the top of the environment. The members are listed in a box to the side of the environment. Your avatar is also visible in the members' list box. Any of these boxes can be altered to be larger or smaller by locating your cursor on the edge of the box and dragging it to the size you want. Each member's name is displayed above their avatar. You cannot see yourself because the program is set up to have you seeing the environment and the members from your eyes.

Microsoft V-Chat is a rich graphics 3-D chat program. You can have hours of fun playing with the various environments, avatars, and gestures that are part of the program. Once you become comfortable with the program you can begin to create your own avatars. The program offers a very nice help file to assist you in learning the program and how to create custom avatars.

Active Worlds Chat

Active Worlds Chat is a 3-D chat that operates through its own browser, Active Worlds Browser. With this program you have a choice of several different avatars you can use to represent yourself.

Active Worlds presents you with several different virtual environments you can explore. Sometimes you find people in these different environments and sometimes you find yourself alone. Each Active Worlds environment is a separate place and is based on the Active Worlds technology. Each environment functions as a different destination, but the basic interface and concept is consistent throughout.

Tip: Moving around in these Active Worlds environments is slow because the pages must update when you move into a new area.

Active Worlds uses what it calls dynamic downloads. This dynamic downloading lets you download an object the first time you come across it and then it's recalled from your disk drive any other time it is needed as part of an environment. Figure 12-3d-9 is an example of one of the virtual environments in Active Worlds.

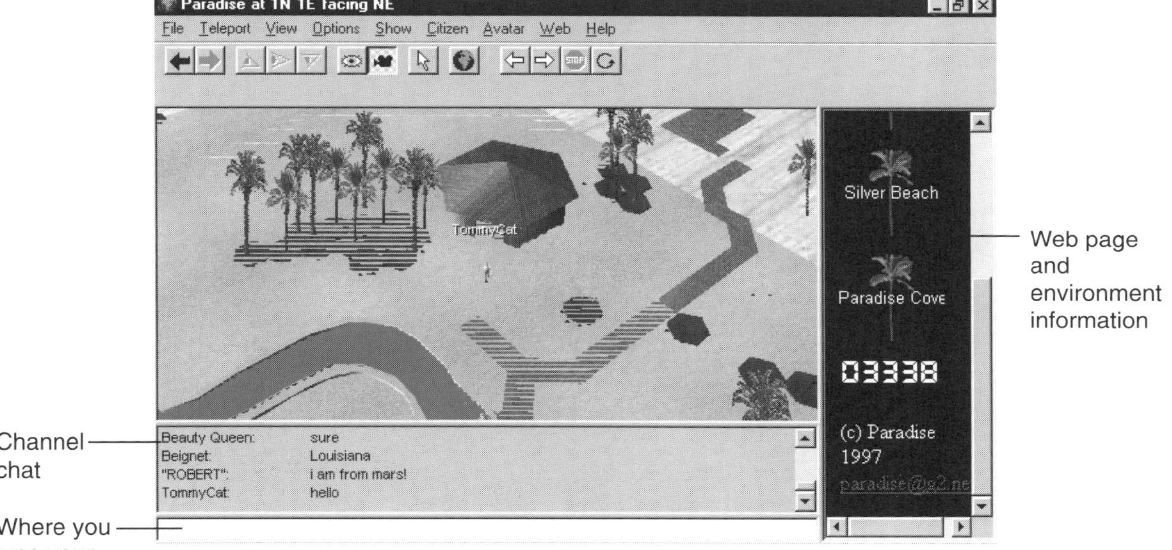

Figure 12-3d-9. Active Worlds Paradise environment

Each time you enter a new virtual environment, you are encountering new objects and new servers. These new items are entered on your hard drive via the dynamic downloading feature of Active Worlds. These are stored in subdirectories Active Worlds creates on your hard drive for you. All of this is performed automatically for you as part of the program.

Within most of these virtual environments you can build things like buildings, huts, or whatever is appropriate for the environment. Once you create your structure it becomes visible for others who visit. These structures you create are saved and sent to the Active Worlds server. This server keeps the database of where objects are located and who is allowed to modify those objects. These objects then become shared experiences that use the Active Worlds Browser as the intermediary and common language. Although many of the virtual environments you visit do let you build in them, there are some that do not.

Before you can begin to explore the virtual environments within Active Worlds you must first register the software. Active World calls this immigration. Active Worlds has set this up as part of the initial setup. When you first log onto the Active Worlds software, you are given a screen that asks you to immigrate. This is done through e-mail and only takes a few minutes. Once you complete the information it asks that an e-mail be sent to Active Worlds. Then you are sent an e-mail back which gives you your citizen ID number.

Now you are ready to explore the Web-of-Worlds that is Active Worlds. When you first log on, you are taken to the main Active Worlds Virtual Environment. This virtual environment is the main gathering place for Active Worlds. Figure 12-3d-10 is an example of this main gathering virtual environment.

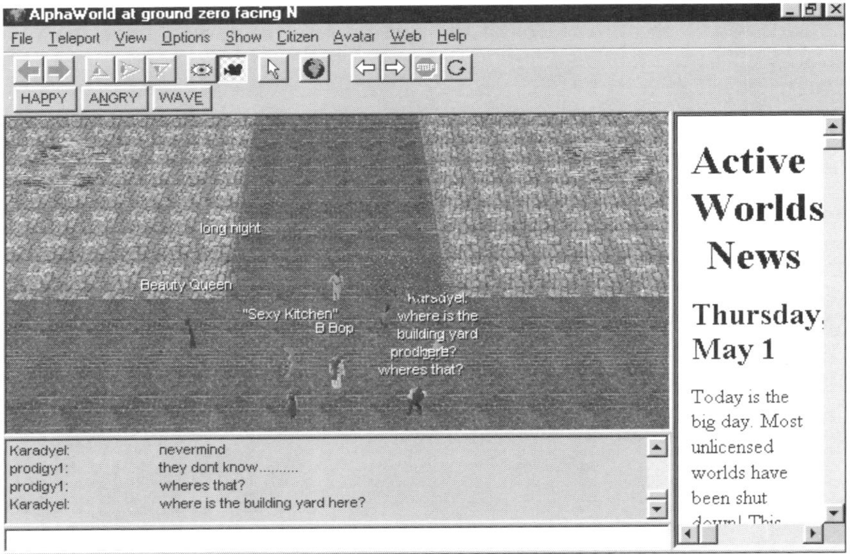

Figure 12-3d-10. Ground zero in Active Worlds

Active Worlds lets you choose how you want to view your environments. You can view them from a first-person viewpoint—as though you are actually seeing everything through your eyes—or from a third-person viewpoint—where you can see yourself as well as everyone else in the environment. In addition you can zoom in and out to see more or less of the environment that you are in. Figure 12-3d-10 is a zoomed-out view of the main Active Worlds environment. See Figure 12-3d-11 for an example of a zoomed-in view of this same environment.

Figure 12-3d-11. Zoomed-in view of an environment

In Active Worlds the conversation is presented in two places. You see it above the heads of the avatars representing the people speaking and you also see it in a text box below the Active Worlds environment. Also notice that the screen is split into three main sections. You have the environment, the text box, and a frame along the right-hand side that contains web page information. You can resize any of these sections by clicking on an edge and dragging it to the desired size. The frame on the right-hand side generally gives you information about the environment you are visiting and directs you to related web pages.

Moving around in these virtual environments is a matter of using the arrow or number keys on your keypad. You can also use your mouse to maneuver within these environments; however, the arrow or number keys work much better and give you better control of your movements.

In most of the virtual environments you visit, you also have options on specific gestures you can use. There generally are standard gestures like wave, angry, and happy. Some of the environments have extra gestures relevant to their theme. When you click on any of these gestures, your avatar performs that gesture.

You can also look around in these virtual environments. You must be in first-person view in order to look around. In first-person viewpoint, you can look up, look down, and look straight ahead. In the toolbar section of your Active Worlds window are the icons that let you do this. You can use your number pad keys (Page Up for look up and Page Down for look down) to do the same activities.

Each time you connect to a virtual environment, you hear music playing in the background, if you have a sound card. Most of the virtual environments have their own background or theme music selected for that environment by the creators. You can also play sounds from your own files. This program supports both .wav and .mid sound files. Be aware, however, that only those with identical sound files on their system are able to hear the sounds you play. All others simply get an error message.

At any time you can choose to move to another virtual environment. In Active Worlds this is called teleporting. To teleport to another environment, select Teleport from the menu bar and then choose the environment you want to change to from the list that appears in the drop-down menu. Figure 12-3d-12 is an example of another environment that was teleported to.

Figure 12-3d-12. Another Active Worlds environment

In addition to the numerous virtual environments in Active Worlds, it also includes rollercoasters and water slides. These are scattered throughout Active Worlds. They are made possible through a special Warp command. You carry your avatar through a trigger point and then you are propelled forward by these warp commands and get to experience the ride as it happens.

Active Worlds is an exciting program that lets you do any number of things. Try it out. If you like the experience of a virtual world with avatars, it has an excellent help file to assist you in learning how to build objects and do many of the activities associated with the program.

OnLive Traveler

OnLive Traveler is a voice, 3-D chat program. It has some very nice graphics, a large number of avatars, and several different worlds you can choose from. However, the program is very slow in loading. It tends to run very slow in almost everything you do.

When you first log onto the program you are taken to its web site via your browser. Therefore you need either Netscape Navigator 3.0 or Microsoft Internet Explorer 3.0. Before you can visit any of the worlds, you must download them first. These do download fairly quickly and can be done from the web site. The help files are also part of the web site.

The drawback is that this program runs so slow that even loading the help pages takes several long minutes. It also takes quite a while for individual pages to load if you have this program open in the background. The tech support suggests that you have nothing open but the program and your browser. This is very sound advice, because the program slows your whole system down. Even if you wanted to you could not do anything else very successfully.

After you download the worlds you want to visit, you can enter through the web pages. I tried this and found the program just wanted to download the program to me again. I opened the world by clicking on the file in my Windows Explorer. OnLive Traveler then proceeds to load the avatar information. The first time you log on you are given a guest avatar which you can use or you can select your own avatar.

To select your own avatar, select the Create New button in the Choose an Avatar dialog box. You are then taken to a screen that lets you select an avatar from the various avatars that OnLive Traveler has to offer. There are avatars under two files, Standard Avatars and OnLiveAvatars. Scan through the various avatars until you find one you would like to represent you in the 3-D worlds of OnLive Traveler. You can change these for each world you visit or use the same one in all your travels. Figure 12-3d-13 is an example of the avatar choice screen with one of the avatars selected.

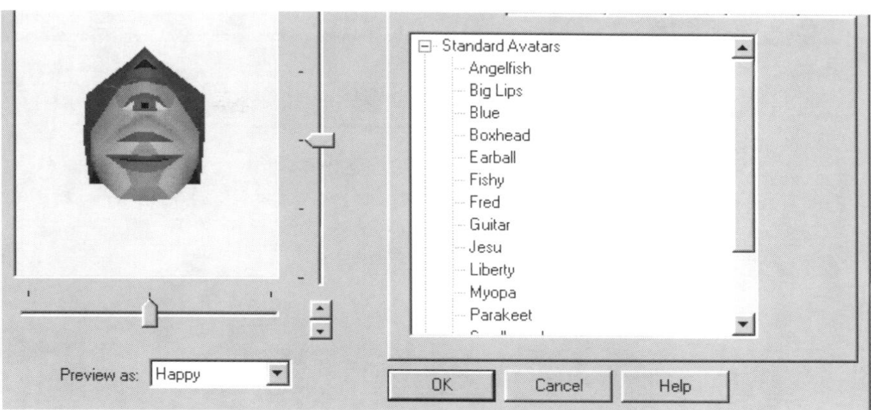

Figure 12-3d-13. Avatar choice screen in OnLive Traveler

After you select the avatar you want you can customize it. You have several choices you can make. You can select the emotion you want your avatar to wear. Your choices here are neutral, happy, sad, and angry. You can view your avatar selection from all angles by dragging the slider on the right of the picture up and down.

In addition to the emotions you can also change the appearance of your avatar, list your user profile information, disguise your voice, and change the settings for the avatar. Each of these choices are represented with a tab at the top right side of the Customize Avatar screen. In the Appearance property tab, you can change the colors and shape of your avatar. Under the Profile tab, you create information about yourself. This tab include boxes that you fill in with your name, birthday, city, e-mail address, web page address, and any comments you want to add. Other users can view this profile on you at anytime you are in any of the OnLive Traveler worlds. With the Voice tab you can modify and test how your voice sounds to others when you are in OnLive Traveler worlds. Under the Settings tab, you can set up a starting space for your avatar. By typing in a URL address for any of the OnLive Traveler worlds you can designate where you want your avatar to start out each time you log onto the OnLive Traveler software.

After you have all your settings in place, click on the OK button and you are taken back to the Choose an Avatar dialog box. At the bottom of this box is a button that says Go Onlive! Click on this button and enter the OnLive Traveler world you selected.

Be patient; it takes quite a while for the program to load all the information for the world you selected. You can go grab a cup of coffee or a soft drink while you wait. You might even feed the cat or scold the kids or make out your shopping list.

While the program is loading you are given a black screen with colored boxes flying around in the space. All your toolbar and menu bar items are inactive. Once the program loads, all those items become active and you get a picture of the world you chose. Figure 12-3d-14 is an example of the Utopia Gateway world in OnLive Traveler.

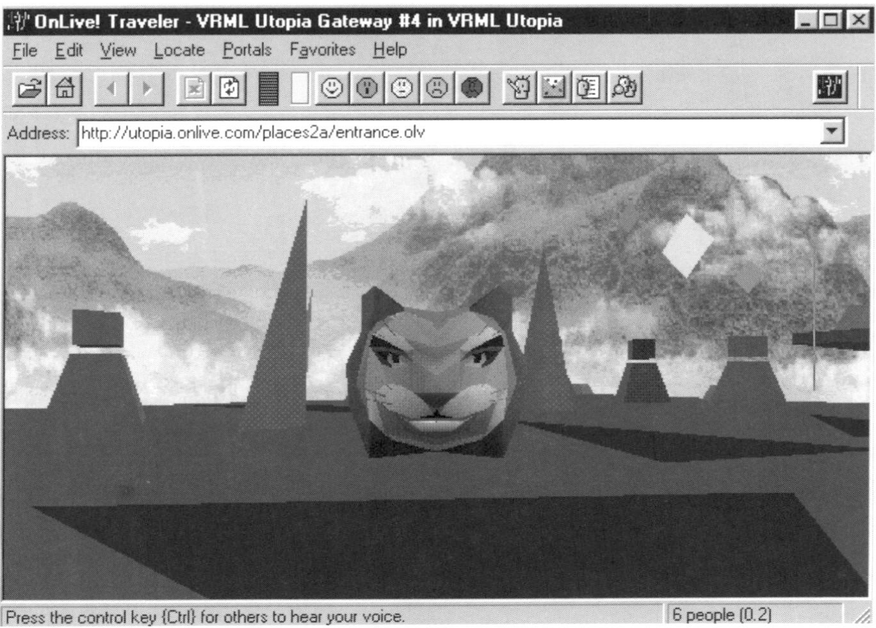

Figure 12-3d-14. Utopia Gateway world in OnLive Traveler

With this program there is no text to go along with the voice chat. Everything is voice chat. If you are having problems communicating through the voice mode you can send text messages to other visitors to the world you're in. Click on the icon in the toolbar that looks like a head with a sheet of paper behind it. This gives you a list of users who are in the world or space you are in. Then you can click on a user's name and the Text Message button. A dialog box pops up that lets you type a short message to the user. When you are ready, simply click on the Send to User button.

Tip: Often the server is lagged for this client, therefore, the conversation is lagged also.

There are several worlds you can visit. This program even hosts special events, such as concerts and special gatherings. Figure 12-3d-15 is an example of the Stonehenge world, which is one of the OnLive Traveler worlds. When a space is full, OnLive Traveler sends you a message box telling you the space is full and to try again later. It also sends you a second message asking you if you want to try another space.

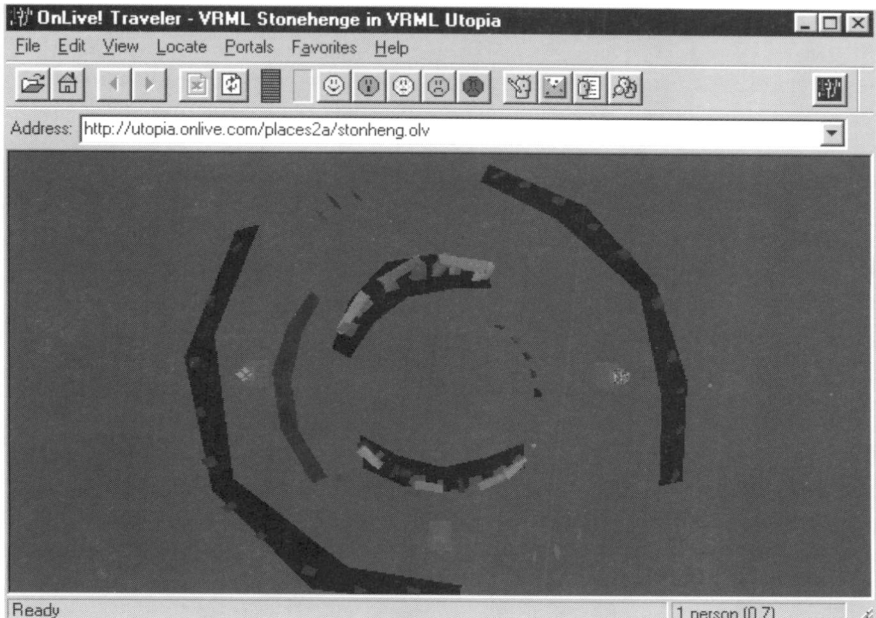

Figure 12-3d-15. Stonehenge environment in OnLive Traveler

Within each of the OnLive Traveler worlds you can access other worlds though what are called portals. These portals are represented by various icons. To enter a portal you can double-click on the portal icon or you can choose Portals from the menu bar and then select the portal you want to enter.

Moving around is fairly simple. You use the arrow keys, the Insert, Delete, Home, End, Page Up, and Page Down keys. You can also use the Alt and Shift keys with these keys to increase your speed of movement or to slide up and down. If you want to change your perspective from first person to third person or vice versa, use Ctrl+I.

OnLive Traveler has the potential to be a very nice 3-D voice chat program. At the moment it is too slow for most users and it does not support Mwave modems. The tech support for the software says it will be supporting Mwave modems in the future. It is a very frustrating piece of software at this time. Hopefully, the designers will work these bugs out of the program and make it easier and faster to use.

Other Chat Programs

There are several text chat programs available for you to download off the web. You may even run across friends on IRC who are willing to send you copies of other programs. We are only covering a few of the other IRC clients in this section. We cover LOL Chat, Microsoft's Comic Chat, Internet TeleCafé, and OrbitIRC Chat. VIRC is covered in more depth in Chapter 10.

The other chat programs available are either similar to the ones covered here or they are designed to perform activities outside the scope of this book. There are several clients you can get off the web that let you communicate with others on the Internet without connecting to any kind of server other than your normal Internet connection. These programs are more appropriate for one-to-one chat than group chat. Therefore they are being left for another time or another book.

The clients covered in this section each have their own unique qualities. They each perform in ways different from other IRC clients. Use this section to help you evaluate what is available, then try a few of these out to see how you like them.

LOL Chat

LOL Chat has its own server(s) and can be used as a one-to-one chat program or a one-to-many program. There are no chat rooms. There is only a common gathering place. You can pull up a list of other users and request chats with them or you can sit back and wait for someone to request a chat with you.

This program also has the capabilities of voice chat. If the other user has Internet Phone already installed on his or her system, you can request a voice chat. However, most of the users of this program do not have voice chat capabilities. They either do not have sound cards installed on their systems or they do not have Internet Phone installed.

It is a decent text chat program nonetheless. It is based on the old talk technology. You can see what the other person is typing as it is typed. Each of you gets your own screen to type in and your messages remain in your screen. See Figure 12-oc-1 for an example of the chat screen for two people in this program.

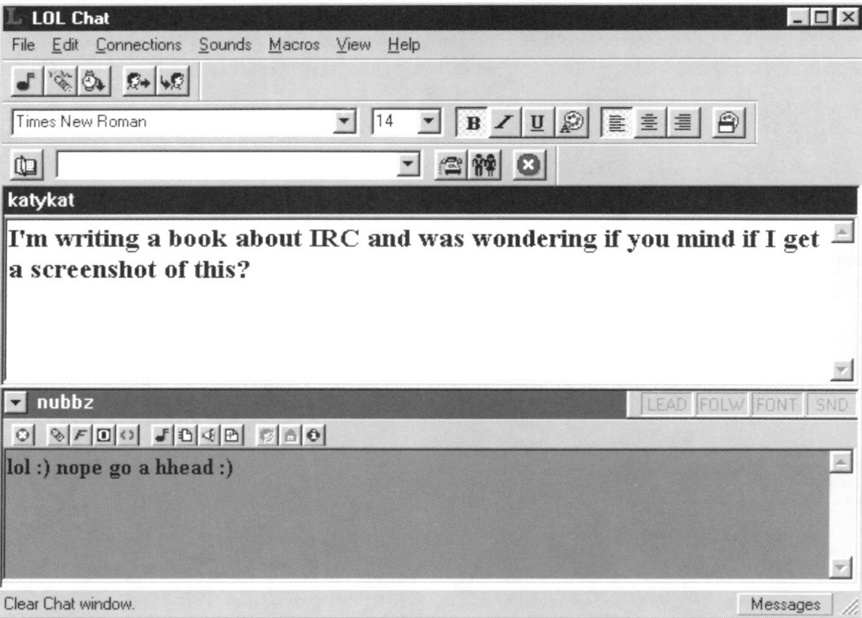

Figure 12-oc-1. Chat window for two users in LOL Chat

With this program you can also surf the web alone or with others you are chatting with. You can lead the web surfing party or you can follow someone else's lead. In the toolbar are two figures—one with an arrow in front of the figure and one with an arrow behind the figure. The front arrow icon lets you lead and the behind arrow icon lets you follow.

LOL Chat also lets you play various preformatted sounds. When you click on the Musical Note icon in the toolbar, you get a drop-down menu which lists the various sounds you can choose from. Click on any of those sound files to play them in your conversations.

You can choose your font style and size with the font box under the toolbar. Simply click on the down arrow button next to this box and choose the font style and size you want your text to appear as. You can also choose a background color and a color for your typed text, as well as other formatting features like bold, italics, centering, and so forth.

LOL Chat has a User List window which shows all users who are currently logged into a server. This User List is where you find other people to talk with. You can access this User List by clicking on the User List icon in the toolbar. This icon is represented by two people, a man and a woman. There are two main parts to this window. The right-hand side of the window is a list of users and the left-hand side is a list of servers. The list of users also includes the number of connections each user is involved in. The letters TS by a user's name means that he or she is with technical support.

LOL Chat contains an Address Book where you can keep names of people you want to search for, as well as notes about those people. The Address Book is found in the Users menu item and has an Address Manager that lets you add, modify, and delete entries.

You can block certain users from calling you. Under the Connections tab in File|Setup in the menu bar, you check the Enable Block list and type in the names of the users you want to block calls from. You can block a selected group of users or you can block everyone. If you choose to block everyone, you can still call others and chat with them. They just can't call you.

In addition to the Address Book, LOL Chat has an Answering Machine. This option lets you create a message that is displayed when someone tries to call you while you are away from your computer. Then they can leave you a message that you can read when you return. This option can be configured using Setup under the File menu. Then you select the Connections tab and choose the Enable Answering Machine checkbox. Simply type your message in the box provided. If you choose not to turn this Answering Machine on, callers do not see your outgoing message and are not allowed to leave you a message.

When more than one person wants to join in conversation with you, the screen splits to accommodate these new chatters. With three people the screen tiles each person's window under yours. As more people join you, screens tile side by side and next to each other. The more people that join your chat, the smaller the screens get for each person. See Figure 12-oc-2 for an example of this split screen feature.

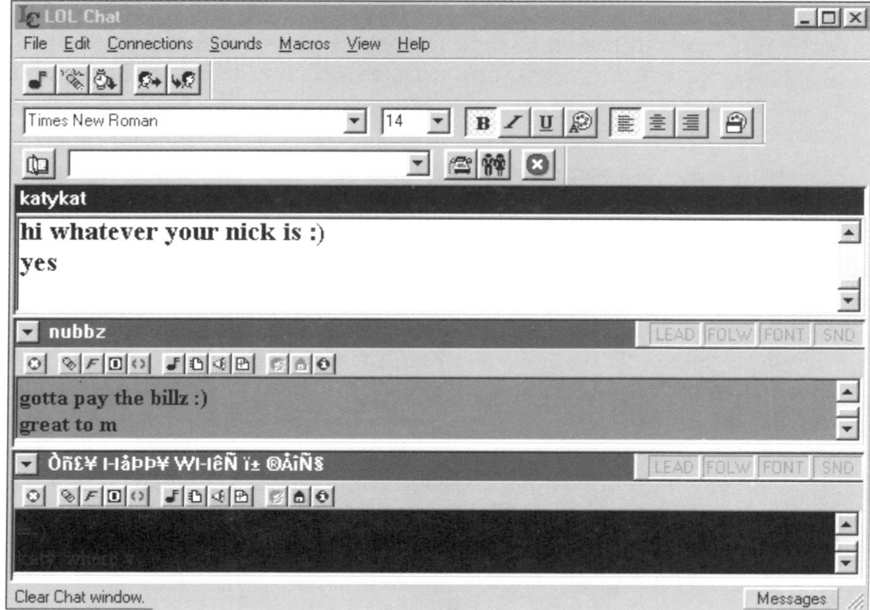

Figure 12-oc-2. Split screen for more than two users

As people begin chats with you, a second toolbar appears under each person's nickname bar. This toolbar lets you do several activities. You can stop the conversation by clicking on the red X icon. You can also clear their screen at any time by clicking on the Pencil icon.

The icon that has two red brackets on it is what you use to whisper to that person alone. Click on that icon and then type your text. When you are finished whispering to that person, click the icon again to turn the whispering off. The whispered text is then displayed in your screen surrounded by red brackets. You can whisper to more than one person at a time by selecting the Whisper icon for each person you want to see your whispered message.

With the Musical Note icon, you can play a sound to that person only. The Speaker icon lets you initiate a voice chat with that person. Using the Person icon you can invite that person only with you to surf the web. The I icon lets you get information on the person whose screen it is in.

You can create macros or shortcuts with this chat client. These macros can contain format changes, text, sounds, or any combination of these. To set up these macros, choose Macro Manager from the Edit menu. Then create the macro you want and associate a key combination to go with it. You can run your macros by using the ABC icon in the toolbar or your keyboard shortcuts.

This client is a nice client if you have a few friends you want to talk to at a given time. Because it is an open forum rather than the channel forum of other chat clients, you can also expect to get requests from other users you don't know. This program is definitely made for anyone who is not shy and enjoys meeting strangers from all over the world. If you're a little shy about joining a room full of strangers, this program is ideal for you. You can connect to the server for this program and wait for others to request chats with you. It is much easier to meet people one-to-one in this program and get to know them without the noise of a busy channel. It is also much easier to keep up with the conversations with this program.

Comic Chat

Microsoft Comic Chat is a program that lets you choose a cartoon character avatar to represent you while you are in chat rooms. You can also choose a background for the rooms you join. This program has its own servers and its own unique society of users.

You can choose from one of three different backgrounds. These are available through the menu bar under View/Options. Once you select Options you get a dialog box that lets you set up how you want your chat session to look, your profile, and your settings, and select an avatar. See Figure 12-oc-3 for an example of this dialog box and the backgrounds you can choose from.

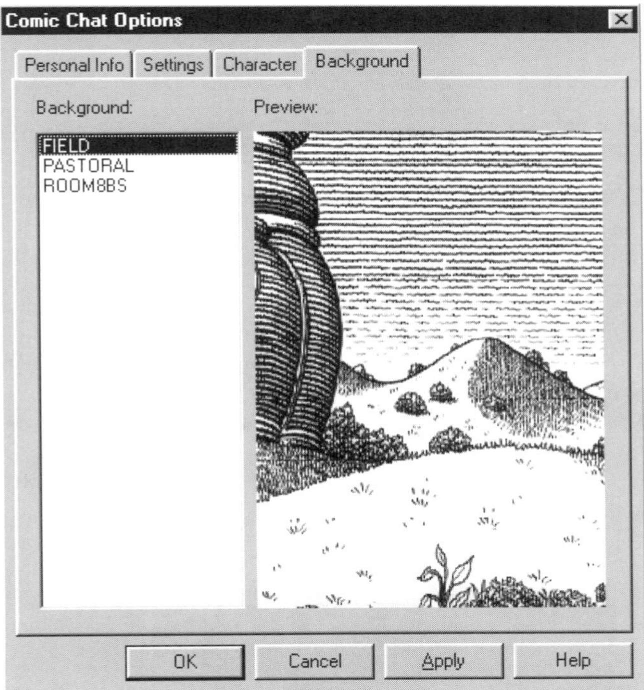

Figure 12-oc-3. Background options in Comic Chat

There are a number of avatars you can choose from. Figure 12-oc-4 shows an example of the avatars that are available. While you are in a chat room, these avatars represent you. You find that due to the limited number of avatars available, there are often several different people with the same avatar. You can check to see who is speaking by placing your cursor on the avatar. Their name displays so that you can then direct comments to them or whisper to them.

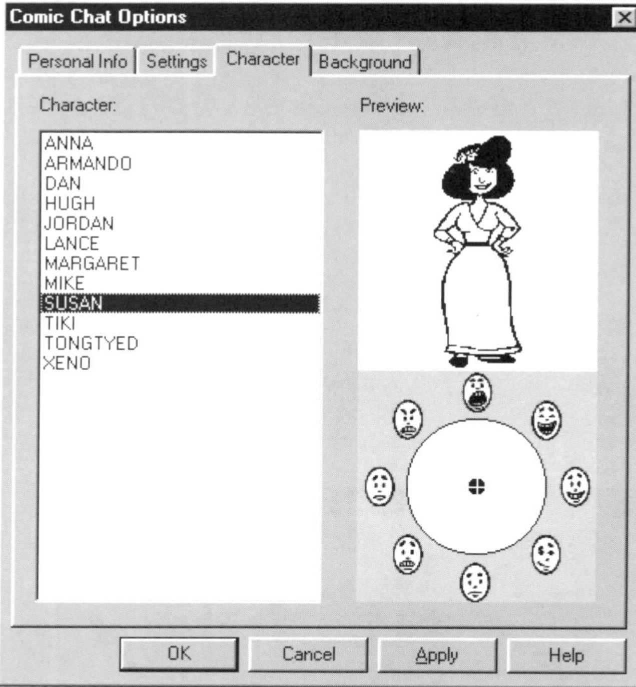

Figure 12-oc-4. Character options in Comic Chat

Along with the background and the avatars you can select you can also use this dialog box to create your settings and your user profile. Figure 12-oc-5 is an example of the other tabs you can use to configure Comic Chat to your preferences. You can create these configurations before you join a chat room or while you are there. You can also change your avatar or the background before you join a room or after you are there.

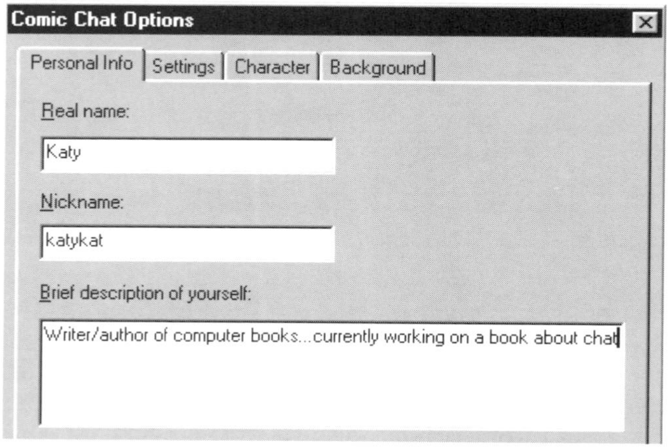

Comic Chat Options

Personal Info | Settings | Character | Background

Real name:

Katy

Nickname:

katykat

Brief description of yourself:

Writer/author of computer books...currently working on a book about chat

Figure 12-oc-5. Personal info options in Comic Chat

Once you are in a chat room and begin your conversations, you can change the expression of your avatar by selecting an expression from the expression wheel in the lower right-hand corner of your window. Each time you type something it appears in a text balloon and your character demonstrates an action appropriate to your text. For instance, when you enter a room and say hi, your avatar waves. If you use exclamation points in your text, your avatar takes on an angry stance with an angry expression.

In addition to these expressions you can pick the type of text balloon you want your message to appear in. The standard text balloon is a spiky or wavy balloon. You can also put your text in a thought balloon, or in an action balloon, which puts a rectangular box around your action statement. See Figure 12-oc-6 for an example of what a chat room looks like and how the conversation is handled.

Figure 12-oc-6. Channel in Comic Chat

In the upper right-hand corner of your screen is a list of all the users in the room you are in. If you wish to stand in front of one of these users as you are speaking you can either highlight their name and avatar in this list and then type your message or you can use their name in your message. It is less confusing, since there are often several users with the same avatar, to include the user's name in the message you are typing.

If you want to whisper to someone, click on that person's name and avatar in the user list. Then type your message and click on the whisper balloon icon at the bottom of your screen. This icon is a balloon with a broken border. When you use this whisper balloon, only the person you indicated sees your message.

When you get bored with the background or avatar you initially chose, select View and then Options from the menu bar. Choose the background and/or avatar you want to change to from the appropriate tabs and then click on the OK button to make your changes. In Figure 12-oc-7, you can see that the background is changed from the one used in Figure 12-oc-6.

Figure 12-oc-7. Background change in Comic Chat

Microsoft Comic Chat is a relatively easy chat client to use. Be aware that you are not connected to regular Internet IRC. You are connected through Microsoft's Comic Chat servers. You can, however, call to another Microsoft Chat user by launching a NetMeeting Internet call from Microsoft Chat. It can also be a lot of fun to chat using these characters, the word balloons, and the various backgrounds.

Internet TeleCafé

Internet TeleCafé is another text-only chat client that uses its own servers. It is a membership-based program. This means that you must register to become a member. With this client there are three types of membership you can choose from—Trial User, Member, and V.I.P. Member. The Trial User can join the Internet TeleCafé and explore to see what kinds of options the program has to offer. When you are satisfied with what you see, join as a Member and there is no fee involved. Members can move through most of the rooms and options of the program. They are restricted from joining certain rooms that are for V.I.P. Members only.

V.I.P. Members have the largest number of options in the client. They also have to pay a fee to become a V.I.P. Member. The fees V.I.P. Members pay are used to improve the Internet TeleCafé environment.

When you first try to connect to Internet TeleCafé, you are asked to register for membership. You can choose at that time which type of membership you want. No matter which membership you choose you are sent a password via e-mail so that you can access the account and use all the options. In order to use all the options the first time you are on, you must leave the program and log back on with your password.

The first place you enter when you log onto Internet TeleCafé is the Lobby. This is a general gathering place and can be quite active. See Figure 12-oc-8 for an example of the Internet TeleCafé window when you join. The screen is broken into three major sections with a task bar section at the bottom of the window. The main screen is where most of the conversations take place. Anything you type appears in this screen. The lower left-hand screen is where any private messages appear that come from other users. And the lower right-hand screen lets you know who is coming and going in the room as well as any invite messages.

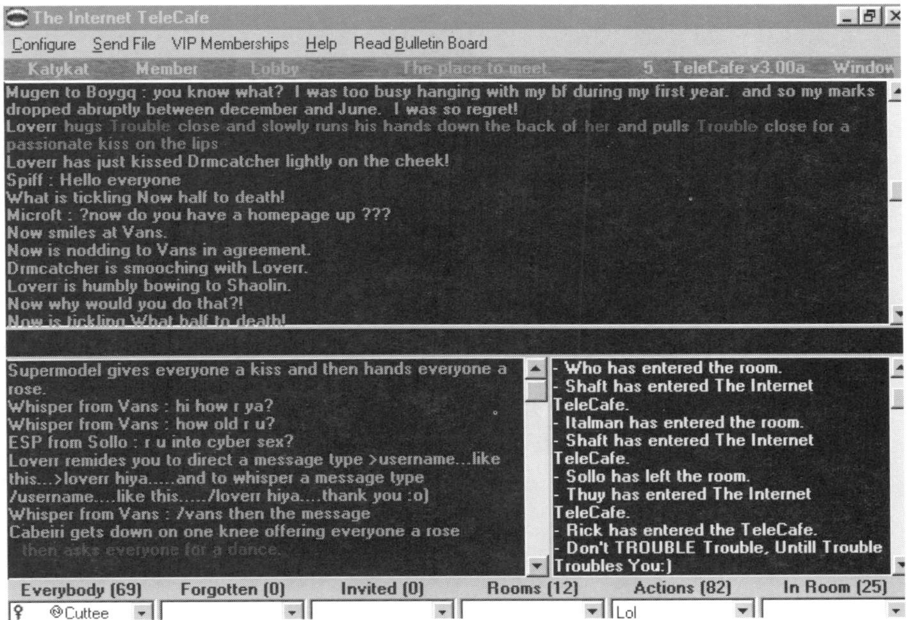

Figure 12-oc-8. Main lounge in Internet TeleCafé

You are not limited to this one room in your selection of chat rooms. There are several you can visit while in Internet TeleCafé. If you click on the down arrow below Rooms in the task bar at the bottom of your window a list of rooms pops up in a menu. You can select any room from that list and double-click on it to have the program take you there. If the room is restricted, you are given a message that tells you so and that you cannot enter that room. See Figure 12-oc-9 for an example of the menu list for rooms.

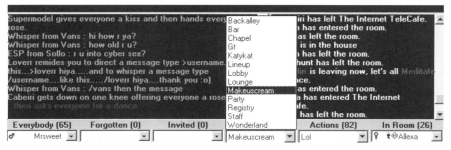

Figure 12-oc-9. Rooms list

Each of the areas in the task bar lets you see a list of who or what is in there and then choose an item from the menu. You can see a list of everyone who is logged onto Internet TeleCafé by selecting the down arrow for Everybody. See Figure 12-oc-10 for an example of this menu.

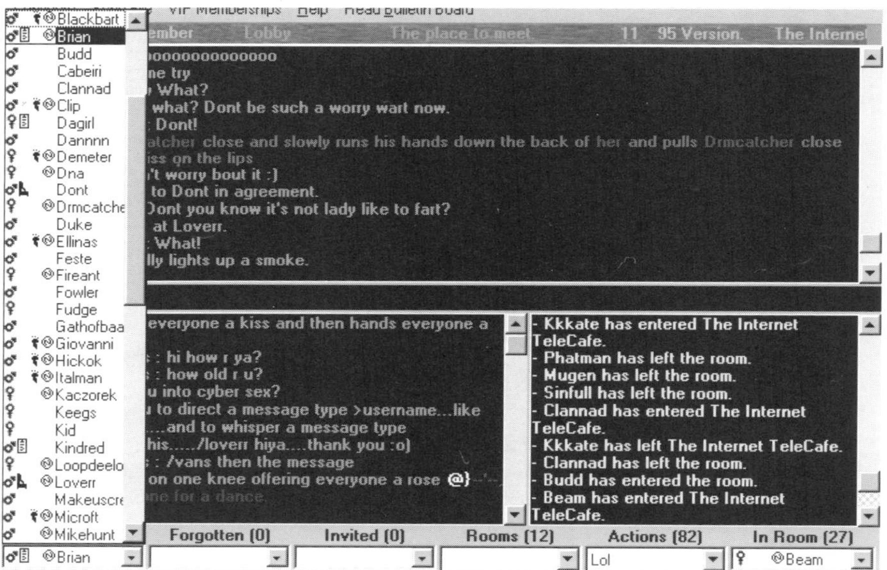

Figure 12-oc-10. Internet TeleCafé user list

You can also see a list of which names are in the room you are in. Click on the down arrow for In Room for the menu of in room names. You can also scroll through the list in the lower right-hand corner of your screen to see who has entered and who has left the room you are in. See Figure 12-oc-11 for an example of the menu list for all the names of the people who are in the room you are in.

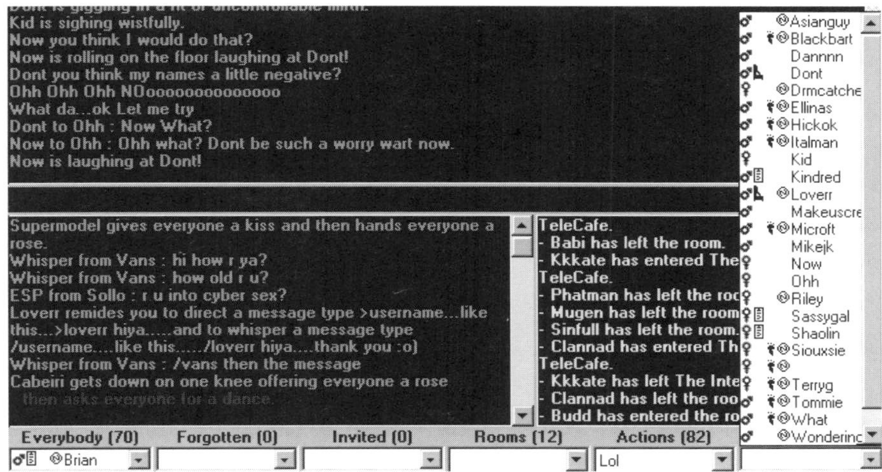

Figure 12-oc-11. Channel user list

This chat client lets you perform actions while you are connected. You can use these actions with text or by themselves. In the task bar at the bottom of your window is an area called Actions. When you click on the down arrow for this area, you get a list of the actions you can perform. Choose an action from the list and double-click on it to perform the action. In Figure 12-oc-12, you see an example of what this Actions list looks like.

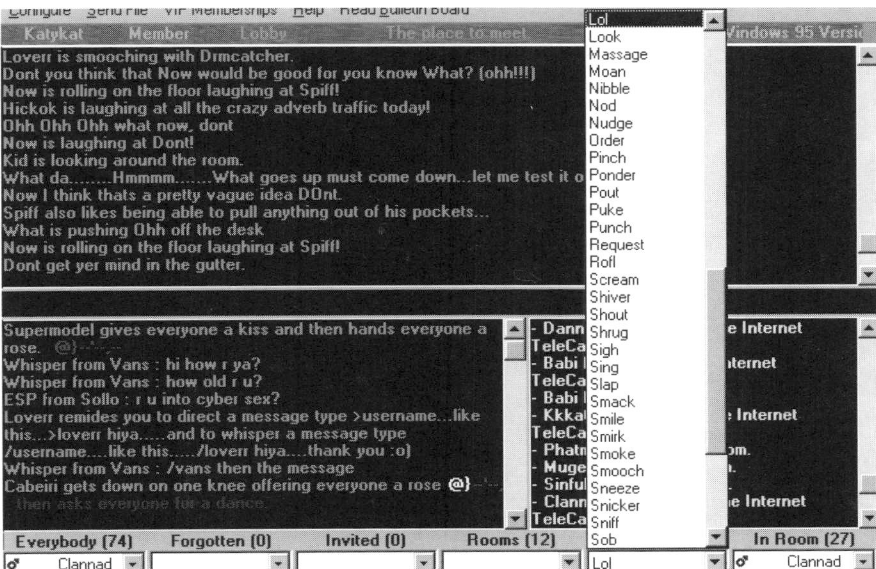

Figure 12-oc-12. Actions list

When you enter Internet TeleCafé a message displays in the lower right-hand screen. This message tells you there is a message on the bulletin board. In the menu bar, you can select Read Bulletin Board to read any messages that are there. When you select Read Bulletin Board, you get a separate window with the bulletin board messages. Figure 12-oc-13 is an example of the bulletin board.

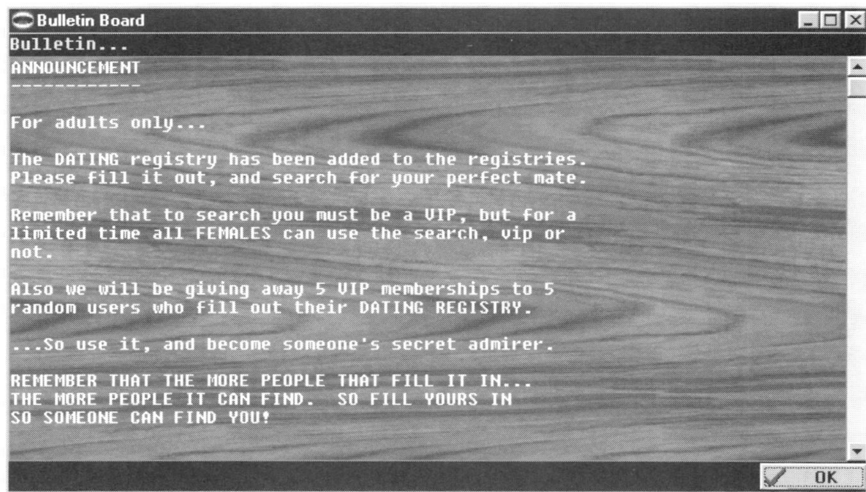

Figure 12-oc-13. Bulletin board

Other than straight text chatting you can perform several commands that are similar to the ones you type in regular IRC. You can access information about these commands in one of two places. Click on the Help menu item. When you click on About Commands you get a listing of the command shortcuts and their functions. When you click on Commands, you get a list of all the commands available. Then you select a command from the list and it is activated for you.

These commands include whispering, exiting, getting a list of rooms, and so forth. Like IRC, most of these commands are prefaced with a forward slash. The commands are usually pretty basic and designed to save you a few keystrokes and time. Figure 12-oc-14 gives you an example of the commands that are available.

```
Commands
Current Commands Available
?              - Use this with any command for more information.
afk            - Lets people know you are not at your keyboard..
apply          - Apply for a free membership.
bulletins  /bu- Allows you to read the bulletin board.
buyvip     /bv- Purchase a VIP Membership using your credit card.
call           - Call something.
config         - Configures your login stuff.
decorate       - Give your room some character.
delnaps    /d - Toss your napkins into the trash.
echo       /h - Turns input echo on or off.
enemy      /e - Puts someone on your enenies list.
forget     /f - Forget/ignore an annoying user.
friend     /fr- Puts someone on your friends list.
gmode      /g - Changes your graphics mode.
help       /? - This listing.
invite     /i - Invite someone to your room.
join       /j - Join a room.
jot            - Write a napkin note to a user.
knock          - Knocks on a door.
list           - Lists information.
```

Figure 12-oc-14. Commands list

This is another simple chat client to learn and use. It too has its own society of users. After you use it a few times, you are sure to become accepted and recognized. It can be a fun way to meet and chat with people all over the world.

OrbitIRC Chat

OrbitIRC Chat is another text-based chat client. You can use this client to access regular IRC. It is designed to be used with any IRC server. When you open the program for the first time you are given a few servers to choose from. You can also add your own servers. Initially you get a free 30-day evaluation program. If you like it, you must register before you can continue using it past the 30-day evaluation period.

When you first open this program you can set up your preferences for the program at that time. You can also import any settings you have from your mIRC client to the OrbitIRC client. In this setup window you can indicate your nick and add or delete servers. This is also the screen you get each time you want to log onto IRC. You connect through this screen. Figure 12-oc-15 is an example of this initial setup/connect screen.

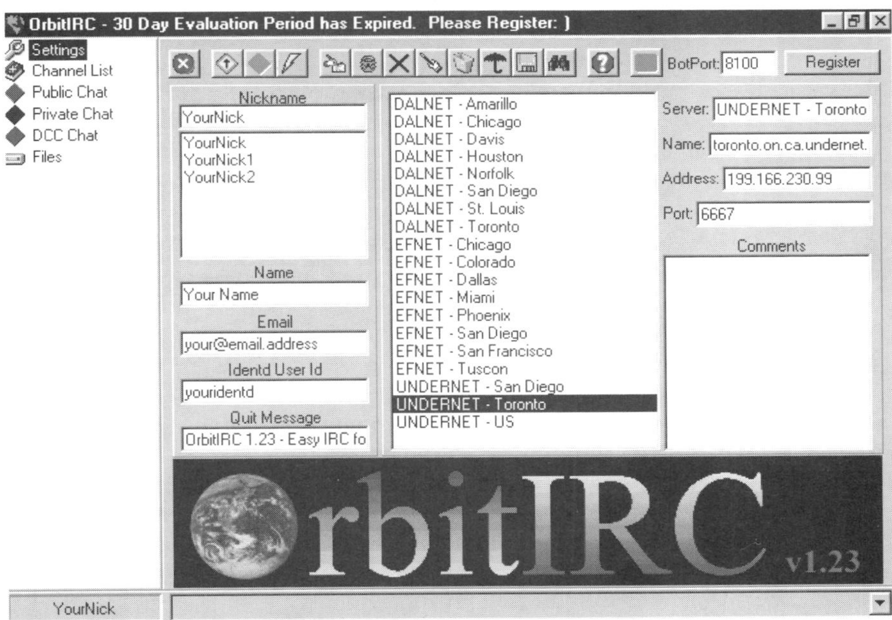

Figure 12-oc-15. Setup and connect window for OrbitIRC

Once you connect to a server you can then join a channel of your choice. You can select a channel from the Channels list or join a channel you are already familiar with.

When you join a channel, you get a large screen in which to type your messages. You can use the default fonts and colors or you can customize your fonts and colors. This is accomplished through the Settings icon in the pane to the left of the

Channel box. Select Settings and then choose Display from the menu. Make your adjustments and click on OK to save and exit.

Each channel you join is added to the Public Chat folder in the left pane beside the channel window. The same is true for private chats and DCC chats. These are listed under the appropriate Private Chat folder or DCC Chat Folder. Each window is hidden behind your active window. When someone types a message to one of the inactive windows, the folder lights up to let you know. Figure 12-oc-16 is an example of the Channel window.

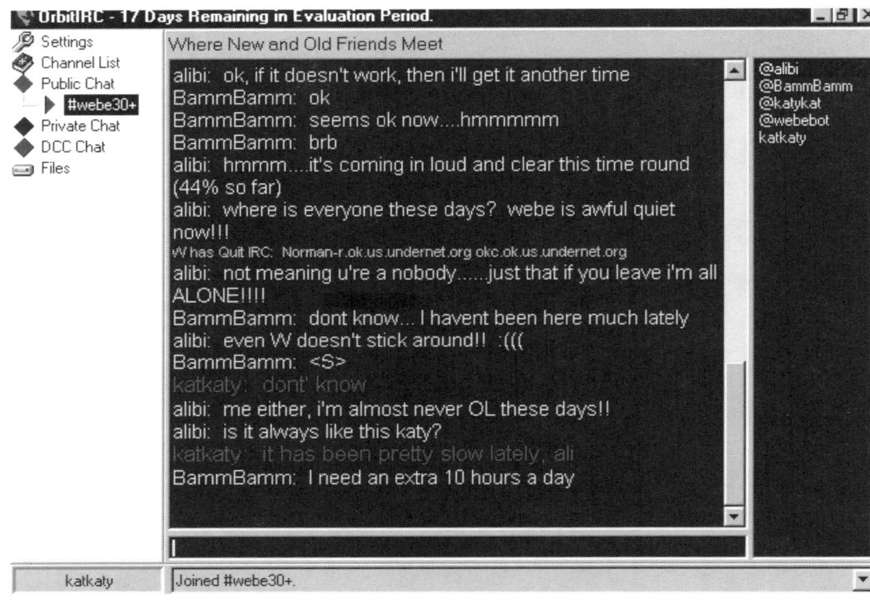

Figure 12-oc-16. Channel in OrbitIRC

If you want to send someone a file from your hard drive, you can click on File in the left pane of the window. You are then given a screen that lists the files on your hard drive. Select the file you want to send, type in the nickname of the person you want to send to, and press Enter to start the send. You can also use this screen to set up how you want to handle incoming DCCs. See Figure 12-oc-17 for an example of this Files screen.

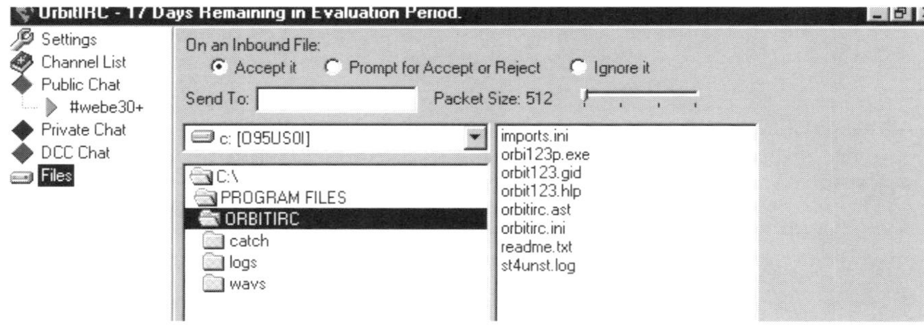

Figure 12-oc-17. DCC options in OrbitIRC

Many of the things you can do with the other chat clients you can do with OrbitIRC also. You can create macros or scripts for frequently used commands or actions. You can set up a file server to automatically send files to other users. You can send and receive sounds and log sessions. But with this program you have an added feature. You can DCC Draw! When you are in a DCC chat with another OrbitIRC user, you can activate the Picturebox and doodle back and forth to each other. This Picturebox feature supports up to 16.7 million colors and various brush sizes. It can break up the monotony of straight text chat.

Chapter 13
Scripts

In this chapter you learn:

- ☑ *What are Scripts?*
- ☑ *How to Create Scripts for mIRC*
- ☑ *How to Create Scripts for Pirch—PIL*
- ☑ *Exercises*

Aliases, popups, and events are an important part of your online chat activities. They can save time and typing. There are different types of aliases, popups, and events you can use or create.

When you first start out, you learn how to set up some of the simpler aliases, popups, and events. As you become more proficient and comfortable using IRC and your client, you start trying to create more advanced ones. Eventually you want to try your hand at creating even more complicated aliases, popups, and events.

These more complicated creations require you to use a form of programming called scripting. This chapter helps you understand what scripts are and how to create them for both mIRC and Pirch. Let's begin by learning what scripts are.

What are Scripts?

There are a couple of definitions for script as it relates to IRC. One definition is the code used in an alias or remote event. Another definition is a coordinated set of remote events, popups, and aliases. In other words, writing mIRC or Pirch aliases, popups, or events is often referred to as scripting. What you are actually doing is using a form of scripting language.

Scripts for mIRC or Pirch usually contain files for aliases and remote events. These scripts can also contain other ancillary files that the script uses. They contain additional information aliases and events need to carry out the command you are creating.

Pirch has given its scripts a special language name, PIL. These PILs use their own special language to perform certain activities and carry out commands. This PIL language is specific to Pirch and was created by its designer.

Full, complete scripts are intended to add functionality to IRC that mIRC or Pirch don't provide. These two clients, as they come to you when you download them, are basic programs. Scripts allow you to add commands to the programs to make them do things that they don't automatically do but that you want them to do.

Scripts can be considered add-ons to your IRC client. They let you add features to the client to help automate certain activities that you normally do or that you want the program to do for you. Some scripts you use to help you manage your channel and some scripts you use to create bots.

Scripts allow you to create conditional statements, loops, and other more complicated expansions to your aliases, popups, and events. These can include the If-then-else statements and variables to create aliases, popups, or events that can perform the activities you want or need them to. You can set up scripts in aliases, popups, and events that react to conditions where you can specify that if certain activities occur, then your alias, popup, or event activates and performs the function you programmed it for.

In essence, when creating scripts, you are using a form of programming. You are essentially programming certain functions and activities as added features that become part of your IRC client.

In order to use scripts you must have a good understanding of how to create aliases, popups, and events. If you have followed along in this book, you have already learned how to create some fairly complicated ones. You are ready now to learn how to add scripts to these activities and create even more complicated aliases, popups, and events.

How to Create Scripts in mIRC

Creating scripts involves using identifiers, variables, and If-then-else statements alone or in combination with each other. Identifiers are built-in commands that return a value, such as $time which returns the current time.

Aliases can be used in the edit box, the area where you normally type commands or anything you want posted to a channel, and you can use them in popups and remote events. You can have aliases call other aliases or call themselves. However, calling aliases within aliases uses a lot of memory, so be advised.

To control the order in which identifiers are read in aliases, you can use evaluation brackets. These evaluation brackets are the [ ] characters on your keyboard. Identifiers you put in these brackets are evaluated from left to right. Nesting brackets lets you evaluate things inside the command any way you want them.

These evaluation brackets force mIRC to evaluate an expression in the order that you specify, by how you place the brackets. By evaluate, we mean compute a math expression, or return the value of an identifier or variable. For instance, when you place the identifier $time in your commands, mIRC *evaluates* $time to the current time.

Here's an example where the identifier $lof (an identifier that returns the length of a file in bytes) won't work without the evaluation brackets. The brackets force mIRC to evaluate the concatenation of the $mircDir and Mirc32.exe *first*, before it gives that data to the $lof identifier. The example is as follows:

```
testeval {
  set %test $lof( $mircdir $+ mirc32.exe )
  set %test2 $lof( [ $mircdir $+ mirc32.exe ] )
  echo 2 -a the value of % $+ test (without brackets) is: %test
  echo 3 -a The value of % test2 (with brackets) is: %test2
  unset %test %test2
}
```

In mIRC you can write an alias and use it just as you would any other identifier. The trick is to use the /RETURN command. Here is an example:

```
WavNick {
 Return ! $+ $me
}
```

This is written just as you write any other alias. Notice the name of the alias *does not* begin with a $. It simply appends your current nick to an exclamation mark. To use it as an identifier, type the following command:

```
TEST { Echo 2 -a Your wave nick is: $wavNick }
```

Figure 13-a is an example of how these scripts look in your Aliases edit box.

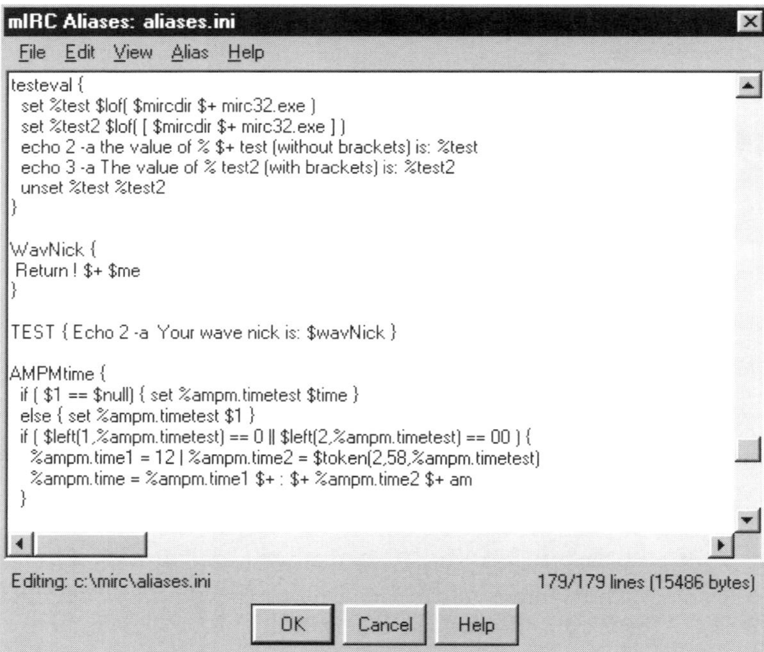

Figure 13-a. Scripts in mIRC Aliases edit box

There isn't a command or identifier in mIRC that returns time in 12-hour am/pm format. The alias example below takes a time value as parameter one, or if parameter one is absent, uses the current time and returns the time in 12-hour format.

```
AMPMtime {
  if ( $1 == $null) { set %ampm.timetest $time }
  else { set %ampm.timetest $1 }
  if ( $left(1,%ampm.timetest) == 0 || $left(2,%ampm.timetest) == 00 ) {
    %ampm.time1 = 12 | %ampm.time2 = $token(2,58,%ampm.timetest)
    %ampm.time = %ampm.time1 $+ : $+ %ampm.time2 $+ am
  }
  elseif ( $chr(58) isin $left(2,%ampm.timetest) ) {
     %ampm.time1 = $remove($left(2,%ampm.timetest),:)
    %ampm.time2 = $token(2,58,%ampm.timetest)
    %ampm.time = %ampm.time1 $+ : $+ %ampm.time2 $+ am
  }
  elseif ( $left(2,%ampm.timetest)  <= 12 ) {
    %ampm.time1 = $left(2,%ampm.timetest)
    %ampm.time2 = $token(2,58,%ampm.timetest)
    %ampm.time = %ampm.time1 $+ : $+ %ampm.time2 $+ pm
   }
  else {
    %ampm.time1 = $left(2,%ampm.timetest) - 12
    %ampm.time2 = $token(2,58,%ampm.timetest)
    %ampm.time = %ampm.time1 $+ : $+ %ampm.time2 $+ pm
  }
  set %ampm %ampm.time
  unset %ampm.*
   return %ampm
}
```

Figure 13-b is an example of how these previous scripts look in your Aliases edit box.

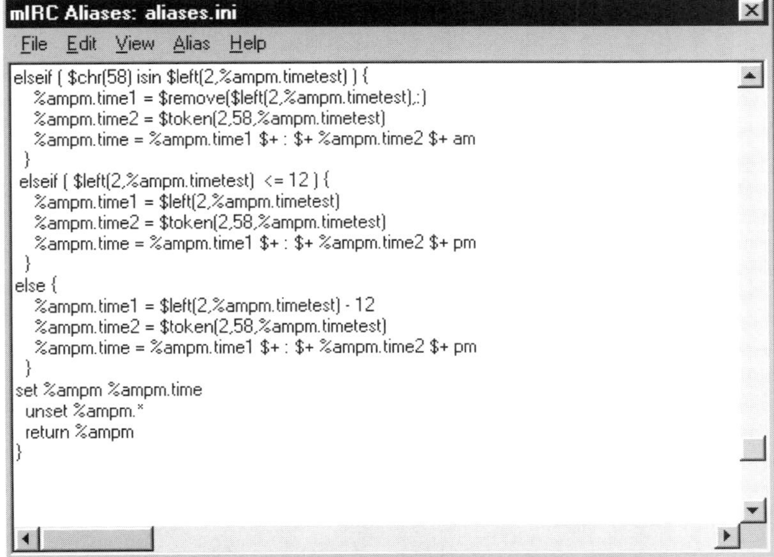

Figure 13-b. More scripts

Following is a test alias to show how to use it as an identifier:

```
test {
 echo 2 -a The current time is $ampmtime
 echo 2 -a 13:00 military time is $ampmtime(13:00:00)
}
```

All variables in mIRC are "global," meaning that any or all aliases and event scripts can use a variable set by any other alias or remote event script. Sometimes, this can cause unexpected results when a variable naming conflict arises, i.e., one alias uses the name of a variable that a different alias doesn't expect to be disturbed. For instance:

```
ctcp 1:PING: { inc %p 1 | echo 4 -s Ping Total is %p }
```

Here we used the variable %p to keep a running total of how many times we've been pinged by someone else. However, if we were to use the variable %p in a different alias, it would upset our ping count total, leading to false ping counts in this case. Sometimes this can be a subtle bug that can be hard to track down unless you are aware of this potential problem.

mIRC has approximately 30Kb worth of space for variables. A good practice is to unset any unneeded variables when your script is finished with them, so as not to accumulate unneeded clutter in your variable file.

It is advisable to use unique names for your various variables. You can use a semi-formal naming convention for naming these variables. By using a naming convention for identifying your variables, you avoid using the same variable names in different places in your scripts and this helps you in bug prevention. It also makes it easier to clean up after that particular alias or event script is done with its variables.

For variables that are "global," the ones that are in constant use by the script and used in more than one alias and/or event script, give the variable a descriptive name. These variables may or may not be cleared at the start of a mIRC session, but usually are never cleared during a session. For example, set %DCC on or set %away off.

For variables that are "local" to a particular alias or not needed elsewhere in the script, prefix the name of the variables with two or three letters and a period. For example, set %go.test 2 or set %go.nick $nick. The period has no meaning in the variable name. As far as mIRC is concerned it's just another character. The letters serve to identify and make unique the variable names for that particular alias. For instance, rewriting the example mass-op alias in mIRC's help file in the If-then-else section looks like this:

```
GiveOps {
  %go.i = 0
  %go.nicks = ""
  :nextnick
  inc %go.i
  if ($snick(%go.i,#) == $null) { if ($len(%go.nicks) > 0) mode #
              +oooo %go.nicks | goto end }
  %go.nicks = %go.nicks $snick(%go.i,#)
  if (4 // %go.i) { mode # +oooo %go.nicks | %go.nicks = "" }
```

```
  goto nextnick
  :end
   unset %go.*
}
```

Figure 13-c is an example of how these scripts look in your Aliases edit box.

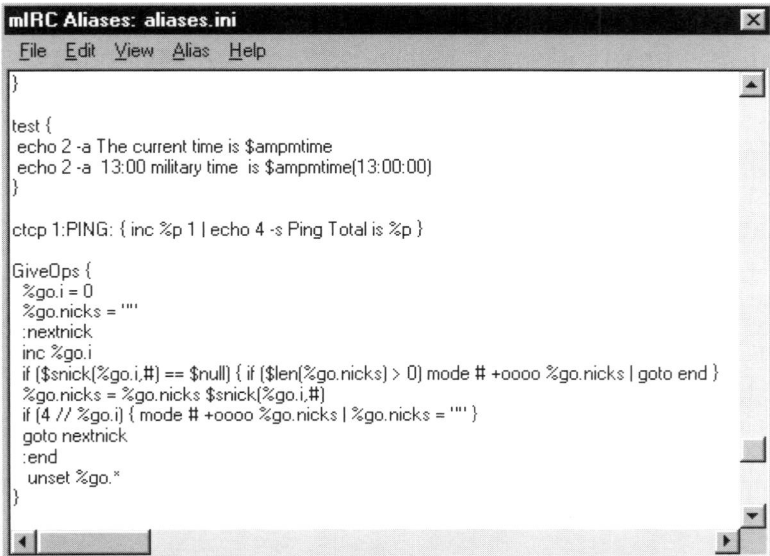

Figure 13-c. Give ops script

In this example the variable name is GO. This is a local variable and the variables are not used again after this alias has completed its task. The reason for this name GO is simply because the name of the alias was Give Ops. This helps avoid the multiple variable name problem mentioned earlier. Also, when this alias completes, it could easily clear them all with the command Unset GO. The unset command allows the use of the * wild card. The unset %go. unsets all variables that start with go. This clears all those variables with one command. It also keeps you from having to remember to unset a handful of different variables one by one.

For variables that are more module in scope and are no longer needed when that particular task is finished, name these variables with the same prefix, either two or three letters or a word, followed by an underscore _. These module variables are ones that require more than one alias or remote script in order for them to work. An example of a module variable is as follows:

```
set %msg_count 1
set %msg_status complete
```

When you see the underscore character in a variable name as you're reviewing code, you know that this is a module variable, not just local to a particular alias, and its name should give you a clue what the script is for. You can also use the unset command to unset all those variables with one command when that task is completed. Or you can initialize them all with beginning values when they should be reset. The command Unset %msg_* cleans up all these variables when they are no longer needed.

It is recommended you use some form of variable naming convention, whether similar to the above or one of your own invention. This naming convention helps prevent you from putting bugs in your scripts, as well as helping you during the debugging of your scripts.

mIRC versions 5.0 and above now allow you to have multiple script files. You might want to consider adding an additional word to the above convention, to show you what script file they belong in. The multiple script files are a great addition to mIRC and allow for easy sharing of scripts and mIRC add-ons. Adding a script file prefix to your variable names helps to ensure unique variable names. This is especially true if you are running scripts from multiple authors. Running multiple script files also gives you the potential of bugs due to nonunique variable names.

Sometimes in scripting it is useful to set a variable name the same as someone's nick, so that later when you see that nick again, you can refer to that same variable. This makes it easier to find the right variable to work with because it's keyed or associated with the nick.

The trick to making a variable name contain a nick is with the use of evaluation brackets. Say for instance you want to count how many times you are pinged by a particular nick. In a CTCP PING event in the Remote/Events editor box, you could type something like:

```
ctcp 1:PING: {
  Inc %ping_ [ $+ [ $nick ] ]  1
  echo 5 -s You have been ping'd by $nick [ %ping_ [ $+ [ $nick ] ] ]
times now.
 return
}
```

The first line increments a variable by one. The name of that variable starts with %ping_ and someone's nick. If you were pinged by a nick, the variable name would be %ping_<nickname>. If you look in your variable file, you see %ping_<nickname> 5 if that nick had pinged you five times.

The second line echoes the message to your status screen and uses an extra set of evaluation brackets. The result of [%ping_ [$+ [$nick]]] evaluates to the contents of the variable as opposed to the name of the variable. These can be referred to as compound variables. These compound variables contain two or more parts. Often, the name of the variable gets calculated as much as the contents of the variable.

You can find that script code gets real confusing when trying to remember how many evaluation brackets to use to return the name of the variable or the contents of the variable. Therefore it is advisable to use two custom identifier aliases to help you keep this clear. Following is an example:

```
VarValue {
  ; cleans up code, by hiding all those [ ] here ... and allows
        "easy" changes,
  ; should mirc change the way it evaluates vars ... ( again) :-)
```

```
  %varvalue = [ % $+  [  [ $1 ] $+ [ $2 ] ] ]
  return %VarValue
}
VarName {
  ; clean up code... returns Variable name i.e. %card28
  ; if $1 = card and $2 = 28
   %varname = % $+ [ $1 ] $+ [ $2 ]
  Return %VarName
}
```

Figure 13-d is an example of how these scripts look in your Aliases edit box.

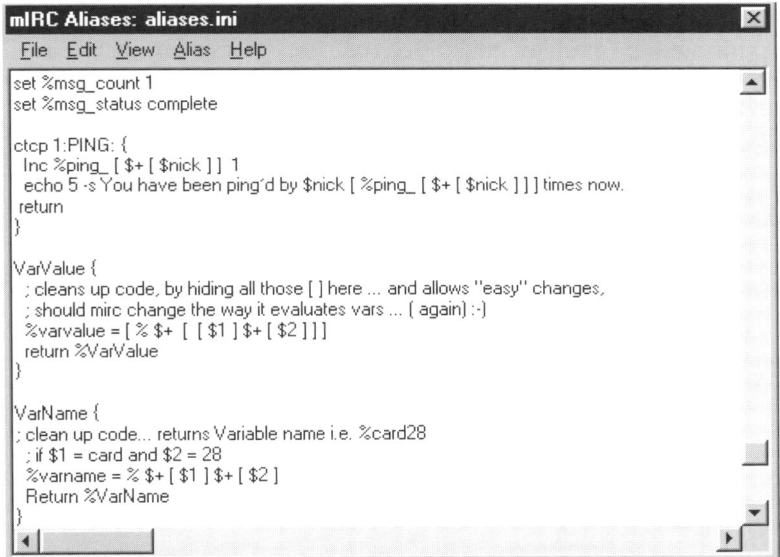

Figure 13-d. Ping and variable name scripts

These two aliases expect two parameters that make up the variable's name. The alias, VarName, returns the name of the variable, while VarValue returns the value or contents of the variable. Aliases presume the leading % variable name character, so don't use that. You can use $varname(Ping.,$nick) instead of $varname (%ping.,$nick). If you rewrite the ping counter example previously described but using these aliases, it looks like this:

```
ctcp 1:PING: {
  Inc $varname(Ping_,$nick) 1
  echo 5 -s You have been ping'd by $nick $varValue(Ping_,$nick)
times now.
 return
}
```

What do you do when an alias or script doesn't work as intended, or doesn't work at all? It's time to put your debugger hat on and figure out what is wrong with your alias or script.

Other than your wits, the most useful tool to debug scripts in mIRC is the echo command. Put echo statements before and after where you think the problem is, and also put in variables or identifiers in your echo statements that the script is working with, so that you can see what it is doing with them.

Are the input parameters to the script as you expected them to be? Do the variables look like you expect? What is the result of an identifier? As you expected? Perhaps a heretofore unexpected result of an identifier?

From there, you can, hopefully, figure out what is wrong with it. Also, look at the status window; you may get a message from mIRC or the server that can give you some clues as to what is wrong.

If you see "UNKNOWN COMMAND _____," where the blank is any command or word, that message came from the IRC server you are connected to. This error message means your script told mIRC to execute an alias and mIRC couldn't find it. Then mIRC assumed it must be a server command and sent it to the server. That often happens when you have a problem with unmatched curly brackets in a script. When you get it working, you can remove or comment out those echo statements that you sprinkled through your code. To comment out a line, place a semicolon at the beginning of a line.

If-then-else statements allow you to make comparisons and decisions in your alias or script code. Get to know this one well—it gives mIRC scripting a lot of power, or flexibility.

If statements always makes a comparison that equate to TRUE or FALSE. The proper formatting of the command is to enclose the comparison test in parentheses and the command in curly braces like this:

```
IF ( ComparisonValue1  ComparisonOperator ComparisonValue2 ) {
command(s) to do if comparison returned True } or:
IF ( 1 < 2 ) { /Echo this will always return TRUE }
If ( 1 <= 2 ) { /echo this is also true }
IF ( 1 == 2 ) { /echo always FALSE-you won't see this! }
```

In order for these If-then-else statements to work, you need to know the comparison operators. They are as follows:

- == — equal to
- != — not equal to
- < — less than
- > — greater than
- >= — greater than or equal to
- <= — less than or equal to
- // — is a multiple of
- \\ — is not a multiple of
- isin — string v1 is in string v2
- iswm — wild card string v1 matches string v2
- isnum — number v1 is a number in the range v2 which is in the form n1-n2 (v2 optional)
- ison — nickname v1 is on channel v2
- isop — nickname v1 is an op on channel v2

- isvo — nickname v1 has a voice on channel v2
- ischan — if v1 is a channel which you are on
- isauto — if v1 is a user in your auto-op list for channel v2 (v2 optional)
- isignore — if v1 is a user in your ignore list with the ignore switch v2 (v2 optional)
- isprotect — if v1 is a user in your protect list for channel v2 (v2 optional)
- isnotifyi — f v1 is a user in your notify list
- && AND || OR — these two let you make multiple comparisons in one if statement

This Goto command is similar to the goto statement in the BASIC programming language, if you're familiar with that. It tells mIRC to jump or skip from one point of your script to another point. Here is an example:

```
/number {
  if ($1 == 1) goto one
  elseif ($1 == 2) goto two
  else goto unknown
  :one
  echo The number ONE
  halt
  :two
  echo The number TWO
  halt
  :unknown
  echo Unknown number!
  halt
}
```

Figure 13-e is an example of how this script looks in the Aliases edit box.

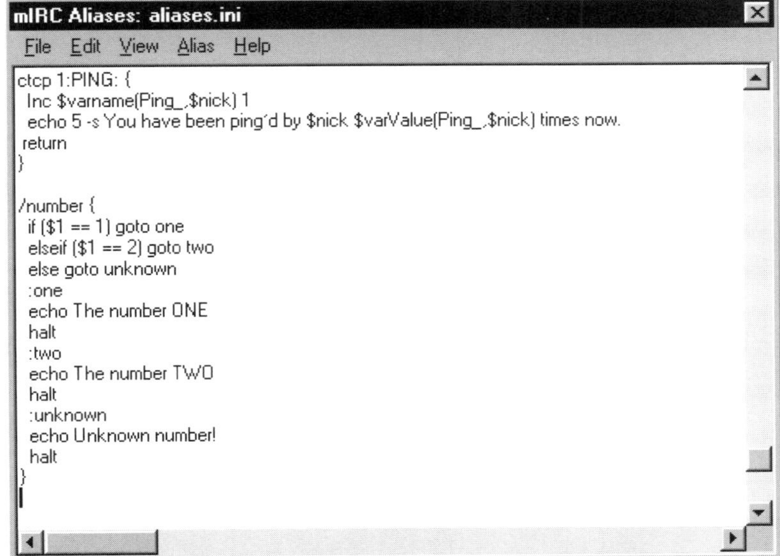

Figure 13-e. Goto command in a script

To use the Goto, you have to specify where to go to with a Label.

As in the above example, Goto One is the label. The label has to be somewhere in your alias and be prefixed with a colon.

The Goto does not go to a label in a different alias or script, only within the current alias. You can make use of the Goto command to perform looping operations.

These are several of the ways you can create scripts in aliases, popups, and events. Use these identifiers, variables, brackets, and If-then-else statements along with the examples included in this section to help you create scripts in mIRC.

How to Create Scripts in Pirch—PIL

Advanced scripting in Pirch is accomplished through the Pirch PIL language. PIL is a bit redundant because it stands for Pirch Interpreted Language. You can view PIL as a bolt-on language to Pirch, separate and different from Pirch aliases. The way you go about writing commands in PIL is different from writing an alias or a remote because the syntax you use is different.

The differences between aliases and PIL don't have to be that confusing. But you won't get too far creating PILs until you completely understand the differences. Before you begin you should have a good grasp of the Pirch commands and built-in variables (identifiers or functions) and how to use them in aliases and remotes. PIL builds on those commands, allowing greater functionality to your scripting.

Having many of the language constructs of a full-blown Windows programming language is actually quite powerful. PIL is based on the Pascal language. If you have ever dabbled in Pascal, PIL is easy to learn. PIL lets you create a variety of windows objects, such as popup windows with list boxes, scroll bars, control buttons, and more.

PILs are created in the Aliases Edit box in Pirch. Because PIL scripts are quite different from aliases, the convention for naming a PIL is to enclose the name in square brackets. This differentiates a PIL script from aliases. For instance, you can name a couple of scripts [MYPIL] or [Script1] instead of MYPIL or Script1.

Again, a PIL is different from an alias. To run an alias, as you already know, you type the name of the alias preceded by the forward slash. To run a PIL you have to use the command /runscript <scriptname>. To run the PIL script named [MYPIL] type /runscript [MYPIL].

You can use parameters with a PIL just as you can with an alias. To run a PIL with parameters add them after the PIL name, separated by spaces. For instance:

```
/runscript [MYPIL] Parameter1 parameter2
```

Tip: If you have a PIL script you use often, create an alias and/or popup for it. For example: /scream /runscript [screamPIL] $1. This runs the PIL script [screamPIL] with an optional parameter as well.

Creating a new PIL is done just as if it were an alias. Go to Aliases, click Add, and give your PIL script a name—remember about the naming convention of using brackets.

Tip: You can also run a PIL script from a remote event.

PIL includes a few standards. These standards include comments, variables, functions, and operators. Each of these standards is an important part of the PIL script.

Comments are usually just that, comments the script writer wrote to help explain what is going on within the script. They are not executable instructions. Comments appearing in a PIL script start with a curly bracket and continue until the closing curly bracket. The ending curly bracket can be many lines later. For instance, { a comment contained between curly brackets }. A space must be placed after the start curly bracket and before the end curly bracket.

Comment brackets are also a useful tool when you need to debug a script. This is called commenting out sections of the script. Instead of deleting these sections and rewriting them later, you can enclose them in curly brackets until you determine where the bug is in your script.

You can use variables in your PIL scripts. With PIL there are two different kinds of variables—string, or text, variables and numeric variables, which are integers only. String variables hold text information, while integer variables hold numbers. String variable names always start with the $ character, for example $myVar.

Variables in a PIL script are set to a value using the := operator. Setting an integer value to equal 2 is written as MyVar := 2;. Notice that the command ends with a semicolon which is a terminator character in scripting.

Another example is $myVar := 'Hello world!';. This variable sets the string variable $myVar to contain the text "Hello World!". In scripting, text has to be enclosed within single quotes.

The previous examples set the variables to what are called literal values, because the numbers or text are literally expressed as 2 or "hello world" as opposed to setting the variable to the result of some other function.

Integer variables are represented as a binary number within the script. String variables are not. String variables can contain numbers. Math operators, such as addition and division, can only be performed on numeric variables, not on string variables. Input parameters to a PIL are in the form of string variables, whether they are numbers or not. You can also use all of Pirch's built-in global variables or identifiers within your PIL scripts.

There are quite a number of functions that you can use in PILs. For a complete list of these functions, see the help file and get familiar with them. In this section we will show you how to use a number of these functions.

Addition, subtraction, multiplication, etc., are some of these functions and they are performed with operators. The most commonly used operators are mathematical operators like:

- \+ addition

- – subtraction
- * multiplication
- / division
- ^ exponential
- mod modulus

Bitwise operators, less commonly used, include:

- shl bitwise shift left
- shr bitwise shift right
- bitand bitwise AND
- bitor bitwise OR
- bitxor bitwise XOR
- bitnot bitwise NOT

The If-then-else statements are one of the most used in scripting. You learned about these and using them in mIRC. They are also available for you to use within the PIL scripts you create.

If statements always make a comparison between two values. If the comparison evaluates to TRUE, then it carries on and does what the statement commands. If FALSE, it jumps down to the Else portion of the statement, if it's there; Else is optional. Here are the comparison operators you can use in creating PILs:

Symbol	*Comparison*	*Example*
=	equal to	(a = b)
>	greater than	(a > b)
>=	greater than or equal to	(a >= b)
<	less than	(a < b)
<=	less than or equal to	(a <= b)

You can also use multiple comparisons within one If statement by using logical operators like the following:

Operator	*Comparison*	*Example*
AND	Logical And	(a and b)
OR	Logical Or	(a or b)
NOT	Logical negation	(not b)

Example 1: A simple PIL

To illustrate how to create a PIL script, we are going to create one with just one line. It uses the PIL function Command() which is one of the most often used functions. It's easier than it sounds. Follow these easy steps:

1. Go to Aliases and click Add.
2. Type [example1] as the name of the PIL script.
3. Add the following line: Command('/display Hello World');.
4. Click Save.
5. In the status window type: /runscript [example1].

6. You should see the words “Hello World” echoed to your screen. Figure 13-f is an example of this script in the Aliases edit box.

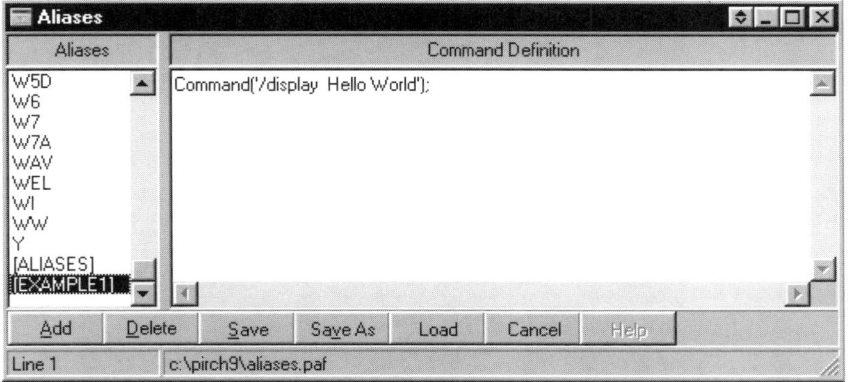

Figure 13-f. Script in Pirch

Command() is one of the most used commands within PIL scripts. You can envision it working as if it typed out the part within parentheses itself in a Pirch window. For instance, Command('/display Hello World'); in a PIL script has the same result as if you typed /display Hello World in the status window yourself. Notice that the command is enclosed in single quotes. As with all PIL functions note that there is also the semicolon terminator character at the end of the command. The Command() function is used to execute IRC and/or Pirch commands such as /join, /msg, etc.

Example 2: Using variables within the Command() function

The previous exercise used a literal command, '/display Hello World'. You can also use variables if you need or want to. The following steps show you how to use variables in a script.

1. Go to Aliases and click Add.
2. Type [example2] as the name of the PIL script.
3. Add the following line: Command('/display ',*1);.
4. Click Save.
5. In the status window type: /runscript [example2] Meow!
6. You should see Meow! painted on your screen.
7. In the status window type: /runscript [example2] George Washington crossed the Delaware. Figure 13-g is an example of this script.

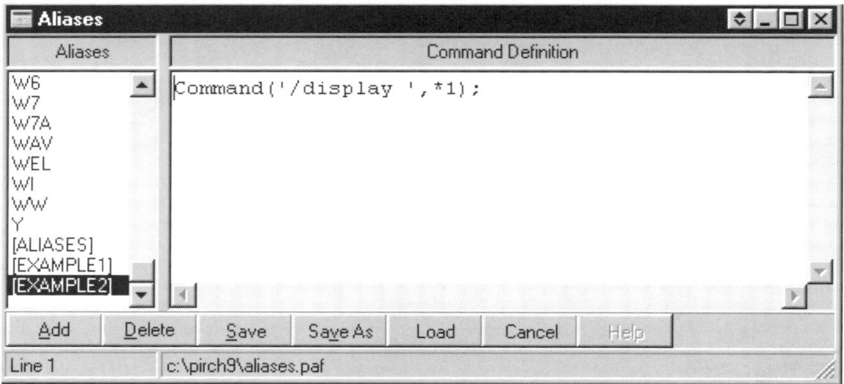

Figure 13-g. Variable within a command script

Here you used the same function. However, in this example you had it use the system variable *1. The *1 means use the first command parameter and all following. And as before, we used the Pirch command /display. This command was enclosed in quotes. Notice that there is a space following the word /display and the ending single quote. If you didn't get yours to work, then that is probably the reason! If you typed /display Meow! on the status line, you have to separate the /display command and the parameter Meow! with a space. The same rules apply when creating a command in a PIL script.

The comma in the command is used to separate multiple items. Notice that the variable is not enclosed in single quotes. You only use the single quotes for literal text.

You can use as many combinations of literal text and variables in the Command() function as you need to. For instance: Command('/msg',' ',$chan,' ','hello all'); is an example of another function command. In this case, the needed space between /msg and the channel name is included as a separate, literal item in the command.

Example 3: If Statement

The If statements are also used quite often. The following PIL script you create takes a number and decides if that number is less than 5.

1. Go to Aliases and click Add.
2. Type [example3] as the name of the PIL script.
3. Add the following lines:

```
test := strtoint($1);
If test < 5 then Command('/display ', $1,' is less than 5');
```

4. Click Save.
5. In the status window type: /runscript [example3] 4. Figure 13-h is an example of this script.

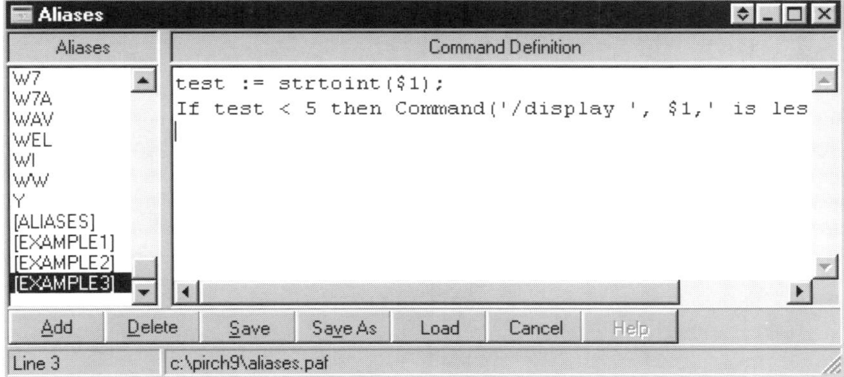

Figure 13-h. If statement in a script

You should see the result 4 is less than 5. Try some other numbers, like 7. How does this script command work? First, you used another PIL command, Strtoint(). That Strtoint function tells the program to convert a string variable to an integer variable. Strtoint stands for STRing TO INTeger. In this example you took the input parameter $1, converted it to an integer type variable, and saved the result in the integer variable Test. Test is an integer variable and does not start with a $.

Test is an integer variable as its name and does not start with a $. There are two types of variables in PIL, an integer and a string. Integers can only hold round numbers (integers) and strings can hold text, words, and numbers. Strings cannot, however, perform math on those numbers, therefore the script treats them as text. The names for string varibles always starts with a dollar sign ($).

Once you convert it to an integer variable—test—then you can compare it with an If statement to see if it is less than 5. If it is less than 5, the If statement continues on and executes the command following the word Then. Should the number be greater than or equal to 5, the program skips the command following the Then.

Example 4: Play a Wave Script

Let's create a PIL script that plays a wave file to the channel and shows the file size of the wav in KB so that other users get an idea about how large the file is.

To do that, we will need to know the file size of the wav file. In the PIL help file, there is the PIL function Filesize(). You use that function in this script. The Filesize function returns the file size in bytes, which is a bit more than you want. Therefore you need to do some math on the result of that function, so you can format the file size in kilobytes, KB. Reading the help on how the Filesize() function works, you learn that if the file doesn't exist, or some error occurred, this function returns -1. You can probably make use of that bit of information too.

The Filesize() function requires the full drive\path\filename so you have to look up what the wave file or sound file path is set to in Pirch on your hard drive. Looking in the help file under variables, you find there is a variable called $soundpath. This is a global variable that tells you the drive and path to the sound files. Once you have the file size, figured some math, and formatted it, you have the script play the wave file to the channel.

1. Go to Aliases and click Add.
2. Type [playWave] as the name of the PIL script.
3. Add the following lines:

```
{ Play a wav PIL }
{ inputs - $1 = wave file (or mid) file name
  $2 = channel or nick to play to
  *3 = optional, additional text
}
{ get file size of wav file }
  $wavfilename := $1;
  $testfile := $soundpath;
  Location := strlen($soundpath);
  StrIns($wavFileName,$testfile,location+1);
  Filelen := Filesize($testfile);
{ test if file exists }
  If Filelen > 0 Then Begin
  { file exists, format file size to kb }
    Kb := Filelen / 1024;
    Decimal := Filelen % 1024;
    $decimal := strcopy(inttostr(decimal),1,2);
  { build up the formatted text string }
    $Formatted := inttostr(kb);
    StrIns('.',$Formatted,strlen($formatted) +1 );
    strins($decimal,$formatted,strlen($formatted) +1);
    $text := '-< ';
    Strins($wavfilename,$text,strlen($text) +1);
    Strins('  ',$text,strlen($text) +1);
    strins($formatted,$text,strlen($text)+1);
    strins('kb',$text,strlen($text)+1);
    Strins(' >-',$text,strlen($text)+1);
  { Let's play it, finally ! }
    Command('/sound ',$2,' ',$wavfilename,' ',$text,' ',*3)
  end;
```

4. Click Save. Figure 13-i is an example of this script.

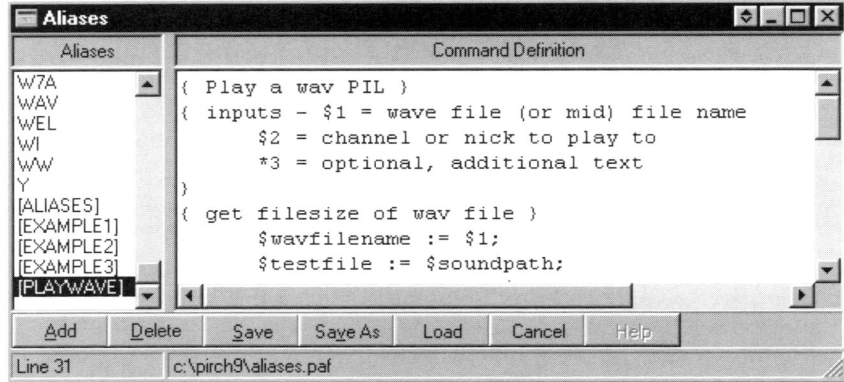

Figure 13-i. Play a Wave script

To run this PIL script, you have to type /runscript [playwav] woohoo.wav #<channelname>. That's not too convenient, so create an alias to make it easier to use as in the following steps:

1. Go to Aliases and click Add.
2. Name the alias.
3. Add the following line to make the alias: /runscript [playwav] $$1 $+ .wav $audience *2.
4. Click Save.

The alias adds the .wav extension to the wav filename.

Now, to play a wav, type /<alias name> <wave name> to play the specified wavename.wav.

This is a PIL script that's a little more involved, so let's tear into how it works. It expects at least two input parameters: the wav/midi filename (filename.wav) and the channel or nick to play it to. The first task is to create a text string that contains the full drive:\path\filename of the sound file. It does that by setting a string variable equal to the global $soundpath variable, then using the strINS() command, which is STRingINSert, appending the filename to the full path where the sound files are stored.

It then uses the Filesize function, the result of which is stored in the integer variable Filelen. Remember, Filesize returns -1 if the file doesn't exist or some other error occurs.

The next line tests to see if the result is greater than 0, figuring that if the file size is 0, it isn't a valid sound file anyhow. If the file size is greater than 0, the script continues, executing the block of lines between Begin and End;. If the result is FALSE, the script skips that block of commands.

First, the script does some math on the returned file size. It determines how many kilobytes there are in the file. The % operator returns the fractional part of the division. Both of these are stored in variables, and then combined later.

Next, it uses the command INTtoSTR to convert the integer variables to string variables, so that you can append those to other text elements. This builds up a text string, bit by bit, in the string variable $text. This is what you want it to look like: -< filename.wav 12.34kb >-. Then, when the script has performed its functions, it sends the /sound command to play the wave and include the file size.

PIL also gives you the ability to create and manipulate many of the window objects, such as control buttons, list boxes, even playing cards. These allow you to create nifty user interfaces for your PIL scripts.

Window objects have several properties that you have to define. These include:

- the location of the window
- the height and width of the window

First you define the location of the object. This is where on the screen it is to show up. You do this with two parameters, Top and Left.

These two points are an X,Y location on the screen. This represents where the top left corner of the window is to be located.

The window coordinates start at 0 for the very top of the screen and increase in number to the bottom of the screen. The value of the bottom of the screen depends on what screen resolution you are using, e.g., 640 x 480 or 800 x 600, etc.

The Left parameter starts at 0 for the left of the screen and increases in number. The Width parameter specifies how wide the window should be, starting from the left and moving towards the right. The Height parameter defines how tall the window or object should be, starting from the top and moving down.

Let's make a window object. It is more obvious how these parameters fit together when you play with one. The command to create a window object is CreateWindow($titletext,top,left,width,height);. This is how the command actually looks:

```
$titleText := 'window example';
top := 10;
Left := 10;
width := 450;
height := 150;
popup := createwindow($titleText,left,top,width,height);
```

Figure 13-j is an example of this script.

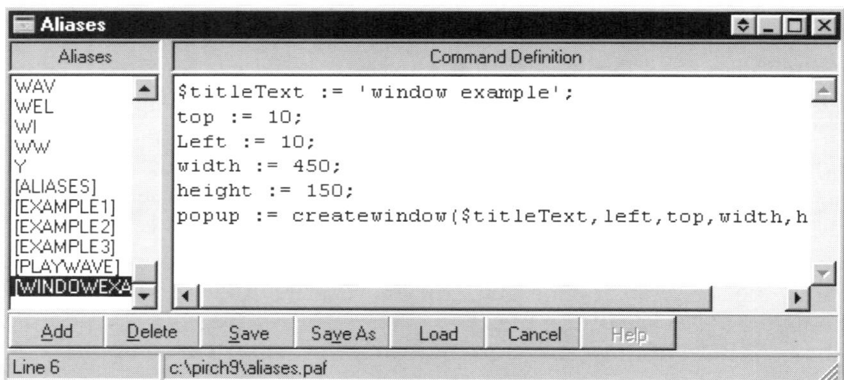

Figure 13-j. Window manipulation script

Now run this script. Try changing the variables for Top, Left, Width, and Height, rerunning the script to see the different effects.

Let's add a control to that window, say a push button. To do this, use the CreateGadget(parent,gadgetType,left,top,width,height) function.

Notice that the result of the CreateWindow function is stored to an integer variable. This value is the WindowID of that window that we can use when creating gadgets.

Read the help file for the function CreateGadget to get a feel for what you can do with it. Notice that the Top/Left parameters for a gadget are now not relative to the screen but relative to the inside of the parent window. In the help file, you see that a button is gadgetType = 4, so let's use that to make one for your window:

```
$titleText := 'window example';
Left := 100;
Top := 100;
width := 485;
height := 140;
popup := createwindow($titleText,left,top,width,height);
button := createGadget(popup,4,390,10, 75,25);
```

When you run that, you should see a click-able button on top of your window. You probably won't see any text on the button yet, however. When you want to set text for these buttons and window captions, use the SetWindowText() function. You should read about this function in the help file and get familiar with it. Since you are adding a gadget, let's add another gadget, a window panel within the window. Make your code look like this:

```
$titleText := 'window example';
Left := 100;
Top := 100;
width := 485;
height := 140;
popup := createwindow($titleText,left,top,width,height);
button := createGadget(popup,4,390,10, 75,25);
panel := createGadget(popup,10,3,3,380,110);
setwindowText(button,'click me');
```

When you type /runscript [windowtest], you see your button with the label "click me" and a panel within the window.

Getting button clicks and other events to do something from window objects requires setting an event. You have to assign an alias or script to run when you click on that particular button. The way to do that is with the setEvent() function. You can read about that in the help file to get more details. To create these getting button clicks, you can use any valid Pirch command, an alias, or another PIL.

If you need to use PIL scripting to handle the event, then you have two choices. You can create a new and separate PIL to handle the event, or you can use the same PIL but with a little extra code. The latter method makes the PIL self contained, or all in one file rather than spread across a collection of files. You can do this by calling the same PIL script and using an input parameter. Examine the modifications to this code segment:

```
IF $1 = 'start' then begin
  { inital startup code here }
  $titleText := 'window example';
  Left := 100;
  Top := 100;
  width := 485;
  height := 140;
  popup := createwindow($titleText,left,top,width,height);
  button := createGadget(popup,4,390,10, 75,25);
  panel := creategadget(popup,10,3,3,380,110);
  setwindowText(button,'click me');
  setevent(button,1,'/runscript [windowtest] click');
```

```
end;
If $1 = 'click' then begin
  { do the stuff you want to do when you click the button here}
end;
```

What are the differences here? One, to run the script, you now have to use the input parameter "start"—i.e., /runscript [windowtest] start. When $1, the first parameter, is equal to "start," it runs the code that puts up the windows and buttons and assigns the button click event to /runscript [windowtest] click.

Now let's add some code so something happens when the button is clicked. There are a large number of attributes that you can change for many of the windows and gadgets. The function to do this is SetWindowAttr(windowid,attribute,value). Take a look at that function in the PIL help file. In this PIL help file you see a large number of attributes that are changeable for each window gadget type. Some of these only apply to certain types of gadgets.

For this example, let's change the background color of the inner window panel. Background color is attribute number 1 and the value of the color can be anywhere in the range of 0 to 16,777,215. That's a lot of color selections!

Using the Random() function, you can pick a random number from 0 to 16,777,215 and then change the color of the panel to that number. Make your code look like this:

```
if $1 = 'start' then begin
  { startup code here }
  $titleText := 'window example';
  Left := 100;
  Top := 100;
  width := 485;
  height := 140;
  popup := createwindow($titleText,left,top,width,height);
  button := createGadget(popup,4,390,10, 75,25);
  panel := creategadget(popup,10,3,3,380,110);
  setwindowText(button,'click me');
  setevent(button,1,'/runscript [windowtest] click');
end;
If $1 = 'click' then begin
  { button click event code here }
  color := random(16777215);
  setwindowAttr(panel,1,color);
end;
```

Figure 13-k is an example of this script.

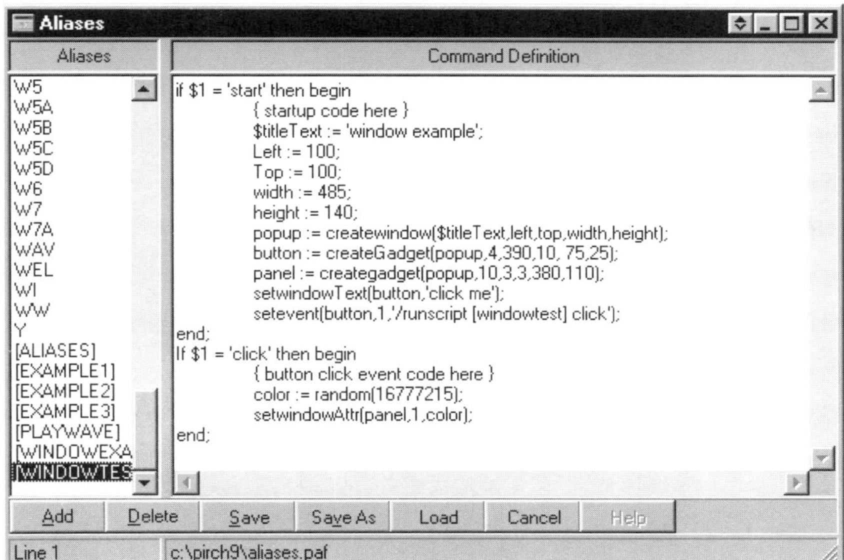

Figure 13-k. Button Click script

Now run this script by typing /runscript [windowtest] start. When you click the button, the color of the panel should change.

Try changing this PIL script around to change different attributes. PIL scripting could fill an entire book, but the best way to learn is by example. Collect other PILs, examine them to learn how they work, and try some of your own.

Several IRC users have created scripts for mIRC and Pirch. You can find these on various sites on the web. Here are a few of these sites:

- http://home.concepts.nl/~renegade/ — Pirch and mIRC scripts
- http://www.rtis.com/ryan/scripts.htm — Pirch scripts
- http://pirch.simplenet.com/scripts/index.htm — Pirch scripts
- http://www.ctfire.com/ — mIRC scripts
- http://www.snip.net/users/matt/MIRC/scripts.html — mIRC scripts

Between what you've learned here about how to create scripts and the scripts you can download from the web, you should be able to alter your IRC clients to do just about anything you want them to. If you have no programming background, learning how to create scripts is not going to be easy for you. This chapter should help you in this endeavor.

Exercises

There were several examples included in the Pirch PIL section so these exercises are for mIRC users only. Use the section in this chapter on mIRC scripts to assist you in creating the following exercises. Also use the help files for mIRC to assist you.

mIRC

1. Create an If-then-else script.
2. Create a script that gives you the length of a file.
3. Create a time script.
4. Create a total pings script.
5. Create a variable for a ping event.

Chapter 14
Bots

In this chapter you learn:

- ☑ *What are Bots?*
- ☑ *How to Use Bots*
- ☑ *Tips on Using Bots*
- ☑ *How to Create Bots*
- ☑ *How to Create a Bot in mIRC*
- ☑ *Automatic Bot Functions*
- ☑ *How to Create a Bot in Pirch*
- ☑ *Running Your Bot*

What are Bots?

Almost from the first time you visit IRC, you notice an anomaly on the channels. This anomaly is something called a *bot*. You either hear the word bot bandied about or you see some of these creatures on some of the channels you visit.

When you ask other users what a bot is or what bot means you get a variety of answers. The technical description or definition of a bot is that it is a self-running program. For the purposes of IRC it is a self-running program that generally handles mundane tasks for you or the other users on your channel. However, bots can come in many different forms and handle many different activities. The function of bots is all dependent on how they are programmed and what they are programmed to do for you and other IRC users.

Bots are basically scripts that are created to respond to commands given to the program by the creator of the bot or other IRC users. They also respond to certain events performed by users on a channel.

For the purpose of this book and your understanding I have separated bots into three categories—channel bots, personal bots, and war and protection bots. Each type of bot has its own functions and uses for you and your channel.

Channel Bots

On several of the nets, like the UnderNet, Starlink, ChatNet, and SuperChat, you can register your channel with the net administrators. Once you register a channel on one of these nets, you get the protection of the net as well as a channel that's open around the clock. The channel bot serves the purpose of providing you with both of these things. It keeps your channel open around the clock and helps to protect your channel.

When you register a channel, you must first apply to the net administrators. They require that you give them information about the channel you want to register such as the name and purpose of the channel. They also request that you have at least ten supporters. For the supporters, they ask for their nicknames and e-mail addresses. This is to make sure that you have enough support for the channel to ensure that it is successful.

Some of these nets let you register any kind of channel that you want and some limit the types of channels they register. Several of these nets do not register or allow channels that are sex or hacker oriented. The UnderNet registers any type of channel a user wants as long as it has supporters and no one objects to the channel.

Each net has a certain amount of time it takes to process your application to register a channel. For instance, the UnderNet takes an average of ten days to review and process your application.

During this waiting period, the administrators notify the supporters on your list to give them an opportunity to protest the registration. They also post your application for a channel to their newsletter to give anyone else an opportunity to protest.

After the waiting period is up, the net administrators send you an e-mail notifying you that your application has been approved. Along with the notification, they send you instructions about how to use your channel bot. You're now ready to invite your channel bot to your channel and start using it. In addition to the instructions for the bot, the UnderNet also offers weekly channel bot classes. In these classes they go into more detail about how to use the channel bot.

The UnderNet has two bots it issues to channels. These are X bot and W bot. The other nets generally have only one bot. Some of the nets let you give your channel bot a name. The UnderNet does not. DALnet has special servers that register channels and nicknames. These special servers are called ChanServe. The server acts the same as a channel bot in many ways.

ChanServe does basically the same thing for you as a channel bot without the bot being physically present in the channel. When you connect to a DALnet server and create your channel, you can send a message to ChanServe to register your channel name. Then each time you log onto DALnet, you find your channel there. When you join your channel, you are automatically given ops because you are the registered channel owner. You can then set up trusted friends to also get ops on your channel from ChanServe when they logon and join the channel.

Once you get your channel registered, it's time to learn how to use your channel bot. Go to the section "How to Use Bots" to find out more about how to use and manage your channel bot.

Personal Bots

Personal bots come in a variety of flavors. They are usually created for one of two purposes. One reason people use personal bots is to keep channels open and to issue ops to them and others on the bot's user list. The other is for fun and games.

There are almost as many types of personal bots as there are people to create them. There are bar bots, poker bots, game bots, and various other personal type bots.

These personal bots are designed to perform certain functions for their creators and channels. For instance, bar bots greet people when they come into a channel and serve drinks and snacks to them. They act like a bartender at a bar you visit in real life. Poker and game bots deal cards or otherwise administer or monitor games for users.

Using scripts and special commands, you can create bots to do just about anything you want them to. They can keep track of when other members of your channel were on last, give you the time, automatically op members, and so forth.

If you can create scripts or commands, you can create a bot to perform activities for you. If you can't create scripts or commands, there is hope. Other people have created numerous kinds of bots. You can find these on the web and use them instead of trying to create your own.

Following are a few sites on the web where you can find bots you can use:

- http://www.rtis.com/ryan/bots.htm — Pirch bots
- http://www.ctfire.com/ — mIRC bots
- http://pw1.netcom.com/~aircool/mirc.html — mIRC bots
- http://www.naz.com/personal/cer/botts.html — mIRC bots
- http://www.inetw.net/~syclops/irc/bots.html — IRC bots
- http://www.intrepid.net/~jpm3/bots.htm — war bots
- http://www.inetone.net/master/mircbots.html — mIRC bots
- http://shoga.wwa.com/~edge/bots.html — IRC bots
- htpp://www.newnet.net/bots.html — IRC bots
- http://www.xcalibre.com/bots.htm — IRC bots
- http://www.digitalsquid.com/digitalsquid/pc/ircbots.html — IRC bots
- http://www.demtrip.simplenet.com/mirc.html — mIRC bots

Later in this chapter, you learn how to create your own bot, as well as how to use bots. These personal bots can be fun and perform mundane activities for you and the other members of your channel. They can add a little excitement to your channel and entertainment for your friends.

War and Protection Bots

Another common type of bot you sometimes see on IRC is the protection or war bot. Some of the war bots are created to cause chaos or havoc on channels. Some of these war bots are used to protect channels from hostile takeovers.

These bots are very aggressive and are designed to take aggressive actions against anyone who tries to take over a channel or who is being unduly annoying or irritating. They are designed to be nasty characters that resort to flooding, kicking, banning, and k-lining anyone who steps over the line and triggers their commands. Users or the owners of these bots can also issue commands to activate the aggressive behavior against another user.

War and protection bots are frowned upon by other IRC users. They are considered a nuisance. We do not show you how to create these type of bots in this book. However, if you really want one of these bots, others have created some excellent ones and you can get them from any of the sites listed in the previous section. Those sites contain both personal bots as well as war and protection bots.

Bots of any kind and especially war bots, as a general rule, are not welcome on most IRC servers on many of the nets. When you log onto an IRC server, pay attention to the MOTD. If a server doesn't allow bots, it tells you in its MOTD. Some servers let you have bots on them if you ask for permission first. You can find e-mail addresses for the server administrators via the MOTD also. Send them an e-mail stating the purpose of your bot and ask permission to use their server for your bot.

How to Use Bots

The three different types of bots have their own unique ways that you use them. Some of them you have to issue commands to, some are activated by events the users in your channels perform, and others require you to message them or send them special characters to activate the scripts or activities they perform.

Channel bots have their own set of commands and how those commands are activated. The different nets have their own versions of channel bots and how those bots work.

It is advisable to get the help files for the bot you are planning to use, no matter which kind of bot it is. Some of these help files can be found on the web and some of them are part of the bot's files. Check the bot's files first and if you don't find a help file there, then go to the web page for the net that owns the bot and search for help pages there.

The personal and war or protection bots should come with a readme file or a help file. Be sure to check for these files when you install the bot and before you begin using it. These files help prevent you from making mistakes while you're learning to use the bot. They can also reduce the learning curve.

Channel Bots

When you register a channel, you become the channel owner and the administrator for the channel bot. As the administrator, you are in charge of the bot. You decide who you trust enough to get operator's status from the bot. As channel owner/administrator, it is up to you to make the decisions about how your channel operates. You make the rules and set the guidelines. Technically, you can do this by yourself or you can collaborate with others like a committee to help you set guidelines for your channel. Refer back to Chapter 4 to refresh your memory on these techniques.

For the purposes of this book, we are only covering the channel bots for the UnderNet. These are the most difficult of the bots to learn. Once you master these channel bots, the others are easier to master.

The UnderNet is set up and run by committees. Two of these committees that are important to you are the UnderNet Channel Service Committee and the UnderNet User Committee.

The UnderNet Channel Service Committee issues one of two channel bots to registered channels. These channel bots are called X and W. They both function exactly the same. These two bots each hold separate user lists for each of the channels they are registered to. These user lists contain the users you designate to have access to your channel bot. You can also give your trusted friends access levels that allow them to use certain functions with the bots.

The highest level access you can give another user is that of channel operator. This person helps you to maintain the atmosphere of the channel. These channel operators have a responsibility to you and to abide by the Channel Service Rules just as you do.

Just because you have a channel bot and establish a user list with the bot doesn't mean you can't give other users ops status through the bot or through the usual means. You can, however, make sure these users do not have access to the channel bot. When you give someone ops or access to the bot, make sure they understand their responsibilities. If they kick or ban the bot from the channel, Channel Service considers that abuse and reacts very quickly. If this sort of abuse continues to happen, they can take the bot away from you and unregister the channel.

There are a few commands anyone can use to get information from these channel bots. For instance, if you want to find out who registered the channel, send a message to either of the bots: /msg x (or w) chaninfo #<channelname>. If you want to find out what access level a user has, type /msg x (or w) access #channelname> <nickname>. This command also tells you if a user has access to the bot. Figure 14-a shows you how the messages look and what you get from the bot when you enter those messages.

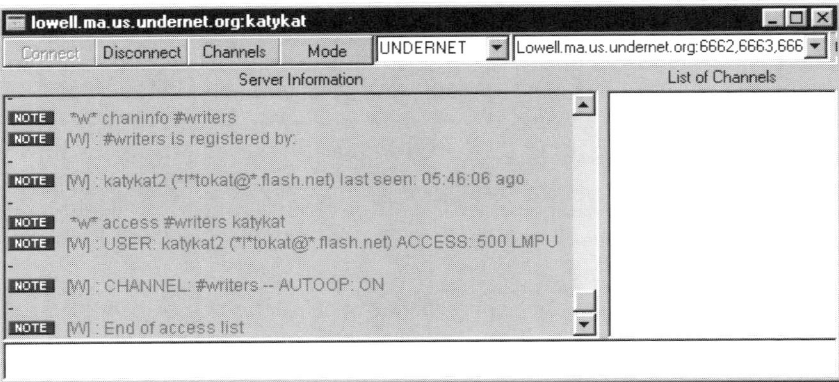

Figure 14-a. Bot messages

When your channel is registered and you are issued a bot, as channel manager you are given 500 level access, also known as Cservice, to the bot by Channel Service. Once you have this access you can add others to the bot's user list and give them access levels. No one can have a 500 level access but you, the owner of the channel. Following are the levels you can assign users and the functions and commands they can use:

- 500 Level — channel owner/manager only. With this level you have full control of the bot and can use all the commands.
- 450-499 Level — trusted channel administrator. These users can add or remove the channel to and from the bot, request the bot join or leave the channel, as well as add or remove users from the bot's user list.
- 400 Level — user list administrator and also trusted channel operators who help with administrative responsibilities. These users can add and remove users from the bot's user list, clear channel mode, modify information and access levels for users in the bot's user list, and get status information on the bot and the channel.
- 100 Level — channel operator. These users can perform through the bot all typical op commands along with a few special bot commands. They can op and deop other users, invite users to the channel, and suspend and unsuspend a user's access to the bot for a specified amount of time, as well as kick and ban/unban other users.
- 50-75 Level — new channel operator or channel regular. These users can also perform through the bot normal channel op commands and a few special bot commands. They can perform the same commands as the 100 level users. However, the 50 level users cannot ban or unban other users.
- 0 Level — all other users not on the bot's user list. These users can only get information from the bot like access levels, ban list, channel information, deauthorization for their password, help, login, map, MOTD, new password on themselves, password, show commands, and show ignores and verifies.

All the higher level ops can do all the commands listed for them as well as any listed for the lower level ops. The higher ops like the 500 level can set protections on the channel and the users. All commands to the bots must be sent as a message to the bot and must use the correct syntax for the command to work. Following are the commands' syntax and the access levels that can use them. These commands are sent to the bot as /msg x (or w) set #<channel name> <variable> <value>.

500 Level variables — this level of user can do all of the following as well as those for the lower level users:

- MassDeopPro — sets the maximum number of deops the bot allows in a 15-second period. Anyone who exceeds this number is deopped and his ops suspended if he is on the bot's user list. The command is /msg x (or w) set #<channel name> MassDeopPro 5.
- FloodPro — sets the maximum number of kicks, topic changes, and so forth that can be done in the channel in a 15-second period. Anyone who exceeds this number is kicked and his ops suspended. This command only works for those events that take place through the bot, not those done in the channel alone. The command is /msg x (or w) set #<channel name> FloodPro 10.
- UserFlag — sets default user settings that are given to new users on a channel. These include 0 for Autoop Off and 1 for Autoop On. The command is /msg x (or w) set #<channel name> UserFlag 0 (or 1).
- NoOp — sets the channel to no ops. The bot deops everyone which makes it the only one with ops on the channel. Users can still access the bot and issue commands through it. The command is /msg x (or w) set #<channel name> NoOp.
- AlwaysOp — sets the bot to always have ops on the channel. The message is /msg x (or w) set #<channel name> Alwaysop. It is advisable to set this command when you first get the bot for your channel.
- OpOnly — sets ops as the only command that users can issue to the bot. However, they can still use normal ops commands, just not through the bot. The command is /msg x (or w) set #<channel name> Oponly.
- StrictOp — sets the bot to only allow those on its user list to have ops. All others are deopped by the bot. Users must send a password to the bot before they can get ops. The command is /msg x (or w) set #<channel name> Strictop.
- Lang — sets the default language for the channel to one you specify. The languages the bot recognizes are en for English, al for Dutch, fe for French, and ge for German. The command is /msg x (or w) set #<channel name> lang en (al, fe, or ge).
- Description — sets the default channel topic. However it doesn't affect the actual topic. The command is /msg x (or w) set #<channel name> description <channel topic>.
- URL — sets the default channel URL which is seen from the chaninfo or the web page. The command is /msg x (or w) set #<channel name> URL <your channel's web page address>.
- AutoTopic — causes the bot to change the topic to the URL and Description every 30 seconds. This topic doesn't work when the channel is idle (when no one is on the channel). The command is /msg x (or w) set #<channel name> Autotopic On (or Off).

450 + Level variables — can set the following commands as well as AlwaysOp, UserFlag, MassDeopPro, URL, and Description:

- AddChan — adds your channel to the bot's database and sets the channel's default modes. You must use this command when you first get your channel bot, otherwise the bot won't remember to come back to your channel after splits or if he's taken down for maintenance or repairs. The command is /msg x (or w) Addchan #<channel name>.
- Join — instructs the bot to join your channel. You use this command when you first get the bot and anytime it does not automatically rejoin the channel after splits or being taken down for repairs. The command is /msg x (or w) Join #<channel name>.
- Part — tells the bot to leave your channel. The command is /msg x (or w) Part #<channel name>.
- RemChan — removes your channel modes from the bot's database. You can use this command when you want to change your channel modes. You do have to ask the bot to rejoin the channel after you use this command. The command is /msg x (or w) Remchan #<channel name>.

400 Level variables:

- Adduser — lets you add users to the bot's user list database and give them access levels. You can only give another user an access level lower than your own. The user must then set his or her password to access the bot and get ops. The bots are now set up to only recognize users that have passwords set up with them. The command is /msg x (or w) adduser #<channel name> <nick> <user@host - the user's address> <level>.
- Clearmode — clears all channel modes. This command is used when the channel gets locked up or someone sets the modes to K (keyed) or L (limited). The command is /msg x (or w) clearmode #<channel name>.
- ModInfo — changes a user's access level and lets you set them up for auto ops and protection by the bot. The command is /msg x (or w) modinfo #<channel name> <variable> <nick> <value>. Variables and values for this command include: autoop on (or off), protect on (or off), access level, match, user@host — changes user's ID, and rempass — removes the user's password.
- Remuser — removes a user from the bot's user list. You have to have higher access than the user you are trying to remove or the command doesn't work. The command is /msg x (or w) remuser #<channel name> <nick>.
- Status — gives you all the special bot modes, channel modes, and the number of users in the channel. The command is /msg x (or w) status #<channel name>.

100 Level variables:

- Deop — deops users on the channel. The command is /msg x (or w) deop #<channel name> <nick or nicks>.
- Invite — uses the bot to invite someone to the channel. The command is /msg x (or w) invite #<channel name> <nick>.
- Op — lets you give ops status through the bot to user. The command is /msg x (or w) op #<channel name> <nick>.
- Suspend — suspends the user's access to the bot for a specified amount of time like seconds, minutes, hours, or days. You can only use this command on users

with lower levels than yours. The command is /msg x (or w) suspend #<channel name> <nick> <user@host> <duration - s, m, h, d>.

- Unsuspend — takes the suspend off a user. The command is /msg x (or w) unsuspend #<channel name> <nick>.

75 Level variables:

- Ban — bans a user from the channel using the bot. When you use this command, the bot bans the user and then kicks him from the channel. You can also include the reason for the ban and how long the ban is to remain in effect. The command is /msg x (or w) ban #<channel name> <nick> <user@host if the user isn't in the channel> <duration in hours> <level — 20-74 keeps them from getting ops and 75 + prevents a user from joining the channel> <reason>. If you prefer not to set the duration, level, and reason, you can just type /msg x (or w) ban #<channel name> <nick>. The bot gives the user a 100 level and bans them for a week by default.
- Unban — removes a user from the ban list. The command is /msg x (or w) unban #<channel name> <nick>.

50 Level variables:

- Kick — kicks a user from the channel through the bot. The command is /msg x (or w) kick #<channel name> <nick> <reason — optional>.
- Topic — changes the topic on the channel. The command is /msg x (or w) topic #<channel name> <your topic>.

0 Level variables:

- Access — lets a user get the access level information on any user, whether they have access to the bot or not, using either a nick or a string. The command is /msg x (or w) access #<channel name> <nick> or <string — *!*@*.host>.
- Banlist — lets a user get the channel's banlist but the user must be on the channel for this command to work. The command is /msg x (or w) banlist #<channel name>.
- Chaninfo — displays who the channel is registered to as well as the default topic and URL if one is set. The command is /msg x (or w) chaninfo #<channel name>.
- Deauth — lets you deauthorize yourself and remove your password. The command is /msg x (or w) deauth #<channel name>.
- Help — gives you help file information and help information about commands. The command is /msg x (or w) help <command>.
- Lbanlist — searches the bot's banlist for a certain string. The command is /msg x (or w) lbanlist #<channel name> <search string — user@host or *!*@*.host>.
- Login — lets you log into the bot and get access. The command is /msg x@channels.undernet.org or /msg w@channels2.undernet.org login #<channel name> <password>.
- Map — gives you a map of connected servers. The command is /msg x (or w) map.
- MOTD — gives the bot's MOTD. The command is /msg x (or w) motd.
- Newpass — lets you set or change your password with the bot. Everyone who gets access to the bot must set a password. The command is /msg x (or

w)@channels.undernet.org (or @channels2.undernet.org) newpass #<channel name> <your password>.

- Pass — sends your password to the bot so you can get access. The command is /msg x (or w) @channels.undernet.org (or @channels2.undernet.org) pass #<channel name> <your password>.
- Showcommands — gives you all the commands you can use with the bot. The command is /msg x (or w) showcommands #<channel name>.
- Showignore — gives you the bot's ignore list. The command is /msg x (or w) showignore.
- Verify — shows you whether a user is a registered Cservice representative. The command is /msg x (or w) verify <nick>.

All the previous commands help you and those you add to the bot's user list with ways to protect yourselves and your channel. These lists help you learn how to use the bots that the Cservice gives you to protect and maintain your channel.

Tips on Using Bots

Create aliases to speed up some often used bot commands. For instance, the UnderNet channel service bots, W and X, have a long login command to identify yourself with them. It is advisable to create an alias for it. In mIRC it is:

/passW /msg W@channels2.undernet.org PASS <YourPasswordHere>

Now typing /passW sends your login to the W bot. This command is so often used that you could automate it fully. In mIRC's perform section (the perform section runs the commands every time you connect to a server), you can have mIRC play a modified version of the above alias:

/passW IF (Undernet.ORG isin $server) { /msg W@channels2.undernet.org PASS YourPasswordHere }

or

/passX IF (Undernet.ORG isin $server) { /msg X@channels.undernet.org PASS YourPasswordHere }

This alias tests to see if you are connected to an UnderNet server first, and if so, then sends the login command to W bot. Put /passW in the perform section of mIRC, and it logs you in as soon as you connect to an UnderNet server. You could also use a function key alias as another way to do this same activity.

You might want to create popups for some of the bot commands to make them faster and easier to use, and because you might not remember the command when the time comes to use it. Here are some sample popups for use in mIRC's nicklist popups. If you implement slight modifications, these work in Pirch also.

```
&W Control
.&W Access:/msg W access # $*1
.&W Adduser 100:/msg W adduser $$1 100
.-
.&W OPs:/msg w op $replace($snicks,$chr(44),$chr(32))
.&W Deop:/msg w deop $replace($snicks,$chr(44),$chr(32))
.&W Kick:/msg W kick $$1 $?="Enter Kick Reason"
.-
.&W ban:/msg w ban $$1 14 99 $?="Enter Reason for Wban"
```

```
.&W ban manual:/msg w ban $$?="Enter ban mask (*!*dude@*.some.com)"
       99 99 $?="Enter Reason"
.&W noOP ban:/msg w ban $$1 14 20
.&W remove w ban:/msg w unban $?="what nick (or mask) to unban?"
.help:{
  echo 6 -a %motif W ban help
  echo 6 -a %motif Sets a ban via Wbot - if you have access for it.
  echo 6 -a %motif w ban manual does too, but you specify the ban mask
  echo 6 -a %motif w noop ban, tells W not to let nick have ops
  echo 6 -a %motif remove ban, removes the ban from W's banlist for nick
       ( or full address )
}
```

Personal, War, and Protection Bots

Once you either create your own bot or get one from one of the sites listed earlier in this chapter, you need to install it onto your hard drive. There are a couple of ways you can do this.

For bots you use with mIRC, copy the mirc.exe file as a new filename. You can name it mirc2.exe. Take the main .ini file for the bot you're going to use and put it in your c:\windows directory and rename it mirc2.ini. Next, run the new .exe file; the bot should load into it.

Another option is to copy the mIRC program into a second and differently named directory. Put your bot files in the second mIRC directory and run the second copy of mIRC. However, if you have the 32-bit version of mIRC, you don't need to use two separate copies of mIRC. You can simply run mIRC twice. With Pirch bots you simply choose a different server and log on to run your bot.

Once you load the bot into your program, connect to a server that allows bots. Other than events the bot automatically responds to, you and users on your channel need to issue commands to the bot to get it to perform the way it is programmed to. For personal bots, all commands can be issued in private messages to the bot or on the channel. All commands begin with an exclamation mark. For instance, if you have a bot set up to tell users when another user was last on your channel, you type !seen <nick>. See Figure 14-b for an example of this command to a personal bot.

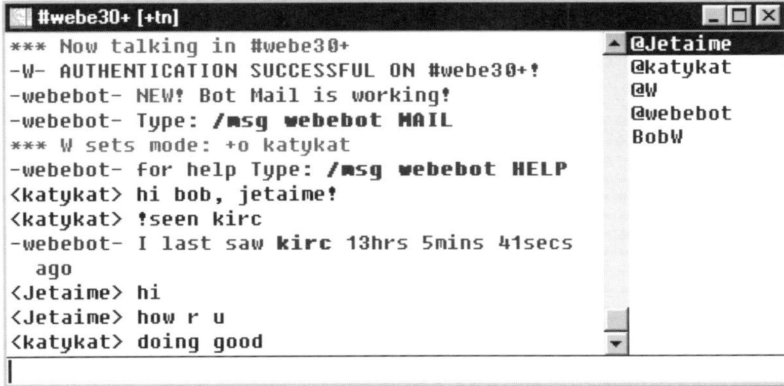

Figure 14-b. Personal bot commands

Each bot has its own set of commands and how to issue those commands. Read the help files and readme files to find out what your bot does and how to make it do the things it does. These files should tell you how to issue commands as well as what events the bot automatically responds to. This is true for personal, war, and protection bots.

How to Create Bots

One of the easiest ways to learn how to create a bot is to read the .ini files for a few bots. See how these bots are set up to work. There are also some useful bot FAQs and scripting FAQs on the web you can get to help you. You can find a bot FAQ at http://www.xcalibre.com/botFAQ.htm and a scripting FAQ at http://www.xcalibre.com/scripting.htm.

When you study other bots to learn how to create your own, be very careful not to take someone else's creations and claim them as your own. Their creators are likely to get very upset with you and could press charges against you for copyright infringement.

Read these FAQs and also use this chapter and the previous chapter about scripts to help you learn how to create your own bot. With the help of this chapter and section, you can learn to create a simple bot to use with mIRC or Pirch.

If you're off to start a new bot, spend a little time thinking about how the bot should react. Is it going to be sharp-tempered? Is it going to be quick to kick people or more mild-mannered? Designing a bot is a lot like designing a machine. It helps to list what you want it to do and how it will react. These define the bot's personality.

Most bots are made up of the following elements:

- set of commands to respond to
- set of IRC events it will respond to
- list of known users that it will accept commands from, usually two or more levels of users

To be effective, most bots have a list of known users, so that only those users can issue it commands, such as grant ops. Often there are two to four levels of users and the commands they can issue to the bot, for instance, bot owner commands, op level commands, friends level commands, and then everyone else.

The user list is a list of users, defined by their user/host address, often with wild cards. Using wild cards ensures that the user can use whatever nick he/she chooses, and the bot still recognizes them. In more sophisticated bots, the users have a password also, which is a more secure method of identifying the user. This is to combat "spoofing." Spoofing is when another user tries to take on the identity of a regular on a channel in order to get ops from the members there or from the bot. For example if you use only the user/host mask, like *!*funnyguy@*aol.com to identify a user, any user from that host could change his or her userID to funnyguy, and gain access to the bot. Having both User@host and a password makes it much more difficult for someone to do this. However, this is harder to code than using the user@host mask only.

Consider how you want the bot to handle the user list maintenance. Decide if you want to manually add people to the bot, or if you need to make a set of commands to let you and others maintain, add, remove, and edit the user list remotely.

The next thing you need to decide is how you want commands that are issued to be accepted by the bot. Are they to be text sent to the channel? Are they to be in the form of messages to the bot? Do you want the bot commands to be issued in DCC chat message windows? Or do you want to use a combination of all of these?

The way commands are processed by the bots becomes easier if the commands have a similarity to them. For instance, all commands to the UnderNet channel bots W and X are performed via /msg. It is easier for the person who programs the bot and easier for the users to remember how to issue commands if the method is universal for all commands. Writing bots in mIRC or Pirch is just like writing scripts. You are writing scripts to make the program perform the way you want it to. You are also setting up remote events to respond to events users perform in your channel.

The purpose of a user list is to help the bot program differentiate between users and the commands they can issue it. For instance, you might want one level for users that have op access to the bot, and another level for everyone else. Once you have a user list with levels set up, you can code the bot to respond differently to events and commands depending on the level of the user issuing the command or performing the event.

How to Create a Bot in mIRC

In mIRC and Pirch, bot scripts make use of the built-in user level mechanism. For instance, let's write an event to give someone ops in a mIRC bot. If they were entered into the user list at the appropriate user level, the command to get ops from this mIRC example bot is: /msg <botnick> op. Next let's say we have only two user levels, op level users at level 10 and everyone else at level 1. The text event in a mIRC bot looks like this:

```
ON 10:TEXT:OP*:?:/mode #<channelname> +o $nick
ON 1:TEXT:op*:?:/notice $nick do I know you?
```

So we have two events, one for level 10 users, one for level 1 users. mIRC defaults to level 1 users for everyone who doesn't appear in your user list. Users that try to get ops get the notice "do I know you" back. Level 10 users, if they are on your channel, get ops. The ? in the event, after the op*: makes the event only respond to private messages, rather than channel text.

For someone to be a level 10 user, they must be added to the bot's user list. The way to do that in mIRC is to type the command in the channel window: /guser 10 <nick> 3. We discussed the /guser command in previous chapters. Refer back to those chapters if you need a reminder on how to use this command.

Typing the /guser command in the bot's channel window isn't always convenient, and not possible for someone who isn't at your computer. So, you may want a few user list maintenance commands to enable remote users to add or delete users from the list. You may even want to make a separate, higher level for users who have access to the commands to let them add and delete other users from the bots user list. For this example bot, we stick to our two user levels. The following are command scripts you create for the bot to enable you to add and delete users from the bot's user list:

```
On 10:TEXT:ADDUSER *:?: {
  If ($2 != $null ) { /guser 10 $2 3 }
  Else { /notice $nick Sytnax: /msg $me ADDUSER <nick> }
}
On 10:TEXT:REMuser *:?: {
  If ($2 != $null ) { /ruser $2 }
  Else { /notice $nick Syntax: /msg $me REMUSER <nick> }
}
```

These two events are simple user list add and remove commands. They respond to a user typing /msg <botnick> Adduser <nick> when they want to add a user to the user list, and /msg <botnick> Remuser <nick> when they want to remove a user from the user list. This script forces the bot to first test to see if a nick was entered; if not, it sends a help message. If the nick was entered correctly, the bot runs a mIRC command to add or remove the nick from the user list. These are simple commands. A more sophisticated way to create a similar command script is to make sure that the nick parameter is a valid nick. In other words, ensure that the nick is actually on IRC or at least on the channel before trying to add the nick. Then you can have the bot send a confirmation message back to the user that the nick has actually been added to the list.

We are going to create a fairly simple bot for this book and you. At any time you can always add to these goals and to the commands for the bot.

To begin we must create the design criteria. The first thing you need to consider is the user list and the levels you want for the various types of users you have coming to your channel. These may include the following user levels:

- Op level users
- Everyone else

Next you need to consider what bot commands these users can issue to the bot. You want to break these commands down into categories for the different level users you have in the bot's user list.

For the purpose of our sample bot, we want op level users to be able to:

- get ops from the bot
- deop someone
- kick and ban people via the bot
- add and delete users from the user list
- get a help list of the commands

Then we want everyone else to be able to use commands to:

- use the !seen command, which shows when a particular nick was last on the channel.

After you set up the user list with levels for users, you need to determine what type of events you want your bot to respond to. For our sample bot, we determine we want it to respond to the following events:

- to kick/ban a non-op level user, should they kick an op level user
- to deop a non-op level user when a server tries to op them

Automatic Bot Functions

In addition to these commands and events you want the bot to respond to, there are automatic functions it needs to perform. After you create the bot and activate it, you want it to join the channel you created it for. You also want it to respond to floods others may try to send it. Therefore, you want to create a CTCP flood protection for the bot. These are pretty simple sets of commands you can set up for the bot to make it do these things automatically. Let's tackle all these commands and events we have discussed so far one by one.

First let's start with the user list and letting your users get ops from the bot. You have already set up your bot's user list to include two levels—level 10 for ops level users and level 1 for everyone else. To write the commands to get ops and perform other commands, you have to decide on the method you want the users to use to communicate with the bot. As discussed earlier you can have users type the command in the channel, in a message, or a DCC Chat message. If you choose to let the users type a command in the channel, you must make sure it is a unique command that isn't likely to be typed in normal conversations, although it can be fun sometimes to have users type "do me bot" in order to get ops from the bot. This was first implemented by a user going by the nick of wastedump. To avoid this problem with our sample bot, we'll have all the op level commands messaged to the bot. Using this method the bot only responds to private messages.

Next you need to set up text events to make the bot respond to events performed by users in your channel. For our sample bot, we use the commands op, deop, kick, ban, help, adduser, and remuser. In mIRC's remote events editor box, the scripts and commands look like the following:

```
on 10:TEXT:OP*:?:/mode #mychannel +o $nick
on 10:TEXT:Deop *:?: {
  If ($2 isop #mychannel { /mode #mychannel -o $2 }
  Elseif ($2 == $null) { /notice $nick Usage: /msg $me DEOP <nick> }
  Else { /notice $nick $2 isn't an op on #mychannel }
}
on 10:TEXT:KICK *:?: {
  if ($2 ison #mychannel) { /kick #mychannel $2 $3- }
  Elseif ($2 == $null) { /notice $nick Usage: /msg $me KICK <nick>
        [kick message]}
  else { /notice $nick $2 isn't on #mychannel }
}
on 10:TEXT:BAN *:?: {
  If ($2 == $null ) { /notice $nick Usage: /msg $me BAN <nick> }
  Elseif ($2 ison #mychannel) {/Ban $2 3 }
  Else ( /notice $nick $2 isn't on #mychannel }
}
On 10:TEXT:ADDUSER *:?: {
  If ($2 == $null ) {/notice $nick Sytnax: /msg $me ADDUSER <nick> }
  ElseIf ($2 ison #mychannel ) { /guser 10 $2 3 | /notice $nick $2
        added to user list }
  Else { /notice $nick $2 isn't on #mychannel }
}
```

```
On 10:TEXT:REMuser *:?: {
  If ($2 != $null ) { /ruser $2 | /notice $nick Removed $2 from
        userlist }
  Else { /notice $nick Usage: /msg $me REMUSER <nick> }
}
on 10:TEXT:Help*:?: { /play $nick $mircdir $+ Help.txt }
```

Figure 14-c is an example of these commands in mIRC's events.

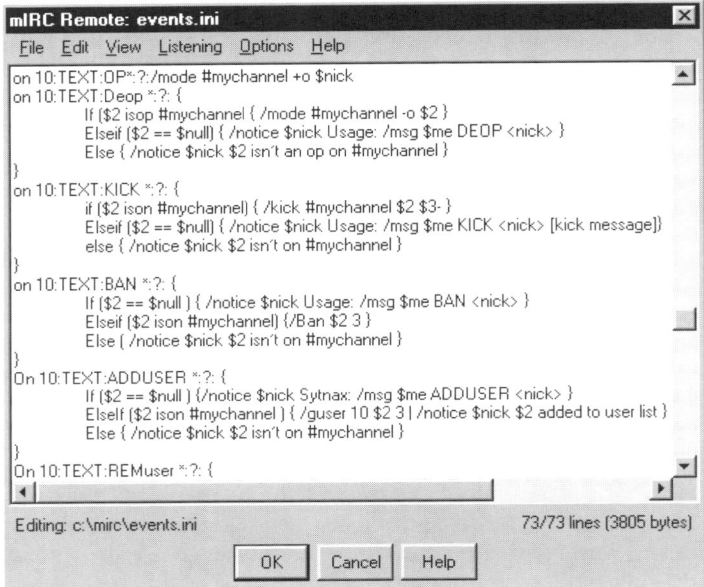

Figure 14-c. Bot scripts in mIRC

These cover the op level commands. The help command plays a help.txt file to the user. This, of course, has to exist first. Therefore you need to create a text file that contains help topics and explanations of the commands you have added to the bots and how the user can access those commands. This help file might contain topics like the following:

- Commands
- Op
- Deop <nick>
- Kick <Nick> [optional message]
- Ban <nick>
- Adduser <nick>
- Remuser <nick>
- Help

Now let's add the kick protection and server op events. Protection is actually a misnomer. The idea is more of retaliation. If someone who isn't an op level user (as entered into the bot's user list) kicks someone who is, the bot kicks that person. To create this kick protection/retaliation event for our sample bot, we use the ON KICK event. In mIRC, it's pretty easy because we have defined the user levels as numbers. Therefore we can prefix the ON KICK event with a left angle bracket (<#level user). This tells the bot that if a 10 level user is kicked by a less than 10 level user to trigger this event. Since we only have two levels, 10 and 1, this works well. The command script looks like this:

```
on <10:KICK: {
 /mode #mychannel -o+b $nick $address($nick,3)
 /kick #mychannel $nick Don't kick $knick $+ !
}
```

Next we want to set up a command in our sample bot to protect our channel from people getting server ops. We set this up in the events of mIRC also. The serverop event triggers when a server ops someone who isn't entered into the op level user list. This includes all user level 1s. Following is the command you use:

```
on 1:ServerOP:/mode #mychannel -o $opnick
```

After you have these commands set up, it's time to consider creating a flood protection command. An effective flood protection is to make the script only respond to a couple of CTCP requests from any given user. Here's a script to do that. Place this flood protection command script in the same remote event file as the others we have created so far.

```
ctcp 1:*:{
  If ($1 == SOUND ) { halt }
  set %ctcpMask Ping Version
  If ($1 isin %ctcpMask ) {
    Inc $varname(ctcp-count,$wildsite) 1 | .timer 1 5 /unset
         $varname(ctcp-count,$wildsite)
    If ($varvalue(ctcp-count,$wildsite) > 4 ) {  Ignore -tu300
         $wildsite |   Halt  }
    return
  }
  else { halt }
}
```

This flood protection works by:

- only responding to PING and version requests
- counting how many requests it gets in a 5-second period; if it gets more than three requests in 5 seconds, it ignores the user for 300 seconds.
- first checking if the CTCP request is a sound request, and does nothing if it is, so as not to ignore those people who play a lot of sounds.

The built-in flood protection in mIRC works well by itself. However, with this script addition, your bot isn't flooded off by someone.

OK, now the seen command. What is it? The idea is to have the bot answer requests from users about when a particular person was last on the channel. To be able to do that, the bot has to keep track of when people leave the channel. For our sample bot, we can do that by making use of the ON PART and ON QUIT remote events. We can write a script code that saves the date and time a particular nick left the channel. This lets the bot recall it when it gets a request for this information.

mIRC and Pirch have commands to read and write Windows .ini type files. These turn out to be handy for this task. INI files have the format: Section Key Value. For example:

```
[Section]
Key=value
```

You've probably seen these files before. For the script for our sample bot, we can use the channel name as the section (or, in this case, LASTSEEN as the section). Then we can use the nick as the key and the date/time as the value. Then the information we want is easily retrievable, and easy to store. Following is how this command script is written for our sample bot:

```
On 1:QUIT:/writeini $mircdir $+ Seen.ini LASTSEEN $nick $ctime
ON 1:PART:#mychannel:/writeini $mircdir $+ Seen.ini LASTSEEN
         $nick $ctime
```

Now that we have a method of storing the information, we need to install the command to retrieve it. Let's use the command format of !seen <nick> as the command the user types to activate the bot to retrieve the information from storage. This !seen is the command users type whether they type it in the channel or as a message to the bot, depending on how you set your bot up to receive commands. This is how you create this retrieval command script for our sample bot:

```
ON 1:TEXT:!seen*:*: {
set %seen.time $readini  $mircdir $+ seen.ini  LASTSEEN $2
  If $2 == $null  { notice $nick who are you looking for? usage:
         !seen <nick> }
  elseif ($2 == $me) { notice $nick Yea, everytime I look in the
         mirror :Þ }
  elseif ($2 == $nick) { notice $nick I don't think I can help you
         … }
  elseif ($2 ison #mychannel ) { .notice $nick Duh! $2 is on
         #mychannel right now!! }
  elseif (%seen.time == $null) { notice $nick I don't know when $2
         was last on ... sorry }
  else {
    set %seen.elapsed [ $ctime - %seen.time ]  | set %seen.elapsed
         $duration(%seen.elapsed)
    notice $nick  I last saw $2 %seen.elapsed  ago
  }
 unset %seen.*
}
```

This script reads the seen.ini file that we saved information on when people left the channel, and stores the result to a variable. That variable either contains date/time information on a person, or it is empty, that is equal to $null, because there was no entry in the file for that particular nick, which means the bot never saw that nick leave the channel.

Then it makes a few tests. If the user entered a nick, the bot gives the information it has on the nick regarding when he was last seen. If not, the bot doles out some help on how to use the command. The bot also gives out a couple of cute responses when the users try it on themselves, the bot, or someone who is already on the channel.

When the bot receives this command it checks its files to see if the date/time information exists. Then the bot calculates how long ago that nick last left the channel, formats some text, and sends the information out to the channel or to the private message window.

Finally, to finish up our design goals, have the bot join the channel on startup. This is easily done by putting a line in the mIRC Perform section. Remember, this Perform section in the General Options performs commands once you are connected to a server for a net. You probably want the bot to do a few more things on connect. You can also create a startup script in an alias, and then have the perform command call that alias, like so:

(put this alias in the same remote script file, as for previous alias scripts)

```
alias Initialize {
  /join #<yourchannel
  /mode $me +i
}
```

Then in mIRC's Perform section, type the following: /initialize. That's it!

How to Create a Bot in Pirch

The bot isn't much different when writing it in Pirch. Since the default User level is 100 in Pirch, we need to change the designated user levels to 200 for op level users, and 100 for everyone else.

To get the commands to work as they do in mIRC, we create some events that respond to the commands. In Pirch we have the events call a PIL script to do the processing for us. The events for op level commands look like the following. Be sure to put these into the events for level 200—create the level and add these events:

```
ON TEXT:OP:?:/mode #testout +o $nick
ON TEXT:DEOP*:?:/runscript [BOTCOMMAND] DEOP $nick $2
ON TEXT:KICK*:?:/runscript [BOTCOMMAND] KICK $nick $2 *3
ON TEXT:BAN*:?:/runscript [BOTCOMMAND] BAN $nick $2 *3
ON TEXT:adduser*:?:/runscript [BOTCOMMAND]  ADDUSER $nick $2
ON TEXT:REMUSER*:?:/runscript [BOTCOMMAND] REMUSER $nick $2
ON TEXT:Help*:?:/playfile $nick Help.txt
```

Figure 14-d is an example of how these bot commands look in Pirch.

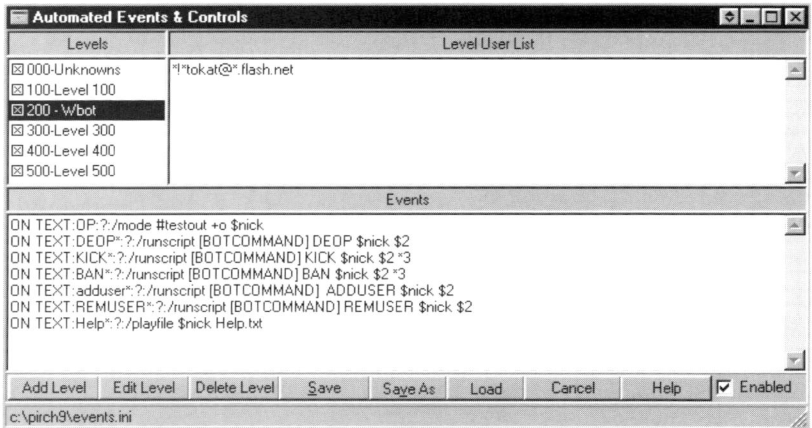

Figure 14-d. Bot commands in Pirch

Most of the commands call a script file, where the bot decides what to do after it receives the command. The Op command and the Help command are handled right in the events section. The PIL script to handle the commands looks like this:

```
{ bot command processor
========================
16 JUN 97
by kIRC
}
{ set $chan to the channel the bot will run on }
  $chan := '#testout;
{ writeln('botcommand fired!',$1,' ',$2,' ',$3);  }
If $1 = 'DEOP' then begin
  {    $2 - Nick     $3 (nick to deop)    }
  If $3 = " then  begin
       { missing parameter, send help message }
       command('/notice ',$2,' Usage: /msg ',$me,' DEOP <nick>');
  end
  else begin
       command('/mode ',$chan,' -o ',$3);
  end;
end
Else if $1 = 'KICK' Then begin
{ $2 - nick $3 - nick to kick      *4 optional message }
  if $3 =" then begin
       { missing parameter, send help message }
       command('/notice ',$2,' Usage: /msg ',$me,'KICK <nick>
            [optional message]');
  end
  else begin
       if $4 = " Then begin
       { create kick message, if none present }
            $kicktext := '_PirchBAWT_';
       end
       else begin
            $kicktext := *4;
       End;
       { kick 'em }
```

```
        Command('/kick ',$chan,' ',$3,' ',$kicktext);
   end;
end
Else if $1 = 'BAN' then begin
   If $3 = " then begin
        { missing parameter, send help message }
        command('/notice ',$2,' Usage: /msg ',$me,' BAN <nick>
                   [optional message]');
   end
   else begin
        if $4 = " Then begin
        { create kick message, if none present }
             $kicktext := '_PirchBAWT_';
        end
        else begin
             $kicktext := *4;
        End;
        { Ban 'em }
        command('/ban ',$chan,' ',$3,' 2');
        { kick 'em }
        Command('/kick ',$chan,' ',$3,' ',$kicktext);
   end;
end
Else if $1 = 'ADDUSER' then begin
   If $3 = "' then begin
        { missing parameter, send help message }
        command('/notice ',$2,' Usage: /msg ',$me,' ADDUSER <nick> ');
   end
   else begin
   { test to see if nick is on channel.  nick to add = $3 parameter }
        count := NickCount($chan);
        { loop through all the nicks on the channel, and see if $3
                   is in the list }
        Flag := 0;
        { Text compare is case sensitive to convert to all lower case }
        $testnick := strLower($3);
        For i := 1 to count do begin
             { WriteLN(Nicklist($chan,i)); }
             If strLower(NickList($chan,i)) = $testnick then begin
                  { yes the nick exists on channel, add to list }
                  Command('/adduser 200 ',$3,' 2 ');
                  Command('/notice ',$2,' Added ',$3,' to User List ');
                  Flag := 1;
             end;
        end;
   { if flag wasn't set to one, then we didn't find nick, alert user }
        If flag = 0 then Command('/notice ',$2,' ',$3,' is not on ',$chan,
                       ' - Unable to add to list ');
   end;
end
Else if $1 = 'REMUSER' then begin
   If $3 = "' then begin
        { missing parameter, send help message }
        command('/notice',$2,' Usage: /msg ',$me,' REMUSER <nick> ');
   end
   else begin
   { test to see if nick is on channel.  nick to remove = $3 parameter }
        count := NickCount($chan);
```

```
        { loop through all the nicks on the channel, and see if $3 is
                in the list }
        Flag := 0;
        $testnick := strLower($3);
        For i := 1 to count do begin
             If strLower(NickList($chan,i)) = $testnick then begin
                  { yes the nick exists on channel, add to list }
                  Command('/REMuser 200 ',$3,' 2 ');
                  Command('/notice ',$2,' Removed ',$3,' from User List');
                  Flag := 1;
             end;
        end;
   { if flag wasn't set to one, then we didn't find nick, alert user }
        If flag = 0 then Command('/notice ',$2,' ',$3,' is not on ,$chan,
                ' - Unable to remove.');
   end;
end;
```

That covers the commands. Next we need to install the protection kicks. We can do this directly in events. In Pirch the ON KICK event triggers on the level of the kicker, not the kickee. Since we want to kick someone who is a non-op level kicker who tried to kick an op level nick, the event belongs in level 100—default users. The event is: ON KICK:<:#:/kick #mychannel $nick Leave $victim alone!

The < sign means that the kicker's level is less than the victim's level which is what we want. Read the Pirch help file for the ON KICK event for details of how this works.

The event to handle serverops is (again, this belongs in the level 100 area events):

```
ON SERVEROP:#Mychannel:/mode # -o $opnick
```

Now let's tackle the !seen command in Pirch. There is a /writeINI command in Pirch and a $readini function. If you read the Pirch help file for /writeINI., the command we need is already written for us!

However, let's add this command to the ON QUIT and ON PART events:

Put this in level 100, the default user area. Change #yourchannel to the channel you will run the bot on. The command looks like this:

```
ON PART:#yourchannel:/writeini $pirchpath $+ seen.ini LASTSEEN $nick
$nick Was last seen on $day $date at $time (EST)
ON QUIT: /writeini $pirchpath $+ seen.ini LASTSEEN $nick $nick Was
last seen on $day $date at $time (EST)
```

These two events take care of writing the data. This time we wrote the entire line of data, instead of just date/time information, to the file.

Now to get the command to read back the data you need to also put the command in the level 100 event area, as the following:

```
ON TEXT:!seen*:*:/notice $nick $readini $pirchpath $+ seen.ini
LASTSEEN $2
```

Make sure to manually add yourself to the bot's user list, so that you can start issuing it commands.

Running Your Bot

Once you have your bot up and running, your next problem is keeping it running. Not all IRC servers allow bots on them. Actually, most of them don't. You have to find servers on your chat network that are bot friendly, or at least tolerant of bots. You have to read the MOTD to see where a server stands with bots. You might also ask around, but don't rely on what you are told alone—read that server's MOTD.

If you intend your bot to run all the time, you want to run it on a computer that has a full-time connection, such as a PC at someone's office. It is possible to run one from a dial-up connection, but it means you have to keep your computer on all the time and put up with occasional to frequent disconnects to your ISP.

If you don't have a full-time connection to the net, and/or don't want to tie up your computer, consider an eggdrop bot. Eggdrop is the name of an IRC client that was written from the ground up to be a bot. A lot of common bot functions and features are already built into the bot. It does have a scripting language called TCL that one can use to modify the bot to do something that you want or need. Eggdrops are probably the most common channel bots, and perhaps the best.

Eggdrops are intended to run from a UNIX machine. The idea is to get a UNIX Shell account (one that will allow running the bot) and have the bot run on the UNIX account. This way the bot is always running on a computer that is always connected to the net. It's a pretty clean setup.

We won't get into the details of setting up an eggdrop here.

To find out more about them, check out:

http://www.valuserve.com/~robey/eggdrop/
http://www.sodre.net/eggdrop/
http://www.xcalibre.com/index.html

TCL scripting documents:

http://sunscript.sun.com/man/tcl7.6/TclCmd/contents.html

A very active mailing list and a good place to ask questions and learn a lot about eggdrops is the Eggdrop list. You can subscribe to this list by sending an e-mail to majordomo@sodre.net and in the body of the message type "subscribe eggdrop" (without quotes).

To find an ISP that lets you run an eggdrop, search through http://www.thelist.com. This web site lists many ISPs and what they offer and don't offer.

Use the information in this chapter to become familiar with the various types of bots that are prevalent on IRC. Learn how to use bots and how to create one of your own. If you choose to use a bot, either one you created or one someone else did, be sure to only put the bot on a bot-friendly server.

Chapter 15

CUSeeMe

Tn this chapter you learn:

- ☑ *What is CUSeeMe?*
- ☑ *How to Use CUSeeMe*

IRC offers you the ability to text chat with anyone anywhere in the world. The World Wide Web also lets you text chat through the web to people around the globe. The 3-D chats let you text chat or in some cases voice chat with others while also letting you move around in a virtual reality world as an avatar. In addition to these, there are programs that let you carry on voice chats with others. There also are programs that let you carry on voice, text, and video chats with people all over the world.

One excellent program that lets you video conference and voice chat with others is CUSeeMe. This program lets you see others when you are talking to them and vice versa. It is a real-time program that lets you have voice conversations with people using the Internet, your computer, and your computer's sound system. When you add video to your computer, you add the ability to see as well as talk. In addition, you can exchange data or use a whiteboard to collaborate on activities with other users.

CUSeeMe lets you have real-time person-to-person or group conferencing with people around the globe. Your computer and this program can help you keep in touch with friends and family through your Internet account or meet new people anywhere in the world.

What is CUSeeMe?

In the simplest terms CUSeeMe is video conferencing software that lets you communicate using video, audio, and graphics with people via your Internet account. You can talk to people one to one or one to many using this software. While you are talking to them you can get live video feeds of them and they can get the same of you. In addition you can also exchange information and graphics with each other using a whiteboard.

You can call individuals or they can call you. Then you can voice chat using this software and your Internet connection. If you prefer you can also text chat with each other. However, the software is designed to allow you to voice chat while viewing video feeds of each other.

In group chats, you can talk to several different people at a time. The program is set up to support up to 100 people at a time for group conferencing. As in the one-to-one chat, you can also exchange data and information with others in the group as well as graphics using the whiteboard. This full-featured program allows you to collaborate on projects with others no matter where in the world they are. However, you must all have this program in order for it to support everyone and afford compatibility.

CUSeeMe version 4.0 requires that you run it on a Windows 95 or Windows NT version 4.0 operating system. You must have a Pentium processor with a minimum of 100 MHz speed. In addition you need a minimum of 16 MB of RAM but 24 MB is recommended. You also need to have at least 10 MB of hard disk space free.

Before you can voice chat you need a 28.8 speed modem and an Internet account. You also need a microphone and a 16-bit sound card and drivers. In order to send video, you must have either a digitizer camera or desktop video camera and a video capture card.

This program can be downloaded from the Internet at either the White Pine site, the site for the developers of this product, or the software site called Tucows. The White Pine site is located at http://www.cuseeme.com and the Tucows site is at http://www.tucows.com.

Once you download the file, double-click on the cuseeme.exe file and it automatically unzips and begins the install process. When it has completed installing itself on your system, it starts by giving you a CUSeeMe Setup Assistant. This Setup Assistant helps you configure the program and prepares you for your first video conference. It also lets you register with an online directory service so that others can find you.

After you finish the setup, CUSeeMe is ready for you to connect to others or to join conferences. CUSeeMe has a built-in phone book that lists several conference servers that you can connect to that are designed for public use. When you double-click on any of the conferences listed in this phone book you are connected to that conference. When you find other conferences you can add them to this phone book to assist you in easily and quickly connecting to your newfound conferences. Figure 15-a on the following page is an example of the start window for CUSeeMe.

CUSeeMe lets you test your video and audio before you connect to a conference or chat with others. It also gives you graphical cards on the other users in the conference or on the conferences. In addition, you create a contact card on yourself. This information is helpful when you try to connect to conferences or to other users. Figure 15-b on the following page is an example of requesting and loading a contact card on another user.

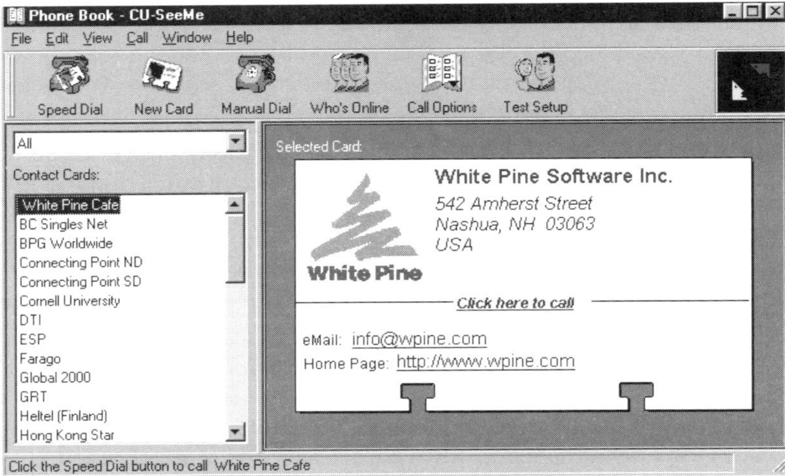

Figure 15-a. Start window and phone book for CUSeeMe

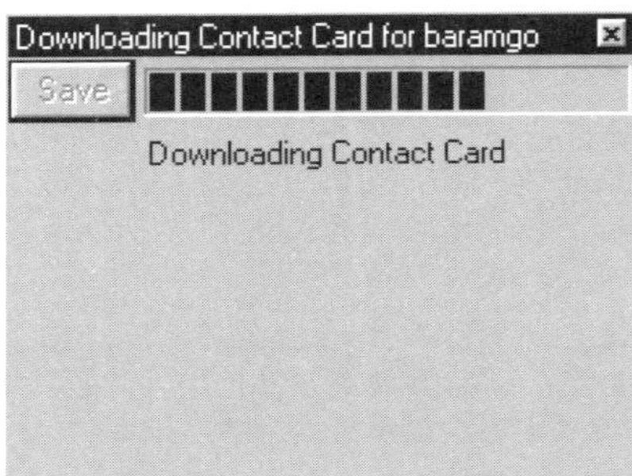

Figure 15-b. Contact card downloading

CUSeeMe combines audio, video, and a whiteboard to let you communicate in real-time live with friends and relatives using the Internet. The audio lets you voice chat with others, while the video lets you see them and lets them see you while you are chatting. The whiteboard lets you collaborate on projects or entertain yourselves while you are chatting. This program can be used for business video conferencing with associates or it can be used for pleasure to talk to friends and family.

How to Use CUSeeMe

When you first connect to CUSeeMe, you initially get a Quick Start & Tips screen that lets you choose how you want to begin your session, unless you choose to connect directly to a conference like White Pine Café conference. By clicking on a button you can choose where you want to go in CUSeeMe. You can choose to connect to the White Pine Café, open the phone book, find a friend, or test your setup. Figure 15-c is an example of the Quick Start & Tips screen.

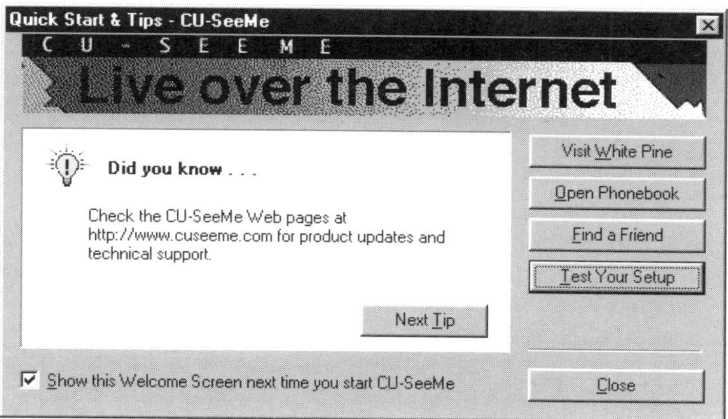

Figure 15-c. Quick Start & Tips window

If you select not to see this screen again, you are taken to the phone book automatically when you start CUSeeMe. This phone book is your main starting place and where you make most of your connections. From this window you make your calls and connect to other users or to conferences.

The phone book stores Contact Cards and IP addresses of places or people you want to call. It is your personal directory. You can store the contact cards of friends, family members, business contacts, and conferences in this phone book. Contact cards contain information on the people or conferences you are trying to call. They contain the e-mail address, home page address, name and/or address, and business card of these people and places. Figure 15-d is an example of the phone book in CUSeeMe.

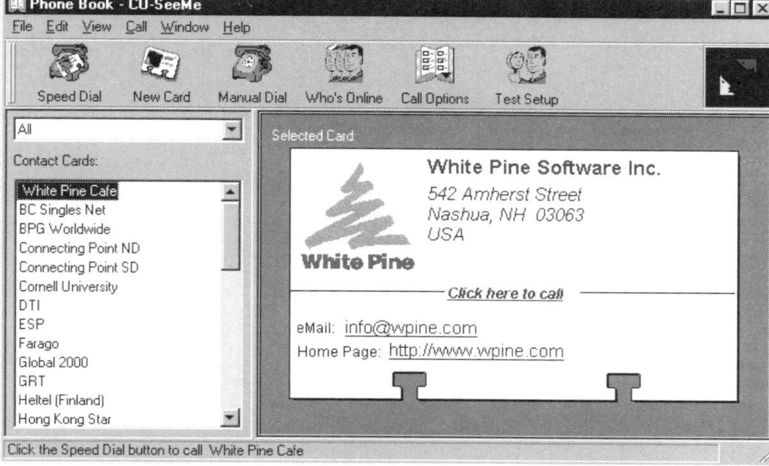

Figure 15-d. Phone book and contact card

Notice on the Contact Card there is an area that says *Click here to call*. This makes it easy for you to connect to the person or place that Contact Card belongs to. This enables you to use a form of speed dialing unique to CUSeeMe. You can, of course, manually dial anyone or anyplace if you prefer. CUSeeMe includes a manual dial feature as part of its program. Simply click on the Manual Dial icon in the toolbar. This is the icon that looks like a telephone. Then follow the prompts you are given.

Another way you can call others is to use the Who's Online feature. Click on the Who's Online icon in the toolbar to get a list of everyone who is connected via CUSeeMe. When you locate someone on the Who's Online list you want to talk to, click on the Speed Dial icon in the toolbar. When the connection is established you get the word Join in the lower right-hand corner of the Connection window. Click on that word and you are ready to start talking to the person you contacted.

If you prefer to join one of the many conferences available with CUSeeMe, simply choose the conference you are interested in. Then click on the Contact Card to join the conference. While CUSeeMe is making the connection, you get a window that lets you know the status of the connection. Figure 15-e is an example of this Connection window.

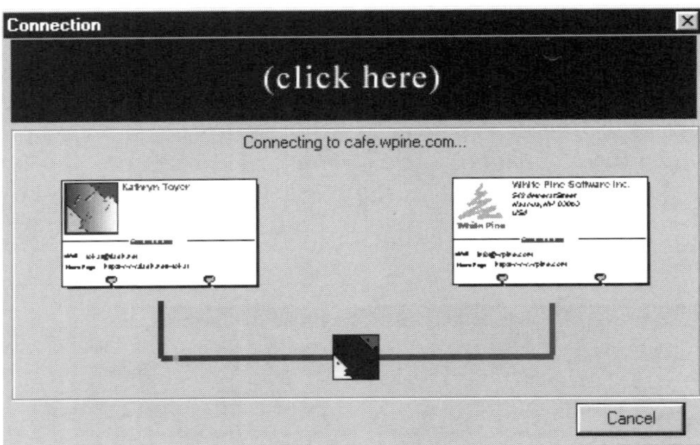

Figure 15-e. Connection attempt window

After the connection is established, you are given a choice of conference rooms you can join. Select the one that interests you and click on the Join button to enter that conference room. After you click on the Join button you get a window that tells you a little bit about the conference room you are about to enter. Once you've read the notice, you can click on the OK button. Figure 15-f is an example of a conference room selection window you see when you connect to a conference.

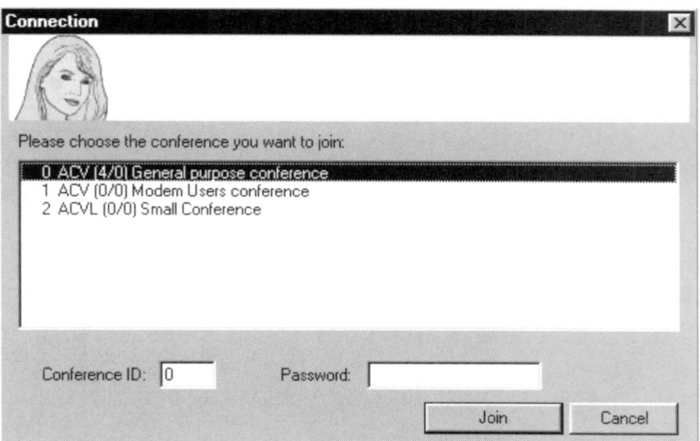

Figure 15-f. Conference Room selection box

Once you click on the Join button, you are transported into the conference room you selected. You then get a new window that lets you see the video feeds from other users there, if they are sending video. You also get a list of everyone who is on the conference. In addition to this you see the status of your microphone and if anyone is talking. Often you also see users text chatting along with voice chatting. Figure 15-g is an example of a conference room window.

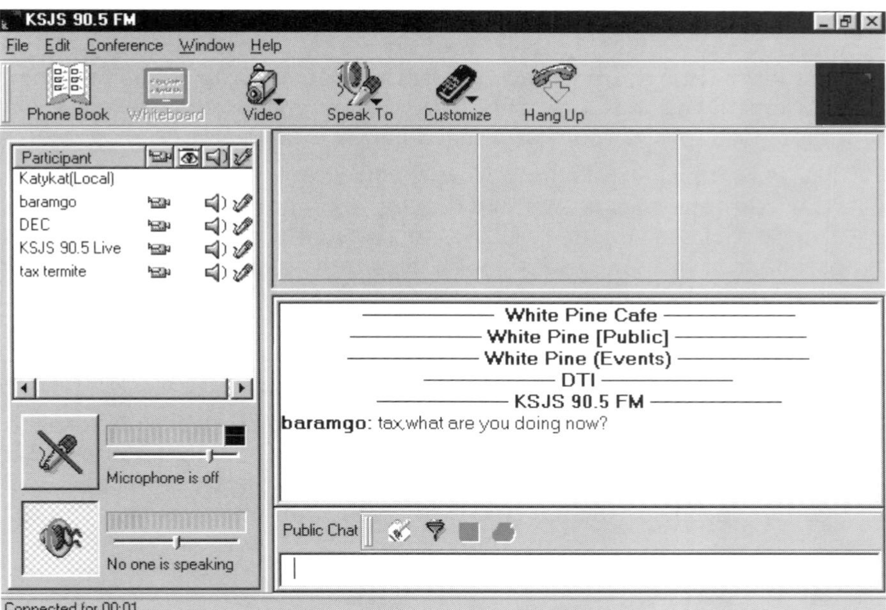

Figure 15-g. Conference room

After you enter the conference room, you can begin chatting with the other users. You can text chat with them or you can voice chat. With the voice chat, you can choose to voice chat with specific individuals or you can voice chat with the whole group of users in the conference room.

In addition to joining conferences or initiating calls, you can choose the Listener option. This allows you to keep CUSeeMe running in the background and receive calls as they come in to you. This option is automatically activated when you start up your computer unless you disable it.

The Listener option works similar to call waiting on your telephone. It listens for any incoming calls and notifies you when someone calls. You can then accept the call, ignore it, or refuse the call. This Listener option also notifies you of calls if you are connected to another user when another call comes in. Listener even works when you are not running CUSeeMe in the background. If you get a call, Listener opens up CUSeeMe so that you can receive the call.

The Whiteboard feature is a separate program that you can access through CUSeeMe. You must download this Whiteboard program before you can use it with CUSeeMe. Once you have it, you can use it with others to share drawings, graphics, and documents. The Whiteboard also lets you and others create or edit information you place on it. All documents you create, open, or import are displayed on the whiteboards of the other user's computers. Any marks, edits, and so forth that you or the other users make on the whiteboard are instantly visible to all who are participating in the collaboration. This feature lets you not only create and edit documents and so forth, it also lets you save those documents to your hard drive or print them out on your printer.

In addition to these chat, video, and collaboration features, CUSeeMe also lets parents rest easy in letting their children use this program. CUSeeMe has a feature that lets them maintain parental control and security of the program. The Parental Control option is a security feature that lets parents use a password to prevent others from performing certain actions with CUSeeMe.

The Parental Control option lets parents restrict communications. They can restrict incoming calls, manual dialing, and multicast conferences. Parents can also restrict the startup of CUSeeMe. By configuring the Parental Control options, parents can set up CUSeeMe with passwords to restrict or allow the functions they want unavailable or available to their children.

CUSeeMe comes with a very thorough help file. It is a fairly simple program to use even though it has many excellent features. It is a very nice program to use if you have the capabilities to voice and video chat with other people. It can be a fun way to voice chat with friends and family. It can also be an excellent tool to meet other people all over the world. You can also use it for business purposes like video or teleconferencing and collaboration on special projects. It's a great tool to use when you have people in distant places who you want or need to keep in contact with.

Chapter 16
PowWow

In this chapter you learn:

- ☑ *What is PowWow?*
- ☑ *How to Use PowWow*

You can chat using text and IRC. You can chat on the web. You can even chat in virtual 3-D environments with an avatar to represent you. You can voice chat with others while also receiving and sending live feeds of each other back and forth. Now you can voice chat with others while surfing the web.

PowWow is a chat software program that lets you voice chat or text chat with others while at the same time you surf the World Wide Web together. It also lets you send e-mail to each other via the program.

With this program you can locate and page other PowWow users. Once you locate someone to chat with, you can not only chat with them either through voice chat or text chat, but you can also view each other's pictures and transfer files. In addition you can join group chats consisting of up to nine people.

This PowWow program lets you search for people to talk to based on their geographical location, age, sex, profession, specific interests, or other similar information. PowWow lets users set up profiles on themselves via White Pages. Other users search these White Pages to locate others with similar interests as their own.

PowWow by Tribal Voice is another great program to use to meet others around the world or to talk to your friends and family. It offers you many excellent features. This chapter tells you what the program is and how you can use it to chat with others.

What is PowWow?

PowWow was designed by Tribal Voice as a chat and communication program for the web. This chat program lets you chat with others using voice and/or text communications. It also lets you send and receive files, view personal web pages, view pictures of other users, and surf the World Wide Web together with other users.

The new versions have an added feature that lets you conference with up to nine other users as a group. In the group you can perform the same activities as you do one on one. You can exchange files, view web pages together, and exchange pictures.

PowWow provides you with its form of an address book which it calls White Pages. These White Pages list everyone who has set up their personal profile and allows you to search them for someone you would like to chat with. New and old users can use these White Pages to locate others to chat with if they don't have someone to chat with when they initially obtain the program. Each user of PowWow can list his personal information including special interests. Then you can search these White Pages for particular types of people or people with similar interests as your own.

While you are waiting on someone to chat with you can entertain yourself by drawing or doodling on the whiteboard PowWow provides you. You can also use this whiteboard to draw on as a group. It allows up to nine people at a time to access and use it.

If you have to step away from your computer for a few minutes, you don't have to worry that you might miss someone trying to reach you. You can let PowWow's answering machine take a message for you. Then when you return to your computer, you can answer your messages. PowWow also collects messages for you when you're offline.

In addition to the public chats you can conduct, you can also participate in private chats with one or more users. Therefore, you can have a public chat or group chats and also hold private chats with individuals simultaneously.

PowWow supports text-to-speech. With this feature you can listen to text spoken through your computer. PowWow also lets you send text-to-speech to other users. When you select to have text spoken while you are in a group chat, the other users also hear the text spoken provided they have their text-to-speech enabled.

PowWow is a Windows-based program and is not compatible with Macintosh operating systems. It supports all the major web browsers like Microsoft Internet Explorer and Netscape Navigator. It also supports some of the other browsers like Attachmate Emissary and Softtronics Softerm.

In order to use PowWow you must have either Microsoft Windows 3.1, Windows NT, or Windows 95 along with a TCP/IP and Internet connection. You must also have a 486 with 33 MHz or faster system. To use the voice chat you should also have a Microsoft Windows compatible sound card, speakers, and a microphone.

PowWow can be downloaded from its web page at http://www.tribal.com or from the Tucows site. After you download the file, double-click on the powwow.exe file to unzip it and begin the installation process. PowWow automatically installs itself on your hard drive and places a file in your Start menu.

When you click on Tribal Voice in your Start menu, you can then select PowWow to start the program. After the program starts, you get a window that lets you choose how you want to communicate with PowWow. You can search the White Pages for other users, connect to a user, or choose a conference to connect to. Figure 16-a is an example of this window.

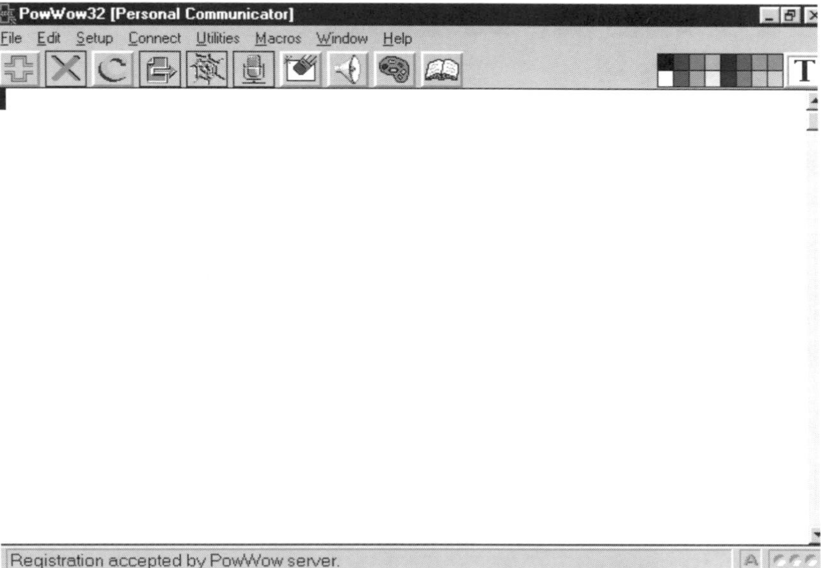

Figure 16-a. PowWow's main window

PowWow has many nice features to let you communicate with friends and family or to meet new friends around the world. Let's go on to the next section and learn how to use PowWow.

How to Use PowWow

Each user of PowWow is registered by e-mail address. When you want to connect or call someone with PowWow, you must know his or her e-mail address. If a person has a fixed e-mail address like tokat@flash.net, you can establish a direct connection with that person. If the address is dynamic, one that is an Internet protocol address which changes each time a connection is made by that person, you cannot establish a direct connection. It may take you a little longer to connect with the dynamic address people.

If you don't know anyone who is using PowWow, you can still find others to chat with. PowWow has what it calls White Pages which lists the profiles of various users of the program. You can search this list to find others to chat with. You can also add yourself to this list so that others can find you.

When you wish to connect to another person on PowWow, select the Connect option from the menu bar. Then select Connect and type in the person's e-mail address. If this is the first time you are contacting this person, you can add them to your PowWow Book by clicking on the Add button before you click on the Connect button. Figure 16-b is an example of the Book dialog box.

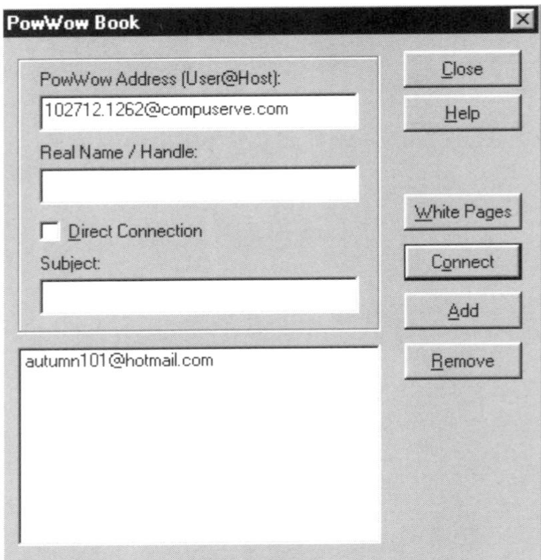

Figure 16-b. Connection window

Once you connect with a user, your screen splits so that each of you has an area to type text messages. Each of you sees what the other is typing as you are typing. You can also establish voice communication by clicking on the Voice icon in the toolbar. This Voice icon looks like a microphone. This is very similar to the old talk programs that preceded IRC. Figure 16-c is an example of the chat window you get when you connect with another user.

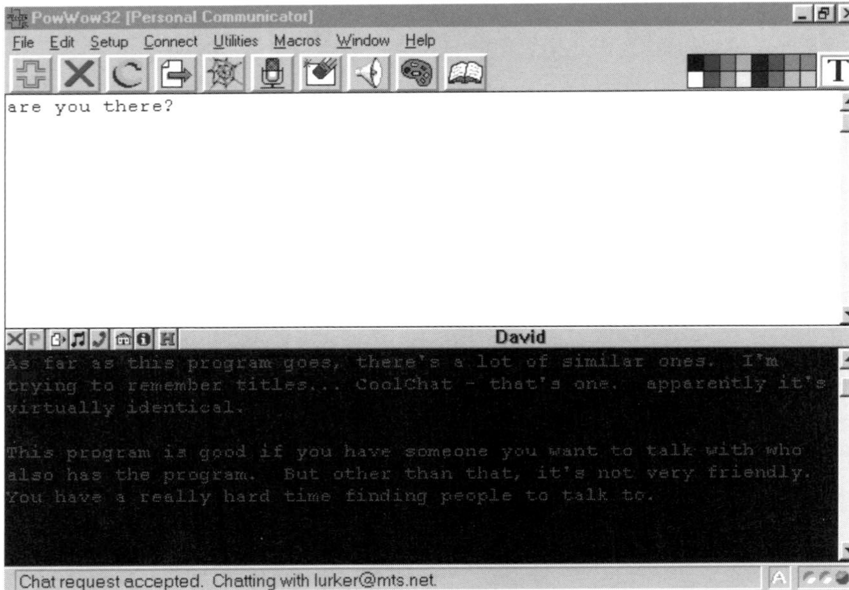

Figure 16-c. Chat window

In addition PowWow has a few prerecorded sounds you can play while you are chatting with someone. You can use these sound files that come with PowWow or you can also play your own sound files. Before the other person can hear these sound files, they must also have the files on their computer. When you want to add sound files to PowWow, click on Utilities and then Sound Add. Type in the name you want for the sound and then add the location of the sound file. You can use the Browse button to search your hard drive for sound files. If you prefer not to hear sounds while you are chatting, you can turn your sound off. Click on the Settings menu item and select Sound Options. Uncheck the Play Sounds box to turn sound off. Figure 16-d is an example of the sound player for PowWow.

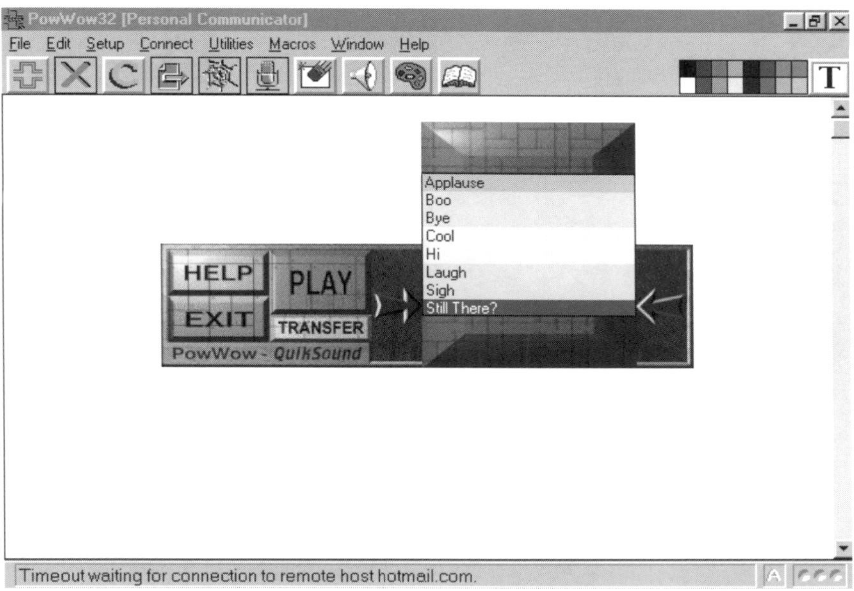

Figure 16-d. PowWow sounds

If the kids start screaming and fighting from the other room or your mate wishes you to cook dinner, you may from time to time need to leave your computer for a while. With PowWow you don't have to worry about missing messages. You can turn the Answering Machine on and let it take messages for you. When you select Setup from the menu bar and choose Answering Machine from the options, you can enter the message you want others to see while you are away from your computer. Then you must select Connect from the menu bar and click Answering Machine On/Off to turn the Answering Machine on. If this selection is checked the Answering Machine is on; if it's not checked it is off.

When you return to your computer you can then view the messages others have left you. If you have any messages, PowWow turns the A in the bottom right-hand corner of your window to red and causes it to flash. To view your messages, select Connect from the menu bar and then choose View Answering Machine from the options you are given. If you want to connect to someone who has left you a message, click on the PowWow button and the program automatically connects you.

While you are chatting with others you can also draw using the PowWow Whiteboard. You can draw by yourself or with others while you are chatting in the Personal Communicator mode. Click on the Draw icon in the toolbar, which looks like an artist's palette. You get a whiteboard with tools to draw and paint with. Each of you can draw on this whiteboard while you are chatting. This whiteboard gives you several options like drawing line width, text, color tools, image options, diagonal lines, and click and drag to resize the whiteboard. Figure 16-e is an example of the PowWow Whiteboard.

Figure 16-e. PowWow whiteboard

If you prefer to talk to many people at a time, you can join a PowWow conference. PowWow's conference mode lets you chat with up to 75 people at a time in a discussion group. Click on the Conference icon in the toolbar. It is the icon that is a blue C. When you click on this Conference icon you are prompted to either Join a Conference in Progress or Host a Conference. If you select to Join a Conference in Progress, you must select one from the White Pages. When you locate a conference you are interested in, click on it and you are transported to that conference.

After you enter the conference you get a chat window to enter your text into. The top portion of this window lets you type what you want while the bottom portion displays the chat messages that are being sent to the conference. If you want to see a list of the users in the conference, click on the Users and Control button in the upper right-hand corner of the window.

To communicate with the other users there, simply type your message and either click on the Send button or press Enter. Through this Users and Control button you can also establish private chats with any of the users in the list. Select the user and then select the option you want to use with them. When you click on the Hear All button, the text is converted to speech via your computer. Figure 16-f is an example of a conference room in PowWow.

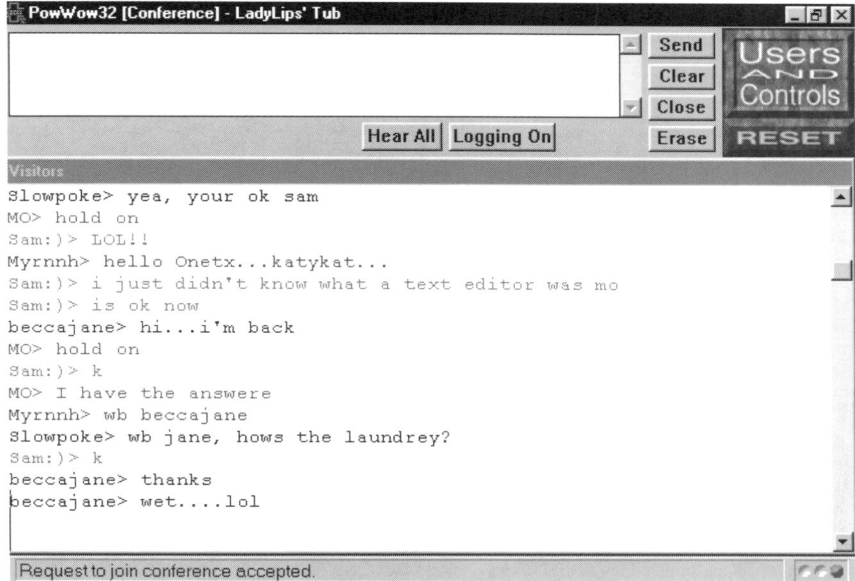

Figure 16-f. PowWow conference room

While you are chatting with others, you can also surf the web with them in tow. To surf the web with a group, click on Utilities in the menu bar. Then select Launch Cruise from the options. After you select the Launch Cruise option, your browser opens if it's not already open. After the browser is opened, the others in your group are notified that you want them to join you in browsing the Internet. They have the option to join you or to refuse the cruise request. When they accept the cruise request from you, their browsers are then opened and once their browsers are opened, they see any sites you, as the leader, select on the web. When you stop cruising, the connections to the browsers are dropped, but the browser remains running.

When you prefer to voice chat with another user, select the Voice Chat icon from the toolbar. Be sure to set up your voice settings before you begin voice chats. From the menu bar, select Settings. Then choose Voice Settings from the options. In the dialog box you get, choose the resolution for the type connection you have—Low Resolution is recommended for all connections and is generally for slower connections and High Resolution for faster connections.

With the Voice Chat feature in PowWow, you can voice chat with one person at a time. You also need a modem speed of 14.4 Kbps or better in order to voice chat. When you are text chatting with more than one person, PowWow prompts you to select who you want to voice chat with. If you want to end the voice chat, simply deselect the Voice Chat menu item.

If you want to establish a private chat with someone, select Connect from the menu bar. Then choose Private Chat from the options. If you are chatting in a group, PowWow prompts you to indicate who you want to private chat with. You can also click on the green P button over the user's screen to establish a private chat with them. Figure 16-g is an example of a chat window and the green P button over the other user's screen.

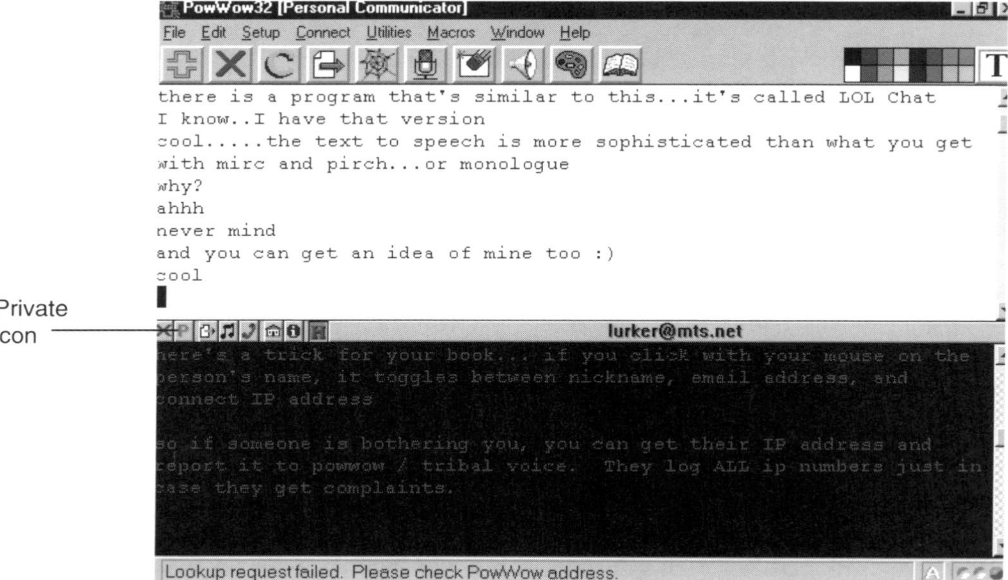

Figure 16-g. PowWow chat window

PowWow also lets you send and receive mail while you are on PowWow and when you are offline. Before you can use this feature, your PowWow address and your e-mail address must be the same and you have to know the address of your mail server. All mail messages are saved in your answering machine. If you are not connected when a mail is sent to you, it is stored and you can retrieve it the next time you log onto PowWow.

Occasionally you run across users that you don't want to communicate with. PowWow lets you block calls from other users. This feature is the Call Blocking Book. To add users to this Call Blocking Book, select Settings from the menu bar. Then choose Call Blocking Book from the options. You get a dialog box that lets you enter the address of the person you want to block. Type in his address and click on the Add button. You can add straight e-mail addresses to this list or you can add IP address or whole domains to block. Once you add these addresses to this Call Blocking Book, you no longer receive connect requests from those users.

As with other chat programs you use on IRC, PowWow also lets you send files back and forth with other users. With this program you can also set up special directories to store the various kinds of files you typically receive. In the Settings menu item, you can select Files and Directories and choose where you want certain types of files to be stored when you receive them from others. When you want to send a file to another user, select File from the menu and click on Send. Then follow the prompts to select and send the file of your choice.

PowWow is a powerful chat program. It gives you the ability to text and voice chat with other users either one on one or as a group. You can also lead others in surfing the web or drawing on the PowWow Whiteboard. This full-featured program is easy to learn and has an excellent help file. Use it to meet and chat with new people around the world or to chat with friends and relatives.

Chapter 17

Voice Chat

In this chapter you learn:

- ☑ *What is Voice Chat?*
- ☑ *Voice Chat Programs and How to Use Them*

The Internet gives you a way to talk live one to one with your friends and relatives. Recent news stories predict that because calls via the Internet are so cheap and efficient, they will eventually dominate the global telecommunications industry.

The technology that lets people talk with voice to others over the Internet is improving. There are still short delays between when a person speaks and when the other person hears the spoken words. Sometime the speech gets garbled and you have to ask the other person to repeat what they said.

These flaws in the technology do happen. However, those who use the Internet to communicate with voice understand this and are willing to work around the inconveniences.

For the cost of an Internet connection and the voice chat software, you can talk to anyone in the world. Many international users also have a per minute charge for the local calls they make to connect to the Internet. But talking to their friends and relatives in distant places using the Internet is still cheaper than what they pay in long-distance charges.

The savings many people see by using the Internet to talk to their loved ones outweighs the inconveniences the technology presents at this time. This is not to say the Internet replaces all the long-distance calls these people make. Quite the contrary. Not everyone has computers or Internet accounts. That leaves a good portion of our society that still uses telephones to call loved ones.

Not only can you talk real-time to friends and family, but you can also meet new people and talk to them using these voice chat programs. Many of these programs are similar to other chat programs in that they offer gathering places for people to meet and chat or talk to each other. They present Internet users with a means to socialize with other people.

In order to voice chat with your loved ones, you must prearrange a time to meet online. With the gathering places provided by these voice chat programs, you can go online at any time of the day or night and find someone to talk with.

What is Voice Chat?

Voice chat is a program you use with your computer and the Internet to allow you to send and receive voice transmissions. These programs let you talk one-to-one or one-to-many in real-time.

For the purpose of this chapter, we are only going to cover the basic one-to-one voice chat programs. The next chapter covers voice chat programs that let you talk one-to-many. Those programs are better used for teleconferencing.

There are several voice chat programs you can download from the web at the Tucows site and other such software sites. This chapter covers a representative number of these voice chat programs but not all of them.

Before you can use any of these voice chat programs, you must have the right equipment. In order to send and receive voice transmission, you need a sound system on your computer. This includes a sound card, speakers, and a microphone.

You must also have enough memory, both RAM and on your hard drive, to store and run these programs. Before you download the voice chat programs you choose, read the system requirements to make sure you have the right equipment and memory to handle the program.

Most of these programs have their own servers. With any of these programs, your computer's sound system, and the programs' servers, you can communicate via voice to other people, either loved ones or strangers. Some of these programs also include video so you can see who you are talking to.

To use the programs that let you send and receive live video feeds, you need a video camera and the software that is compatible with the program you want to use, or some kind of video setup on your computer. Again, read the system requirements for the program before you download it to make sure you have the right equipment.

With these video and voice chat programs, you don't have to have video to use them. You can still receive video, if you have a Windows 95 or NT operating system. You just can't send video of yourself to others.

The following section covers several of the voice chat programs that are available for you to use. Some of these programs are simply voice chat programs while others combine voice chat with video. Most of these programs are shareware programs. Read this chapter carefully and decide which ones you want to try. If you like them, be sure to register your copy and send the developers their fee for the programs.

Voice Chat Programs and How to Use Them

There are many different voice chat programs that you can download from the web at various software sites. We cover several of these programs here. We do this to give you an idea of what is available. To begin with, we cover the voice chat programs that are straight voice chat. Then we move on to the voice chat programs that also include video.

Technique: Make sure you have a fixed IP address before you use these voice chat programs. These fixed IPs help other users connect to you.

The straight voice chat programs offer you the ability to talk live with other people. They have their own servers that you are connected to when you open the software. You use their servers and their phone books to locate people to talk to. If you have friends and family you want to talk to using these programs, you have them meet you at a specific time on their copy of the software.

Gather Talk

Gather Talk is a fairly simple voice chat program to use. Once you download and install it, the program is automatically loaded into your Start menu. This means that each time you start your computer, Gather Talk is one of the programs that automatically tries to start. It opens your Internet Access Dialer. If you click on Connect in the dialer, Gather Talk remains open in the background.

With Gather Talk open in the background, you can then receive calls while you are working on other things. You can also place calls at any time. If you prefer not to have Gather Talk open in the background while you work, left-click on the Gather Talk icon in the task bar at the bottom of your window. Then click on Close. This shuts the program down. I suggest doing this before you connect to the Internet. Otherwise when you click on Close Gather Talk, it tries to close your connection to your provider. If you have other Internet applications open it asks you if you want to close your connection to your provider. It saves you time and steps to close Gather Talk before you connect to the Internet.

Tip: You need at least a 14.4 modem for these voice chat programs. However, the faster modem you have the better for you and the people you voice chat with.

This program offers different areas of interest or languages for users to gather and talk. These areas are broken into General, and then into various languages. When you select a topic, you get a list of users who are also interested in that topic or speak that language. Figure 17-a is an example of this Connect dialog box that lists users under the various topics with Gather Talk.

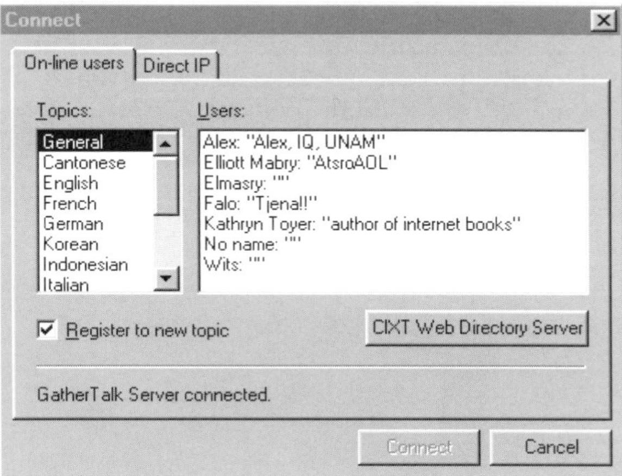

Figure 17-a. Gather Talk topics

After you open Gather Talk, you get a window that lets you place a call or receive a call from someone. This is the main window for Gather Talk. When you do connect with another user, an icon with his or her name or nick appears in this window to let you know who you are talking to. At the top of the window are two icons. One is a green phone handset and the other is a red phone handset with a jagged line through it.

Clicking on the green phone handset takes you to the Connect dialog box. There you select someone you want to talk to by highlighting their name and clicking on the Connect button. When someone calls you, click on the green handset icon if you want to accept the call. If you don't want to accept the call, simply ignore it and eventually it will stop ringing and that person will try someone else. Figure 17-b is an example of the Gather Talk main window.

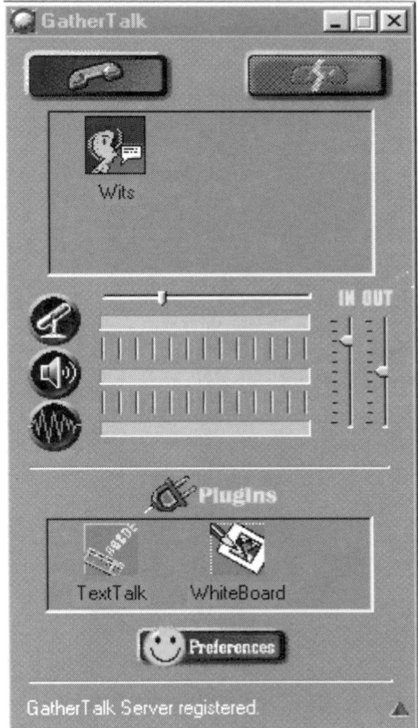

Figure 17-b. Gather Talk main window

If you are unable to hear the other person or he or she is unable to hear you, this program has a way for you to still communicate with each other. You can choose to text talk instead. Simply click on the TextTalk icon at the bottom of the Gather Talk window. You then get a TextTalk window in which the two of you can use text to chat with each other. Figure 17-c is an example of the TextTalk window.

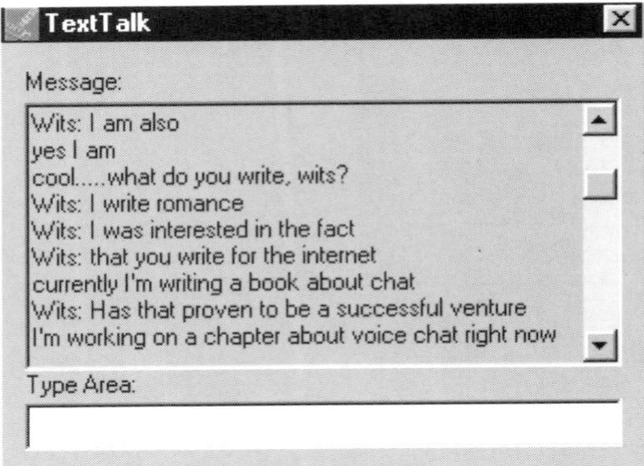

Figure 17-c. Gather Talk text chat

While you are talking to others you can also use the whiteboard to draw and doodle. You can also talk to more than one person at a time. Myself and others found this program seems to have problems with the modems and microphones working properly. Most of the time I was unable to establish voice communications. The program could be a good program provided all the bugs are worked out of it.

InterPhone

InterPhone is a voice chat program that lets you dial other users or lets them dial you to establish voice communication. There is no directory for this program or gathering place like there are for other voice chat programs. Therefore you must know the address, e-mail or IP address, in order to contact someone with this software.

The program does allow you to set up speed dial numbers under the One Touch Dialing feature. You can also add names and addresses under the Phone Book option for easy reference and dialing. If someone leaves you a message while you are on another call or away from your computer, you can retrieve it from the Message Center. InterPhone also has an option that lets you log your conversations with other. Figure 17-d on the following page is an example of the main window for InterPhone.

Tip: Before talking to specific friends and family members, set up a date and time to meet online. This saves each of you time and frustration.

InterPhone is a nice program if you already know the address of the people you want to contact and talk to. This is a good program for those who want to talk via the Internet to their loved ones.

Figure 17-d. InterPhone main window

Televox

Televox is another straight chat program. After you have downloaded and installed this program, you click on the desktop icon for Televox to open the program. The first time you use Televox you are taken through several steps to configure it to your preferences and establish a profile on yourself.

This setup process also includes testing of your sound system to get the volumes adjusted correctly to your environment. After you have completed all the setup screens for Televox, the program opens for you to begin your communications. The main screen presents you with several options. You can sit and wait for someone to call you or you can use the Call button to bring up a list of other users you can talk to with Televox. Figure 17-e is an example of the main Televox window.

When you click on the Call button in Televox, you get a Call window which lists all the users who are online at that moment. You can scan through this list to find someone you want to call and talk with. This listing gives you the user's name or nickname, e-mail address, and a comment. Once you find someone you wish to speak with, highlight the user's name and click on the Dial button at the bottom of the Call window. Televox then attempts to connect you to that person. Figure 17-f is an example of the Televox Call window.

Figure 17-e. Televox Pro main window

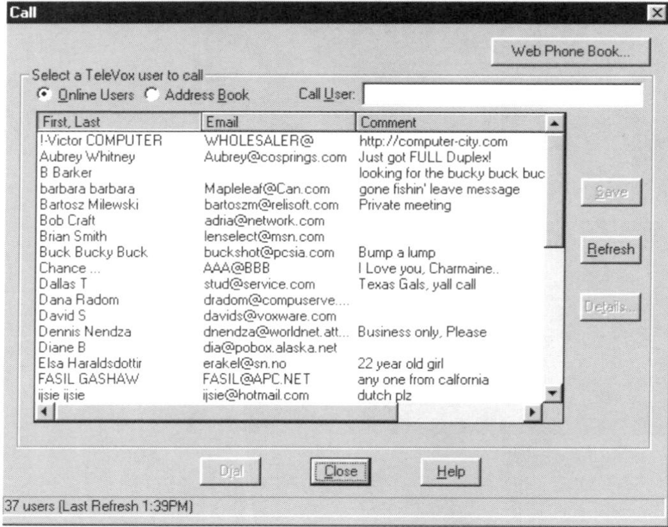

Figure 17-f. Televox call window

Each time you call someone or they call you, their name is displayed for you in the Televox main window after the connection has been established. The program also tracks the time you are online with this caller. If the two of you are having problems communicating via voice, you can switch to text chat by clicking on the ABC Text Chat button in this main window. Figure 17-g is an example of what the main window looks like after you establish a connection with another user.

Technique: Headphones are suggested to help you understand the other party better through the distortion and delays that are common with voice chat.

While you are chatting with someone, you can also transfer files back and forth to each other. In addition, if you prefer to change the sound of your voice, you can. Televox offers you the option of Voice Fonts to change your voice. Click on the Voice Fonts icon in the Televox main window and then select the Voice Font you want to use.

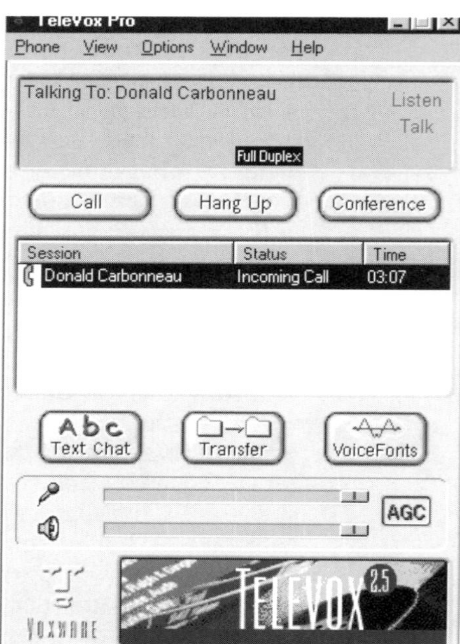

Figure 17-g. Televox connection

The few times I received calls from anyone, the quality of the transmission was very bad. The transmissions came across very slow and garbled. The other person could not hear me at all and was too impatient to wait or use the text chat. You may have better luck with this program than I did.

Internet Phone

Internet Phone is one of the voice chat programs that comes with video also. It also includes some nice graphics to help you know what is going on when you are chatting with others. It lets you know when the other person is talking, when you are on hold, when you have an incoming call, and so forth. You can also send and receive videos of the people you are talking to.

Be advised: This is one program that has its own server and has gathering places set up. These are similar to the chat channels in IRC. However, most of these are made up of sex-related chats. Therefore, if you have children, you want to monitor them very closely with this program. Even in the General chat areas, you can be contacted by someone who has something different in mind than you do.

After you download Internet Phone and install it on your hard drive, you can open the program. When it opens it begins connecting you to its server. Once the connection has been made, you are automatically dumped into one of the General chat areas. You do not have to stay in this chat area. You can leave it and find another one more suitable to your tastes. You can also stay there and join other chat areas too.

You can find other users online or chat areas by looking through Internet Phone's Global Online Directory. This lists all the chat areas that are available and how many users are in each area. Use this to find a chat area you are interested in. Figure 17-h is an example of the Global Online Directory.

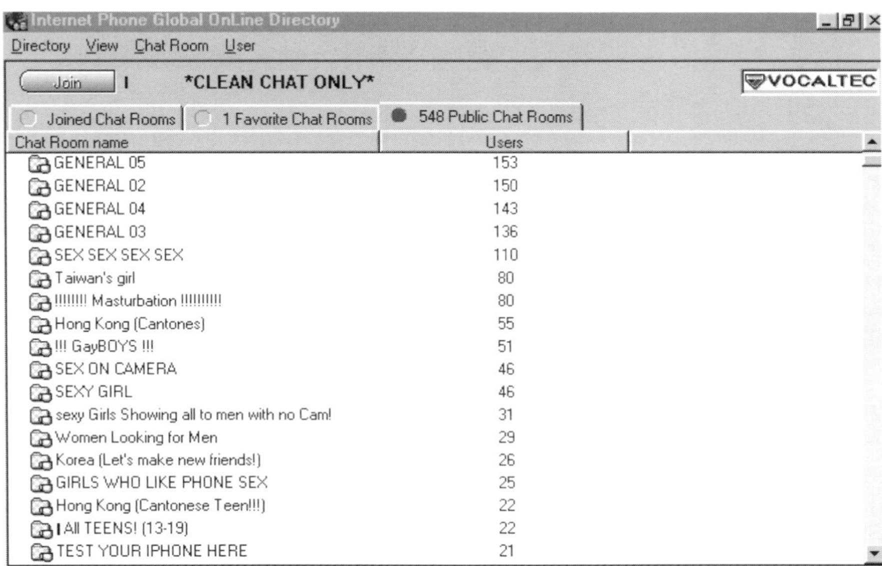

Figure 17-h. Internet Phone global directory

When you join a chat area, you get a listing of everyone who is in that room. This information includes profile data the users provided on themselves. You see what their nick is, what their real name is, and any other information in the way of comments they chose to include. Figure 17-i is an example of what the chat areas in Internet Phone look like.

Technique: Play around with your codec settings in the program you choose to use to adjust the quality of transmissions and receptions.

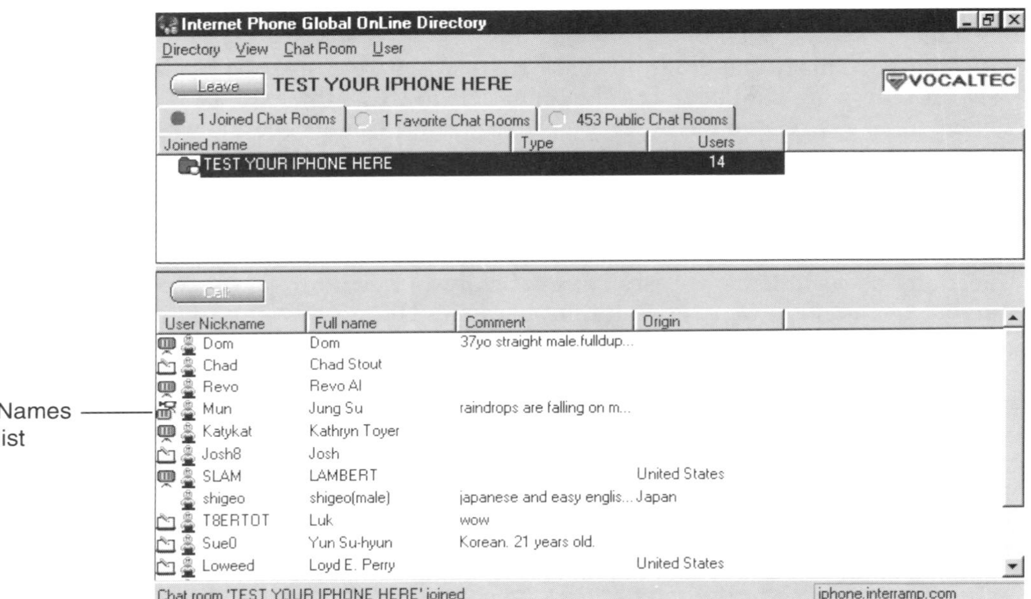

Figure 17-i. Chat room

While you are waiting to connect to another Internet Phone user, you get an Internet Phone screen which gives you your status with Internet Phone. If you are not connected to anyone, calling someone, or being called by someone, the screen tells you that it's waiting for a call. Figure 17-j on the following page is an example of this waiting Internet Phone window.

Each activity that happens in Internet Phone gives you a different screen that keeps you informed. When someone connects to you, the screen changes to reflect the two of you talking. The upper half shows two people connected via a telephone. This screen also tells you when someone is talking, when someone is listening, or when no one is talking. At the bottom of this screen, you also get a status of all calls you have connected as well as any that you received during your session with Internet Phone. If you want to contact someone you spoke with before, you can highlight their name in that status area and click on Phone to initiate a call. Figure 17-k is an example of this screen when you are connected to a caller.

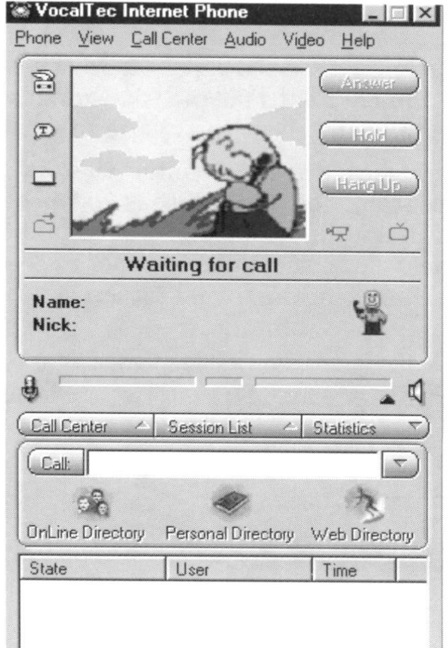

Figure 17-j. Waiting for call window

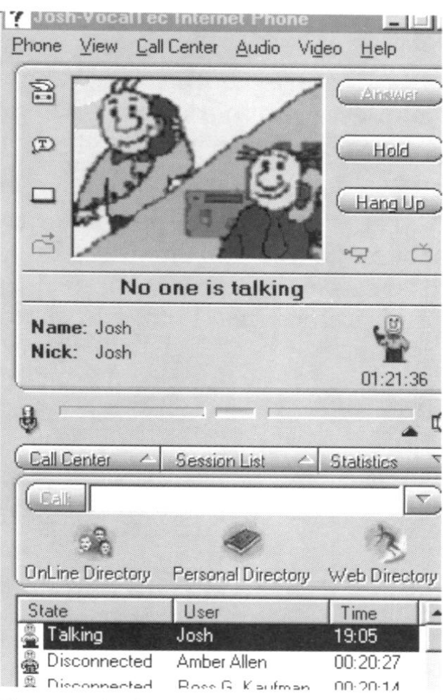

Figure 17-k. Connected call window

With Internet Phone you can receive calls while you are talking to someone else. It gives you the option to put one person on hold while you answer another call. When you put someone on hold or you are put on hold, Internet Phone changes your status to On Hold. When someone is trying to call you while you are talking, Internet Phone tells you that you have a call waiting. When you choose to answer the other call, you put the first caller on hold automatically. Figure 17-l is an example of the Internet Phone screen when you are on hold with a caller.

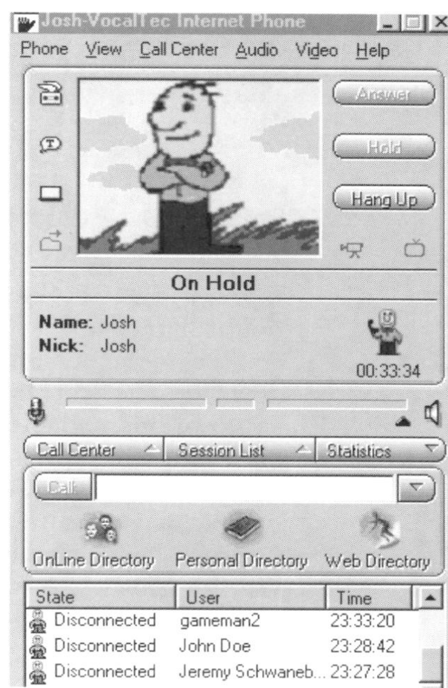

Figure 17-l. On hold window

Tip: These voice chat programs work better utilizing the full-duplex capabilities built into them.

Internet Phone is one of the best programs out of all the voice chat programs available. It is the most stable and has the best quality of transmissions and receptions. If you have video capabilities, you can add live video feeds to your conversations. If you don't have video capabilities, it's still an excellent program to use to voice chat with others and you can still receive live video feeds from others.

Iris Phone

Iris Phone is another voice chat program with video capabilities. This program connects you to its server. Then you can chat with people you know or you can do a search of who is connected to Iris Phone and talk with anyone there.

When you open Iris Phone, you are presented with a window that lists the technical support or sales people for the program. You can call these people and talk to them. Or you can choose to do a search and find someone else to talk to. This initial screen is how you connect to others. It is also where you set up your options and preferences. Figure 17-m is an example of the initial screen you get with Iris Phone.

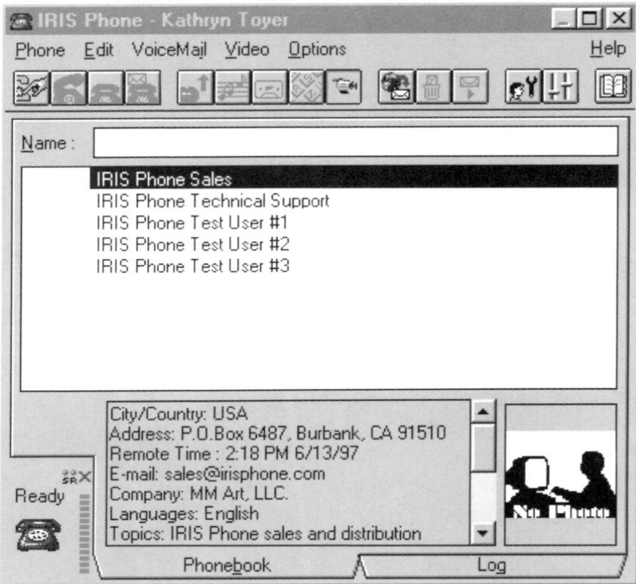

Figure 17-m. Iris Phone main window

If you want to do a search of Iris Phone's White Pages to see who is on that you might like to talk with, click on the Call icon in the toolbar of the initial screen you get. This icon is a blue phone with a hand dialing on it. Iris Phone gives you a window that lets you choose how you want to search for others on its server. Enter your options and click on the Start button. Once it connects to the server and completes its search, Iris Phone lists its Search Results in the right-hand portion of your White Pages window. You can then select who you want to talk with by highlighting their name. Once you highlight their name, you can add them to your Address Book or you can call them. Figure 17-n is an example of Iris Phone's White Pages window.

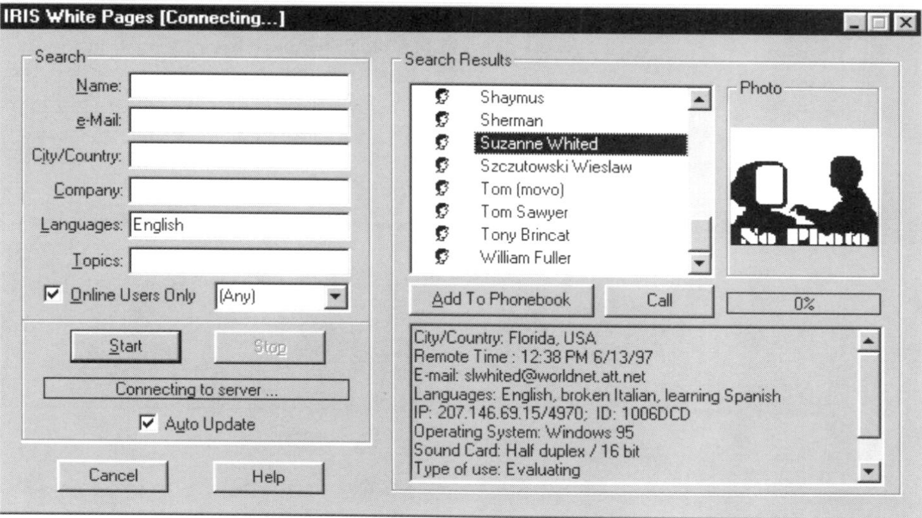

Figure 17-n. Iris Phone White Pages

Iris Phone also allows you to use video if you have video capabilities. Then you can see who you are talking to and vice versa when you connect with someone. It is a nice program to use to voice chat with your loved ones or to meet new people and voice chat with them.

VDO Phone

VDO Phone combines voice chat with video and text chat. You can register with the program so that your name or nick is displayed on a web page for other VDO Phone users to find you. Beware: This is one program that seems to attract those interested in chatting about sex as well as sending you video of them in various states of undress, usually completely undressed. When you tell these people you are not interested in chatting about sex or phone sex, they quickly disconnect from you and move on to other prey.

When you open the program for the first time, you go through a setup and test process. Part of this process is to set up a password. This is to keep your children from accessing this program, and for good reason. Then each time you open this program, you must supply your password before you can access it. After you enter your correct password, VDO Phone gives you its main window. It is through this window that you perform all of your activities. If you know someone to call, you can do it from this screen. If you don't know anyone, you can access VDO Phone's Directory Services through this screen. Simply click on the Who's Online ball in this window. Figure 17-o is an example of VDO Phone's main window.

Figure 17-o. VDO Phone main window

After you click on the Who's Online ball in the main VDO Phone window, your web browser opens and takes you to the VDO Phone Directory Services. On this web page you can search for others with similar interests. Simply enter the values you want it to search for and click on the Search button. You then get a page that lists all the VDO Phone users that are online at the time. Figure 17-p is an example of the VDO Phone Directory Services.

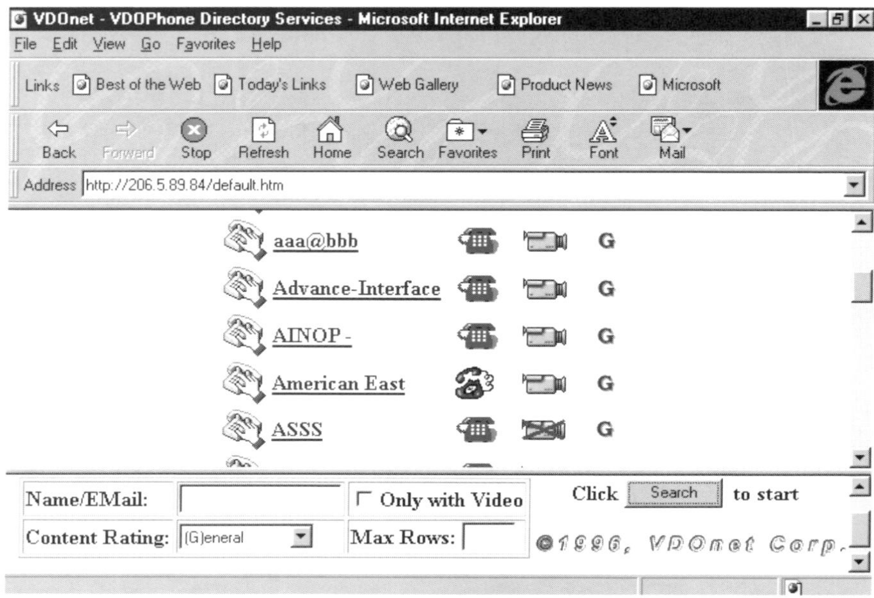

Figure 17-p. VDO Phone directory

Once you search through all the users online with VDO Phone and you select the one you want to chat with, you click on the Yellow Phone icon. VDO Phone then attempts to connect you to that person. Once a connection has been established, you can start talking to each other. If you have video capabilities, you can send live video feeds to each other.

If either of you are experiencing trouble with the voice reception or transmission, VDO Phone lets you use text chat to communicate. The users of this program are not too shy to use text chat if the voice transmissions aren't up to par.

VDO Phone is a nice program that could have a lot of potential. However, the amount of sexually oriented conversations that go on in this program make it undesirable for those who aren't interested in that sort of talk or who have children.

HoneyComb

HoneyComb is a voice chat with video program that you can use with IRC. It lets you connect to the EfNet and to ChatNet. When you connect to HoneyComb, you get its main Greetings window. From this window you set up your options and connect to meeting rooms. This window is your central point of activity. Figure 17-q is an example of HoneyComb's Greetings window.

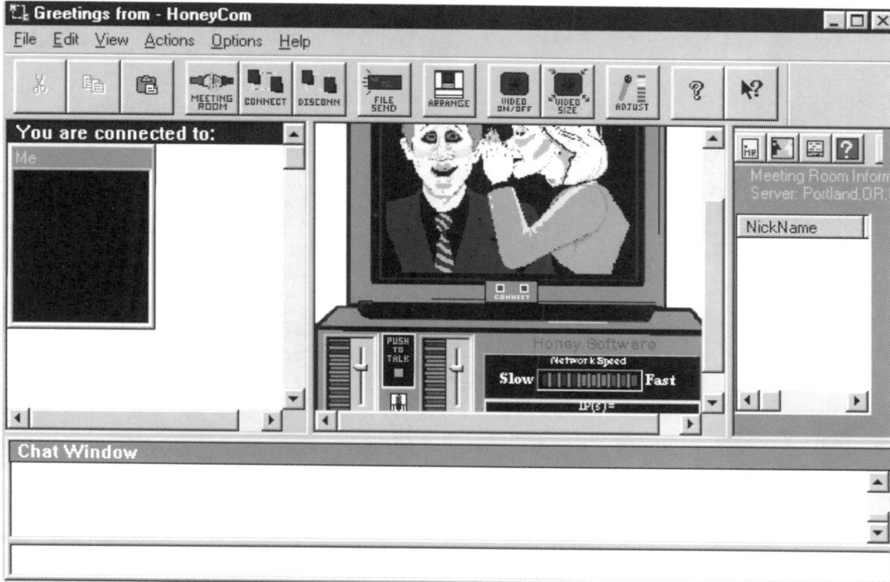

Figure 17-q. HoneyComb's Greetings and main window

When you want to connect to a meeting room, click on Actions in the menu bar and then select Join a Meeting Room or click on the Meeting Room icon. HoneyComb then gives you a connection window. This window gives you the status of your connection attempt and lets you know when you are connected to the server. Figure 17-r is an example of this connection window.

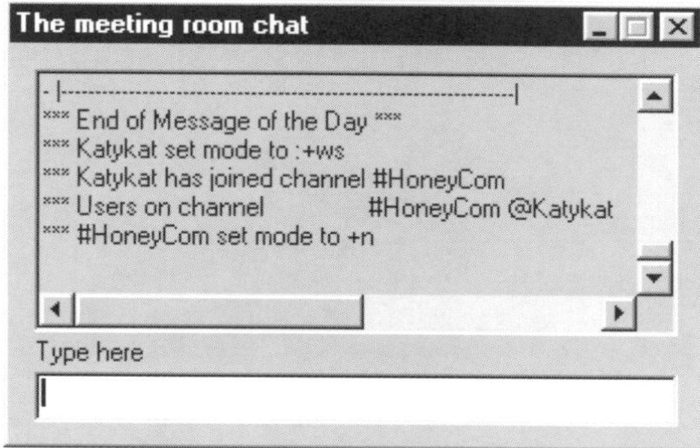

Figure 17-r. HoneyComb's server connection

Once your connection is established, HoneyComb dumps you into the channel #honeycomb. In this channel, you can text chat with others or you can voice and video chat with them. Although the window doesn't look much different from the Greetings window, it is. Notice that your nick now appears in the right-hand side of the window. When there are other people on the channel, their nicks appear there also. Then you can initiate voice chats with them or simply text chat.

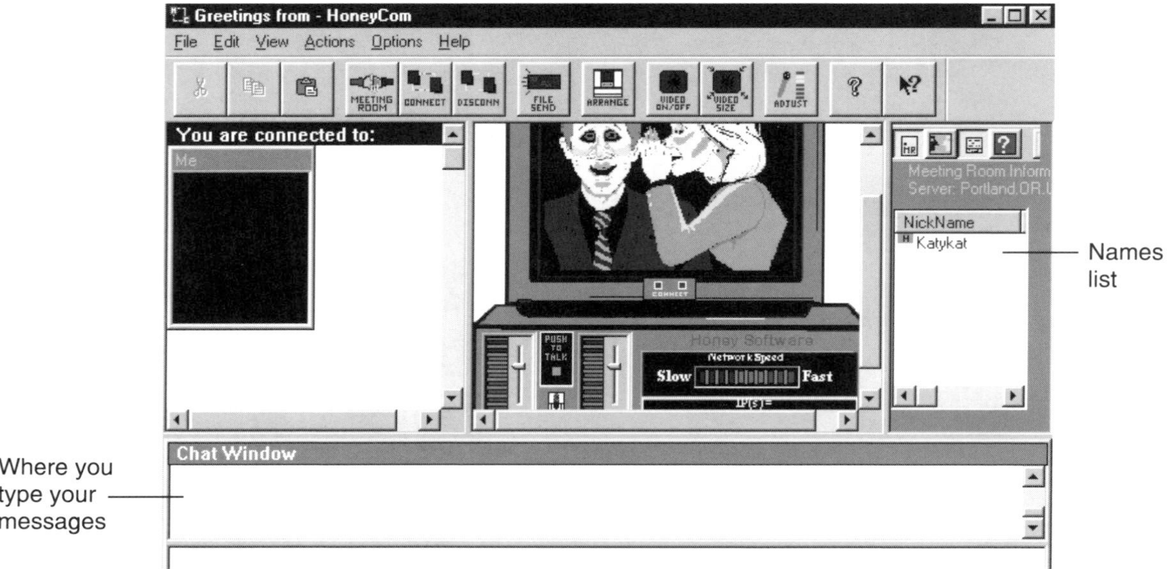

Figure 17-s. HoneyComb channel window

HoneyComb is a nice enhancement to IRC. It offers you the ability to use IRC for both text and voice chat with video as an extra bonus. It could prove to be a popular program once it catches on.

Study these voice chat programs. Test a few out for yourself. Find one that you like and that performs the way you want. Then use it to meet new people or to voice chat with your loved ones.

Chapter 18

Internet Teleconferencing

In this chapter you learn:

- ☑ *What is Internet Teleconferencing?*
- ☑ *Tools for Internet Teleconferencing and How to Use Them*

The Internet gives businesses a way to keep in touch with distant employees. E-mail is one way businesses can keep in touch, but the Internet also provides a way for businesses to keep voice contact with those employees. With the voice chat programs, businesses can have employees report in for assignments or discuss the day's activities. The Internet takes voice communications even further.

Businesses can use the Internet to hold sales meetings, conferences, training sessions, and workshops. Anything a group can do via the telephone and conferencing can be done on the Internet. To conduct teleconferencing on the Internet, businesses need an Internet account, teleconferencing software, and the video equipment and software.

These Internet teleconferencing programs let businesses, educators, and trainers use the capabilities of the Internet to give real-time, live presentations. Several businesses, educators, and trainers have already discovered how to use the Internet to teleconference and televideo conference. The increasing demand from users for reliable and effective teleconferencing and televideo conferencing products has encouraged software developers to design products to meet these needs.

What is Internet Teleconferencing?

Internet teleconferencing is using the Internet and special software to voice conference with other people. The special teleconferencing software allows a group of users to meet via a special server so that they can converse together. Internet teleconferencing is very similar to teleconferencing using conventional telephones. Although the quality isn't up to the quality of telephone service teleconferencing, it has improved over the past year or two and continues to improve.

These teleconferencing programs allow the group to talk in real-time to each other just as they would if they were talking over a telephone. They also let the group collaborate on and share projects. With video added to the mix, the group can see each other as they are talking or the group leader can put on a demonstration or training session or conduct a meeting.

The teleconference can be conducted wherever the members of the group have computers or laptops. Some of the members may be in their motel rooms, some may be hooked up through a connection at an Internet café location, and others may be coming to the conference through their connection from their homes. With Internet teleconferencing, no one needs to make the expensive trip back to the home or regional office location to sit in a stuffy meeting room.

The time and expense it takes to take all these people out of their territories and transport them to the meeting location is saved when businesses use Internet teleconferencing. Generally, when a company holds a sales meeting, for instance, they have to pay to have all their sales reps leave their territories and travel to and from the meeting site. For all the reps who have territories outside the meeting area, the business has to also provide overnight accommodations for them for the duration of the meeting.

With Internet teleconferencing, no one has to leave their territory. They can all stay where they are and use their computer and the special net-based conferencing software to participate in the meeting. There is no need for time lost traveling to and from the meeting. Nor is there the added expense of motel rooms for the group while they attend the meeting. No matter where the rep is, he can participate in the teleconference once he establishes his connection to his Internet account.

Even conventional videoconferencing can run a company over $1,000 a seat. It is more cost effective for many business to expend under $300 per computer for video conferencing than it is to hold meetings at a remote location or videoconference via conventional means. Businesses that are adept at using whiteboards for presentations and collaborations are much better candidates for televideo conferencing.

The quality of televideo conferencing over the Internet is not as high as it is for conventional videoconferencing. However, the quality is improving and is also dependent upon the type of connection the company uses and the type of equipment it chooses for the videoconferencing. The adage "You get what you pay for" is very true when selecting the equipment you plan to use for televideo conferencing over the Internet.

The higher quality of equipment and lines you use, the better your transmission and receptions are. The best camera for this purpose is the CCD-PC1 PC Cam with the second best being The QuickCam from Connectrix. If you prefer to use your own videocam with a capture card, then the software you choose to use it with becomes equally important. The next section covers the teleconferencing software available to use with your videocam and the Internet. The best connection is through the Ethernet with an ISDN line being the second choice for speed and quality of the connection.

The video cameras for Internet use range from $200 to $2,000. It is advised that cameras that cost under $600 don't provide the quality of synchronized video and audio of the higher priced cameras. If what you are looking for is quality of transmission in sync with audio and no blurring when there is movement, the higher priced cameras are the better purchase. However, if you're not concerned with full-motion video presentations, the lower priced cameras are sufficient. This is especially true if you are planning to conduct most televideo conferencing using a whiteboard.

After you consider the video equipment you have or need to use, it's time to consider the software to use with the Internet to make these televideo conferences happen. There are a few very good products available.

Tools for Internet Teleconferencing and How to Use Them

There are several software programs available to help you use the Internet for teleconferencing or televideo conferencing. This section covers a couple of these products and shows you the basics of how to use them. One of the products this chapter highlights is Microsoft's NetMeeting. This section also tells you about some of the other products available but does not go into detail about those products.

CUSeeMe was detailed in its own chapter previously in this book. It can also be used as a televideo conferencing tool. It offers several nice tools to assist businesses in televideo conferencing. These include the collaboration tools of a whiteboard, a file transfer utility, and a text-based chat option. It does not, however, allow the group to share documents.

CUSeeMe lets you put up to twelve video windows on your screen at the same time, letting you view up to twelve group participants at once. The only drawback is that the performance degrades in proportion to the number of video windows you add. This product is a good choice if you need multiuser audio and video capabilities and don't need the collaboration capabilities of some of the other products.

Internet Conference Professional by VocalTec is a good collaboration program. This program does not have video capabilities, however, the developers of this product are working on a new version that does include video.

Internet Conference Professional lets you connect to one of its servers. Then you can set up a private conference room and invite the rest of your group to join you. The others in the group must type the name of the room into their copy of Internet Conference Professional.

This program does allow document sharing and collaboration. This lets the group make and see changes almost instantaneously. For this feature to work in editing documents, all the parties in the group must have the same application. But that is pretty standard anytime you want to edit or work with any document. To make it easy for its users, Internet Conference Professional includes icons for inserting documents onto the whiteboard as part of its program. This program is an excellent product for teleconferencing and collaborations on documents.

Before we get into learning about NetMeeting, let's look at what you should look for in a teleconferencing product. Following is a list of features you want to look for:

- Easy setup — Is the product easy to set up? Does it let you test the audio and video performance? How easy is it to install? Does it adapt to the speed of your connection?
- Invites — How easy is it to invite others in your group to join you in a conference? Does the product offer speed dialing or an address book feature to make it easier for you to connect to your group?
- Multiplatform support — Does it support the various operating systems like Windows 95, Windows NT, UNIX, Macintosh, Windows 3x? Does it support H.323 which is the standard that allows cross-packaged conversations?
- Conferencing with a group — Does it meet all your needs for a teleconferencing or televideo conferencing tool? Does it have all the features you want like text chat backup, file transfer capabilities, a whiteboard, and/or document sharing and collaboration? Does it support the International Telecommunication Union's T.120 standard? This is important to be able to perform collaborations and file transfers.
- Collaboration — Does it have a whiteboard? Does the whiteboard give you easy-to-use mark-up tools? Does the program include a separate chat window for users to type comments? Does it let you share documents? How fast does the program perform updates on shared documents when the group is collaborating?

Use these questions to help you find the product that best suits your needs for teleconferencing over the Internet. Following is one product that provides some nice features for teleconferencing and televideo conferencing. It is highlighted here to give you an idea of what's available and how to use the products.

NetMeeting

NetMeeting by Microsoft is a full-featured Internet teleconference software package. This program looks very much like Microsoft's Internet Explorer which gives those users easier interface with NetMeeting. This program allows real-time audio, video, and data communications via the Internet.

Before you can begin to use NetMeeting you must make sure you have the proper equipment and system to handle the program. The system requirements include:

- Microsoft Windows 95 or NT
- 486/66 or faster computer with 8 MB of RAM or more; a Pentium with 12 MB of RAM is recommended and a must if you plan to use video
- Sound card, speakers, and a microphone
- Video-capture card and a camera or video camera that connects through your computer's parallel port, if you want to send video

You can download this program from any of the software sites on the web like the Tucows site or you can download it as part of the Microsoft Internet Explorer program or separately from the Microsoft site. This is a freeware program so when you register it, you need not send any money for the program. After you download the program, install it on your hard drive. It is a self-extracting file that installs itself automatically on your hard drive while creating a menu item for you in the Start menu.

Once you have NetMeeting installed, click on the menu item and start the program. When the program loads, it gives you a main window and tries to connect you to one of the Microsoft NetMeeting servers. The main window is designed to give you easy use of the program and its features. Figure 18-a is an example of the NetMeeting main window.

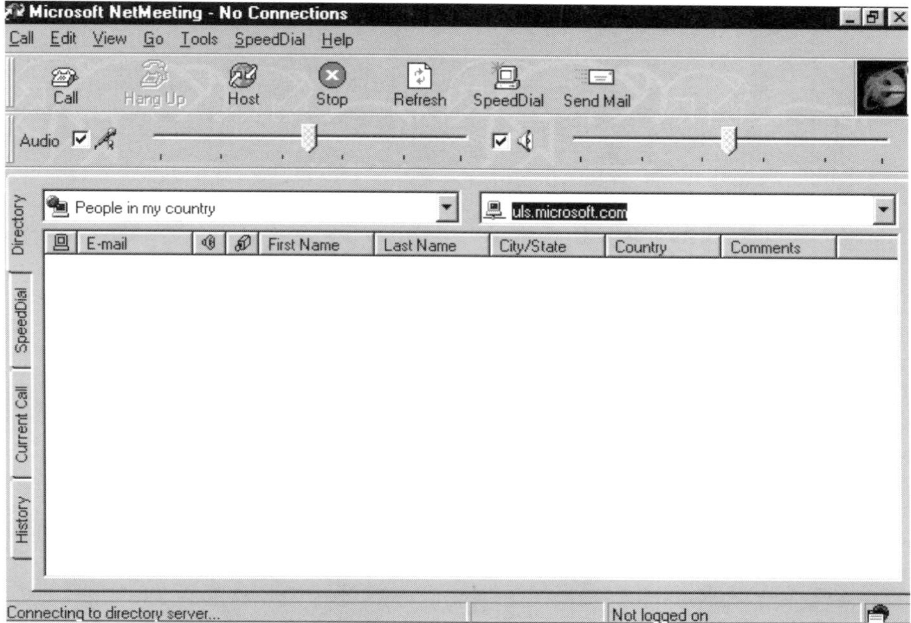

Figure 18-a. NetMeeting main window

NetMeeting gives you toolbar items to help you activate its features. It also includes tabs along the left-hand side of the window for easy access and viewing.

After you connect to the Microsoft server, you get a list of the people who are connected to that server via NetMeeting. You can select how you want to view those users. You can view them All, or you can view them by People in a call, People not in a call, People with audio and video, People with audio, and People in my country. Once you make your selection, NetMeeting displays those users in the window for you to scan through. Figure 18-b on the following page is an example of the window with the users listed.

You can use this directory to locate the others in the group and add them to your Speed Dial list. Adding users to the Speed Dial is a simple process of locating their name or e-mail address in the directory and right-clicking on it. Then choose Add to Speed Dial from the options you are given. Each time you come on, you can check this Speed Dial list to see if any of your group is on. Figure 18-c is an example of the Speed Dial list.

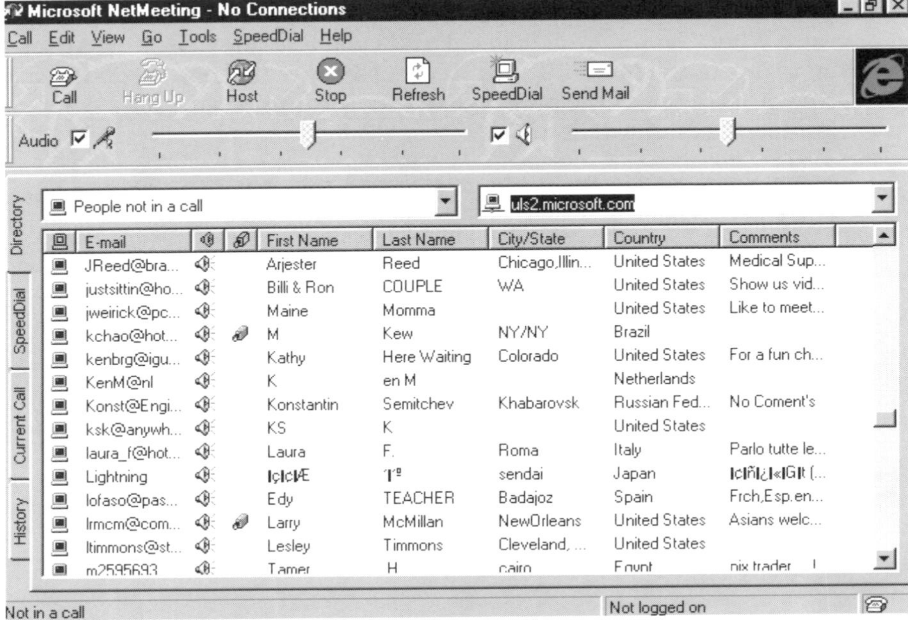

Figure 18-b. NetMeeting server directory of users

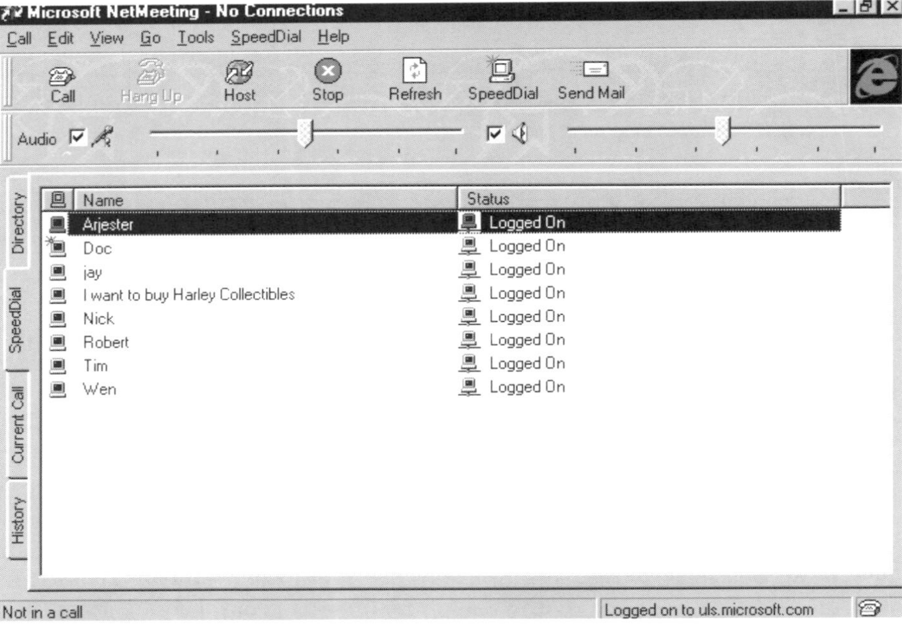

Figure 18-c. Speed Dial list

From the Speed Dial list you can then begin calling each user you want to conference with. Simply click on their name in the list and click on the Call icon in the toolbar. Before you begin inviting others to join you, you need to establish a place to meet. Click on the Host icon in the toolbar and click on OK when it asks you if you want to host a conference. NetMeeting then gives you a private conference room to conduct your business in. Figure 18-d is an example of the conference room you get in NetMeeting.

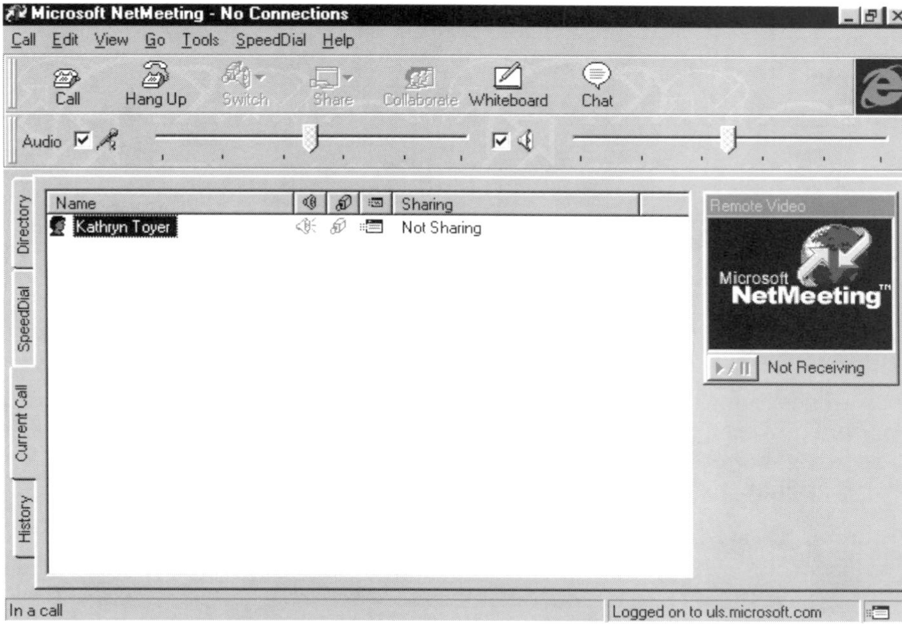

Figure 18-d. NetMeeting conference room

When everyone has joined you can then begin your meeting and using the tools NetMeeting gives you to assist you in your meeting. One of these tools you use to demonstrate or collaborate with the group is the whiteboard. With the whiteboard you can draw, highlight, add colors, import documents, and edit or work on them. It also allows you to add text, point to objects or areas on the whiteboard, and lock the contents so that the other users can't edit or change anything you do on the whiteboard. This is a great tool for demonstrations or for collaborations. Figure 18-e on the following page is an example of NetMeeting's whiteboard.

Along with this whiteboard, everyone in the group can share an application with each other. The person who wants to share the application clicks on the Share icon in the toolbar, after they have started the application on their own system, to start the Sharing an Application function. Then everyone in the group can participate in changing a document or creating one from scratch in this application. Be careful using this feature and sharing a Windows Explorer window like My Computer. Remember you are sharing all the Windows Explorer windows you have open when you do this. Therefore, anyone could change things in those applications that you don't want changed.

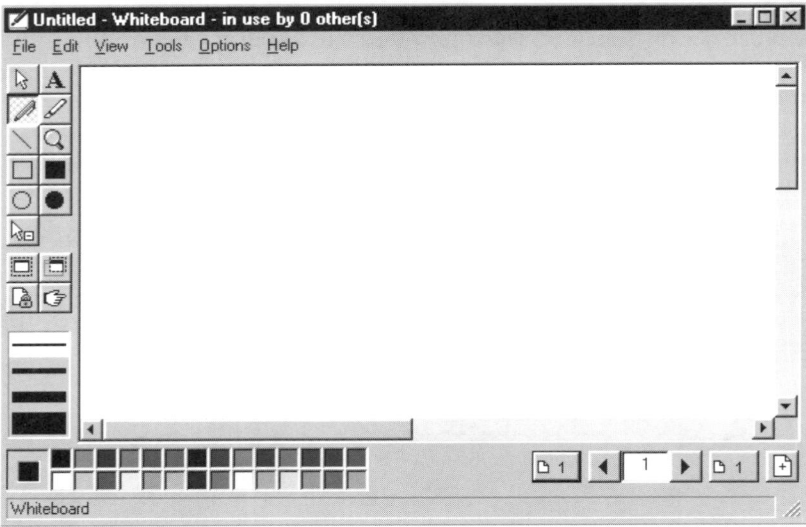

Figure 18-e. NetMeeting whiteboard

In addition to these collaboration activities, NetMeeting gives you and the others in your group the ability to text chat. This allows everyone the capability of adding text comments to the projects you are working on. Figure 18-f is an example of the text chat that is available with NetMeeting.

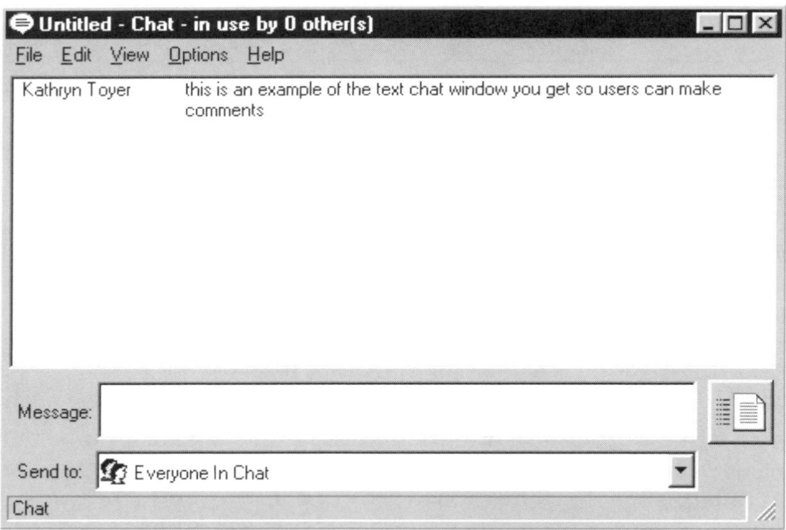

Figure 18-f. NetMeeting text chat

NetMeeting also lets you create a link on your web pages so that others using Internet Explorer or NetMeeting can call you. If someone wants to establish a voice connection to you while they are traveling on the web, they can do this through your web site. However, if you're not online at the time, they are unable to connect to you. Of course, then they can leave you an e-mail message.

With the video feature of NetMeeting, only two people can send and receive video at a time. Therefore, this feature of the program is best used for presentation or demonstration purposes. However, one person can send video for the whole group to see. The receivers do not need to have video on their end in order to receive video. The person or persons who want to send video are the only ones that need the video capabilities. The audio features of NetMeeting are limited as well. Only one person at a time can speak. Therefore, the text chat comes in handy when you are sharing applications and collaborating.

NetMeeting is a very nice program that enables you to conduct meetings, perform demonstrations, or train a group of users. It allows you the privacy of a private conference room. It also lets everyone in the group participate in collaborative efforts. If you plan to try using the Internet for videoconferencing or teleconferencing, this is a product to try.

Chapter 19
Putting It All Together

In this chapter you learn:

- ☑ *Putting It All Together in mIRC*
- ☑ *Putting It All Together in Pirch*

IRC offers you a lot of potential activities you can perform. The IRC client you use offers you even more potential. Many of the activities you perform while you are on IRC are pretty simple and basic. However, there are many advanced activities you can perform once you learn how to do them.

This book is designed to help you learn how to do some of these advanced type activities. This book has covered a lot of material. In this chapter we take what you have learned in each of the chapters and put it all together for each of the IRC clients mIRC and Pirch.

Putting It All Together in mIRC

If you have been using IRC for a while and have used mIRC as your primary IRC client, then you have probably experimented with some of the things you can do in mIRC to enhance your time on IRC. You have probably already created several aliases, popups, and events to take care of some of the more mundane tasks you normally do.

At some point you probably thought to yourself how nice it would be if only you could do such and such. You think there must be a way to do that in an alias, a popup, or even an event. You may even see other users doing things you wish you could do. If only you knew how. This book is designed to help you learn how to do the things you wish you could do but don't know how.

In order to become proficient at all the things you want to do in mIRC, you must take it a step at a time. Learn each of the different features of mIRC and you can become as expert at getting mIRC to do things automatically for you as some of those other users have.

The first step is to learn all the commands. Then you must learn all the special mIRC commands, identifiers, and so forth. After you learn these, you need to begin learning how to create different kinds of aliases. Since this book deals with advanced activities, this chapter covers how to put it all together with advanced functions in aliases, popups, and remote events and controls.

Aliases

Since you have been using IRC for a while, you have already learned how to create some of the easier and basic aliases like ones for joining or parting a channel. In Chapter 1 you learned how to create more complicated aliases and in Chapter 13 you learned how to create scripts to use in aliases to perform even more complicated alias functions.

Aliases are designed to give you shortcuts you can use to have the client perform certain activities for you. You want to keep these shortcuts short and easy to remember. Then create aliases that make your life simpler and easier while you're on IRC. Use aliases to perform mundane or repeated activities that require you to enter long command strings.

Let's review what you learned and practice a few alias functions you can create and learn so you can begin creating your own. To begin with, open the Alias Edit box in mIRC. Type a shortcut for the alias you are going to make. Let's name this one Tester1. After the shortcut type in a command to read a random line from one of the text files on your system.

The command should look like this: /<shortcut> /say $read <directory\path\filename>.

Now create another alias to put that read alias on a timer to display random lines of text to the channel every three minutes. Review timers and how to set them from mIRC's help file or from Chapter 1. The command should look similar to this: /<shortcut> /<timer#> 0 <seconds to = 3 minutes> /describe $chan $!read <directory\path\filename.

Next, review Chapter 1 and create a unique color-coded alias. Remember to use Ctrl+k preceding the numbers for color changes. Use some of the shifted characters to create some ASCII art to go along with your special alias.

Lastly, let's create a script in the Alias edit box. Create a script that evaluates the size of a file in your mIRC directory. Pick any file you want. Name this script Tester2. The script should look similar to this with your values inserted in the angle brackets:

```
tester1 {
  set %test $lof( $mircdir $+ <yourfilename> )
  set %test2 $lof( [ $mircdir $+ <yourfilename> ] )
  echo 2 -a the value of % $+ test (without brackets) is: %test
  echo 3 -a The value of % test2 (with brackets) is: %test2
  unset %test %test2
}
```

Refer back to the chapter often and the help files in mIRC to help you in creating aliases. Try your hand at a few of your own. If they don't work the first time, keep trying different things until you get them to work. A big part of creating these aliases in mIRC involves trial and error. Following is a list of things you can do to help you create advanced aliases.

- Learn all the IRC commands
- Learn all the mIRC commands
- Learn all the mIRC variables and identifiers
- Create the shortcut identifier you want to use
- Create the command for the alias
- Learn how to create and use scripts

This list is applicable to Pirch also, with the exception that you learn Pirch identifiers and variables as well as the PIL scripting language for Pirch. After you master aliases, go on to popups and learn how to master them.

Popups

Popups are very similar to aliases, but they let you use a drop-down menu to select the command or activity you want to use rather then typing a shortcut. After you've had a taste of creating some of the simpler popups, you are ready to create some of the more complicated popups.

Click on the Popups toolbar item to open the Popups edit box. Remember to give your popups menu names and submenu names. Each of these submenus are preceded by a dot or a series of dots depending on where they fall in the submenus.

Let's try creating a few popups. In the menu bar of the Popup Edit box, select View and choose Nickname list from the options. Now copy the color-coded alias you created earlier to your popups. Don't forget to give it a submenu name.

Next, click on View again in the menu bar of the edit box and select Status from the options. Now create a timer popup to set yourself away and leave a message in the channel every five minutes. Refer back to Chapter 2 to refresh your memory about how to create this popup. The command should look similar to this: .<popup name>:/ame is Away ($+$?= <your message> $+) | /away <your message> | /timer<#> <# of time to display> <time in seconds> /ame is away (<your message>).

Lastly, create a timer page for your away message. You select which popup area to put this popup into. The command should look like this with your variables inserted in the angle brackets: .Away and Record Pages:/away $$?="What is your away message?" | /timer<#> 1 0 <time in seconds> /.play -c -11 pages.txt 500.

Remotes and Events

Remotes and events are commands that react to things you or other users do while you are in IRC or in a channel. This area of mIRC lets you automate many activities and frees you up to do more serious chatting.

To begin creating events you must select the Remote Events icon from the toolbar. This gives you the Events edit box. Then you must select the area you want to create the events for. You do this through the View and Listening menu options.

Begin by creating a users list. Select the correct area to put the users list in. Then enter the levels you want to use for this users list. Create popups so you can add users to this list.

Next create an event that sends a user's ping time back to him when you ping him. Select the correct area to put this event command in. Be sure not to put yourself in a continuous loop situation. The command looks similar to this:

```
1:CTCPREPLY:PING*    {
  if ( $nick != $me ) {
    %pt = $ctime - $parm2
    /notice $nick **Your ping reply is %pt seconds
  }
```

Refer back to Chapter 3 and the help file for creating events. Create a few of your own. Try to determine how some you have seen others using work. Then try to set them up in the Remote Events edit box. Keep trying until you get it right. Events are fairly straightforward and easy to set up in mIRC. You should have no problems.

Putting It All Together in Pirch

Aliases

Pirch has its own set of identifiers and variables. You need to learn those, as well as the IRC commands in order to master creating aliases. Then read the PIL help file to help you learn how to create scripts and the PIL scripting language.

Many of the aliases you create in Pirch are very different from the ones you create in mIRC. Be sure to get familiar with Pirch's variables and identifiers. Learn how they work so that you can use them to create aliases.

Let's try a few examples to test what you've learned so far in this book. Begin by opening the Pirch Alias edit box. Type in the name you want for the shortcut for the alias you are creating. Then type in the command for the alias.

Create an alias to read a line from a text file in your system followed by it reading another line from that same text file. This involves setting up two aliases. The first alias should look like this: type the alias name in the alias name box, then type /notice $1 <your message> #<channelname>, then on the next line type /<the name of the second alias>. Then in the second alias you type $read -L<#> <directory\path\filename> and on the next line type the name of the third alias you want this alias to go to if you want it to go to another alias. Keep following these steps until you have the aliases set up the way you want them.

Next set up an alias using the color codes and add some ASCII art in it. Play around with the color codes and the ASCII art until you get something you are pleased with.

Lastly, set up a timer alias. Remember to read the help file in Pirch to get a good understanding of how this command works. It may take you a few tries to get this down. Try putting a timer on the read command. Keep trying until you get an alias that works and learn from your mistakes and how Pirch works.

Popups

To create popups in Pirch, first click on the Popups toolbar icon. Then select the area you want to create the popup for. As with mIRC, you create menus and submenus set off with dots. Then you type in the command for the popup you are creating.

Begin by creating an away message on a timer. Select the Server Window tab and type in the command. This away with timer command should look something like this: .<popup name>:/timer<#> <timer variables> /away | /me is away <your message>.

Next copy the color-coded alias you created earlier over to the popups. Choose the right tab for this new popup and create a menu and submenu item for it. If you prefer you can create a totally new color-coded popup command.

Lastly, try to re-create a popup you have seen someone else use. Test it and if it's not right, keep trying until you get it right. If it gets too frustrating, ask your friend to copy it to a channel for you and see where you went wrong. This should help you learn how to create these popups. Trial and error is often the best teacher.

Events and Controls

Events and controls in Pirch are very similar to those you can create in mIRC. Most of the event commands are the same. To begin, open the Events and Controls panel by clicking on the Events icon in the toolbar. Then select the level you want to create the event in.

Create a pager event for when you mark yourself away. As you are creating this event, also add a command to play a sound file when someone pages you. The command should look similar to this: ON PAGE:/playmedia <directory\path\filename for a sound file> | /notice $me \-31 $nick is paging you | /notice $nick ($+ $date - $time $+) $me has been paged, please leave a message | /msg $nick <your message>. Insert your variables into the angle brackets.

Next create an event to automatically send requested sound files to other users. Choose the level you want this event to go into. Refer back to Chapter 3 if you need to refresh your memory. You can also refer to the help file for assistance.

Lastly, create an event to send a message to the person to whom you are sending a file via DCC when the file has been successfully sent. Be sure to include the different types of files you typically send. The command could look like this: ON DCCSENT:*:.<file extensions>:/notice $nick File $filename transferred successfully $+ , the average speed was $rate CPS.

Now, try to create some that are unique to you and how you use IRC. Use the help files and this book to assist you in creating these events. Work on getting your client setup to be unique to you and your activities. You probably won't use everything you can do with IRC or everything that is covered in this book. Determine how you use IRC and your client and customize it to your needs.

If you feel particularly industrious, try creating aliases, popups, and events in a few of the other programs covered in this book. None of these things were covered here so you are on your own. However, if you learn quickly, you should be able to at least create some simple aliases, popups, and events in these programs. Most

IRC clients use similar commands, identifiers, and variables. Again, if something you try doesn't work, try something else until you find something that does work. Test what you have learned here and what you know against these two programs and some of the others available for IRC.

Happy IRCing!

Index

3-D chat programs, 146-159

A

Active Worlds, 4, 152-156
Advanced commands, 74-89
Advanced mIRC, 113-124
  Address book, 116-117
  Colors, 114-115
  DCC options, 120
  File servers, 117-120
  On connect, 123-124
  Text to speech, 121-123
Advanced Pirch, 103-112
  Autoexec command, 104-105
  Channels list parameters, 111-112
  Colors, 105-107
  Fetch command, 112
  File servers, 107-109
  IdentD server, 112
  Text to speech, 110
  Video, 109
Aliases, 14-26
  How to create, 17-25
  in mIRC, 18-21
  in Pirch, 22-25
  What are, 14-17
Alleviating lag, 94
Alpha World, 4

B

Bot friendly servers, 219
Bots, 197-219
  Creating in mIRC, 209-215
  Creating in Pirch, 215-218
  How to use, 200-206
  Personal, 199, 207-208
  Tips on using, 206-207
  War and protection, 200, 207-208
  What are, 197-198
Button function scripts in Pirch, 193-195

C

Channel bots, 198-199
  Commands for, 202-206
  How to use, 201-206
  User levels for, 202-206
Channel ops, 67-72
  Banning users, 70
  Channel bots, 71-72
  Channel modes, 67-69
  Kicking users, 71
Chat programs, 4-8, 141-173, 227-250
Comic Chat, 7, 163-166
Creating a mIRC bot, 209-215
  Add users, 210
  Automatic bot functions, 211-215
  Command scripts, 210-215
  Flood protection, 213
  Last seen command, 214-215
  Op level commands, 210-213
  Perform on connect command, 215
  Remove users, 210
Creating a Pirch bot, 215-218
  Bot events, 214
  Last seen command, 218
  On kick command, 218
  PILs for bot commands, 216-218
  User levels, 215
Creating events and controls in Pirch, 55-63
  Miscellaneous commands, 63
  ON commands, 55-63
Creating remotes and events in mIRC, 39-55
  Commands for event commands, 43-44
  Events, 47-54
  Event commands, 43-46
  Identifiers for event commands, 43-44

ON events, 47-54
Raw commands, 55
User events, 39-42
Variables, 42-43
Creating scripts in mIRC, 175-184
aliases and scripts, 184
Goto commands, 176
Identifiers, 175
If-then-else statements, 175
Variables, 175
Creating scripts in Pirch, 184-195
CUSeeMe, 220-226
Conference room, 225
Contact card, 223-224
How to use, 222-226
Listener option, 226
Phone book, 223
What is, 220-222

D

DALnet, 8-9, 12
DALnet servers, 12
DCC, 96-101
and sound, 96-102
Drag and drop, 97-98
Extension map, 101, 110-111
TDCC command, 99
XDCC command, 98-99

E

EfNet, 8-9, 12
EfNet servers, 12
Eggdrop bots, 219
Events and controls in Pirch, 55-63
EZ-IRC, 8

F

Fancy aliases in mIRC, 18-19
Fancy aliases in Pirch, 23-24
Flood protection aliases in mIRC, 18
Foiling stalkers and hackers, 83-87

G

Gather Talk, 238-240

H

Handling splits, 94-95
HoneyComb, 248-250
Meeting room, 249

I

Internet Phone, 243-245
Chat areas, 243-244
Global online directory, 243
Screen, 244
Internet TeleCafé, 5, 166-171
Internet teleconferencing, 251-259
Tools for, 253-259
What is, 251-253
InterPhone, 240
IRC commands, 88-89
Iris Phone, 246-247

J

Java applets for web chat, 142

L

Lag, 90-91, 94
LOL Chat, 5, 160-163

M

Managing multiple channels in mIRC, 136-137
Managing multiple channels in Pirch, 137
Managing multiple nets in mIRC, 138-139
Managing multiple nets in Pirch, 139
Manipulating windows scripts in Pirch, 191-193
Mimix, 7
mIRC, 3
mIRC client commands, 75-79
Monologue, 110
Multiple channels and nets, 135-140

N

Net Meeting, 254-259
People lists, 255
Servers, 255
Sharing applications, 257
Speed dial list, 255-257
Text chat, 258
Video, 259
White board, 257
Web page links, 258
Nets, 8-13

O
OnLive Traveler, 8, 156-159
Operator's status, 65-73
  Responsibilities of, 66-67
  What is, 65-66
Orbit IRC chat, 6, 171-172
Other nets, 10-13

P
Personal bots, 199, 207-208
PILs, 184-195
  Alias scripts, 185
  Comments, 185
  Functions, 185
  If statement, 188-189
  If-then-else statements, 186
  Operators, 185-186
  Using variables within the command function, 187-188
  Variables, 185
Pirch, 3
Pirch client commands, 79-83
Play a wave script in Pirch, 189-191
Popups, 27-37
  How to create, 27-37
  What are, 27
Popups in mIRC, 28-32
  Channel window, 29
    Action, 30
    Invite, 30
  Channels List, 30
    Add, 31
    Flood Control, 31
    Fsend, 31
    Fserve, 31
    Logging, 30
    Msg, 30
    Notice, 30
    Play, 30
    Quit, 31
    Say, 30
    User, 30
  Nickname List, 31
    Fancy greetings, 32
  Status window, 28
    Away, 28
  Query/Chat windows, 28,31
    DCC send, 28
    Ignore, 29
Popups in Pirch, 33-36
  Channel (Names List), 34
Pirch fancy popups, 34
  Action, 34
  Channel (Main Pane), 35
  Channel (Private Msg/DCC Chat), 36
  Invite, 34
    List of channels, 34-35
    Msg, 35
    Notice, 35
    Play, 35
    Picture, 35
    Quit, 35
    Request, 35
    Say, 35
    Send, 35
    View, 35
PowWow, 227-235
  Answering machine, 232
  Call blocking book, 234
  Conference, 233
  Connection option, 229-230
  File send, 234
  How to use, 229-235
  Launch cruise, 233
  Send and receive mail, 234
  Sounds, 231
  Voice chat, 233-234
  White board, 232
  What is, 227-229
  White pages, 229
Putting it all together, 260-265
Putting it all together in mIRC, 261-263
  Aliases, 261-262
  Popups, 262
  Remotes and events, 262-263
Putting it all together in Pirch, 263-265
  Aliases, 263
  Events and controls, 264-265
  Popups, 264

R
Read a file aliases in Pirch, 22
Read aliases in mIRC, 19-20
Remotes and events, 38-64

in mIRC, 39-55
What are, 38

S

Scripts, 174-196
in mIRC, 175-184
in Pirch, 184-195
What are, 174-175
Simple PIL, 186-187
Software, 3-8
Sounds, 102
Speak Freely, 8
Splits, 91-93, 94
SuperChat, 8,10,12
SuperChat servers, 12

T

Televox, 241-243
The Globe, 145
The Palace, 5, 147-151
Timer aliases in mIRC, 20-21
Timer aliases in Pirch, 24-25
Tips on using bots, 206-207

U

UnderNet, 8-9, 12
UnderNet servers, 12

V

V-Chat, 151-152
VDO Phone, 247-248
VIRC, 6, 124-134
Aliases, 129-131
Client setup, 127-129
DCC, 133-134
Events, 131-132
How to use, 126-134
Popups, 132
Video, 133
What is, 125-126
Voice chat, 236-250
Voice chat programs, 238-240

W

War and protection bots, 200, 207-208
Web chat and other chat programs, 141-173
Web chat programs, 141-146
Westwood Chat, 7
Winsock IRC, 8
World Village web chat, 143

Z

Zia chat, 144

CD-ROM with mIRC and Pirch Software

The CD-ROM included with this book holds the shareware versions of mIRC and Pirch IRC software. As shareware, you are requested to submit the appropriate funds to the developers of these pieces of software. The funds, nominal as they are, enable these developers to continue bringing you excellent software and upgrades.

If you choose to use the mIRC software, please remit $20 to the following:

Khaled Mardam-Bey
23 St. Mary Abbots Court,
Warwick Gardens,
London W14 8RA,
Great Britain

For the Pirch software, remit $10 to the following:

Northwest Computer Services
309 North LaBree Suite #9
Thief River Falls, MN 56701
Attn: PIRCH

Each of these two excellent chat clients on the CD-ROM are in executable formats. To install them on your computer, simply place the CD-ROM in your CD drive. Double-click on the My Computer icon on your desktop. Then double-click on the CD drive. Select the program you want to install and double-click on it. Because these are executable files, they automatically install themselves on your computer and give you icons or shortcuts, as well as items in your Start menu.

Once the program or programs are installed on your computer, you're ready to configure them to your preferences. Then you're ready to start using them and trying out the projects covered in this book. Have fun!